New Catholic Feminism

Roman Catholicism exerts a continuing influence on the culture and politics of the world's nations, and never more so than on issues of gender and sexuality. If the Catholic Church is to continue to be relevant to modern women, it needs to go beyond its traditional anachronistic sexual stereotypes and hierarchies, to present the Gospel in a way that is attentive to the questions, needs and values of the age, without surrendering the central truths of Christian faith.

New Catholic Feminism is a radical and dramatic feminist enactment of the Catholic faith. Engaging with feminist theory and postmodern feminist theology, Tina Beattie offers a detailed and often disturbing analysis of Catholic neo-orthodoxy in its representation of gender and sexual difference. Through encounters with thinkers such as Judith Butler, Luce Irigaray, Martin Heidegger and Hans Urs von Balthasar, Beattie explores Catholicism's gendered imagery and sacramentality in the context of language, sexuality, prayer and the body, questioning the assumptions upon which neo-orthodoxy rests in its resistance to women priests, and its theological models of masculinity and femininity. Having confronted the conflict between feminism and the Vatican and Pope Benedict XVI, Beattie proposes a new theological approach to the encounter between feminism and Catholicism, for the twenty-first century.

Tina Beattie is Reader in Christian Studies at Roehampton University, where she also convenes the MA programme in Religion and Human Rights. A leading Catholic and Marian theologian, she is the author of *Woman* (New Century Theology, Continuum, 2003); *Eve's Pilgrimage* (Continuum, 2002); *God's Mother, Eve's Advocate* (Continuum, 2002); *The Last Supper According to Martha and Mary* (Burns & Oates, 2001); and *Rediscovering Mary* (Burns & Oates, 1995).

New Catholic Feminism

Theology and theory

Tina Beattie

Routledge
Taylor & Francis Group

LONDON AND NEW YORK

First published 2006
by Routledge
2 Park Square, Milton Park, Abingdon, Oxon OX14 4RN

Simultaneously published in the USA and Canada
by Routledge
270 Madison Ave, New York, NY 10016

Routledge is an imprint of the Taylor & Francis Group

© 2006 Tina Beattie

Typeset in Perpetua by
Taylor & Francis Books
Printed and bound in Great Britain by
Antony Rowe Ltd, Chippenham, Wiltshire

All rights reserved. No part of this book may be reprinted or reproduced or utilised in any form or by any electronic, mechanical, or other means, now known or hereafter invented, including photocopying and recording, or in any information storage or retrieval system, without permission in writing from the publishers.

British Library Cataloguing in Publication Data
A catalogue record for this book is available from the British Library

Library of Congress Cataloging in Publication Data
A catalog record for this book has been requested

ISBN10 0–415–30147–5   ISBN13 9–780–415–30147–3 (hbk)
ISBN10 0–415–30148–3   ISBN13 9–780–415–30148–0 (pbk)

T&F informa

Taylor & Francis Group is the Academic Division of T&F Informa plc.

Contents

Preface ix
Introduction 1

PART I
The middle 17

1 – Catholicism, feminism and faith 19

The Vatican and feminism 20
Catholicism and the end of feminism? 23
Secular theory and feminist theology 26
The secularization of knowledge 29

2 – Feminist bodies and feminist selves 33

The disembodied self 33
Butler's absent God 37
Sex, gender and the secular body 40
Rethinking essentialism 42
The self as gift 45

3 – Gender, knowing and being 49

Heidegger and the question of Being 50
Sexual difference, being and language 54
Feminist theology after Heidegger 57
Towards a feminist Thomism 60
Gendering apophaticism 65

4 – Knowledge, desire and prayer — 68

The secularization of vision 70
The problematization of prayer 72
Desire and reason 76
Praying as a woman 81

PART II
The end — 89

5 – Incarnation, difference and God — 91

Balthasar and Irigaray: engendering difference 92
Language and embodiment 95
Irigaray and the otherness of God 96
Balthasar's theo-drama 99
Balthasar and the otherness of woman 101
Eve, Mary and the Church as woman 103
The end of woman 107

6 – Masculinity, femininity and God — 112

Acting up: man as material girl 113
Sexual difference in eastern and western Christianity 117
Sexual difference and the imago Dei *121*
Sexuality and sacramentality 126

7 – Cherchez la femme: gender, Church and priesthood — 129

The nuptial significance of the priesthood 130
The Marian and Petrine Church 133
Justifying the male priesthood 137
The sacrament of the body 139
Sacramentality and the female body 142
Cherchez l'homme: Balthasar's sexual paradoxes 145

8 – Desire, death and the female body — 149

Balthasar's suprasexuality 150
Woman, sex and time 152
Sex, death and the polarities of human existence 155
Kenosis, sex and death 158
Kenosis, masculinity and vulnerability 161

9 – Sex, death and melodrama   163

Sexual role models? Hans Urs von Balthasar and Adrienne von Speyr 163
Hell and the female body 167
Balthasar's struggle 170
Casta meretrix *173*
The female sex as other 179
The indictment of theology 182

PART III
The beginning   185

10 – Being beyond death   187

Befriending death 188
Beyond necrophilia 190
Lacan, Heidegger and death 197
René Girard: desire and violence 201
Girard and the peace of Christ 204

11 – Maternal beginnings   208

The maternal sacrifice 210
Maternal abjection 212
The maternal subject 215
The incineration of meaning 220

12 – Redeeming fatherhood   225

God, suffering and sacrifice 225
Masculinity and violence 229
Christ the dragon-slayer 231
Peace and martyrdom 233
God's origins 234
The compassion of the father 239
The community of the father 242

13 – Redeeming motherhood   246

God and the status quo 246
Balthasar's motherly God 249
Maternity and natality 253
The maternal Church 256
The cosmic mother 260
The Church as Eve 265

14 – Redeeming language — 269

The silenced sex 269
The body that speaks 273
Redeeming the nightmare 277
The elemental matrix 281
Difference beyond death 284
Theology beyond feminism 287

15 – Redeeming sacramentality — 290

The fire and the rose 292
The knowledge of angels 293
The liturgical body 298
The maternal priest 302
Fecundity and sacrifice 304
God's grandeur and the body's grace 310

Notes	312
Bibliography	357
Index	370

Preface

In 1999, when Graham Ward examined my doctoral thesis, he pointed out that I was somewhat dismissive of Hans Urs von Balthasar, and he wondered if I might have offered a more developed analysis of his theology. I replied that I thought life was too short to analyse Balthasar. (By that time I knew I had passed, so I could afford to be flippant.)

In the years since then, Balthasar has become increasingly significant for Catholic theology and for some Anglican thinkers, although he has been largely ignored by feminist theologians. As I encountered Catholic theologians who seemed to be almost in awe of Balthasar, I began to wonder if perhaps I had been too quick to dismiss him. Maybe I had missed something. Maybe he really was, as some would argue, the Catholic Church's answer to feminism. This idea engaged me more, the more dissatisfied I became with both liberal and postmodernist feminist theologies, which often subordinate the doctrinal and existential content of Christian faith and worship to the secularized perspectives of liberal feminism and feminist theory respectively.

Six years later, having plumbed the depths of Balthasar's sexual theology, I think I was probably correct in my initial evaluation. Nevertheless, given his growing influence, and given the extent to which, almost without exception, the theologians who engage with him as translators and interpreters seem oblivious to the violence inherent in his theology with regard to female sexuality, I hope that this book will make an original contribution to feminist theology, while providing a source of provocation and challenge to those theologians – women as well as men – who have fallen under his spell. Despite the severity of my criticism, in seeking ways of bringing a feminist reading to Balthasar's theology and symbolism, I have discovered quite astonishing resonances between postmodern psycholinguistic theory and neo-orthodox Catholic theology, so that I hope that this book does suggest a genuinely new way of doing feminist theology, beyond both liberal feminism and feminist theory. Even if there have been times of intense struggle in grappling with deeply disturbing theological ideas, this has felt like an exhilarating intellectual journey through relatively unexplored territory, where I have discovered much to celebrate as well as much to criticize.

During the book's long gestation, I have been more grateful than I can say for those many friends and colleagues who have encouraged me to keep going, and who have allowed me to explore controversial questions in a supportive intellectual milieu. In particular, the Catholic Theological Association of Great Britain has been a source of intellectually rigorous debate and warm friendship, providing replenishment and sustenance for the sometimes lonely task of doing theology in the conflicted terrain between the authoritarianism of the contemporary Church, and the secularism of the contemporary academy.

To begin to list names is always to risk leaving out those many people – friends and family as well as students and colleagues – who form the matrix within which theological ideas are nurtured and explored. However, my thanks go to Pamela Sue Anderson, Sarah Jane Boss, Beverley Clack, Julie Clague, Gavin D'Costa, Philip Endean, Harriet Harris, Grace Jantzen, Sebastian Moore, Marcus Pound, Janet Martin Soskice and Frank Turner, who have all provided encouragement and feedback during the course of writing this, and to Sarah Butler, Fergus Kerr, Michael Kirwan and Nicholas Lash for their information and advice. As members of the National Board of Catholic Women Bioethics Subcommittee, Mary Hallaway, Mary McHugh, Patrica Stoat and I have put the world and the Church to rights many times during the mellow warmth of late-night conversations over bottles of wine and good food, reminding me that doing theology among friends can be one of the richest of shared interests. Ali Green's research has provided an interesting insight into the ways in which some of the ideas explored in this book might be interpreted from the perspective of an Anglican theology of women's ordination. Gerard Loughlin has been a soulmate and source of continuing inspiration, both in the grace of his theology and in the many conversations and e-mail exchanges which have provided a space of shared humour and consolation in the ongoing struggle to be fully human and fully Catholic. In the years since Ursula King supervised my doctoral studies, she has remained a loyal and generous friend and critic. She serves as a reminder to me that it is possible to combine a profound commitment to feminist scholarship with a generosity and abundance of living in which there is always time for family and friends, as well as a continual enthusiasm for encounters with new faces and places. I am truly indebted to her for all that she has done to inspire and encourage me in my personal and professional life.

My thanks are due to the Leverhulme Foundation, for providing me with a Research Fellowship which enabled me to finish this book. I am also grateful to the editors I have worked with at Routledge, and most particularly to Lesley Riddle and Gemma Dunn for their encouragement and patience over the last year. As my Head of School at Roehampton University, Lyndie Brimstone has vigorously defended the time needed for academic research against the ever-encroaching demands of modern academic bureaucracy, and I am grateful for her understanding and support.

Finally, there is my family, but that word seems too domesticated to describe the group to which it refers, a sprawling community of people aged 2 to 87, spread across three continents, bound together by memories and stories as much as by genes and bodies. One of the exciting experiences of having adult children is the constant expansion of boundaries – metaphorical and real – to accommodate new people, new visions, new challenges and new possibilities. If this book explores strange and sometimes abstract theoretical concepts, it has nonetheless been nourished in the sacramentality of everyday life with all its muddles and compromises, and its epiphanies of grace experienced in the most ordinary details of living and loving. I hope that something of that world shows through the gaps. I doubt if those I know and love most will read this (life is, after all, too short!), but without them I could not have written it, for they have provided me with a space of stability and security that has made it possible to let go of a great many certainties and wade out into intellectual waters which have at times seemed too deep and too dark for comfort.

This book is for all my friends and family who, in eucharistic encounters where the kinship of food and wine, of shared hope and suffering, overflows the boundaries of doctrine and liturgy, nonetheless have helped me to see that there is after all some profound connection between the practices of everyday life and the Church's liturgical performances of faith, which will always elude the power of the grizzled old men who seek to control the vulnerability and fecundity of Christ among us. Above all, this book is for Dave – because he is different.

You need only observe the kind of attention women bestow upon a concert, an opera or a play – the childish simplicity, for example, with which they keep on chattering during the finest passages in the greatest masterpieces . . . [I]n lieu of saying, 'Let a woman keep silence in the church,' it would be much to the point to say, 'Let a woman keep silence in the theatre.' This might, perhaps, be put up in big letters on the curtain.[1]

Introduction

The final writing of this book has taken place during a year when the Catholic Church has rarely been out of the news. From the improbable alliance between conservative Catholics and Protestant evangelicals which helped George W. Bush to win the 2004 American elections, to the death of Pope John Paul II and the subsequent election of Pope Benedict XVI, Roman Catholicism exerts a continuing influence on the culture and politics of the world's nations.[1]

Although the Catholic Church has become increasingly radical in its social teachings, particularly under the papacy of John Paul II, and the gulf between the Church and the western democracies on issues of economics, war and social justice has widened as the military and economic dominance of the western nations has increased, the Church's political impact in these areas has been relatively small. Its continuing power to influence western politics has been most apparent, not on issues of justice and peace but on issues of gender and sexuality, at least insofar as contemporary American politics is concerned. Thus, a president whose position on a range of issues from the environment and economics to war and capital punishment stands in stark opposition to Catholic social teaching found support among Catholics primarily because he was not John Kerry, a Catholic who was seen to support abortion and whose Democratic Party was perceived as being dangerously liberal with regard to issues such as homosexuality, marriage and the family, even though Kerry had a good voting record on issues of social welfare, global poverty and the environment that some might say should be of equal concern to Catholic voters.[2]

This increasing conservatism of the Catholic Church was given added impetus with the election of Pope Benedict XVI. Peter J. Boyer, writing in *The New Yorker*, claimed that 'For many Catholics, the white smoke that curled into the Vatican sky in the early evening of April 19th quickly came to be seen as a distress signal.'[3] It is too early to assess the influence of the new papacy on questions concerning the role of women in the Church. Although Cardinal Ratzinger was known as a harsh authoritarian when he was head of the Congregation for the Doctrine of the Faith, his homilies and statements since becoming Pope suggest at least the possibility of a more dialogical approach. In his inaugural homily, he spoke inspiringly of what he saw as his pastoral mission:

> The pastor must be inspired by Christ's holy zeal: for him it is not a matter of indifference that so many people are living in the desert. And there are so many kinds of desert. There is the desert of poverty, the desert of hunger and thirst, the desert of abandonment, of loneliness, of destroyed love. There is the desert of God's darkness, the emptiness of souls no longer aware of their dignity or the goal of human life. The external deserts in the world are growing, because the internal deserts have become so vast. Therefore the earth's treasures no longer serve to build God's garden for all to live in, but they have been made to serve the powers of exploitation and destruction. The Church as a whole and all her Pastors, like Christ, must set out to lead people out of the desert, towards the place of life, towards friendship with the Son of God, towards the One who gives us life, and life in abundance.[4]

This is a vision that many Christian feminists might applaud, but the challenge is how to communicate to the Catholic hierarchy that the 'holy zeal' of the Church's pastors is, for a growing number of faithful women, part of the problem and not part of the solution. For many of us, 'the internal deserts' become more vast as the Church's sacramental life becomes more arid. We seek full participation in the vision that the Pope so eloquently sets before us. We share his faith in the redeeming love of Christ, and his passionate concern for a world where so many suffer under the 'powers of exploitation and destruction'. But until women are recognized as full and equal participants in the life of faith, until we are acknowledged as persons graced with the image of God, capable of representing Christ to the world as fully and effectively as men do, the Church herself will continue to be a spiritual desert where men's fears and fantasies lead them to refuse the grace that female sacramentality might bring to Catholic liturgical and institutional life. Pope Benedict XVI went on to say that 'All ideologies of power justify themselves in exactly this way, they justify the destruction of whatever would stand in the way of progress and the liberation of humanity.'[5] For some of us, struggling for the progress and liberation of our womanly humanity in a Church where the heavy hand of the hierarchy shadows our every move, those words cannot help but have a certain irony.

At such a time, it might seem that the most pressing task confronting feminist theologians is that of political struggle and resistance in the name of liberal values of freedom, democracy and equal rights, over and against the rising tides of religious and political conservatism. Sometimes during the last year I have wondered what I was doing, huddled over my desk exploring the dense, dark regions of Hans

Urs von Balthasar's theology and psycholinguistic theory, while my liberal Catholic friends shook their heads in dismay as the promises and hopes of Vatican II faded in the face of the Church's increasingly reactionary tendencies. Surely, it would have been better and more profitable to rush off and write a book about feminism, theology and politics than to plough on with this intellectual struggle to produce a book that might at first glance seem far removed from and perhaps even irrelevant to the most urgent questions that Catholic women face in the contemporary world?

Yet I hope that this feminist psycholinguistic probing of the symbolism and sacramentality of the contemporary Church might ultimately be a more political act than the overtly political rhetoric of feminists such as Rosemary Radford Ruether and Elisabeth Schüssler Fiorenza, and there are several reasons for this. Having spent ten years teaching and studying feminist theology, while I do not entirely agree with those Catholic so-called new feminists who proclaim that feminism has failed (see Chapter 1), I think that the feminist theological vision has begun to stagnate and stands in need of revitalization. Unlike the new Catholic feminists, I do not believe that neo-orthodox Catholicism,[6] informed by the theology of Balthasar and John Paul II but also manifesting the kind of social and sexual ideologies that are a feature of contemporary American politics, holds the key to such a feminist revival, but it has a significant contribution to make, if only through its capacity to stimulate close critical engagement with the Catholic tradition in a way that might liberate new meanings and possibilities for feminist theological reflection.

Western feminist theologians have to a large extent remained captive to a highly politicized and often agnostic theology, shaped by the priorities and commitments of a generation of liberal American Catholics whose ideas were formed in the aftermath of the Second Vatican Council, and whose power to define the parameters of contemporary theology remains significant.[7] Rebecca Chopp suggests that American feminist theology needs to be understood within the wider context of American philosophical and political pragmatism on the one hand, and American public theology on the other: 'feminist theology, placed as it is in the history of pragmatism and American public theology, works for the transformation of political and personal life away from patriarchy into freedom'.[8] Chopp argues for a shift towards a more postmodern approach to questions of language and knowledge, calling for 'productive strategies of transformation in terms of a critique of the depth texture of patriarchy'.[9] This means recognizing that

> we cannot simply change metaphors or add new experiences to our dominant theological stew and stir, but that we must transform the very terms, patterns, and ordering of how language, culture, politics, and subjectivity work. We can criticize gender opposition and affirm theological practices of

4 *Introduction*

> difference by opening up the realm of meaning and the rules of meaning-making.[10]

In setting about the kind of task that Chopp describes, I seek a way beyond the politics of western liberal feminism, in order to develop a feminist theology of grace informed by a sense of the sacramentality of creation and by an awareness of the significance of prayer, revelation and faith for Christian ways of knowing, through a critical feminist refiguration of contemporary Catholic theology. This invites a feminist return to a European Catholic heritage, which is I believe more capable of expressing the complexity, depth and intellectual rigour of the Catholic tradition than the kind of American pragmatism to which Chopp refers. I include within this European heritage not only the mystical and classical theologies of thinkers such as Catherine of Siena and Thomas Aquinas, but also recent quasi-Catholic theologies produced by psycholinguists such as Luce Irigaray, Julia Kristeva and Jacques Lacan.

If feminists are to understand and challenge the misogyny that forms a dark undercurrent to the Catholic theological tradition, we must go beyond politics in order to ask why the Catholic hierarchy is so resistant to acknowledging the sacramentality of the female body in its capacity to reveal Christ. There is a profound fear of female sexuality that infects the celibate Catholic imagination, and I believe that this lies behind many of the Church's other failings, not least her failure to challenge war and violence with the same unyielding absolutism with which she challenges abortion and contraception. Although feminists have done much to diagnose the symptoms of this sexual malaise, they have done relatively little to explore its possible causes.

Paradoxically, as the reader will discover in what follows, the language of post-Catholic psycholinguistics has the most profound resonances with the language of neo-orthodox Catholic theology as far as sexuality, embodiment, desire and death are concerned. Perhaps this is because all the thinkers I engage with in this book – theologians and critical theorists – acknowledge a continuum between the innermost workings of the human psyche and the structures and systems which order our world. For Christians, as for psychoanalysts, it is through the healing and conversion of our psychic wounds that we become persons capable of living at peace with ourselves and with one another, through our attentiveness to the power of language to reveal and shape the worlds we inhabit. If this risks an individualistic ethos, both in Christianity and in psychoanalysis, it also invites recognition of the interdependence of psychology, politics and theology. Feminist theologians will not bring about a transformation in Christian politics and values by simply turning up the volume of their political sermonizing. Indeed, if American politics are any indication, this may be counter-productive, producing a backlash through a resort to forms of religious and political conservatism which have the power to eradicate the fragile equalities gained by women during the last century. There is a need to go beyond the rhetorical smokescreens of political discourse, in order to excavate some of the deeper layers of language and symbolism within which fear and desire are coiled together, emanating energies that have the power to corrode our most committed struggles for peace, justice and sexual equality.

When psycholinguistics and neo-orthodox theology are brought into intimate dialogue with one another, the confusion which surrounds the place of the female body in Catholic symbolism and sacramentality begins to burn with a dark intensity. This illuminates an unexplored space – virgin territory perhaps – which is at one and the same time charged with the most profound and threatening irrationality, but also with a sacramental and sexual potency that might yet bring about the transformation of the Catholic vision.

To undertake such a task, one must go beyond any moralistic formulation of right and wrong, true and false, to recognize the pervasive and insurmountable instability of the Christian story, particularly in its Catholic version. This story is a weaving together of multiple 'texts' – performative narratives of faith extending in time and space across two thousand years of histories and localities – and it must be read simultaneously as a narrative of damnation and redemption, of poison and cure. Like Derrida's reading of Plato's *pharmakon*,[11] it is untranslatable from the perspective of those who seek linguistic exactitude and philosophical precision, for ultimately it is undecidable, subject to a 'strange logic'[12] which makes it resistant to translation into any other 'language' – whether that is the language of philosophy, politics, psychology or gender theory. Outside of this story, one is neither saved nor damned, neither poisoned nor cured, any more than one is poisoned or cured by a drug that one does not swallow. It is only from within that one recognizes redemption and damnation, cure and poison, as the two sides of the fabric out of which faith is woven. It is through accepting the promise of redemption that one risks damnation, and through seeking the cure that one risks being poisoned. That is faith's mystery, and it means that the Christian story is the locus of a dynamic, transgressive and dangerous volatility, sacramentally and socially embodied in the material world. Here we encounter God and Satan, the beatific and the demonic, the redeemed and the damned, and in historical, human terms they are inseparable. From the perspective of human reason, Catholic Christianity is an impossible paradox.

Perhaps nowhere was this paradox more apparent than in the exuberant excesses of mourning and celebration that surrounded the dying of John Paul II. Even the British media – not normally noted for their pro-Catholic bias – were seduced into covering events in Rome with an aura of what sometimes felt like hushed awe and amazement, suspending critical judgement to show us the Catholic Church at prayer, lingering on images of candlelit vigils and weeping nuns, suggesting a Church made up of millions of devout and obedient believers brought together by the dying of a much-loved Pope. But the Catholic Church was also at play that fortnight, and perhaps media sensibilities attuned to a post-Protestant culture in which religion and moral conformity are seen to go hand in hand were less attentive to this other side of Catholicism, which is more medieval than modern in its unruly abundance.

For the dying of John Paul II was also a carnival of love and desire, of yearning and faith, erupting in the gaps of Catholicism, in the enigmatic meanings encoded within its devotions, practices and beliefs, suggesting a surge of life within this creaking institution that refuses to be controlled or silenced or eliminated. How many babies were conceived in Rome that week, in that vast human coming together? How many legitimate and forbidden sexual encounters sought to express a hope beyond death, enigmatically glimpsed in the stubborn charisma of a man whose faith at the end disrupted all the boundaries he so vigorously sought to defend? How many condoms were secretly disposed of in the Vatican's litter bins? How many erotic couplings happened in the shade of Bernini's columns? How many adulteries? How many gay embraces? How many furtive gropings of yearning and delight beneath the papal windows? Faith, sex and death. They feed on one another and fecundate one another, and our ability to accept any one must surely entail an ability to accept the other two, beyond violence, sacrifice and fear. This is the mystery and the paradox of the Catholic faith, beyond its institutions and hierarchies.

In opening up a dialogue between feminist and psycholinguistic theories and Catholic theology, I seek to demonstrate that the radical instability of Catholic Christianity is a potent resource for feminist theological reflection, but this depends upon keeping open the horizons of revelation and faith, against the closures of secular modernity. Unlike many postmodern feminist theologians, whose work I discuss in more detail in Chapter 1, my intention is not to subordinate theology to theory. Rather, I ask how feminist theory can help Catholic theologians to forge a new and more radical theological vision, through the sacramentality of a faith that seeks understanding in the *aporia* between the divine mystery and a graced creation – an epistemological space that tradition tells us is populated only by human reason and angels, but that today we also know as the rich and mysterious terrain of the unconscious, home to our hidden hauntings of ecstasy and abjection. Our postmodern secular culture has much more to say on the subject of angels than Christian theologians and worshippers, but Christianity needs to rediscover the potency of angelic mediations to inform a liturgical theology which draws on the insights of psychoanalysis in its understanding of language and desire, as the key to a revitalized sense of worship and sacramentality.

Nancy Dallavalle refers to the tendency among feminist theologians to seek 'a reformulation of Christian tradition in the light of the emancipation of women, a position that continues to rest on an ethical, not a theological, basis'.[13] She argues that

> Catholicity . . . can not be simply about justice. Rather it is primarily about sacramentality. Indeed, orthodoxy's call to the right worship of God involves

not only the understanding that faith seeks but also a considered setting-aside of the norms of humanity for the grace of basking in the mystery of what human norms can never measure. Whatever universality or catholicity might imply, it is, finally, a mystery in which we are joined by 'an account of your hope' [1 Pet. 3:15] and in which neither the account (tradition) nor the hope (redemption, deification) are objects for our manipulation and comprehension.[14]

A feminist sacramental vision needs to refocus its lens beyond liberal feminism's primary concerns of justice and equality, in order to recognize that faith, hope and love provide a more textured language for the mystery of our humanity than justice alone. If Christians profess a concern for the human person made in the image of God, then the very least we must do is to seek justice with all who share a similar concern for human well-being. But that is not what Christianity is ultimately about, nor is it in any sense unique to Christians to be concerned for justice. Christianity's uniqueness, its particularity and its identity, derive from the drama it performs in the world – the drama of God incarnate who is carried in the womb of a virgin, who becomes the helpless infant at her breast, who eats, drinks, loves and laughs with ordinary people, who is tortured and put to death because the world does not understand him, and who gathers together all these incarnate human realities into a story of resurrection, reconciliation and the hope of eternal life. This story provides the narrative context within which Christians understand what justice requires of us, and it focuses the demand for justice on the vocation to recognize God in that which the world overlooks, abandons and forgets.

In a critique of feminist theology that focuses with particular severity on the work of Rosemary Radford Ruether and Elisabeth Schüssler Fiorenza, Susan Parsons argues that 'nihilism shadows the writing of particular feminist theologians',[15] expressing itself through an over-reliance on the human power to achieve social transformation, and through a resistance to any understanding of faith that would offer hope beyond the Nietzschean death of God and the postmodernist fragmentation of meaning. Without such hope, Ruether's

> moral exhortations . . . to establish a code of conduct based on some spurious notion of 'solidarity in struggle' is itself a postmodern, and thus a nihilistic move, acknowledging, by what it refuses to speak, its own lack of anything at all to say in the face of the absence of God, and masking itself with humility.[16]

In place of Ruether's rhetoric of justice, Parsons invites a turning

> to the anguish of the world which waits with eager longing, and to the coming of God who raises from the dead and who calls us into a transcending

thinking that may even lose the cloak of its own assumptions in its running for joy.[17]

She calls for feminist theologians to 'think anew what it is to be orthodox, to be informed by a tradition and embodied in its thinking, and to engage in a work of apologetic theology for our day that is sensitive to the feminist critique'.[18] In particular, this brings with it a requirement to 'think redemption anew',[19] in order to articulate a hope that is 'altogether more strange'[20] than the optimism of post-Enlightenment liberal humanism.

With Parsons, I go in search of the strange hope of the Catholic faith, in order to 'think redemption anew'. I suspect that I am less sanguine than she is about the capacity of Catholicism to yield up its promises to feminist theology without a prolonged and intense struggle with its symbols and sacramental practices, and this book is written in the form of such a struggle. I invite the reader to accompany me on a quest through a labyrinth of conflicting and contested meanings, a linguistic landscape which inevitably becomes more uncanny and disorientating the more we explore its hidden depths, so that the style as well as the content of the book becomes increasingly exploratory and searching as we feel our way towards a clearing in the forest of faith, where a woman's body might come into being.

This involves a style that is elliptical and even repetitive in places, for it presents itself not as a work of systematic theology but as a psycholinguistic probing of the underside of theological language and symbolism. As I seek to unearth hidden meanings and to listen to enigmatic silences and garbled expressions of denial and desire, I must often loop back on myself, revisiting some texts repeatedly from different angles, allowing ideas to emerge in different contexts, so that they yield up multiple meanings and interpretations. This also involves quoting extensively from key sources, for this is intended to be a multi-vocal theology which emerges through encounter and dialogue, and sometimes through conflict and contradiction. Lurking behind these 'conversations' is the awareness that meaning is constantly refigured anew in the process of translation, interpretation and combination. Beneath the illusory coherence of a monolinguistic study there are questions about the subtleties which are sacrificed as texts are translated between cultures, languages and generations, particularly with regard to gendered interpretations. Nevertheless, although I have consulted some texts in their original languages when I have been uncertain as to the reliability of the translation, my primary concern is to discover the potential of theological language to inform a bodily, sacramental performance of faith, and this means that language must be supple, capable of sculpting itself to the body's grace, porous enough to allow its meanings to be expressed in gesture, speech and touch, and open to as many translations and interpretations as there are bodies to perform them.

Introduction 9

The style and structure of the book are intended as a parodic feminist staging of Hans Urs von Balthasar's idea of theo-drama. I ask what it means to take seriously his claim that the Christian story is God's own story, played out on the world's stage, in which our roles are determined to a very large extent in terms of sexuality and gender. By performing the woman's role, I seek to expose the inconsistencies and contradictions in his theology, both in order to challenge the ways in which some new feminists cite his work as Catholicism's response to feminism, and in order to ask how a feminist deconstruction of his theo-drama might open up different ways of interpreting the theological and sacramental significance of the sexual human body.

Seeking to avoid the kind of agnostic or atheistic assumptions inherent in much feminist theological discourse,[21] I ask how feminist theology might rediscover the intimacy and otherness of the God of Christian revelation whom we encounter in the writings of mystics such as Catherine of Siena, for whom God was a 'mad lover' who pursued her through all the struggles of her often tormented spirituality, and in Aquinas for whom creation was a wondrous window into the love of an utterly unknowable God. This invites a rediscovery of the language of mysticism and prayer as channels into new ways of knowing and being, beyond the ontotheologies which still haunt the work of feminist theologians such as Ruether, who defines God as 'the source of being that underlies creation and grounds its nature and future potential for continual transformative renewal in biophilic mutuality'.[22] Such language remains trapped in the kind of metaphysics that has become increasingly problematic for theology after Heidegger, implying as it does a de-personalized, de-mysticized philosophical concept from which all language of desire has been evacuated. Heidegger was right when he suggested that

> Man can neither pray nor sacrifice to this god. Before the *causa sui*, man can neither fall to his knees in awe nor can he play music and dance before this god. The god-less thinking which must abandon the god of philosophy, god as *causa sui*, is thus perhaps closer to the divine God.[23]

Feminists refuse to sacrifice before the *causa sui* of man's theology, but in their theologies many have also forgotten how to play music and dance before God. Beyond the puritanical political polemics of much feminist theology, we need to rediscover how to play as well as how to pray, and I suggest that this invites an opening up of the horizons of feminist theological discourse to a form of post-Heideggerian apophaticism, informed by the critical perspectives of psycholinguistics and gender theory.

This means that I enter into critical dialogue across a range of frontiers which are very often regarded as unbreachable by feminist thinkers. Through a serious engagement with psycholinguistic feminist theory and postmodern feminist theology, I offer a detailed and often disturbing analysis of Catholic neo-orthodoxy in its representation of gender and sexual difference. Yet I also allow Catholic theology to question and challenge the extent to which feminist theory, at least in its Anglo-American versions, is subservient to a secular ideology that is, I suggest, inimical to some of the ethical aims and deconstructive strategies of feminism. Thus I invite both feminist theory and postmodern feminist theology to go beyond an implicitly modernist acceptance of the secularization of knowledge, to ask how Catholic theology might contribute towards a transformed epistemology that would be more radical and transgressive than the secularized parodies of identity that feminist theorists perform before the closed horizons of modernity.

For those who approach what follows from a secular theoretical perspective, I invite the suspension of disbelief, a willingness to play theology's language games, if only in order to discover that these are more complex and dynamic than secular thinkers acknowledge. If modern Catholic theology is an awesome and sometimes terrifying force for feminists to grapple with, it is also, I believe, an inexhaustibly rich source for feminist reflection and analysis – a source of *jouissance* as well as abjection, and I have experienced both in writing this. There have been times when I have felt sick with dread at where my analysis is leading, finding myself in linguistic spaces that are far more sticky and visceral than the stylized sexual morphologies of an Irigaray or a Kristeva, because they are not safely contained exercises in inter-textuality. The language is sacramental rather than symbolic. It has a performative dimension, and seeds itself deep in the body's responses and desires. For women, these seeds have sometimes flowered in joyous expressions of faith and creativity, but for too many others they have brought physical or metaphorical death, and a burning away (literally or symbolically) of the body's grace. So there has been a sense of risk, even of fear, and an occasional overwhelming urge to withdraw to a safer, cleaner, more rational space. Yet there were also many times when I felt a sense of exhilaration at the promises unfolding before me, finding myself swept up in something that I was beginning to see through not seeing, and to know through not knowing, and I knew why it mattered so much to me to write this book, to stay in the dark spaces, and to trust the light which is always just beyond the focus of our human vision.

For those who approach this work from a faith perspective – and I dare to hope that this might include some new Catholic feminists – there will undoubtedly be much that causes profound shock and dismay. Again, I can only invite the reader to go along with me, and to suspend judgement until the end. For if I cannot possibly offer a confident affirmation of the truths of the Catholic tradition, I know that the writing of this book has been a personal journey of faith which has made me aware of the extent to which the Catholic tradition truly does encompass the heights and the depths of our humanity – its darkest fears, and its most eloquent hopes – beyond the most extensive probings of psychoanalysis, which nevertheless provides the guiding light through which I have sought to make this journey. I do not set my own work over and against Catholic thinkers whose understanding of feminism is very different from my own, because in being against them I am also with them. Although my theological 'voice' is often mimetic and ironic, it is at the same time a subjective exploration of faith, informed not only by the demands of academic scholarship, but also by my ongoing commitment to the Catholic Church. So, while I hope I have been rigorous and faithful to the professional demands of the academic community, I hope that I have been no less rigorous and faithful in recognizing my responsibilities and commitments to the worshipping community of which I am also a part.

Unlike many books on feminism and gender theory, I address the question of masculine as well as feminine subjectivities and identities in some detail. While a great deal continues to be written on theology and women, one cannot address the question of gender without close attentiveness to constructs of masculinity as well as femininity. This is particularly important given the extent to which gender functions as a metaphor for human and divine relationships in the Catholic theological tradition, so that whether one is 'male' or 'female' depends less on the body than on the position one occupies in relation to the human or divine other. This means that there is a high degree of slippage when it comes to gendered identities, at least as far as the male body is concerned. The closer one looks, the less certain one can be about where 'man' ends and 'woman' begins, for the two seem to morph in and out of each other with quite remarkable versatility, giving rise to a multiplicity of gendered roles and identities in which only the female body remains fixed, although whether or not this body is 'woman' remains to be seen.

Catholic theology is radically different from Protestant theology in its treatment of gender and sacramentality, and for this reason I avoid the broad ecumenism that informs most feminist theologies, in favour of a focused and in-depth analysis of Catholic sacramental theology. While I realize that this might strike some readers as too exclusive, I think it is a betrayal of both feminist and theological scholarship to airbrush out these differences in order to present a superficial appearance of unity or universality. Several times in what follows I argue that, however problematic it might be, the Catholic theological tradition is a rich resource for the construction of gendered identities and subjectivities beyond the reductive influences of both the Reformation and the Enlightenment. Rather than minimizing difference, I suggest that it is in acknowledging our differences that feminists might enter into dialogue and debate, but this entails speaking from a particular position which does not seek to colonize or speak for those who occupy other contexts and positions, whether these are secular or religious.

I begin in 'The middle', bearing in mind Derrida's suggestion that we begin '*Wherever we are*: in a text where we already believe ourselves to be'.[24] The middle is the point at which the theological polarities which structure Balthasar's theology might encounter one another beyond his violent sexual dualisms. It is also 'the broken middle' which, according to Gillian Rose, is a space of diremption and ambiguity that we must inhabit if we are to go beyond binary dualisms in order to accommodate the paradoxical contrasts which position us in the world. The 'broken middle' resists the 'holy middle', a hypothetical space of unbounded peace which is in fact a space of totalizing power, because it refuses to accommodate the imperfection inherent in the necessary institutions and laws of society, in favour of an idealized and illusionary eschatology.[25] The middle sets the scene for what follows, allowing me to take up a position in the space of conflict and mutual resistance between feminist theory and Catholic theology. This means breaking new ground, allowing this to become a 'broken middle' where feminism might go beyond theological and secular antagonisms, in order to offer women a space of becoming in the situation in which we find ourselves, inescapably positioned by the institutions, laws and values of our cultural and religious heritage, but also positioned by the visions of peace, wholeness and personal transformation which both feminism and Catholicism hold out before us in different ways.

I start by offering a critical survey of both Catholic new feminism and feminist theology. As examples of new feminism, I refer to the document published by the Congregation for the Doctrine of the Faith on 31 July 2004, titled 'Collaboration of Men and Women in the Church', and to a collection of essays edited by Michele Schumacher, titled *Women in Christ*, also published in 2004.[26] In assessing the state of feminist theology, I refer primarily to a collection of essays titled *Horizons in Feminist Theology*, edited by Rebecca Chopp and Sheila Greeve Davaney.[27] I seek to show that many of the postmodern feminist theologians whose work is represented in this book allow their ideas to be positioned by secular feminist theory, in such a way that their theology fails to represent the subjectivities and contextualities of women of faith. This leads me to the larger question of what is at stake in the widespread conformity of Anglo-American feminist theory to post-Enlightenment epistemologies, which deny any significance to theological perspectives in the formation of knowledge. In Chapter 2, I focus this question on the relationship between sex and gender and nature and culture in feminist debate, bringing Schumacher's new Catholic feminism into critical encounter with Judith Butler's gender theory. I then consider the problematic question of essentialism, in order to ask how the Catholic understanding of the self as gift might contribute towards a more relational feminist understanding of subjectivity, premised upon the idea of the primal giftedness of the human in relation to God and the sexual other.

In Chapter 3, I move towards a feminist theological epistemology informed by postmodern readings of Heidegger and Aquinas, and focusing on the significance of language, desire and revelation. This theme is continued in Chapter 4, where I ask how prayer might be understood from a feminist perspective, as a way of coming to know which necessarily involves desire and an opening of the self to the other. Engaging primarily with Sarah Coakley's study of prayer and *kenosis*,[28] and with Pamela Sue Anderson's feminist philosophical account of the 'rational passion' of women's religious yearning,[29] I suggest that prayer is a fundamental but neglected resource for feminist theological reflection on the relationship between the self, creation and God.

'The end' begins in Chapter 5, where I move to a more critical engagement with Balthasar and the new feminism, from a perspective informed by a wide range of feminist theorists and theologians, including Irigaray. I devote a considerable amount of space to Balthasar and to his relationship with the mystic/hysteric Adrienne von Speyr, because together they have had a significant influence on the contemporary Church's teachings on theology and sexuality. Michelle Gonzalez suggests that 'Perhaps no other figure in Balthasar's life has provoked more confusion and sometimes disdain than the medical doctor Adrienne von Speyr.'[30] My male theological colleagues often try to minimize the more problematic aspects of Balthasar's sexual theology by attributing these to Adrienne's influence, as if Hans without Adrienne is a much more worthy theologian. Yet my research has led me to believe that Balthasar was correct when he said that his work was inseparable from hers.[31] In seeking to unravel the complexities and instabilities of his theology with its violent sexual undercurrents, it has been important to situate this in the context of his intimate relationship with Speyr which, even if it did not find physical sexual expression, was in no small measure responsible for the growing sexualization of his work after their relationship began in the early 1940s. Given that conservative Catholics sometimes point to these two as models for contemporary relationships between men and women, I have felt justified in bringing theological enquiry to bear on what would otherwise be a rather disturbing private story of two people struggling to reconcile a visceral sexual Catholicism with a commitment to a life of mutual abstinence.

'The end' is intended as a *double entendre*, signifying as it does both the *telos* and the termination of the female body in the story of salvation. In Chapter 5, I develop a mutually critical encounter between Balthasar and Irigaray, allowing his theology to expose her denial of the otherness of God, and allowing her theory to expose his denial of the otherness of woman. In Chapter 6, I go further in this deconstructive enterprise, by showing that the challenge which faces feminist theology is not so much the absence of woman as the absence of masculinity from the Catholic understanding of creation, in a long tradition of theological reflection informed by the association of masculinity with transcendence, divinity and reason, and femininity with immanence, humanity and the body. Thus the only 'man' in creation is the priest who vicariously represents the masculine divinity of Christ, while all other men are in fact 'women' and 'brides' in their humanity. Here, we go back to patristic theology in order to begin to unravel the complexity of the Catholic understanding of gender, so as to demonstrate the impossibility of using this in any coherent sense to support a sacramental theology based on an essential biological or psychological difference between the sexes. I develop this theme further in Chapter 7, where I challenge new Catholic feminism to provide an adequate account of the sacramentality of the female body. I

14 *Introduction*

suggest that resistance to women's ordination is having a highly distorting effect on Catholic theology, producing an incoherent and contradictory range of arguments which belie the reconciling promise of the story of salvation. The result is a process of denial which, I argue in Chapter 8, leads Catholic theology to reproduce the 'necrophilia' and violence which thinkers such as Grace Jantzen and Beverley Clack associate with the western intellectual tradition, in its understanding of death, sex and immortality. In Chapter 9, I follow this theme through to its darkest and most violent images in Balthasar's theological representation of Christ in hell and of the Church as *casta meretrix* or chaste whore, in order to argue that the denial of female sacramentality ultimately leads to the symbolic identification of the sexual female body not only with death and hell, but also with all forms of otherness which have historically threatened the Catholic Church, including pagans, Jews and heretics. 'The end' thus ends with an exposure of the extent to which some of Balthasar's most ostensibly innovative and daring theological insights are in fact premised upon an extreme and violent form of misogyny to which his many theological interpreters and translators apparently remain oblivious.

'The beginning' begins with Chapter 10, representing a move beyond deconstruction towards the reconstruction of meaning through the feminist refiguration of Catholic sacramentality and symbolism. Drawing upon the ideas of René Girard, Paul Ricoeur, Charlene Spretnak and Sarah Boss as well as Irigaray, Kristeva and Balthasar/Speyr, these six chapters explore ways of speaking about God, fatherhood, motherhood, the body, death, sex and priesthood in order to ask how Catholic sacramentality and liturgy might go beyond both the nostalgia for a pre-modern form of faith that refuses any of the insights of the modern world, and the modern, rationalizing effects of the Second Vatican Council which many believe have led to the impoverishment of Catholic life and worship. I explore ways in which a maternal sacramental priesthood might liberate male and female bodies together to enact the story of Christ on the world's stage, through a transformed liturgy capable of inspiring new ways of being in the world in a graced celebration of the divinization of the human and the sacramentality of creation.

As we enter more deeply into this story of gendered being and becoming, of salvation and damnation, of insider and outsider, of body and spirit, we discover that nothing is as it seems. Bodies elude us, flowing in and out of one another, together and apart, as couples and communities and as solitary, mutating beings before God. Divinity and humanity encounter one another in gendered couplings, unions, partings and separations, in a restless flight of language and becoming that beats its wings against the caged confines of theological necessity, requiring ever more violence and force to keep it enclosed. In unmasking this violence, I seek to demonstrate that the liberation of theology cannot come about without the liberation of the female body from the silence and animality to which men have consigned her, in order for them to perform their feminine parodies as brides of

Christ and women before God. Only when the sacramental significance and grace of the female body is recognized as equal to but different from that of the male body will we be able to recognize our sexuality as a gift, orientated not only to procreation but more importantly to the creativity of worship, devotion and prayer. Only then might we begin to explore the mystery and wonder of our own being, as beings made in the image of God who is also mystery and wonder, simultaneously revealed and concealed within and beyond all that is.

If the Church has any hope of being listened to by modern women, it needs to go beyond its present anachronistic sexual stereotypes and authoritarian structures, to present the Gospel in a way that is attentive to the questions, needs and values of the age, without surrendering the central truths of the Christian faith. This entails recognizing that much of what presents itself as tradition and truth in neo-orthodox Catholicism is neither: it is a modern sexual ideology, shot through with contradictions, inconsistencies and distortions, which obscures the luminous possibilities of the Catholic faith and binds tradition to its own narrowly defined understanding of human nature. Only by freeing the theological vision of the Church from this sexual stranglehold will it be possible to listen with prayerful attentiveness to the questions that women are asking today with regard to the role of women in the Church, and the sacramental significance of the female body in the liturgical performance of the story of salvation. As I shall show, this has profound ramifications for men as well as women, and it invites a new appreciation of the ways in which Catholic sacramentality and liturgy can express an eschatological hope that manifests itself in the graced interstices of everyday life, where human creatures are called to be priests of creation and lovers of God.

Part I
The middle

1 Catholicism, feminism and faith

The relationship between feminism and Catholicism is not new, but in a rapidly changing cultural environment the nature of the debate has shifted significantly in recent years. Some of the most influential pioneers of twentieth-century feminist theology, such as Mary Daly, Elisabeth Schüssler Fiorenza and Rosemary Radford Ruether, were Catholic women whose work first appeared in the decade following the Second Vatican Council (1962–5), when many Catholics responded eagerly to Vatican II's shift towards a more open and liberal understanding of the Church. However, since then, deep divisions have opened up in Roman Catholicism between liberals who see the Council as a triumph for democratization and modernization, and neo-orthodox Catholics who believe that the initial enthusiasm for the Council's reforms must be tempered with a greater respect for the Church's sacramental and hierarchical traditions.

While feminist theologies continue to proliferate, representing an ever wider diversity of perspectives and contexts but mostly situated towards what Nancy Dallavalle refers to as 'the social-liberal'[1] end of the theological spectrum, an alternative version of Catholic thinking about women has begun to take shape since the mid-1990s. This is sometimes called the 'new feminism' in recognition of Pope John Paul II's call for women to promote 'a "new feminism" which rejects the temptation of imitating models of "male domination", in order to acknowledge and affirm the true genius of women in every aspect of the life of society, and overcome all discrimination, violence and exploitation'.[2] Although feminist theology has not been officially censured by the Vatican in the way that liberation theology was in the 1980s, the impact of feminism on Roman Catholicism might be assessed by the extent to which it has triggered this new attentiveness among conservative theologians to questions of sexuality, gender and embodiment. These theologians tend to present their work as an irenic engagement with feminism, although on closer scrutiny it usually amounts to a subtle way of silencing or rejecting feminist arguments through a confident reassertion of the authority and wisdom of the Catholic tradition.

The Vatican and feminism

Although it makes only one explicit reference to feminism, the thinking which informs the new Catholic feminism is clearly evident in a letter written by the Congregation for the Doctrine of the Faith (CDF) in May 2004 and published on 31 July 2004, under the signature of Cardinal Ratzinger and sanctioned by Pope John Paul II, titled 'Collaboration of Men and Women in the Church'.[3] In its opening sentence, the letter describes the Church as 'expert in humanity', and it goes on to say that 'the Church is called today to address certain currents of thought which are often at variance with the authentic advancement of women'. It begins by setting out a biblical theology of sexual difference in which man and woman are described as equal persons made in the image and likeness of God; it affirms the body – soul unity of the person, and it represents the conflict between the sexes as a consequence of original sin which might be healed through the rediscovery of the spousal love between man and woman, understood in the context of the relationship between Christ and the Church.

The content of the letter is not antithetical to some feminist arguments, and indeed it reveals how many unacknowledged resonances there are between feminism and Catholic theology. It affirms the inherent relationality of women – described as 'a "capacity for the other"' – which, although couched in essentialist terms that feminists might reject, echoes many of the theories found in feminist writings.[4] While asserting the primary responsibility of women towards the domestic sphere and the need to have this fully recognized by society, the letter also defends the right of women to find fulfilment in work outside the home. Not only that, but it describes the positive contribution that women might make to the transformation of society, arguing that 'women should have access to positions of responsibility which allow them to inspire the policies of nations and to promote innovative solutions to economic and social problems'. Again, such ideas would find widespread support among feminists.

But the whole bias of the letter is implicitly anti-feminist. For a start, it is produced in the name of one exclusively male group (the CDF is made up of twenty-five cardinals, archbishops and bishops),[5] and addressed to another exclusively male group (the bishops of the Catholic Church). Its title bears little relation to its content, which says hardly anything about men or about collaboration, but instead focuses almost entirely on the nature and role of women. Not surprisingly, perhaps, it was widely publicized in the secular press as the Vatican's hardline reaction to feminism. Instead of seeking a balanced engagement that would acknowledge affinities as well as dissonances between Catholicism and feminism, the letter sets the (male) authority of the Catholic hierarchy over and against feminism, in such a way that all feminists are discredited and the Church's expertise in humanity is confidently asserted.

Although it has much to say about violence, antagonism and hostility between the sexes, the letter offers no acknowledgement that a history of male dominance in the Church as well as in society might bear at least some responsibility for this, nor does it acknowledge that nearly all the perpetrators of violence in today's world are men, and the overwhelming majority of victims are women and children. Rather, it implies several times that feminism is to blame for the animosity between the sexes. It refers to 'new approaches to women's issues' which tend to 'emphasize strongly conditions of subordination in order to give rise to antagonism'. There is no recognition that the subordination of women to men (a doctrine that prevailed in the Catholic tradition until it was replaced by a doctrine of complementarity in the 1950s and 1960s) might itself be a cause of antagonism between the sexes. Instead, the feminist protest against women's subordination is not only held responsible for creating antagonism, its whole purpose is interpreted as antagonistic – it is '*in order* to give rise to antagonism'.

The letter claims that, as a result of these new approaches to women's issues, 'women, in order to be themselves, must make themselves the adversaries of men. Faced with the abuse of power, the answer for women is to seek power.' Such criticisms might well have some validity if they were more focused, but couched in these general terms they become an unfounded attack on feminism as a whole. It is demonstrably not true that those concerned with women's issues have in recent years adopted the kind of adversarial politics that the letter refers to. Indeed, if anything, the contrary may be true. The radical separatist feminism of the 1970s, associated with thinkers such as Mary Daly, has yielded to a more diverse and complex feminist landscape, which encompasses a growing plurality of perspectives. If there are some forms of feminism that are not compatible with Christianity, there are many others in which women and men together seek new ways of relating, not through a struggle for power over one another, nor through regarding one another 'as enemies to be overcome', but in a shared endeavour to understand and unmask the dynamics of power, domination and oppression as these affect the relationship between the sexes. If the letter had acknowledged this, it might have offered a more balanced and convincing critique.

The letter also expresses concern about the ways in which sexual differences have come to be 'viewed as mere effects of historical and cultural conditioning. In this perspective, physical difference, termed *sex*, is minimized, while the purely cultural element, termed *gender*, is emphasized to the maximum and held to be primary.' This results in 'a new model of polymorphous sexuality', which contradicts fundamental Christian beliefs about human nature, sexual difference and family life, and makes 'homosexuality and heterosexuality virtually equivalent'. But the relationship between sex and gender is by no means straightforward in the Church's own theology, as is clear from this letter. After celebrating the feminine characteristics associated with Mary, 'with her dispositions of listening, welcoming, humility, faithfulness, praise and waiting', the letter points out that 'the feminine values mentioned here are above all human values'. So, the feminine traits which are lived by women 'with particular intensity and naturalness' should in fact 'be characteristic of every baptized person'. In other words, there is no necessary relationship between sex and gender, if everything that can be said of women in terms of maternal femininity can be said of men as well. As I shall argue later, this fluidity of gender roles in Catholic theology means that feminist debates about sex and gender can make a significant contribution to the Church's understanding of its own sexual symbolism, while some of the arguments of new feminists such as Michele Schumacher also pose a significant challenge to some feminist thought in this area.

The letter affirms the indispensable contribution that women can make to society – women have an 'irreplaceable role . . . in all aspects of family and social life involving human relationships and caring for others' – but it also claims that 'the reservation of priestly ordination solely to men does not hamper in any way women's access to the heart of Christian life'. Is this because the priestly hierarchy does not involve 'human relationships and caring for others'? Is it because the ordained men of the Church, being 'expert in humanity', know all there is to know about women so that women have nothing to teach them, however necessary their contribution might be to the rest of society? In the only sentence that might be interpreted as a call to collaboration, the letter tells the bishops that 'The witness of women's lives must be received with respect and appreciation, as revealing those values without which humanity would be closed in self-sufficiency, dreams of power and the drama of violence.' This is an ironic exhortation when it is addressed to a male hierarchy in a Church which still prohibits women from being members of the magisterium, from administering the sacraments, or from preaching the homily during Mass. In other words, the most important areas of the Church's intellectual and sacramental life remains closed to the active witness of women's lives. As this book unfolds, I will ask to what extent this results in a Church that is closed in 'self-sufficiency, dreams of power and the drama of violence', precisely because of the ongoing struggle to keep women under male ecclesiastical control.

If Catholic thinkers want to contribute to feminist debate, then they need to respect the rules of good scholarship and reasoned argument, including the imperative to negotiate disputed claims with an informed and balanced understanding of the issues. The fact that many feminists are guilty of ignorance and prejudice in their dealings with religion does not justify a similar level of ignorance and prejudice when theologians deal with feminists. Neo-orthodox Catholics who engage with feminism still have an anachronistic tendency to appeal to a kind of ecclesiastical authority which has no currency in secular discourse, and which is likely to antagonize even further a secularized culture that is already deeply sceptical if not openly hostile towards religiously informed arguments. As long as Catholic pronouncements on feminism are marked by the kind of defensive authoritarianism that is a feature of many Catholic writings on the subject, it is hardly surprising that many secular feminists view the Catholic Church as the enemy of women's struggles for equality. The pity is that potentially valuable insights and arguments risk being ignored, because their Catholic authors are so one-sided and hostile in their approach.

Catholicism and the end of feminism?

Although the CDF letter makes no direct reference to the new Catholic feminism, it is possible to situate it in the broader context of anti-feminist arguments that have been taking shape among some Catholic thinkers in recent years. In particular, a collection of essays titled *Women in Christ*, edited by Michele Schumacher, appeared in 2004 a few months before the publication of the CDF letter, and it offers a more comprehensive insight into the concerns and perceptions that motivate this Catholic backlash against feminism.

Apart from Francis Martin, all the contributors to *Women in Christ* are women, and this serves as a reminder of the extent to which many Christian women, far from being converted by feminism, are actually alienated by its claims and arguments. It would be easy to caricature the new feminism as it is represented in this volume, but whatever the manifold shortcomings in its treatment of feminist ideas and arguments, it is also an attempt to set out a vision of women's dignity and sexual mutuality as persons made in the image of God, through an appeal to the Catholic tradition. This means recognizing that 'authentic self-realization should be understood vertically as well as horizontally, an understanding which requires a certain balance between nature and culture (nurture) on the one hand and nature and grace on the other'.[6] Although several of the essays are marred by anti-feminist polemics and by sweeping generalizations, there are also rich insights, particularly in the essays by Schumacher, which invite further reflection with regard to the relationship between sex and gender and between feminism and faith. But although there are aspects of the new feminism which might make a significant contribution to feminist theological reflection and which highlight particular failings in recent feminist theory, this would depend upon a genuinely respectful Catholic dialogue with feminist theory. As it is, this ostensibly dialogical encounter between feminism and Catholicism is a thinly veiled attack on contemporary feminism, based on a highly superficial and at times distorted reading of feminist sources.

The new feminism claims some affinity with 'the "old" brand of feminism . . . associated with the women's liberation movement',[7] but it also presents itself as an answer to a feminist vision that has, according to most of the authors, failed and even, to quote Mary Ann Glendon's endorsement on the back cover, become 'defunct'. According to Elizabeth Fox-Genovese, 'That we are in sore need of a new feminism can hardly be doubted, and the answer to why we need one could hardly be more disconcertingly simple: the old one has failed.'[8] The extent of this alleged failure can be judged by the two essays in which Prudence Allen surveys the legacy of feminism, and identifies two women in history who can be regarded as authentic feminists: Christine de Pizan (1364–1430), and Edith Stein (1891–1942). Stein features repeatedly in these essays – along with Pope John Paul II and Balthasar, she is one of the primary sources for the new feminism. But those who represent contemporary feminist theology and theory are dismissed by most of these authors (except Schumacher) in their entirety. Their works are plundered for 'sound-bites' but never discussed or analysed in any detail, and at times the invective against them amounts to an embittered and narrow-minded assault that casts serious doubt on the scholarly integrity and judgement of the authors. For example, Beatriz Vollmer Coles claims that

> Because twentieth-century feminism has had no solid philosophical foundation, it has been driven to skepticism if not absurdity. There has been no other goal, standard, or concept than 'war against patriarchy'; and even then, there is ambiguity as to what feminists mean thereby.[9]

Coles's main target is what she calls 'gender feminism', which she describes as the successor to earlier forms of radical feminism:

> In the 1980s and 1990s radical feminism was renamed *gender feminism*. This new form redefined 'equality' to no longer refer to dignity, rights, and opportunities; instead its meaning was reduced to mathematical equality for statistical ends. Its political lobby even pushed some governments to impose quotas and affirmative action in an attempt to pervade all spheres, including the home.[10]

Coles gives no reference for the term 'gender feminism', although she may be referring to postmodern, deconstructive theories of gender such as those associated with Judith Butler or Luce Irigaray. Gender feminism has, claims Coles, 'brought about a postmodern dualism, exalting one sex over the other, but it has also encouraged homosexual lobbies, new witchcraft, and other extreme ideologies, which exist almost exclusively in contemporary Western culture'.[11]

Other contributors are more restrained in their anti-feminist bias, but nonetheless, there are slippages which expose the prejudices behind many of the essays. Fox-Genovese says of 'dissident Catholic feminist theologians like Rosemary Radford Ruether and Elisabeth Schüssler Fiorenza' that 'Their demands begin with the sexual liberation of women, grounded in the right to abortion, and extend to women's ordination to the priesthood.'[12] There is no reference in

Catholicism, feminism and faith 25

support of this claim, but to say that Catholic feminist theologians' work is 'grounded in the right to abortion' is simply not true, since references to abortion are largely absent from their work. This silence on an issue of such profound ethical significance might in itself be cause for criticism, but it cannot be claimed that feminist theology is 'grounded in the right to abortion'. Yet Prudence Allen, usually a fine scholar who has written an impressive series of studies on the concept of woman in western thought,[13] suggests that

> once feminism explicitly separated itself from relations with God, and when it set itself up in antagonism with organized religion, it began to think of getting rid of other people. It saw certain groups of people as enemies and saw nothing wrong in eliminating them.[14]

It is hard to explain how a careful philosopher can be reduced to this level of polemic in her antagonism towards feminism. However legitimate Catholic concerns about abortion might be, to dismiss the whole secular feminist movement as genocidally motivated is pernicious. Elsewhere, Allen refers to feminists who 'indirectly oppose Jesus Christ by saying they are following him while acting contrary to the content and witness of his teachings: they call themselves Catholics or Christians, but they choose contraceptives'.[15]

It is tempting to dismiss any book that contains so many inaccuracies, insults and distortions. However, I think it is important for feminist theologians to engage with the new feminism, for several reasons. First, the prejudices expressed in *Women in Christ* are not uncommon. They are typical of what any feminist will encounter in the Catholic Church, and indeed among many other religious groups as well. The writers of *Women in Christ* are playing to a particular audience. Their intention is not to offer a balanced and mutually enriching dialogue between feminism and Catholicism, but to promote an authoritarian form of Catholicism that emerged under the papacy of John Paul II, heavily influenced by the then Cardinal Ratzinger, based on the belief that true Catholicism entails absolute, unquestioning loyalty to the Pope and to the teachings of the Church, and that any form of criticism, however conscientious and well informed, constitutes a form of disloyalty that calls into question one's very right to be Catholic. If one is to challenge these assumptions – which may gain added power under the papacy of Benedict XVI – then one must engage with the arguments and ideas behind them.

Second, the fact that these 'new feminists' include highly educated and articulate women must at least invite a recognition from feminist theologians that they do not and must not claim to speak for all women. The new Catholic feminists serve as a reminder that many women – not just Catholics, but across all churches and indeed in all religions – find in conservative forms of religion an alternative to the nihilistic and materialistic tendencies inherent in modern western culture.

While liberal churches are losing numbers, those which preach certainties and absolute truths seem to have a certain appeal to many modern believers, whether these are the absolute truths of evangelical fundamentalists or of Catholic popes. Feminists might wish this was not the case, but it is dishonest simply to ignore this phenomenon or to condemn it out of hand.

Third, for all their provocations, some of these 'new' feminists – Schumacher in particular – pose a challenge to the assumptions and methods of secular feminism, and that is also why I believe that their approach invites reflection from those who would seek to reconcile a commitment to feminist ideals with a commitment to the Christian faith. There is in much liberal and postmodern feminist theology a certain barrenness surrounding the question of faith. Prayer is rarely mentioned, and the whole idea of the theologian being open to the revelation and otherness of God tends to be set aside, either because the appeal to women's experience has taken the place of scripture, revelation and prayer as the primary source for the Christian understanding of God, as is the case in liberal feminism, or because postmodern feminist theologians have uncritically conformed to the methods and criteria of feminist critical theory, in such a way that their theological insights are silenced through what might perhaps be seen as an over-enthusiasm for the latest trends in secular academia.[16] A critical but creative engagement with women theologians who are more assertive about their faith might restore to feminist theology the neglected language of prayer and revelation.

Secular theory and feminist theology

The work of some of the most influential postmodern feminist theologians appears in a collection titled *Horizons in Feminist Theology*, edited by Rebecca Chopp and Sheila Greeve Davaney. In her concluding essay to *Horizons*, Chopp points out that 'feminist theory, in its modern and postmodern varieties, is quite devoted to the Enlightenment resistance to theology'.[17] She goes on to observe that many of the Christian feminist theologians who contributed to the volume

> indicate a similar disenchantment with or even resistance to theological symbols and theological doctrines. Many of our authors are Christian theologians engaged, at some level, with the symbols of Christian practice and belief. Yet the articles rarely mention the language or imagery of Christian symbols, let alone belief and practice.[18]

This raises the question of representation, particularly with regard to the potentially conflicting demands of the Church and the academy, for there is a risk that feminist theological scholarship distorts and misrepresents the values, practices and beliefs of women of faith, in its secularized academic discourses.

Mary McClintock Fulkerson, who is one of the few writers represented in *Horizons* whose work maintains a faith perspective,[19] raises the question of power and representation in her book *Changing the Subject*. In a Foucaultian critique of feminist theological discourse, Fulkerson argues that feminist theology fails to acknowledge the multiplicity and plurality of discursive relationships of power and resistance, as a result of which it

> implicitly silences voices of other women of faith: texts' meanings are fixed, power is monarchical. Those whose experience differs from the model of 'women's experience' are not accounted for, or constitute a lobotomized casualty of patriarchy, one of Mary Daly's 'fembots'.[20]

In order to become more critically nuanced in its critique of power and oppression, feminist theology needs to be more attentive to 'the constructed character of reality':[21]

> Power is not just in the hands of oppressors; power has an internal relation to knowledge. What this means is that one cannot step outside of discourse to make judgments about what ought to be, because one is always already in discourse. For Foucault, this means that truth and knowledge are relations of power . . . [I]n any dominant discourse the terms of truth (that is, what counts as true) are defined by the discourse . . . If we cannot step outside of discourse, there is no place outside of the power that attends it, no realm free of the effects of the productive character of power.[22]

Fulkerson argues that feminist theology 'is about meeting women whose struggles are for physical survival rather than for the feminist transformation of the academy'.[23] In her critique of the appeal to women's experience, she points out that, while the production of feminist theological texts entails using the rhetoric of pluralism, inclusivity, liberation and solidarity with the oppressed, such texts are produced within an academic domain that is by nature exclusive and elitist:

> the institutional capacity to host the discussion and provide chairs at the table — or to shut down the building altogether, so to speak — is the site where real authorizing power is located . . . [T]hose without the skills required to participate in the table discussion will . . . not have their experience of the divine articulated, or will have it articulated by 'experts' who represent them.[24]

In this context, it is interesting to note the Roundtable Discussion that was published in response to *Horizons in Feminist Theology*, in which a number of feminist theologians debated the theological value of feminist theory. Referring to *Horizons*, Emily Neill writes,

> The theoretical wrangling that takes place in the volume, much of which is written over against earlier feminist thinkers – and quite hostilely in certain essays – seems almost completely void of a feminist commitment to use theory and the construction of knowledges to transform structures of oppression and domination.[25]

Central to Neill's critique is the charge that the shift to a theoretical perspective in feminist theology represents a desire for academic acceptability rather than an ongoing commitment to the struggle for justice. Such a move 'positions feminist theology and its goals more in line with a modern debate on epistemology that is going on very much within the academy, and not necessarily in resistance to its structures of domination'.[26]

This suggests that the challenge that confronts feminist theologians is the need to hold together the demands of academic rigour and objectivity positively construed as critical reasoning and argument, and one's responsibilities and commitments to communities of women, children and men who represent diverse and often contradictory ideas and values, and whose lives may be untouched by the rhetorical games of the (post)modern academy. If one takes as the barometer of modern female identity a Judith Butler or a Luce Irigaray, one is confusing a highly stylized and dislocated form of academic rhetoric with questions of identity, belonging and meaning that actually situate women in the lived world of human relationships, economic realities, cultural expectations and religious practices.[27] It could be argued that some of the concerns expressed in postmodern theories of subjectivity are premised more upon the preoccupations of affluent western academics than upon the wider dilemmas of human subjects struggling for survival against the sometimes annihilating forces of the modern world. To confuse the multiple self of academic discourse with the female person who lives, loves, suffers, yearns and struggles in the context of everyday life is to assume too direct a relationship between cultural theory and personal identity. Janet Martin Soskice writes,

> Feminist theology is sometimes attacked by others in feminist fields as a theoretical backwater. If this is true, it may be part of the price paid for keeping an ear to the ground. 'A theologian,' goes a Christian Orthodox adage, 'is one who prays' – and on this reckoning there are many theologians who have minimal access to education of any sort, much less to theological education. Feminism in theology may lack the theoretical frameworks of some of its sister subjects, but its prospect for reaching millions of lives, including those of the world's poorest women, is immense.[28]

The relationship between theology and theory is problematized if one seeks to introduce a sense of communal responsibility or a faith perspective. Rather than agreeing to play by the rules of secular feminist theory or ignoring its insights altogether, feminist theology might have an important contribution to make by calling into question secular feminism's resistance to theology, and its capacity to silence or marginalize theological voices. For if feminism seeks to represent the interests of women worldwide and not simply to provide a megaphone by which the values of western secular individualism can be broadcast to the world, then there needs to be a much greater recognition by feminist theorists of the extent to which religion continues to shape the lives and identities of the majority of the world's women. Rather than uncritically marrying feminism to secular ideology, theology can provide a perspective from which to interrogate the history and oppressive power relationships inherent in secularism itself, allowing for a more mutually respectful sense of dialogue and creative debate between feminist theology and feminist theory.

The secularization of knowledge

Lorraine Code describes the ways in which academic disciplines are sustained but also limited through maintaining invisible ideological boundaries. She writes, 'A network of sociopolitical relationships and intellectual assumptions creates an invisible system of acceptance and rejection, discourse and silence, ascendancy and subjugation within and around disciplines.'[29] Quoting Foucault's observation that 'within its own limits, every discipline recognizes true and false propositions, but it repulses a whole teratology of learning', Code argues that 'A discipline defines itself both by what it excludes (repulses) and by what it includes. But the self-definition process removes what is excluded (repulsed) from view so that it is not straightforwardly available for assessment, criticism, and analysis.'[30] In its self-definition, feminist theory both excludes and hides from view (and therefore from analysis) any engagement with theological questions, while postmodern feminist theology masks its own relationship to faith, in a futile struggle to gain a hearing from the secular sisterhood.

There is extensive feminist literature which seeks to go beyond the autonomous, masculine subject of post-Enlightenment thought by introducing more relational, less rationalist concepts of subjectivity.[31] However, it is interesting how resistant feminist theorists are to theological alternatives which might challenge the post-Kantian inversion of the relationship between reason and faith, in which the hegemony of the man of reason was asserted over and against the man of faith, so that faith was first subjugated to and eventually eliminated by reason. (Women were of course marginalized or excluded from both accounts of reason.)

J.B. Schneewind attributes to Kant the invention of 'the conception of morality as autonomy',[32] arguing that Kant devised an innovative solution to the challenge of finding a basis for moral philosophy that did not rely on the belief that morality is 'one aspect of the obedience we owe to God'.[33] In arguing this, Schneewind suggests that religion, rather than the scientific developments of the sixteenth and seventeenth centuries, was the primary impetus for the development of modern moral philosophy. He observes that

> The conception of morality as self-governance provides a conceptual framework for a social space in which we may each rightly claim to direct our own actions without interference from the state, the church, the neighbors, or those claiming to be better or wiser than we. The older conception of morality as obedience did not have these implications.[34]

Many feminist theorists would reject the excessive individualism inherent in Schneewind's description, but few if any would question its secularism, or would ask if perhaps the autonomous individual of post-Enlightenment thought is inextricably bound up with the secularization of the subject, for it was this that finally brought to birth (after a long gestation perhaps) the modern man of reason. To what extent is it possible to question the autonomy and individualism of this 'man', without also questioning 'his' secularism which, at least in Anglo-American feminist theory, is also 'hers'?

Penelope Margaret Magee argues that, in resisting any engagement with theological discourse and in perpetuating the dichotomy between the sacred and the profane, secular feminism is trapped in a system of binary oppositions that fails to deconstruct the relationship between language, knowledge and power.[35] She sees the resolute avoidance of the theological in feminist theory as betraying 'a desire to totalize "theology" in Absence',[36] and she points to the critical reception of Irigaray's religious language by feminist theorists to illustrate her argument.

Magee proposes a feminist onslaught on the bastions of theology. Referring to Anthony Wilden's idea of the 'Imaginary Other' as maintaining 'hierarchized oppositions' encoded within closed systems of thought, she argues, 'There is, in mainstream English-speaking feminism, no sign of deconstructive and practical energy in relation to the secular/religious and the sacred/profane, which are fundamental categories of the Imaginary Other.'[37] She goes on to suggest that

> Traditional philosophers, theologians and clergy have already achieved much success keeping the sacred and the profane (as defined by them) at war with one another, and we know who are the colonized. Feminism should not sell arms to the combatants.[38]

Yet although Magee offers a cogent critique of secular ideology, she is more positioned by secular feminism's contempt for religious faith than she acknowledges.

Her approach to religion is unequivocally deconstructive, and her 'Imaginary Other' is situated on the side of masculine power struggles, with no recognition that it might also be the locus of liberating forms of faith and practice for women. Citing scholars who argue that 'the violence of sacrifice [is] the foundation of the sacred', Magee suggests that 'the politics of subversion' entails 'the pleasure and the terror of keeping our shoes on and striding towards the burning bush'.[39] But if 'the burning bush' is a metaphor for all that the human being perceives to be most holy because it is touched by the fire and the presence of God, then at the very least a respect for the religious other should challenge this call to profanation. Feminism, including much feminist theology, has failed to take seriously enough the extent to which prayer and devotion may have shaped women's religious lives far more profoundly than doctrine and theology, and may indeed have been the site of women's prolonged struggles to elude the control of male religious hierarchies and their theological concepts.

For a feminist theologian, to seek to live out her personal faith story as one which might involve a complex weaving together of different narratives, informed not only by the demands of academic scholarship and social engagement but also by prayer and desire for God expressed in the context of a worshipping community, need not be to reinscribe theology within a narrow confessional framework. It might rather be to keep the horizons of feminist theology constantly open to the new and unexpected sources of transformation and renewal that Christians call grace, through a vision inspired by an awareness of the primal relationality of the human creature as a being created in and for love. The feminist quest for a relational self might therefore invite that most transgressive of moves – a transgression beyond the rigid boundaries of secularism, to reopen the question of God.

When Kant erected an epistemological barrier between faith and reason, he brought to completion the progressive desacralization of the world that some would argue had begun with the institutionalization of the Church in the twelfth century as a result of the Gregorian Reform,[40] and had been given added impetus by the emergence of nominalism in the fourteenth century, and a century later by the Reformation.[41] It was a small step for the great thinkers of the nineteenth and early twentieth centuries to evacuate God from 'his' redundant position behind the scenes of human reason.

But now there has been another change of scene, and 'reason' has given way to the constantly shifting settings and stagings of the postmodern condition, in which the absence of God glimmers between the cracks and gaps in the structures of knowing. 'God' is no longer the noumenal, inaccessible *a priori* who lends coherence to the logic and ethics of rational 'man', but neither is God the redundant creator and psychological illusion of Darwin and Freud respectively. Rather, 'God' haunts the gaps and teases the silences of our post-Nietzschean, post-Heideggerian reflections, so that it has been said of Heidegger that his work is 'one of a number of postdoctrinal, postsystematic theologies',[42] and Jacques Derrida, consummate master of the deconstructive enterprise, finds himself in uneasy solidarity with apophatic mystics and negative theologians.[43] As Denys Turner observes:

> In much continental philosophy, from Heidegger to Levinas and Derrida, it is acknowledged, with varying degrees of unease at having to concede the point, that the predicaments of our culture have an ineradicably *theological* character . . . [I]t is by no means as easy as it was once thought to deny the existence of God.[44]

So what if there is truth in Irigaray's claim that 'To posit a gender, a God is necessary'?[45] According to Irigaray, 'Divinity is what we need to become free, autonomous, sovereign . . . If women have no God, they are unable either to communicate or commune with one another.'[46] Where is such a God to be found, and what might her relationship be to women's being and becoming?

In asking this question, I begin with the question of the body because, when all is said and done, it is the body that positions women in language. The negation of the significance of female embodiment by both Catholic theology and postmodern theory has to be resisted if a language of female personhood is to be allowed to emerge from the mirrors, shadows and silences that have until now constituted 'her' place in the world.

2 Feminist bodies and feminist selves

I have considered some of the failures of both postmodern feminist theology and new Catholic feminism to provide an adequate response to questions of female subjectivity and personhood that press with such urgency upon contemporary society, politics and ethics. The new feminism, which claims to offer a solution beyond feminism, confidently asserts that, if women would only open themselves in faith to the light of revelation, mediated through the Church's doctrines and teachings, they would find an answer to their questions in the essential nature of their God-given femininity. At the other extreme of the feminist spectrum, women are invited to unmask all ontologies and essentialisms as discourses of power by means of which society reproduces the heterosexual body through the manufactured illusions of identity, interiority, nature and sexual embodiment. Women's liberation from these deceptions might enable them to celebrate their transgressive potential in a disruptive, anarchic performance of gender that overthrows the established orders by way of a parodic mimesis of their own humanity, transcending their limitations and finitude through a Manichean contempt for the materiality and situatedness of their bodily selves.

The disembodied self

High priest of this movement is the critical theorist Judith Butler, who writes that

> acts, gestures, and desire produce the effect of an internal core or substance, but produce this *on the surface* of the body, through the play of signifying absences that suggest, but never reveal, the organizing principle of identity as a cause. Such acts, gestures, enactments, generally construed, are *performative* in the sense that the essence or identity that they otherwise purport to express are *fabrications* manufactured and sustained through corporeal signs and other discursive means. That the gendered body is performative suggests that it has no ontological status

> apart from the various acts which constitute its reality. This also suggests that if that reality is fabricated as an interior essence, that very interiority is an effect and function of a decidedly public and social discourse, the public regulation of fantasy through the surface politics of the body, the gender border control that differentiates inner from outer, and so institutes the 'integrity' of the subject. In other words, acts and gestures, articulated and enacted desires create the illusion of an interior and organizing gender core, an illusion discursively maintained for the purposes of the regulation of sexuality within the obligatory frame of reproductive heterosexuality.[1]

Here, the body itself becomes a mirage, inaccessible and unknowable beyond the veils of linguistic performances that have become the costumes and guises of the infinitely mutable self. The body is neither inert sexual matter upon which the maps and meanings of gender are inscribed, nor is it a source of revelation that might, in its very givenness, shape our understanding of its meanings. Rather, the body materializes – 'matter is always materialized'[2] – through its production within the linguistic and cultural constructs of heterosexual domination and control. To defy this linguistic order, to change our ways of speaking, to act differently, is to be different, because there is no 'be-ing' beyond the acts we perform.

Seyla Benhabib asks what this vacuous performance means in terms of women's quest for a sense of self:

> If this view of self is adopted, is there any possibility of changing those 'expressions' which constitute us? If we are no more than the sum total of the gendered expressions we perform, is there ever any chance to stop the performance for a while, to pull the curtain down, and let it rise only if one can have a say in the production of the play itself?[3]

Benhabib refers to 'a complete debunking of any concepts of selfhood, agency, and autonomy',[4] leading to a Nietzschean position which offers

> a vision of the self as a masquerading performer, except of course we are now asked to believe that there is no self behind the mask. Given how fragile and tenuous women's sense of selfhood is in many cases, how much of a hit and miss affair their struggles for autonomy are, this reduction of female agency to a 'doing without the doer' at best appears to me to be making a virtue out of necessity.[5]

This suggests that, between the complacent essentialisms of Catholic 'new feminism', and the nihilistic performativities of feminist postmodernism, women remain persons in want of a discourse, individuals in search of a self.

But let me go beyond this preliminary positioning of two apparently polarized responses to the question of what it means to be or to become a woman, in order to explore these different perspectives in more depth. For the question of anthropology (i.e. the question of woman/women), hinges on the question of theology (even or especially *in absentia* – resistance to theology is a subliminal but potent influence on feminist theory), which brings back into focus the question of the relationship of women to God, which is inseparable from the elusive question of being itself. For, notwithstanding feminism's resistance to questions of theology and faith, the theoretical discourses that position postmodern feminism are haunted by the question of God.

An author such as Butler, whose prose seems to revel in its own obscurity, is open to different readings, some more positive than others. As with many feminists, her work develops through dialogue and responsivity to the arguments of her critics, and therefore it is an evolving and ongoing project. In *Bodies That Matter*, she attempts a more developed exploration of the body and materiality in relation to the language of sex and gender than she initially offered in *Gender Trouble*, and in *The Psychic Life of Power* she seeks, through psychoanalysis, to offer a more nuanced exploration of interiority. In the preface to the 1999 edition of *Gender Trouble*, she responds to her critics by clarifying her position in some areas and modifying it in others. She explains the motivation for her work as follows:

> To the extent the gender norms (ideal dimorphism, heterosexual complementarity of bodies, ideals and rule of proper and improper masculinity and femininity, many of which are underwritten by racial codes of purity and taboos against miscegenation) establish what will and will not be intelligibly human, what will and will not be considered to be 'real', they establish the ontological field in which bodies may be given legitimate expression. If there is a positive normative task in *Gender Trouble*, it is to insist upon the extension of this legitimacy to bodies that have been regarded as false, unreal, and unintelligible.[6]

Sarah Coakley points out the extent to which 'Butler's theory of the "body" is capable of serious distortion'.[7] Coakley explains, 'Language cannot *create* bodies (that would be an odd claim indeed); rather, Butler is insisting that there is no access to bodies that is not already a gendered access.'[8] Butler maintains that her intention is not to suggest that the body is reducible to discourse with no remainder, but to make clear how problematic it is to think or to live the body outside the discursive heterosexual boundaries imposed upon it – boundaries that imprison and dehumanize bodies perceived to be abnormal or unnatural, condemning them to 'the violence of the foreclosed life, the one that does not get named as "living", the one whose incarceration implies a suspension of life, or a sustained death sentence'.[9]

36 *The middle*

But notwithstanding the nuances that invite a close (and patient) reading of Butler's work, it is not surprising that the new feminists see this 'gender feminism' as the arch enemy of Christianity, nor is it difficult to find evidence in some of their writings to support Butler's thesis that compulsory heterosexuality is the means by which a certain politics of power reproduces itself through the linguistic production of nature and the body. Indeed, Butler's argument is considerably strengthened by claims such as the following: 'Gender feminists – following the tracks of poststructuralist philosophers – are interested in deconstructing, among other things, language, family relationships, reproduction, sexuality, work, religion, government, and culture in general.'[10] This suggests that compulsory heterosexuality is indeed the loom upon which the social fabric is woven, so that everything from family relationships and reproduction through to work, government and 'culture in general' is threatened by those who question the essential heterosexuality of human 'nature'.

The reaction of the new feminists and Ratzinger's CDF to 'gender feminism' confirms the extent of Butler's influence, particularly in American gender politics, and the threat that this is perceived to pose to religious institutions that are heavily invested in traditional socio-sexual values. Coakley observes that

> Butler's work continues to exercise an uncanny degree of influence. Somehow it is the allure of gender liberation (not now sexual liberation, note) that has fascinated the late-twentieth-century mind, the prospect of an escape from stereotype, the hope of an elusive personal transformation beyond normal human expectations and restrictions.[11]

However, without denying the insights of Butler's theory, there is a level at which her project remains fundamentally flawed, because it is trapped in the very materialism that it seeks to escape. Her performance of identity politics might entail a wrecking of the props and scenery of the established order as far as sexual identities are concerned, but it is also a thoroughly secularized performance that does not transgress or call into question the conditions that sustain secularism and the extent to which secularism itself might be implicated in the perpetuation of modern sexual identities and their oppressive effects. As a result, Butler's political vision cannot amount to more than a vague utopianism deprived of any ultimate hope, because it is always vulnerable to the powers that it seeks to escape and parasitic upon the structures that it seeks to destroy. The self that refuses itself in the interests of the constant unmaking and remaking of self becomes a form of solipsistic exhibitionism that cannot break free of the constructs that constitute its deconstructive goal. In common with many other feminisms, Butler's secularism must pit itself against any possibility of an opening into transcendence or metaphysics, and this involves a sustained resistance to theology and an evasion of the questions that theology might pose to her enterprise.

Butler's absent God

In hoping for 'a coalition of sexual minorities that will transcend the simple categories of identity, that will refuse the erasure of bisexuality, that will counter and dissipate the violence imposed by restrictive bodily norms',[12] Butler acknowledges the pervasive influence of power – '[t]here is no political position purified of power'[13] – and the risk of the politics of identity itself 'becoming an instrument of the power one opposes'.[14] Foucault's influence on her work has led to an increasing preoccupation with the power of power itself, leading Coakley to observe that 'it is a post-Foucaultian analysis of "power" that comes to the fore in her analysis, and at points suggests comparison with the "Yahweh" of her Jewish heritage who still lurks at the corners of her discussion'.[15] But power thus constituted is a tyranny that offers no escape, save for what Coakley summarizes as Butler's 'insistence that speech can effect occasional punctures in existing power relations'.[16]

In a densely argued chapter in *Bodies That Matter*, Butler problematizes the understanding of the Lacanian real in the work of Slavoj Žižek and Ernesto Laclau. In Lacan's linguistic appropriation of Freud, the real is a consequence of the oedipal crisis. It is the abjected and forbidden desire that is banished by the threat of castration, and that constitutes the most profound and unspeakable dimension of our psychic make-up, being that which is denied access to the symbolic order constituted by the laws that govern language and the speaking subject.[17] Associated as it is with the primal desire for the mother, the real is closely identified with femininity, so that 'woman' comes also to signify the non-signifiable, non-representable other of the symbolic order, whose subject is masculine.

Butler's language is redolent with implicit theological questions, as she interrogates the concealed ideological functions of the Lacanian real as 'the unspeakable, the unviable, the nonnarrativizable that secures and, hence, fails to secure the very borders of materiality'.[18] She refers to Žižek's 'invocation of a certain kind of matter, a "rock" or a "kernel" that not only resists symbolization and discourse, but is precisely what poststructuralism, in his account, itself resists and endeavours to "dissolve"'.[19] She points to the slippage in Žižek's language, so that

> the 'real' that is a 'rock' or a 'kernel' or sometimes a 'substance' is also, and sometimes within the same sentence, 'a loss', a 'negativity'; as a figure it appears to slide from substance to dissolution, thereby conflating the law that institutes the 'lack' and the 'lack' itself.[20]

38   The middle

This leads her to ask,

> How are we to understand this figure of a rock which is at once the law and the loss instituted by that law? The law as rock is to be found in the Hebrew prayer in which God is 'my rock and my redeemer', a phrase that suggests that the 'rock' is the unnameable Yahweh, the principle of monotheism.[21]

Here, Butler reveals the extent to which a certain secularizing and defining power exerts itself through her text. In her critique of Žižek, she refers to his treatment of

> 'the Marxist – feminist criticism of psychoanalysis' and in particular 'the idea that its insistence on the crucial role of the Oedipus and the nuclear family triangle transforms a historically conditioned form of patriarchal family into a feature of the universal human condition'.

But, she continues,

> Žižek then asks the following question, but asks it through a figure which makes the rock of the real speak: 'Is not this effort to historicize the family triangle precisely an attempt to *elude* the "hard kernel" which announces itself through the "patriarchal family" – [then in caps] the Real of the Law, the rock of castration?' If the real of the law is precisely what cannot speak, the traumatic site foreclosed from symbolization, then it is with some interest that the real speaks here, qualified here as the real of the law, and that it is Žižek who, it seems, revives the word from the rock, and brings it down the mountain to us.[22]

But Butler too becomes a Moses figure, permitting the real to speak, or speaking the real, by confusing analogical with representational language. It is nonsensical to suggest that 'the law as rock' *is* 'the unnameable Yahweh', for if Yahweh is unnameable then Yahweh is *not* the rock: Yahweh is not the law but the giver of the law. Moreover, by introducing a third term into this biblical analogy – 'the principle of monotheism' – Butler imposes yet another concept, one whose philosophical language is alien to the Hebrew understanding of Yahweh, thereby offering a cluster of definitions that ensnare the real in representational language: the unnameable Yahweh becomes the law, a rock and a principle. This is to freeze the real, not this time by making a universal necessity of the oedipal law that brings the real into being through its banishment while covertly permitting it to speak in the name of the patriarchal family (as she suggests in her critique of Žižek), but by permitting the real to speak on behalf of a secularism that refuses the theological revelation of the scriptural analogy, and divests 'Yahweh' of the creative and redeeming power that the scriptures seek to express. By equating Yahweh, the giver of the law, with the law and with the principle of monotheism (a principle is surely an effect of the law and a donation of the law giver), Butler too is guilty of 'conflating the law that institutes the "lack" and the "lack" itself'. 'Yahweh', like the real, thus becomes complicit in the secular politics of power which always and everywhere militate against the freedom of subjective becoming. There is, in this account of the real and/or of God, no redeeming power save their undoing through a perpetual process of interrogating the ideologies that they conceal, the powers that they exert, and the identities that they secure.

In her determination to expose all that is hidden and unknowable to the relentless glare of the deconstructive, all-knowing mind, does Butler perhaps reveal the extent of her struggle against a religious desire that her obedience to the secular diktat prohibits her from acknowledging? Might this desire be the forbidden expression of the ultimate *eros*, the yearning of the sexually unstable body for its union with God beyond gender? Reading Butler in engagement with Gregory of Nyssa's disruption of gender binaries in the service of an erotic eschatology, Coakley points out that 'Butler speaks little of death; yet death, as Gregory well sees, is the most incisive test of a person's life . . . [D]eath for Gregory is merely a passage into a further "bodily" – albeit de-genitalized – life.'[23] Coakley describes 'Gregory's eschatologically-oriented theory of gender'[24] in terms of a bodily continuity between this life and the next, because of its 'divine referent that forms the final point of meaning'.[25] She quotes Rowan Williams, who thematizes this as 'that fundamental *eros* for the endless God that binds the polyphony of our intentionality into some sort of unity'.[26] Coakley asks,

> Do we not perhaps detect a yearning for such completion in Butler's remorselessly sophisticated and tortured maneuvers? . . . [W]hat seems to be being enacted is the gesturing to an eschatological horizon which will give mortal flesh final significance, a horizon in which the restless, fluid post-modern 'body' can find some sense of completion without losing its mystery, without succumbing again to 'appropriate' or restrictive gender roles.[27]

Butler's transcendent performativity suggests a one-way spirituality – a liberation of the human soul through its escape from the confines of the body, so that it is free to do whatever it will, unfettered by the body's restraints. The new Catholic feminism offers the opposite as far as women are concerned, for (as we shall see) it robs the female body of all possible transcendence and signification, making her the mute matter to be plundered by him for the signifiers that will situate 'him' as 'her' before God. This results in a performative transgendering of the male body which has far more in common with Butler than the new feminists acknowledge, but which leaves the female body without language, sacramentality or representation.

However, I have already suggested that Schumacher offers a more nuanced critique of feminist theology from the perspective of the new feminism than some of the other contributors to the collection edited by her. I want to consider in more detail now her critique of what she calls 'gender feminism' (implicitly referring to Butler), and its failure to acknowledge the significance of the body.

Sex, gender and the secular body

In Schumacher's essay, 'The Nature of Nature in Feminism, Old and New', she argues that, through its denial of human nature, feminism perpetuates 'the *dualistic conception of nature* which is itself, many feminists claim, a product of the "divide-and-rule" mentality of Enlightenment thought and "androcentric logic"'.[28] Feminism, 'in its rightful refutation of the reductionist claim that anatomy is destiny . . . has deprived nature of any "real" (essential) content and thereby accepted the "patriarchal" division of nature and culture which denies nature of [sic] its traditional metaphysical dimension'.[29] To recognize that grace is inherent in nature, and that human nature itself is inherently relational, is to understand that we attain to personal self-fulfilment, i.e. we fulfil our human nature, through our culturally constituted commitments and relationships: 'Nature both requires culture and contributes to culture.'[30] Even if one acknowledges that nature might be socially determined to a large extent, it retains its own sphere of meaning, so that there is a 'delicate but absolutely necessary balance between nature, conceived as an essential reality, and nature, conceived as a socially determined reality'.[31]

Feminism's failure lies in its denial of the 'essential reality' of nature, including human nature, as a result of which its arguments have 'evolved from the social construction of *gender* to the social construction of *nature*'.[32] This means that

> The delicate balance between nature and nurture – already upset (if we accept the feminist critique) by patriarchy's reduction of the former to the physiological realm – is further threatened (this time in the other direction) by feminism's insistence upon the overbearing power of culture.[33]

According to Schumacher, this has serious implications for our understanding of human freedom.

Schumacher refers to Simone de Beauvoir's famous maxim, 'One is not born, but rather becomes, a woman.'[34] She interprets Beauvoir's feminist existentialism as entailing 'a break from nature as man has conceived it',[35] and she explains:

For Beauvoir, as for Sartre, a nature opposed to reason — and thus freedom — is a nature which must be denied; and when nature is lost, all that remains is freedom itself. The human being *is* freedom: a freedom whose only goal is to will itself. Freedom invents its own values and gives meaning to a life having no a priori meaning.[36]

I am not convinced that this criticism of Beauvoir is entirely justified,[37] but Schumacher's argument is more persuasive when it is considered from the perspective of Butler's performative politics. According to Beauvoir, nature, liberated from its ideological function, is simply a fact of life for men as well as for women. The problem is the asymmetrical identification of woman with the body and nature, and the denial that man too might be identified in this way:

> Woman has ovaries, a uterus: these peculiarities imprison her in her subjectivity, circumscribe her within the limits of her own nature. It is often said that she thinks with her glands. Man superbly ignores the fact that his anatomy also includes glands, such as the testicles, and that they secrete hormones.[38]

For Butler, nature cannot be spoken of at all outside its culturally constructed, ideological function, and therefore it provides no possible basis for the expression of a freedom or subjectivity that is not already defined in the terms it seeks to escape. From the perspective of Butler's secular materialism, God and nature are both perceived as constructs that militate against human freedom, so that autonomy can only be asserted through the overcoming of religion and nature. Butler's 'Yahweh' is the Lacanian real which, like 'nature', must be deconstructed in order to unmask its functions of oppression and exclusion: 'the symbolic law in Lacan can be subject to the same kind of critique that Nietzsche formulated of the notion of God: the power attributed to this prior and ideal power is derived and deflected from the attribution itself'.[39] All is politics and power, and freedom finds its only expression in defiance.

Schumacher (referring to Beauvoir) writes that 'this secular denial of nature — because of its affiliation with divine grace — parallels the religious emptying of nature of its properly human content: its capacity for self-realization based upon free will'.[40] It is Luther, suggests Schumacher, who, in his overpowering of nature by grace, prepared the way for secularism's 'overpowering of grace by nature'.[41] In other words, secular feminism, in its assimilation of nature to culture, brings to its logical conclusion what Luther began in his denial of the inhering grace of creation, and his insistence that the human being can make no contribution whatsoever to Christ's saving work:

> Ironically, [the Lutheran] attempt to preserve grace of human influence by granting it virtually full dominion over nature may have effectively led to its

(grace's) estrangement from the natural realm. 'By Lutheran decree, divine grace has been forbidden to *take root* in our human earth. Henceforth our world is cleared of the sacred.' . . . Nature is no longer regarded as revelatory of God; creation no longer points to the Creator.[42]

Thus nature, evacuated of intrinsic meaning and grace, becomes at best inert matter, and 'in the absence of grace, is capable of nothing but evil'.[43]

But Schumacher, like the other new feminists, is selective in her engagement with feminist thinkers and captive to an uncritical allegiance to neo-orthodox Catholicism. However incisive her critique of some aspects of feminism, she does not offer a viable solution to the problems that she identifies with some insight in the feminist denial of nature. In order to rediscover a form of Catholic sacramentality that can acknowledge the body's grace without undermining the viability of a feminist critique of tradition, I want to consider Nancy Dallavalle's call for a 'critical essentialism', informed by a discussion 'that brings the important insights of gender theory into a deeper and more mutually critical conversation with the profound resonance of biological sexuality in the Catholic theological tradition'.[44]

Rethinking essentialism

In her essay, 'Neither Idolatry nor Iconoclasm: A Critical Essentialism for Catholic Feminist Theology', Dallavalle summarizes what she sees as a polarized approach to the significance of sexual difference:

> From gender theory comes the position that not only have we no access to uninterpreted biological sexuality, the division of humanity into male-and-female is itself a patriarchal social construction with only incidental biological moorings . . . In contrast is the fundamentalist essentialism of conservative Catholic theologians and much official Catholic teaching, which argues that the gender constructs 'masculine' and 'feminine' are well grounded in, and representative of, biological sexual duality, a duality best understood by an anthropology of complementarity.[45]

Although critical of the ways in which the modern Catholic magisterium interprets the significance of the sexual body, Dallavalle argues that the Catholic belief that there is theological as well as anthropological significance in the claim that male and female bodies are created in the image of God invites feminist reflection:

> While men and women share and suffer much in common . . . we live our lives not 'embodied' generically, but as male and female. And while the Catholic tradition contains a variety of anthropological reflections about the significance of bodiliness for humanity, it is the aspect of being created male

Feminist bodies and feminist selves 43

and female that bears the burden and distinction of being viewed as a profound locus for theological reflection.[46]

Dallavalle insists that the development of a critical essentialism is a task of Catholic theology. She situates this task in the context of the continuing tradition of the Church's reflection on the significance of human sexual embodiment, in a way which

> retains the centrality of the doctrine of creation, with its ancient insight about the importance of humanity's creation as male and female, while giving full import to the fact that this ancient insight is never received apart from the ongoing life of the reflecting Church.[47]

The term 'critical essentialism' is not one with pretensions to philosophical or scientific universality, since it takes seriously the constructed and contextual nature of knowledge, and it therefore functions to express 'not comprehensive explanation, but "catholic" exploration'.[48] Thus, 'while we have no unconstructed human access to the meaning of our creation as male and female, we can and should continue to plumb the mystery of biological sexuality as "holy work"'.[49] This entails recognizing that theological reflection on male and female humanity is 'an interpretive act by creation on creation',[50] in which, beyond the reductive and distorted readings that have been produced by a patriarchal and androcentric culture, there is an 'ongoing polyphony of creation and tradition and economy'.[51]

This quest for a form of essentialism that might be compatible with feminism finds secular expression in the work of Christine Battersby, who proposes a fluid essentialism which would be compatible with an idea of 'the *female* – not *feminine* – subject position in western modernity' as 'a historically and socially emergent norm that changes over time'.[52] Battersby argues for a greater appreciation of the potential multiplicity of models of the self, based on the recognition that 'the male [imaginary] has acted as both norm and ideal for what it is to count as an entity, a self or a person'.[53] To introduce the question of gender into western concepts of identity means recognizing the incapacity of an Aristotelian understanding of essence to accommodate the fluctuating norms of the embodied female self, since it posits 'an "essence" as an underlying "real" that secures identity and that persists through a variety of changed circumstances'.[54]

Battersby appeals to the 'ontological significance'[55] of birth, as the basis for a philosophical understanding of female subjectivity based on the recognition that 'becoming a woman involves a privileged relationship to a bodily morphology . . . it is in terms of a relationship with her body that female identity is secured'.[56] Female embodiment entails a relational, fluctuating sense of identity: 'for a woman "self" and "not-self" are sub-contraries, not contradictories, when considered in logical terms . . . [I]t might be possible (when pregnant) to be both self and not-self. "Self" is capable of interpenetration by "otherness".'[57] This involves respecting

> the profound links between 'being a woman' and fleshiness . . . To talk of a woman remaining the same self from birth to death involves an emphasis on fleshy continuity, rather than structures maintained by – or provided by – the *cogito*. As such, female identity is non hylo-morphic: it erupts from flesh, and is not a form (*morphe*) imposed on matter (*hyle*) by the mind in a top-down way.[58]

In particular, Battersby suggests that to take as normative 'the body that can birth'[59] requires a relational understanding of female subjectivity:

> We need to explore what happens if we retain the notion of essence, but allow within it the kind of fluidity that can encompass female difference – and also the type of female embodiment in which self can be impregnated with otherness.[60]

Battersby offers a richly nuanced critique of Butler's readings of Nietzsche, Irigaray and Lacan, but she argues that Butler's radical disavowal of any metaphysics or essentialism leaves her thought trapped within its own ironic resistance to an overly homogenized concept of a patriarchal system narrowly defined in terms of 'the Lacanian and Hegelian communities of "man"'.[61] She questions how politically radical Butler is, since her 'ironic laughter offers political hope, but only through the acceptance of too much despair'.[62] Seeking to move beyond both 'Butlerian parody and deconstruction', and 'the modes of utopian remembrance that characterize the late Irigaray', Battersby argues for the need 'to ally a metaphysics of becoming with an account of the historical and cultural factors that help configure the female subject-position in its diverse specificities'.[63]

However, although Battersby appeals for contingent and variable models of selfhood based on an acknowledgement of the diversity that operates within concepts such as patriarchy, she does not consider the contribution that theological writings have made to concepts of the self. As a result, potentially fruitful alternatives to the modern understanding of the subject are not considered, even although they belong within the intellectual and cultural diversity of western thought.

By recognizing that a significant dimension of western thought – the Catholic theological tradition – has always explored questions of identity in terms of fluctuating concepts of relationality, bodiliness and maternity, Battersby might have entered into a mutually critical dialogue with Catholic theology, particularly given her engagement with Kristeva and Irigaray whose writings are permeated with theological references. Her idea of a fluid essentialism informed by the concept of an embodied self 'impregnated with otherness' may well invite reflection on the significance of prayer, in which a woman's bodily self is open to God and allows itself to be impregnated by the divine Other, not in order to negate the self, but in order to arrive at a more profound, relational conception of the self (see Chapter 4). As it is, Battersby's arguments are limited by her failure to include incarnational theological perspectives among her resources, since she allows herself to be positioned by the secularist discourses of Anglo-American academia which deny her access to the potential of theology to open up different ways of knowing and reasoning.

This exclusion of theology indicates a failure of feminist theory in its historicization and contextualization of knowledge, even although postmodern feminists claim that awareness of the situatedness of knowledge is central to feminist epistemology. For feminists seeking alternative ways of conceptualizing the relationship between the body and language, pre-modern theology provides a rich resource for the postmodern refiguration of knowledge beyond modernity's literalisms. This is particularly so if one bears in mind the arguments of those such as Sarah Boss and Carolyn Merchant who claim that the shift from a theological to a rational scientific world view represented a transition from an organic to a mechanistic understanding of the material world, which had profound implications for the understanding of nature and the female body.[64]

One of the most important consequences of this change was the coming into being of the autonomous modern subject, for whom the moral life is orientated towards duty, not happiness, and freedom is achieved not through the disciplined practice of a virtuous life informed by natural law, but through the assertion of the individual will in conformity to a moral law that operates over and against the laws of nature. Human nature thus becomes separated from all other forms of nature, and the power of reason becomes that by which man must control, exploit and subdue nature, rather than the faculty that enables the human being, through the eyes of faith, to experience the revelation of God through a right understanding of creation. But to suggest this is to raise the question of the feminist self, not now in relation to the body but in relation to God.

The self as gift

Theology is inseparable from prayer and faith. It does not offer a way of knowing that can simply be appropriated by the secular, autonomous subject for her own purposes, and perhaps this is why feminism is so resistant to theology. Theological ways of knowing involve a reopening of questions of relationality, interdependence, vulnerability and *kenosis* which have been deeply problematized by feminist theology as well as feminist theory. The feminist theological body is neither the highly symbolic, disembodied 'body' offered by gender theorists such as Butler, nor is it the essentialized feminine body offered by the new

Catholic feminists. It is a sacramental body, which discovers its meaning through its incorporation into the performative narration of the Christian story in liturgy, worship, prayer and everyday life. This entails reflection on the capacity of the body to communicate God's grace, through an understanding of the self as a gift to be given.

The idea of the self as gift is central to the theology of Pope John Paul II, with its strong emphasis on the significance of the body for our understanding of personhood. In his catechesis on the Book of Genesis, John Paul II refers to the 'hermeneutics of the gift',[65] and he interprets the creation of the male and female human being as signifying the 'nuptial meaning of the body',[66] with nakedness representing 'the original goodness of God's vision'.[67] In the naked man and woman's joyful discovery of one another, human relationality is revealed to be 'an image of an inscrutable divine communion of Persons',[68] in a way which expresses 'the gift as the fundamental characteristic of personal existence'.[69] From this perspective, shame constitutes a 'boundary' experience in human consciousness,[70] obscuring the original meaning of the body, distorting human sexuality and opening the way to relationships in which the sexual other becomes an object of possession rather than a person. Nevertheless, the original innocence of creation remains deeply rooted in every human being, so that a recovery of the self as gift to the other is possible, although 'man and woman must reconstruct, with great effort, the meaning of the disinterested mutual gift'.[71]

This understanding of the bodily self as gift is as promising as it is problematic for feminist theology. Insofar as it leads to a reaffirmation of a highly conservative understanding of marriage, procreation and motherhood, it invites critical feminist analysis, but as part of a project of reclamation rather than rejection of its claims. In other words, it is possible for a feminist to acknowledge the ways in which this theology of the body can contribute towards theological reflection, while questioning the dynamics of power and control which allow a celibate male Pope, writing in the context of an exclusively male hierarchy, to claim authority to speak about the incarnational significance of the female body. By the logic of John Paul II's position, only women themselves have the God-given authority to do this. Indeed, the very existence of such an exclusive male authority structure which appropriates to itself the divine right to interpret revelation and formulate doctrine, and which has a long history of the abuse, silencing and exclusion of women, suggests that the context out of which a Pope speaks is profoundly distorted by the shame which John Paul II describes with such insight.

With feminist theologians, John Paul II acknowledges the significance of bodily experience for revelation:

> In the interpretation of the revelation about man [sic], and especially about the body, we must, for understandable reasons, refer to experience, since corporeal man is perceived by us mainly by experience . . . [O]ur human experience is, in

this case, to some extent a legitimate means for the theological interpretation, and is, in a certain sense, an indispensable point of reference.[72]

He also acknowledges that the meaning of sexuality requires recognizing masculinity and femininity as if there are 'two different "incarnations", that is . . . two ways of "being a body" of the same human being, created "in the image of God" (Gn. 1:27)'.[73] At the very least this means that, until experiencing female bodies are given equal authority to men to undertake the prayerful task of reflection and interpretation with regard to the incarnational significance of sexuality, the Church's sexual doctrines remain veiled by the sin and shame of the fall. But as I shall show, in Catholic theology no less than in postmodern gender theory, there are many ways of being a gendered body, and the potential of the Catholic understanding of gender lies not in its sexual dualities but in its capacity to open up a dazzling proliferation of relational performances in the gap between male and female bodies.

Schumacher argues that

> Even among those feminists who hold a relational model of the human person, there is strong objection to the idea of a woman being perceived or presented in terms of her relationships with others . . . In order to be truly free, she must – it is reasoned – be thought of as an independent being, as her 'own' person. As such, she is thought of as related to others only in virtue of her *own choice*. Hence, although relationality remains an important concept in feminist thought, it is in no way to be mistaken as constitutive of, or essential to, the human (and thus the feminine) person as such. The person, in most feminist thought, is always prior to and ultimately free with regard to these relationships which . . . remain a consequence, or product, of his or her choosing.[74]

One must balance the validity of this critique with an appreciation of the historical and social contexts in which it has become necessary for women to carve out a space of autonomy in resistance to relationships of subordination, ownership and control which fall far short of the kind of gifted relationality described by John Paul II. Nevertheless, a recovery of the sense of the essential giftedness of the self, which brings with it an absolute valuing of the dignity of the self as the gift of God, made in the image of God, may offer feminist theology a new model of relationality that is not parasitic upon the autonomous subjectivities of modernity, nor prey to the many forms of subordinationism and subjugation which haunt the Christian theology of woman.

Schumacher describes the subject of the new feminism as '[t]he authentically liberated woman . . . who experiences herself as eternally loved and forgiven, and thus as authentically free'.[75] She suggests that this means the cultivation of a sense of a self that is both possessed and given:

> 'Self-possessed' in this sense, she is really capable of giving herself to God and to other human persons; for one cannot truly give what is not in one's possession, what is not one's own, even where the possession is one's identity itself.[76]

According to the new feminists, such awareness of the freedom of the self to become gift to the other situates the sexually embodied female person in the context of her primordial relationships to God and to other human beings, informed by 'the old scholastic maxim *anima forma corporis* – the soul is the form of the body',[77] and by the Thomist insight that 'grace does not destroy but perfects and completes nature'.[78] The body is endowed with grace so that nature (including human nature) might be truthfully known through the body's dispositions and characteristics, and human nature is itself 'understood as open to – if not actually orientated toward – grace: a participation in divine life'.[79]

However problematic the new feminism might be in its uncritical acceptance of sexual stereotypes and essentialisms, this insight into the graced relationship between the bodily self and God is vital for the development of a feminist sacramental theology. Feminist sacramentality needs to begin not with woman's experience but with the body's grace. It needs to incarnate hope beyond nihilism by rescuing the female body from the weary truths of an exhausted religion, as a potential catalyst for sacramental transfiguration.

But this means the refiguration of knowledge, through a reopening of the theological horizons beyond metaphysics and beyond modernism. If we never know except through our bodies, it is also true, as Butler and others suggest, that the relationship between language and the body is perhaps the most mysterious of all, and it is a mystery that is inseparable from the mystery of God.

The quest for a theology beyond patriarchy, beyond metaphysics and beyond violence invites a post-Heideggerian return to Aquinas on the far side of modernity, for it is Heidegger who creates a clearing in which it becomes possible to rediscover the wonder of being. It is through that sense of Heideggerian wonder at the beingness of beings that we might discover Aquinas beyond patriarchy's dominion, as an angelic doctor of women's becoming. With this in mind, the next two chapters explore the possible opening up of a path from Heidegger to a rediscovered Thomism, by way of a new feminist understanding of prayer.

3 Gender, knowing and being

Although Heidegger has had a far-reaching influence on theology, to such an extent that one might argue that nearly all modern theology is to some extent positioned by his challenge to metaphysics and ontotheology,[1] there has been little explicit acknowledgement of his influence by feminist theologians. Susan Parsons is one of the few Christian feminist thinkers to situate her questions about gender in the context of the Heideggerian question of Being. She invites us to ask how we are to understand the paradox of our being as something given and therefore something beyond our control or our choosing, and our being as an orientation towards freedom that involves personal responsibility, decision and choice. What happens to this already imponderable conundrum when the quandary of gender is introduced? What is the project of our becoming, and how are we to speak of ourselves when we become conscious of '[t]he dispersal of Dasein into bodies and sex'?[2]

> And this dispersal is one by which I am bound, to which I am somehow betrothed as my portion, for which I am curiously responsible without having done anything to deserve it. What are these ties in the midst of which I already find myself and how did they come to be formed? What is my obligation to them as things that have been formative of who I am but that seem still to await my taking them up, living into them and with them? In what way have they become decisive for me, with an elusive decisiveness that may only appear as I think about them and so I seem to be free in relation to them, and yet may astonish me with the strength of their hold upon my life, and their resistance to my manipulation? Such questions are indications of the forms of comportment to that which is already given to me, to the bonds of relationship in which I already find myself as a worlded being.[3]

Heidegger's *Dasein* is manifest only through its dispersion into beings for whom a full understanding of being is forever beyond reach: 'To seek understanding of the being of being human is for the one who thinks, the one who philosophizes, to throw oneself beyond oneself, in one's own existence to reach out towards the limits.'[4]

We never arrive at those limits, we never grasp what it means to be, because Being always recedes from scrutiny. At one end of the spectrum, the 'I' becomes ever more elusive and mysterious the more we try to penetrate beyond its linguistic veils and performative acts to find an essential or ontological self. At the other end of the spectrum, the transcendent or metaphysical reality of Being fragments, in the shadow of Heidegger, into the postmodern suspicion of all grand narratives, so that any philosophy or theology that would seek to anchor itself between the fixed poles of bodily beings and metaphysical Being is condemned as yet another illusion of power, tainted, from a feminist perspective, by the pervasive influence of patriarchy: 'Patriarchy and metaphysics – the latter especially with regard to so-called postmodernists – are used to suggest structures of domination by which thought is silenced.'[5]

After Heidegger and Nietzsche, we cannot escape the scepticism of our age. We are compelled to ask where meaning is to be found and how hope is to be spoken of, if all is meaningless and life is a tragi-comic performance played out in front of the impenetrable curtains of death. In this era when we have wiped away 'the entire horizon'[6] and 'unchained this earth from its sun',[7] in this time of terror and emptiness, women are asking the question of Being for the first time. But how is woman to become, when man and God have already ceased to be? Dare we hope, with Irigaray, that the Nietzschean death of God opens a passage to a new beginning, a divine rebirth, 'a gay science of the incarnation'?[8] If so, how are we to speak of this fruitful beginning? What language can we use, and how indeed might God open our lips that we may praise her name, beyond sacrifice and murder?

> O Lord, open my lips,
> and my mouth will declare your praise.
> For you have no delight in sacrifice;
> if I were to give you a burnt offering, you would not be pleased.
> The sacrifice acceptable to God is a broken spirit;
> a broken and contrite heart,
> O God, you will not despise.
>
> (Psalm 51:15–17)

Heidegger and the question of Being

The question of Being that Heidegger opens up makes a persistent claim upon theological reflection, but it also has the potential to bring woman and God together in a space of encounter that shimmers with mutual mystery and unknowability. Heidegger invites feminist thought to enter into a more radical space of risk than it has dared so far, not only by calling into question 'woman' (as feminist theory does), or 'God' (as feminist theology does), but by allowing the question of Being to flood through the space of encounter between the two with a strange and awesome potency.

After Heidegger, Christian theology has had to ask to what extent the Christian understanding of the mystery and otherness of God has been compromised by the projection of concepts of being onto God, in such a way that God becomes an ultimate entity or being in a universe of lesser but fundamentally similar beings. Feminist theology is premised on the claim that this includes the projection of maleness onto God, so that the mystery of God becomes circumscribed within an androcentric and patriarchal concept of the being of God. God becomes, in common parlance, 'the man in the sky', leading Mary Daly to argue that 'if God is male, then the male is God'.[9]

The challenge posed by Heidegger continues to be interpreted in many different ways by Christian thinkers, but I am concerned with the potential of Heidegger's question of Being to invite deeper reflection by feminist theologians on the relationship between revelation, nature and gendered embodiment in the life of faith, in order to expose the ways in which patriarchal and androcentric language continues to prop up an unacknowledged metaphysics in much Christian thought, but also in order to rediscover the dimension of prayerful mystery in the human encounter with God that has by and large been neglected in much western feminist theology. So-called third world women's theologies often communicate a more profound awareness of prayer and faith at the heart of their theological reflections, but this can result in a descriptive approach that is not sufficiently developed in terms of theological analysis. Heidegger's question of Being opens up new possibilities for theological reflection in the space of encounter between Catholic theology and feminist theory, in a way that allows the language of prayer and revelation to suffuse a critical theoretical analysis of the lingering metaphysics of presence that haunts the texts of both feminist and neo-orthodox Catholic theologies.

What happens when a woman stands with Heidegger to share his sense of astonishment and wonder at the 'isness' of being, his 'ceaseless, circling, inward-driving query: "Why is there? Why is there not nothing?"'[10] How might we learn to experience the being of ourselves and of God if, with Heidegger, we learn to stand 'soul- and spirit-deep in immanence, in that which is, and in the utter strangeness and wonder of [our] own "isness" within it'?[11] Or is it possible that to be 'woman' is already to be in that space, and if so, then what does woman have to say to Heidegger, and what does Heidegger's Being have to say to woman?

Although Heidegger's thought continued to develop after the publication of *Being and Time* in 1927, becoming more lyrical and even quasi-mystical in his later writings, the central concern that runs through all his work is the philosophical history of Being, and the ways in which the Greek understanding of 'being' has undergone semantic mutations from its pre-Socratic origins, by way of Plato and Aristotle, to its formative role in western philosophy and theology. George Steiner writes that 'the voluminous totality of Martin Heidegger's argument bears on one single topic: what he calls "the being of Being"'.[12]

Heidegger seeks to demonstrate that the development of metaphysics suppressed the experience of Being as being-in-the-world, and led to a highly conceptualized and abstract form of knowledge that fails to appreciate the wonder of the everyday coming into being of Being. In particular, Christian ontotheology posits the idea of a supreme Being or God as origin, first cause and ground of being, so that God becomes an entity among other entities in a way that erases the difference between beings and Being, amounting to a forgetting of Being. Western thought has lost the sense of wonder that, for the pre-Socratics, was associated with the mystery of Being as it emerges out of the past and moves towards the future, unveiling its presence in the presence of beings so that in the everyday world we encounter Being in a multitude of beings, and never otherwise than in the temporal and spatial entities that surround us and of which we are a part.

Although we are beings among beings, the human is *Dasein* (literally, *Da-sein*, being-there, or is-there), because it is a being uniquely endowed with the capacity to question Being.[13] As a being that is aware of the fact of its being, '*Dasein* has been thrown *into existence*',[14] in the awareness 'that it is' but not knowing the 'whence' and the 'whither' of its being.[15] *Dasein* experiences the dispersal of being through its practical involvement with and relationships to other beings, and thus the being of *Dasein* is 'Being-in-the-world', which brings with it the call to be 'Being towards the world',[16] experienced as care: '*Dasein*, when understood *ontologically* is care.'[17] Care, in this sense, refers not to the colloquial sense of being emotionally concerned or anxious (although it has these associations), but primarily to the awareness that comes about through the day-to-day encounters and relationships between *Dasein* and the ready-to-hand, the everyday beings that constitute the environment in which we act and in which we experience Being.

In our forgetfulness of Being, we have neglected the kind of knowledge that would constitute a constant attentiveness to this being of everyday life, in favour of ontological speculations that have little bearing on our experience of being in the world. Instead of knowing the world through the wonder of the continuous unveiling of Being in beings, we have developed a representational theory of knowledge in which we seek knowledge about the world through its relationship to abstract concepts that obstruct our openness to being-in-the-world.

In recognition of this forgetfulness of Being, the task of the present era is that of recollection. This is not a historical quest for the origin of Being, but rather a quest to discover the history of Being through the history of philosophy, in order to learn to think differently about Being. This means that we need to think of Being not in terms of past origination, but in terms of an origin that is always ahead of us, because, as the origin of beings, it is always coming into being:

> The essence of truth is at the same time the truth of essence. Being and truth belong to each other just as they belong intertwining to a still concealed rootedness in the origin whose origination opening up remains that which comes.
> That which is original occurs in advance of all that comes. Although hidden, it thus comes toward historic man as pure coming. It never perishes, it is never something past.[18]

This learning to think anew about Being entails living the history of Being in the present, through an awareness of its past and its futurity. It invites reflection on the particular relationship of human being to Being, while bearing in mind that 'At times Being needs human being, and yet it is never dependent upon existing humanity.'[19] To the human is given the task of expressing the truth of Being, and, because Being is never manifest except in its coming into being, this means that 'The history of Being . . . is solely Being itself.'[20] Thus thought does not seek the rediscovery of Being in the past, but must rather move forward in order to discover anew the distinction between Being and beings, not before but beyond metaphysics. This entails a transformation in our way of knowing the world, beyond the reification of beings represented by mechanization and technology, in which 'man takes on the role of the authoritative being' and 'Knowledge thus becomes calculation.'[21] But what kind of knowledge might take the place of philosophy and metaphysics, that would enable human thought once again to discern the truth of Being as it reveals itself in beings?

Heidegger explores this question in the context of Goethe's maxim: 'Look for nothing behind phenomena: they themselves are what is to be learned.'[22] In order for this learning to take place, it is first necessary for Being to open a space or create a clearing in which its presence can manifest itself, in the way that a forest clearing creates an opening that is 'not only free for brightness and darkness but also for resonance and echo, for sound and the diminishing of sound. The clearing is the open region for everything that becomes present and absent.'[23] The phenomenon is the clearing created by Being as it becomes present in being, and it is only by recognizing this openness for Being in the phenomena of beings that human thought itself becomes open to the manifestation of Being. Heidegger expresses this with reference to Parmenides' idea of unconcealment (*aletheia*), as

> the clearing that first grants Being and thinking and their presencing to and for each other. The quiet heart of the clearing is the place of stillness from which alone the possibility of the belonging together of Being and thinking, that is, presence and apprehending, can arise at all.[24]

54 *The middle*

The foregoing summary of the main contours of Heidegger's thought is inevitably too condensed and over-simplified, but it is sufficient to situate feminist questions about womanly being in a postmodern context that takes seriously the challenge to both theological and philosophical metaphysics posed by Heidegger.

Sexual difference, being and language

There is a question as to how far woman has ever had a share in the philosophical concepts of being described by Heidegger. Whether philosophically or theologically, 'woman' has traditionally been understood as that which is not fully included in the metaphysical or ontological nature of being, and one must therefore ask, with Irigaray, if the forgetting of sexual difference requires the reopening of thought to a question that Heidegger never asked, but that might be 'the issue in our time which could be our "salvation" if we thought it through'.[25] As Lorraine Code argues,

> Not only has it been taken for granted that knowers properly so-called are male, but when male philosophers have paused to note this fact, as some indeed have done, they have argued that things are as they should be. Reason may be alike in all men, but it would be a mistake to believe that 'man', in this respect, 'embraces woman'. Women have been judged incapable, for many reasons, of achieving knowledge worthy of the name. It is no exaggeration to say that anyone who wanted to *count* as a knower commonly had to be male.[26]

Excluded from philosophical speculation, woman's domain has been that of everyday being in the world, constituted by her mundane relationships of care. So does 'woman' not already mark that space of the immanence of Being that Heidegger claims has been covered over and rendered inaccessible and unthinkable? Who has covered over her being, that she remains so invisible, even to Heidegger himself in his quest for other ways of being? Western philosophy and theology have always associated woman with being rather than doing, with immanence rather than transcendence, so might 'woman' be uniquely positioned in her ability to rethink Being from the position of Heidegger's beingness, and what might the implications be for our understanding of the relationship between human and divine being?

Parsons makes the point that, for Heidegger, the question of sexual difference barely registers in the face of the question of Being:

> explanations of how we got here, by socialization, by choice, by genetic code, are *after the fact* and so do not take us into our beginning, to the roots of our coming to be from out of that which cannot be seen for itself because it lies ahead of us in the future . . . Gender is an experience of thrownness and of

belonging already to being, of already finding oneself in the midst of the ontological difference as oneself the site of its particular appearance, its there-being.[27]

Derrida misrepresents Heidegger, Parsons argues, in his essay, '*Geschlecht*: Sexual Difference/Ontological Difference', when he claims that Heidegger's neutralization of the question of sex reveals his *Dasein* to be, in Parsons' words, 'wearing a manly mask of indifferent emptiness'.[28] According to Derrida, Heidegger's *Dasein* remains implicitly male. Derrida proposes that

> If *Dasein* as such belongs to neither of the two sexes, that does not mean that its being is deprived of sex. On the contrary: here one must think of a predifferential, or rather a predual, sexuality – which does not necessarily mean unitary, homogeneous, or undifferentiated.[29]

In this 'one must think', Parsons argues that Derrida 'reinstates the one who knows . . . as the one who transcends to the realm of the always already given to us in order to know how it is with being'.[30] Over and against Derrida, she suggests that Heidegger's understanding of 'metaphysical emptiness'[31] does not provide a theoretical space from which we can project back some theory about a 'primordial pure pre-difference',[32] but rather, 'the neutrality of Dasein is positive because it is potency of being and of coming to be in the many dimensions of existence that Geschlecht signifies'.[33] Our reflections on gender do not look back to some original ground of being or essence; rather, they are orientated towards futurity, arising out of the givenness of our experience of being as bodily and sexual, so that 'we are not looking back to a past but rather reaching out into what recedes from us into the future'.[34]

But, as Irigaray recognizes, questions of sexual difference cannot escape the positioning of the subject in language, and this raises questions about the extent to which sexual difference is already encoded within the language that situates us in the world, and therefore in our ability to think Being. In his later writings, Heidegger increasingly emphasizes the significance of the relationship of language to Being:

> Thinking accomplishes the relation of Being to the essence of man. It does not make or cause the relation. Thinking brings this relation to Being solely as something handed over to it from Being. Such offering consists in the fact that in thinking Being comes to language. Language is the house of Being. In its home man dwells.[35]

If this is so, then to open ourselves up to Being is to allow Being to express itself in language, and the neutralization of gender would require a neutral language in which Being might manifest itself in ways not marked by sexual difference. But, according to Irigaray, we have no access to such neutral language, and therefore the question of Being always begs the question of sexual difference. There is no neutral language in which neutralized Being might speak. If, then, gendered Being comes towards us as our future origins, we must ask how such Being is to reveal itself to thought, when it has no language in which to speak.

However, like Heidegger, Irigaray views her subject from a philosopher's perch, high above the *bricolage* of beings in the world. She sees only the large picture, as he does, abstracted from the ways in which relationships of care – including sexual relationships – express themselves in the mundane activities of everyday bodily living, which are too inconsequential to catch the attention of the distant philosophical gaze. Irigaray and Heidegger see a smooth and unbroken tradition as they peer at life through the haze of philosophical texts and arguments that surround them – a tradition that, for Heidegger, leads to the forgetfulness of Being, and for Irigaray, to the forgetfulness of sexual difference. But what forgetfulness informs their vision, that they can perceive such uni-directional movements amidst the flux and fluidity of human becoming?

Heidegger and Irigaray confuse philosophy with living. Philosophy's power to construct the world is extensive but not without limit, and while the ideas and concepts of philosophy and theology might spill over in manifold ways to impinge upon the perceptions of beings in the world, they do not and never have controlled the many ways in which human beings experience Being. Particularly for women, who have been institutionally and intellectually excluded from the conceptualization of Being, a question remains as to how relevant Heidegger and Irigaray really are for the daily business of being in the world. Why should women play this philosophical game of problematizing something that has arguably never been a problem for women at all?

In a feminist critique of postmodernism, Seyla Benhabib argues that

> much of the postmodernist critique of western metaphysics itself proceeds under the spell of a metanarrative, namely, the narrative first articulated by Heidegger and then developed by Derrida that 'Western metaphysics has been under the spell of the "metaphysics of presence"' at least since Plato.[36]

Benhabib goes on to ask if 'the philosophical tradition [is] so monolithic and so essentialist as postmodernists would like to claim'.[37] She suggests that

> In its strong version the 'death of metaphysics' thesis not only subscribes to a grandiose metanarrative, but more significantly, this grandiose metanarrative flattens out the history of modern philosophy and the competing conceptual schemes it contains to the point of unrecognizability.[38]

Benhabib's critique can be extended back over the western history of ideas, which is considerably more plurivocal and diverse than either Heidegger or Irigaray acknowledges. This raises the question as to how far they contribute towards the forgetfulness of Being (Heidegger) or of sexual difference (Irigaray) through their inattentiveness to the particularity of bodily being in the world that will always elude a philosophical gaze focused too intently on concepts rather than beings.

Feminist theology after Heidegger

Although Heidegger and Irigaray are arguably both Catholic theologians of a sort, they approach the history of philosophy from a perspective informed by one way of interpreting Being – that is, thinking conceptually about Being – without taking into account the extent to which classical Christian theology is primarily orientated towards thought in the service of prayer and revelation, bodily expressed in the sacramentality of liturgy and worship. Even if one accepts the argument that theology lost its way after Aquinas to become enmeshed in metaphysics and ontotheology,[39] this is only true if we restrict our definition of theology to an academic pursuit that became increasingly remote from the prayerful theology of everyday life, which still remains partially accessible to us in the writings of some of the saints and mystics, many of whom were women. Irigaray recognizes the language of mysticism as a potential site of sexual otherness, but, like Lacan (another Catholic theologian of sorts), she attends to the mystic's voice through the veils of psycholinguistic analysis, so that prayer and revelation are muffled by added layers of theory and interpretation which domesticate the unsettling strangeness of the mystical encounter with the otherness of God.

But this brings us back to the central question. How is a woman to approach the incomprehensible otherness of God in order to articulate her relationship to Being and to language, when she has no access to a language that does not already inscribe her into its theological and sexual hierarchies as the feminine other '*to the economy of the Same*',[40] constructed around the projections of the masculine subject? Even if Being in the beings of women may elude the philosophical forgetfulness of Being that concerns Heidegger, as long as womanly being rests at the level of being in the world without philosophical or theological mediation, it remains inaccessible to thought and therefore outside the history of Being that is the history of thought. Indeed, the great change effected by forty years of feminist scholarship has been the gradual transformation of academic discourse by the emergence of different questions and perspectives that arise when the question of Being presents itself as gendered, disrupting the categories and boundaries of thought that have prevailed in one form or another since the time of Aristotle, through a multi-disciplinary, polyglot approach to scholarship and learning. Already, the history of Being is coming into being in the shape of consciously gendered language, suggesting that the future origin of Being may be altogether other than that which Heidegger might have anticipated.

A post-Heideggerian feminist theology entails the negotiation of two potentially conflicting claims. On the one hand, it entails an acknowledgement of the primacy of language as that which positions the body in the world and renders it meaningful. On the other hand, it also entails that, unless we acknowledge the body as a site of potential significance beyond language, it is difficult to see how one could begin to construct a language of womanly being in the world if all language is inherently patriarchal or phallocentric in its structures and meanings. As Margaret Whitford points out in her study of Irigaray, 'one cannot alter symbolic meanings by *fiat*; one cannot simply step outside phallogocentrism'.[41] Ultimately, one has to go beyond the mimetic strategies and parodies of Irigarayan woman, to affirm the mystery of the body itself, and I would reiterate that this cannot be separated from the mystery of God.

I have suggested that the rediscovery of a language of grace might provide a resource for feminist reflection on the sacramental significance of the female body, by acknowledging the revelatory potential of the body in relation to God. However, this entails attentiveness to the ways in which androcentric and patriarchal concepts of God have made Christian theology complicit in the perpetuation of social structures and liturgical practices which negate the role of the female body in the story of salvation. The task is therefore twofold: it is to create a space for feminist theological reflection by acknowledging the divine mystery concealed behind the patriarchal masks of the theological tradition, and it is to create a clearing in language in which the being of woman might at last speak from the site of a body which has until now been silenced and excluded from manifesting its meaning as an unveiling of Being in the world. This invites a consideration of the ways in which Heidegger's critique of theology has led to a rediscovery of the potential of Thomas Aquinas for post-Heideggerian theology.

If the content of Aquinas's theology reflects a world view unquestioningly ordered around the sexual and social hierarchies of the medieval world, his theological method provides a rich resource for feminist reflection on the mystery of God, from the position of the graced body whose senses are aroused by desire for God. Indeed, insofar as secularism blinds feminist theorists to pre-modern theological resources, it denies them access to what may be one of the most fruitful alternative epistemologies available to those who would challenge the autonomous masculine individual of postmodern philosophy and culture through an appeal to more relational, bodily ways of being in the world. In contrast to the Cartesian 'I', the Thomist subject's knowledge of self is derivative and dependent upon her sensory, material relationships with the rest of creation. We learn who we are, not by a process of introversion premised upon a radical mistrust of the world revealed to our senses, but by trusting our bodily way of being in the world: our senses are gateways to God.

Fergus Kerr argues that, in contrast to the Cartesian view of the person as

> privileged and unified locus of self-consciousness, facing an array of objects out there . . . Thomas has 'a non-subject-centred' approach to human experience, in the sense that he never pictures the mind as projecting significance on intrinsically unintelligible and valueless objects but always rather as the actualization of intellectual capacities by potentially significant objects, according to the axiom '*intellectus in actu est intelligibile in actu*': our intellectual capacities actualized *are* the world's intelligibility realized.[42]

According to Kerr, this means that Thomism offers an alternative epistemology to 'the "naïve" realist' view that 'the world (reality) is altogether independent of our knowledge of it'.[43] Instead,

> the Thomist wants to say that knowledge is the product of a collaboration between the object known and the subject who knows: the knower enables the thing known to become intelligible, thus to enter the domain of meaning, while the thing's becoming intelligible activates the mind's capacities. Knowing is a new way of being on the knower's part; being known is a new way of being on the part of the object known.[44]

For Aquinas, Kerr argues, 'Our experience of things is not a confrontation with something utterly alien, but a way of absorbing, and being absorbed by, the world to which we naturally belong.'[45]

Aquinas's affirmation of the significance of the material world, and his positive view of philosophy and the natural sciences as limited but truthful paths to knowledge, suggest the possibility of a more irenic and productive dialogue between feminist theory and feminist theology than either the new Catholic feminists or secular feminist theorists acknowledge. In his critique of feminist theology, Francis Martin argues that, in the dialogue between faith and reason,

> The light of faith is an integrating and transforming factor in the dialogue and the light of reason is the integrated and transformed factor. In the words of Aquinas . . . 'Those who use the work of the philosophers in sacred doctrine by bringing that work of the human mind into the service of faith, do not mix water with wine, but rather change water into wine.'[46]

While this challenges the perspective of postmodern feminist theologians whose work reverses this relationship, integrating theology into theory so that the dimension of faith and revelation yields to secular reason, it also affirms the significance of feminist theory and philosophy for theology. In announcing the death of feminism, the new feminists resist this insight and deprive theology of a valuable resource for its own intellectual development.

Towards a feminist Thomism

In Part I of the *Summa Theologiae*, Aquinas explores the relationship between the ultimate truth of Christian revelation, and philosophical knowledge of the world which can be acquired by the natural sciences through the use of reason. Although knowledge begins for Aquinas with the truths of Christian revelation, which are discoveries of faith and do not lend themselves to rational explanation or justification,[47] philosophy can yield truthful knowledge about the world, because 'all things are said to be seen in and judged by God, insofar as we know and judge all things through participation in God's light, for the light of natural reason is itself a participation in the divine light'.[48] Thus, although we cannot know the being of God from the world around us, we can know that God exists as the cause of all that is. Insofar as sensible things are caused by God and depend on God, 'we can be led from them so far as to know of God "whether God exists", and to know what must necessarily belong to God',[49] even although God far exceeds all that is.

There is, however, a difference between this natural light of reason and the 'light of glory',[50] so that 'We have a more perfect knowledge of God by grace than by natural reason.'[51] The light of glory brings about a deeper knowledge of God because, through it, 'the rational creature is made deiform'.[52]

The believer is increasingly conformed to the likeness of God through responding in faith to a desire for God which is kindled but not satisfied by our experience of the material world. Ultimately, this increasing knowledge of God becomes a form of not knowing, for it leads us to the awareness that God is beyond all naming and conceptualization within the parameters of finite human knowledge. Aquinas expresses this in paradoxical language:

> Although by the revelation of grace in this life we cannot know of God 'what He is', and thus are united to Him as to one unknown; still we know Him more fully according as many and more excellent of His effects are demonstrated to us, and according as we attribute to Him some things known by divine revelation, to which natural reason cannot reach, as, for instance, that God is Three and One . . . Faith is a kind of knowledge, inasmuch as the intellect is determined by faith to some knowable object. But this determination to one object does not proceed from the vision of the believer, but from the vision of Him who is believed.[53]

Faith, then, is ultimately beyond rationalization. It offers a way of knowing that can be trusted but cannot be explained, and this provides the context within which it becomes possible to use reason to gain a more truthful understanding of

Gender, knowing and being 61

creation as the work of God, and therefore as a revelation of God's creative love. The knowledge of God that is attainable through the use of natural reason is therefore deepened by grace, in such a way that 'grace does not destroy nature but perfects it'.[54]

Denys Turner argues that Aquinas, in his famous five arguments for the existence of God, is not seeking to define God but to demonstrate the unknowability of that which is called by the name of God, to such an extent that 'We do not know . . . how "other" God is.'[55] For the Christian who is drawn into the unknowability of God it becomes 'a sharing in its nature as love, so as to share it in friendship with God. It is a darkness, therefore, which for the Christian is deepened, not relieved by the Trinity, intensified by the Incarnation, not dispelled.'[56]

But this mystical encounter between the knower and God suggests that, the more we become conscious of the mystery of God, the more we become conscious of the mystery of our own being before God. One could argue that, according to Aquinas, true knowledge knows itself to be boundaried by mystery – the mystery of God, and the mystery of the self as it is drawn more closely into union with God. I want to explore some of the implications of this Thomist epistemology for feminist theology.

In her book *She Who Is*, Elizabeth Johnson argues that Aquinas provides a resource for feminist theological reflection beyond the androcentric and patriarchal projections of traditional Christian theology. She quotes Aquinas's argument that 'we cannot know what God is, but only what God is not; we must therefore consider the ways in which God does not exist, rather than the ways in which God does'.[57] Johnson interprets classical theology to mean that, even in the light of revelation, 'the highest human knowledge about God is to know that we do not know, a negative but entirely valid knowing pervaded by religious awareness'.[58] It is against this mystery, informed by an awareness of the analogical nature of religious language, that women might 'emancipate speech about God',[59] drawing on a polyphony of cosmic and female images of God from different traditions and sources, for the creation of new forms of theological discourse.

Seeking to challenge the idolatrous 'stranglehold on religious language of God-He',[60] Johnson sets out to explore the new possibilities that open up when theological language is understood in the context of a God who is always beyond conceptual knowledge, but who is truthfully known in love:

> The God who is utterly distinct from all creatures and hence better known intellectually by negating all symbols is nonetheless deeply known in human love, as love itself . . . In the end, we are united to God as to an unknown, savoring God only through love.[61]

Balanced against her repeated assertion that God is beyond all intellectual knowledge is this repeated insistence that we know God through love: 'Lest we despair of ever knowing the divine will in any way at all . . . Augustine consistently pushes the necessity of nescience to its genuine religious goal, the knowing of God through love.'[62] In surrendering ourselves to the mystery of this love, individually and in community, we discover new, non-oppressive ways of relating to God:

> God is that on which you lean your heart, that on which your heart depends, 'that to which your heart clings and entrusts itself', in Martin Luther's memorable phrase. As the focus of absolute trust, one to whom you can give yourself without fear of betrayal, the holy mystery of God undergirds and implicitly gives direction to all of a believing person's enterprises, principles, choices, system of values, and relationships. The symbol of God functions.[63]

The truth content of speech about God is, according to Johnson, relational rather than conceptual, dynamic rather than static, and analogical rather than literal. In the analogical process of affirmation, negation and double negation – 'negating the positive and then negating the negation' – 'an unspeakably rich and vivifying reality is intuited while God remains incomprehensible'.[64]

Nevertheless, while Johnson is careful to maintain a dialectic between mystery and revelation as far as God is concerned, it is her interpretation of this in terms of feminist principles that makes her vulnerable to the criticisms of those such as Martin, who argues that, like other feminist theologians, she is guilty of a foundationalist epistemology which is inconsistent with the classical theological tradition. Theology and anthropology are ultimately inseparable in Christian reflection on the relationship between God and the human made in the image of God, and I would suggest that it is in her anthropological understanding of women before God that Johnson's theology reveals its weakness.

Martin claims that 'it is impossible to decide whether, for Johnson, speech about God has any truth content or is rather to be judged for its subjective suitability. Johnson's position is simply not clear.'[65] Indeed, he dismisses her work because, despite its 'several valuable insights [he never identifies what these are] . . . , the agnostic context in which they are developed means they must be rethought in the light of a better understanding of faith as a way of knowing'.[66] These claims are demonstrably unfounded even on a cursory reading of Johnson's theological approach, but I think Martin is on stronger ground when he argues that Johnson, like other feminist theologians, makes women's experience the foundation for knowledge – even though she is careful to insist that this refers to the interpretation of experience, and not to experience itself. Johnson's finely nuanced presentation of a theology which balances an apophatic not-knowing with a knowing of God as love is not entirely consistent with her tendency to interpret faith in terms of a series of prescriptive feminist ideals as the condition by which one comes to know God. For example, Martin's claim that her use of the idea of conversion is not in keeping with the 'classic notion of conversion'[67] has some legitimacy, when one looks closely at how Johnson interprets the personal transformation brought about by faith.

Johnson understands conversion as being brought about by way of a dialectic between the contrast of oppression by sexism and the confirmation of self-worth through the reclamation of women's narratives of empowerment and solidarity in the Christian tradition.[68] She describes conversion as a 'foundational experience', understood as 'the breakthrough of power occurring in women's struggle to reject the sexism of inherited constructions of female identity and risk new interpretations that affirm their own human worth'.[69] As a result, 'women's awakening to their own human worth can be interpreted at the same time as a new experience of God, so that what is arguably occurring is a new event in the religious history of humankind'.[70] The articulation of this awakened feminist consciousness invites '[n]arrative remembrance'[71] which creates 'a solidarity of sisters' through the reclamation of 'the history of women's empowerment', by a weaving together of past and present stories of women's 'courage', 'power', 'creativity', 'leadership' and 'prophecy'.[72] This unleashes 'a positive type of history . . . by forming communities of discourse' through which women come to an awareness of themselves as 'genuine subjects of history'.[73]

But Johnson also insists that this conversion experience must be different from 'that of classical theology where it typically connotes the process of disowning oneself or divesting oneself of ego in order to be filled with divine grace'.[74] Given the feminist argument that this idea of self-emptying is not applicable to women but to 'the ruling male whose primordial temptation is likely to be the sin of pride or self-assertion over against others',[75] Johnson argues that, for those who are already marginalized and excluded, 'language of conversion as loss of self, turning from *amor sui*, functions in an ideological way to rob them of power, maintaining them in a subordinate position to the benefit of those who rule'.[76] Rejecting this model of conversion, Johnson suggests that women's conversion must involve 'a turning away from demeaning female identity toward new ownership of the female self as God's good gift'.[77] In terms of moral values, this entails 'the affirmation that women are human persons with the capacity to exercise moral agency',[78] while it 'eschews the vision of the isolated moral agent so prized by the dominant view of man in Western culture'.[79] The alternative feminist vision is that of 'relational autonomy, which honors the inviolable personal mystery of the person who is constituted essentially by community with others'.[80]

Johnson is attentive to the mediated nature of women's experience insofar as she acknowledges the extent to which theology is discursively and linguistically constituted, and she recognizes the task of feminist theology as one of constructing alternative narratives about women and God. Nevertheless, in common with other liberal theologians, she risks succumbing to a reductive and moralizing banality with regard to feminist representations of the female self in relation to God, premised upon a thoroughly modern understanding of the self-made woman – autonomous, rational, free, and exercising enough control over her own circumstances to make informed and responsible choices about who she is, what she believes, and how she behaves. It is difficult to find in her work any acknowledgement of the extent to which we might discover the mystery of God where we least expect to find it – in the woman who is broken, whose life is chaotic, whose sexual relationships might be part of that chaos, whose mental or physical health is too damaged to experience the kind of conversion experience that Johnson describes. It should also be pointed out that the vast majority of those converted to Christianity in the modern world (women as well as men) are attracted not by liberal feminist versions but by the doctrinal certainties and devotional exuberances of different forms of Pentecostal Evangelicalism, which are usually highly conservative with regard to sexual values and roles.[81] By ignoring this reality, Johnson is to some extent guilty of using the power of the academy to silence voices of otherness, in the way that Fulkerson describes in her critique of feminist theology (see Chapter 1).

Conversion refers to the mysterious ways in which a person is awakened to the call of the living Christ, and it cannot be interpreted exclusively in terms of liberation from sexism to an affirmation of self-worth, even if this is indeed how many modern women experience conversion. It is an experience that reaches into the visceral depths of our humanity, beyond all socio-political realities, although feminist and liberationist theologians are surely right to point out that individual conversion must translate into a concern for justice in politics and society. But Johnson's account of women's conversion offers insufficient recognition of the vast psychological and spiritual complexity of the ways in which grace and sin, alienation and hope, resonate through the language and experience of faith in the subjective and communal aspects of the Christian life. To appreciate this complexity means letting go of the idea of the experiencing feminist subject as a reliable yardstick against which to measure our knowledge of God and of the world, and recognizing instead that knowledge is a dynamic coming into being that unfolds in the mysterious encounter between the unknown self and the incomprehensible God, an encounter that comes about through love and desire, and sometimes through darkness and chaos – not through power and control. It is a process in which the self, God and creation are caught up in the mystery of being, and it is the human mind that has the blessing and the curse of being conscious of that mystery through its own awareness of being, in a way that does not always translate into the visions and values of liberal feminism.

This entails reopening questions of prayer, *kenosis* and vulnerability, which are deeply problematic for feminists. As we become more like God, we become more conscious of the mystery of our own being. Insofar as much feminist theology lacks this mystical dimension in its socio-political anthropology, it remains closed to the possibility that faith not only recognizes God as the ultimate Other, it also renders us 'strangers to ourselves',[82] to borrow a phrase from Kristeva that I shall elaborate upon later.

Gendering apophaticism

To pray as a woman is to enter bodily into the process of theology, to bring to theology all the insights, questions and revelations that arise from the site of the female body. This means that the acting out of the role of woman in the Christian story requires a complex negotiation between feminist theoretical and Catholic theological insights, ever attentive to the risk of emptying oneself to a God whose presence is veiled by the texts and practices of masculinity. Before such a God, a woman may fear that she will become like the person described by Jesus:

> When the unclean spirit has gone out of a person, it wanders through waterless regions looking for a resting place, but not finding any, it says, 'I will return to my house from which I came.' When it comes, it finds it swept and put in order. Then it goes and brings seven other spirits more evil than itself, and they enter and live there; and 'the last state of that person is worse than the first'.
>
> (Luke 11:24–6)

For a woman to seek prayerful knowledge of God means seeking herself beyond the not-self that she discovers in the haunted language of a tradition that offers her no space of habitation, in the knowledge that this might risk ever greater hauntings and madness in the spaces beyond self. For how does she know that, if she empties herself of her fragile, unformed sense of self, all the demons of patriarchal religion will not rush in to take 'her' place? Ultimately, it is only trust in the love of God, in God as Love, beyond all the knowing and naming of patriarchy, that might allow a woman to listen to that unknowable other whose silence speaks as the shadow of language, as a negation of meaning that must be negated, in order to affirm that woman too might arrive at not being, in order to discover how to speak truthfully of being. This means that, within the silence of contemplation, we must discover a language that allows us to speak of God in all the fecundity and desire of our material being in the world, for this is how we come to know God.

Turner appeals to pseudo-Denys's *Mystical Theology* to explore the task of theological language, arguing that, for pseudo-Denys, the more worldly theological language is, the less likely it is to 'seduce us into supposing its adequacy'.[83] Thus, 'theological language is at its best, its least misleading, when it is most concrete, imaginative, and even carnal'.[84] It is only through the simultaneous proliferation, negation and double negation of images and ideas about God that we might come close to expressing the inexpressible mystery of God:

> our language leads us to the reality of God when, by a process simultaneously of affirming and denying all things of God, by, as it were in one breath, both affirming what God is and denying, as he puts it, 'that there is any kind of thing that God is', we step off the very boundary of language itself, beyond every assertion and every denial, into the 'negation of the negation' and the 'brilliant darkness' of God.[85]

Developing this theme with regard to Aquinas, Turner points to 'the incarnational character of his theology':[86]

> Thomas was happy to anchor the negative, apophatic 'moment' of his theology in just the same secure bedrock in which is anchored the affirmative, incarnational moment: for both, what we *must* say about God and the fact that all that we say about God fails of God derive with equal force from the same necessities of thought, and converge in equal measures, in a sort of 'two-sidedness' of theological speech.[87]

As Johnson argues, Aquinas's apophaticism invites a proliferation of female language about God, for the ultimate mystery of God not only challenges all theological language – it also liberates theological language from the illusion that some ways of speaking express a more certain knowledge of God than others. Knowledge of God is darkness and unknowing, and thus God must be able to tumble into speech through every possible way of being in the world, as a reminder that God is infinitely other than being in the world.

But in order for this to happen, woman needs to find a space in which to express her difference, so that the mystery of her own being goes beyond the negation that she encounters in the texts of theology, to a 'negation of the negation'. The 'two-sidedness of theological speech' may need to become at least three-sided, if it is to reflect the fact that woman's unknowing of God may be different from man's unknowing of God, particularly given that man has often conflated woman and God as the mysterious and unknowable Other (as we shall see when we come to consider Lacan). A gendered apophaticism leads to a proliferation of negations and counter-negations, setting in play an incandescent prism of language through which meaning is refracted, multiplied and illuminated. As Irigaray suggests, this entails a creative appropriation of the language of 'woman', a form of inessential essentialism in which woman parades and parodies herself, as a way of showing that there is a self beyond the parody. Even as we acknowledge that that self is hidden in the mystery of God – 'There is no such thing as *The* woman'[88] – we need to take up the position of the woman in order to understand our own negation, to explore our absences and our silences, and to rescue our bodies from the grave of men's desire.

Between the apophatic silence of contemplative *kenosis*, and the cataphatic unveiling of women's joy and lamentation, desire and loss, we come to new ways of knowing through new ways of praying. This might involve the dissolution of the modern female subject of feminist theology into an altogether more mystical and unpredictable space of womanly becoming, through an exploration of what Sarah Coakley describes as the '"dark" knowing beyond speech' of the Christian mystics, which challenges 'the smugness of accepted anthropomorphisms for God', and probes 'to the subversive place of the "semiotic"'.[89]

In Heidegger's attempt to create a clearing beyond the metaphysics of Being, he offers feminist theology a space for theological reflection on the ways in which woman's becoming might emerge from the history of her own non-being, as an event which calls to us from the future of Being. In this sense, prayer needs to be understood not only as the conscious setting aside of time and thought before God, but as the cultivation of a habitual attitude of wonder at being in the world, before the all-encompassing, incomprehensible otherness of God. This is an adventure that lures the self beyond the illusory props and safeguards of modern culture, beyond the security of knowing who we are and where we belong, beyond the postmodern self with its fictitious parodies of difference and otherness, to the wilderness where the Wholly Holy Other comes to meet us:

> And I will enter this darkness
> where I have never walked before
> And I will submit into this darkness
> to a terror never dared before
> And I will yield into this darkness
> to a loving never ventured before
> And of her darkness I must know and I must know nothing
> And in this darkness I must be made and I must be unmade
> And of her darkness I must be possessed and dispossessed of all things.[90]

4 Knowledge, desire and prayer

In modern epistemology, there is a close relationship between knowledge and power. To know the world is also to control the world. It is to pit the masculine, rational mind over and against femininity, nature and the body, in order to have mastery over them.

For Aquinas, knowledge is not about power but about desire and love. We come to know God through the attraction of creation which opens our hearts and minds to the creator. Timothy McDermott points out that 'Thomas connects willing with loving',[1] since it is our will that orients us towards the good, even although sin distorts our appetite for goodness.[2]

McDermott points out that Aquinas's understanding of will primarily as an inclination towards the good and only secondarily as directed towards action does not associate will with power but with desire:

> the word *will* for Thomas does not first connote a power to dominate things but a *willingness* to be attracted by them. The fundamental activity of will is not making decisions, choosing between things, but the activity of loving, of consent to their creation.[3]

One could say, in Heideggerian terms, that it is in letting things be, in becoming aware of our being among beings, that we become aware of the question of Being, which leads us to the mystery of God. This is a prayerful way of knowing, for it suggests that our relationship with the material world is a continuous conversation with God.

But Heidegger, who could think only in the forgetting of prayer and the denial of God, positions his desire against a refusal of the kind of hope that faith might invite. Steiner asks to what extent his resistance to theology manifests itself in the violence of his struggle with language:

> The question is: what is the role in Heidegger's thought and language, these two being strictly inseparable, of the renunciation and refusal of the theological? Could there, in fact, be a communicable, an arguably intelligible,

articulation of an ontology of pure immanence? . . . The violence of neologism, of grammatical compaction in Heidegger's discourse materially reflects the endeavour, under persistent strain, to forge a language of ontological totality in which the theological presence would not intrude.[4]

To what extent might one ask a similar question of feminist theorists such as Butler, whose vigorous resistance to theology drives her theory to the point of linguistic exhaustion with its frenetic quest for new ways of being against nothingness?

The peace of letting be is our 'amen' to the world, for what is prayer if not 'the clearing that first grants Being and thinking and their presencing to and for each other'?[5] To pray is to enter 'The quiet heart of the clearing' which is 'the place of stillness from which alone the possibility of the belonging together of Being and thinking, that is, presence and apprehending, can arise at all'.[6] This is nothing less than the transformation of thought into prayer, if we understand thought as the rational activity of the philosophical mind in its quest to order the world, and prayer as the contemplative stillness of the thinking heart in its quest to interpret the world as the revelation of the Wholly Other God.

Heidegger describes what thinking truly should be:

> Thinking does not become action only because some effect issues from it or because it is applied. Thinking acts insofar as it thinks. Such action is presumably the simplest and at the same time the highest, because it concerns the relation of Being to man. But all working or effecting lies in Being and is directed toward beings. Thinking, in contrast, lets itself be claimed by Being so that it can say the truth of Being. Thinking accomplishes this letting. Thinking is *l'engagement par l'Être pour l'Être* [engagement by Being for Being].[7]

It has often been observed that one can substitute 'God' for Heidegger's 'Being', but one can also substitute 'praying' for Heidegger's 'thinking'. What he reiterates here is nothing other than the Christian belief that God prays in us, inspired by Paul's reflection on prayer in Romans: 'for we do not know how to pray as we ought, but that very Spirit intercedes with sighs too deep for words' (Rom. 8:26). Prayer acts insofar as it prays; prayer, in contrast to thinking, lets itself be claimed by God so that it can say the truth of God; prayer is *l'engagement par Dieu(e) pour Dieu(e)*.

In this chapter, I want to explore the potential of prayer, informed by feminist consciousness, with this Heideggerian possibility in mind. Might the quest for a feminist epistemology beyond modernity invite a reappraisal of the ways in which prayer might open the mind to new ways of knowing, informed by the perspectives that Heidegger offers to theological reflection?

The secularization of vision

In its critique of modern concepts of autonomy, knowledge and subjectivity, feminist theory is, I have suggested, profoundly resistant to the aspects of relational being that open up through theological reflection on the self and the world. Positioned by a post-Kantian secular ideology that renders inaccessible the theological hinterland of revelation and faith, feminist theory gropes towards but fails to reach a theological understanding of the self beyond patriarchy's dominion. Feminist theologians have access to a wider range of resources for the postmodern reconstruction of knowledge and subjectivity, but many of them are also post-Kantian moderns at heart, to the extent that they use the rhetoric of 'God' without the relational dimensions of prayer and revelation that constitute the only possibility of an encounter between the human creature and the divine other.

In order to illustrate this feminist resistance to the idea of prayer, I want to consider Ellen Fox's reading of Simone Weil in her essay, 'Seeing through Women's Eyes: The Role of Vision in Women's Moral Theory'. Fox refers to Weil as an example of 'the recurring theme of *vision*'[8] in women's writings on moral philosophy: 'To see and to be seen clearly, with sensitivity to rich detail and subtle moral nuance, has been identified by women from different traditions as profoundly important to a well-lived life.'[9]

Referring to Weil's essay titled 'Reflections on the Right Use of School Studies with a View to the Love of God', Fox writes that

> one of the most important reasons for learning to concentrate on one's studies is that such concentration aids in developing the concentration needed for prayer. And prayer, for Weil, is a certain form of extremely pure attention, or attentive seeing.[10]

She goes on to quote 'a telling passage' in which Weil writes:

> The love of our neighbor in all its fullness simply means being able to say to him: 'What are you going through?' It is a recognition that the sufferer exists, not only as a unit in a collection, or a specimen from the social category labeled 'unfortunate', but as a man, exactly like us, who was one day stamped with a special mark by affliction. For this reason it is enough, but it is indispensable, to know how to look at him in a certain way . . . This way of looking is first of all attentive. The soul empties itself of all its own contents in order to receive into itself the being it is looking at, just as he is, in all his truth.[11]

Fox explains that

> For Weil, the foremost reason for learning to see rightly is that it is our only means of finding God . . . She has no qualms at all about the soul 'emptying itself of all its own contents' since she has confidence that God will fill her being with his presence and truth. For Weil, proper attention does not mean active searching; she argues that attention really consists of a kind of open, receptive waiting, where the self does not intrude or try to take a more forceful, participatory role in the pursuit of God. We must simply set our hearts on God, or the truth, and then wait.[12]

However, Fox quotes a further passage in which Weil describes the young student, working at his Latin prose, as becoming like a slave, 'faithfully waiting while the master is absent, watching and listening – ready to open the door to him as soon as he knocks. The master will then make his slave sit down and himself serve him with meat.'[13] This, for Fox, is an unacceptable metaphor as far as feminists are concerned, and it must be replaced by a more appropriate secular interpretation:

> It is fairly clear why no contemporary feminist should be willing to accept Weil's notion of attention without some important modifications. The posture of the attentive slave *might* work when directed toward God, or the truth, but when directed toward other human beings, it is a recipe for disaster. Particularly when practiced by women toward men, it has not, historically, produced the reversal described by Weil in which the master serves the slave with meat. Thus, though Weil's development of and emphasis on the notion of attention and attentive seeing are powerful and evocative, the notion needs to be reworked for secular use.[14]

Weil's imagery is inspired by lines from George Herbert's poem, *Love III* – 'You must sit down, sayes Love, and taste my meat: So I did sit and eat' – a poem which surely unmans God in its delicate reversal of roles of servitude and humility, so that Christ becomes the one who lovingly serves at the table of the soul. But Fox makes no attempt to differentiate between prayerful attentiveness to a God who, for Weil as for Herbert, offers a space of welcoming and nurturing love to the hesitant soul, and the kind of servile attentiveness that women have been encouraged to display towards men, in the Christian tradition as much as in any other. A feminist theologian would agree with Fox's suggestion that the master–slave metaphor is to be rejected when it translates into social or sexual relationships, and she might also ask to what extent such enslaving relationships have been legitimated by the Christian understanding of God. But it does not necessarily follow that the only alternative is to rework the notion 'for secular use'. Might another alternative be to reclaim the space of prayerful attentiveness as one in which a woman can empty herself before God, confident that 'God will fill her being with [her] presence and truth'?

To suggest that Weil's capacity to look with love on the suffering other can be secularized without loss of meaning, is to miss the point. For Weil, prayer and openness to God make possible the dispossession of self and love of the human other. Thus care for the other begins, not with the individual's response to a moral imperative, but with the awareness that before one ever becomes a gift to the other, one is already given by God. If, as Fox suggests, 'To see and be seen clearly . . . has been identified by women from different traditions as profoundly important to a well-lived life', then Weil must be allowed to challenge the secular assumption that this entails no transcendent dimension. For her, it is the consciousness of being created and seen through the eyes of love, which enables us to love the suffering other who is also already seen and loved by God.

The problematization of prayer

However, Weil's understanding of prayerful learning as the soul's 'emptying itself of all its own contents' does raise questions from a critical feminist perspective. To risk the loss of self, to surrender power and allow oneself to be shaped by a knowledge that one receives but cannot control, is, as many feminist theologians have argued, deeply problematic in the context of a Christian tradition that has often if not always deprived women of knowledge, power and self.

In Valerie Saiving's influential article of 1961, 'The Human Situation: A Feminine View', she questions the Christian understanding of sin, arguing that it is informed by masculine concepts of sin experienced as 'the unjustified concern of the self for its own power and prestige'.[15] However, as far as women are concerned, Saiving argues that a lack of any sense of self-worth, and a denigration of the self in its servility to others, might constitute a more accurate description of feminized forms of sin. She suggests that 'a woman can give too much of herself, so that nothing remains of her own uniqueness; she can become merely an emptiness, almost a zero, without value to herself, to her fellow men, or, perhaps, even to God'.[16] This kind of critique, reiterated in many feminist writings, suggests that women should be extremely cautious of a male-dominated religious tradition that advocates a spirituality of *kenosis* and self-negation.

The problem that feminists of faith must negotiate is that, without some form of the giving of self in prayer and in human relationships, the modern, autonomous subject remains the foundation upon which the postmodernist self constructs its ostensibly deconstructive parodies and performances. Indeed, one might argue that only a self that is thoroughly secure in its identity and its economic and social setting can risk the kind of transgressiveness advocated by theorists such as Butler. For the vast majority of women who might derive their sense of self primarily from the communities to which they belong – including the family – the sacrifice of identity in the interests of gender politics may be not a form of liberation but a violent betrayal of relationships of dependency and care.[17]

The challenge is to discover a way of being that preserves the fragile sense of self that women are beginning to acquire in modern culture, while allowing that self to willingly abandon herself to God in the confidence that this God is an Other who participates in our personal becoming and makes us more rather than less the selves we seek to be. This is a God whom Johnson describes as 'the focus of absolute trust, one to whom you can give yourself without fear of betrayal, the holy mystery'.[18] With this suggestion in mind, I want to consider Sarah Coakley's understanding of *kenosis* and prayer, in which she seeks to go beyond feminist critiques to offer a new understanding of kenotic prayer based on the vulnerability of God revealed in Jesus Christ.

Coakley quotes Hampson's critique of the Christian idea of *kenosis*:

> That it [*kenōsis*] should have featured prominently in Christian thought is perhaps an indication of the fact that men have understood what the male problem, in thinking of terms of hierarchy and domination, has been. It may well be a model which men need to appropriate and which may helpfully be built into the male understanding of God. But . . . *for women, the theme of self-emptying and self-abnegation is far from helpful as a paradigm*.[19]

Coakley argues that feminists such as Hampson misunderstand the potential of *kenosis* for feminist spirituality, partly due to confusion about the meaning of the word. She suggests that, amidst the multiple and often contradictory ways in which *kenosis* has been understood, the word needs to be interpreted from a christological perspective. Coakley bases her analysis on different interpretations of Philippians 2:5–11, which refers to Christ who 'did not regard equality with God as something to be exploited, but emptied himself, taking the form of a slave, being born in human likeness, And being found in human form' (Phil. 2:6–7). Coakley suggests that, rather than interpreting this in terms of 'the "two nature" Christology of later "orthodoxy"',[20] the scriptural text invites a narrative reading of Christ as 'choosing *never to have* certain (false and worldly) forms of power – forms sometimes wrongly construed as "divine"'.[21] In other words, rather than seeing this as the emptying out of God's masculine, divine power in the incarnation, Coakley suggests that Christ challenges the very association of God with such power from the beginning. When we come to consider Balthasar's idea of *kenosis*, we shall return to this suggestion.

74 *The middle*

Coakley argues that Hampson's critique is premised upon more modern, philosophical interpretations of *kenosis*, and she sees Ruether's understanding of the *kenosis* of patriarchy as a more faithful feminist representation of this narrative Christology: 'Jesus promoted values quite different from those of *machismo* or worldly power. In his ethical example patriarchy was emptied out (not, we note, Christ himself emptied out).'[22] Thus, suggests Coakley,

> If Jesus' 'vulnerability' is a primary narrative given, rather than a philosophical embarrassment to explain away, then precisely the question is raised whether 'vulnerability' *need* be seen as a 'female' weakness rather than a (special sort of) 'human' strength. As in Ruether's standpoint, so here: Jesus may be the male messenger to *empty* 'patriarchal' values.[23]

In her analysis of the different ways in which theologians and philosophers have sought to explain or justify Christ's *kenosis*, Coakley identifies two interpretative tendencies which she refers to as '"new" (theological) "kenoticism" on the one hand, and analytic (philosophical) "anti-kenoticism" on the other'.[24] Arguing that both have 'several – though very different – drawbacks from a feminist perspective',[25] she writes that

> Whereas the 'new kenoticism' appears to make 'God' both limited and weak (by a process of direct transference from Jesus' human life to the divine), and so endanger the very capacity for divine transformative 'power', the analytic 'orthodoxy' clings ferociously to a vision of divine 'omnipotence' and 'control' which is merely the counterpart of the sexist 'man' made in his (libertarian) image. One model seems propelled by masculinist guilt; the other by unexamined masculinist assumptions. Neither considers – any more than does Hampson – the possibility of a 'strength made perfect *in* (human) weakness' (2 Corinthians 12:9), of the normative concurrence in Christ of non-bullying divine 'power' *with* 'self-effaced' humanity.[26]

Coakley argues that Hampson's criticism of *kenosis* fails on two counts: it does not take into account the idea that Jesus refuses masculine power from the outset, and it appeals to the same gender stereotypes that it claims to reject, by accepting 'the alignment of "males" with achieved, worldly power, and women with lack of it'.[27] But, asks Coakley, 'what . . . if true divine "empowerment" occurs most unimpededly in the context of a *special* form of human "vulnerability"?'[28]

Coakley acknowledges the extent to which Christian ideas of vulnerability have served to legitimate abusive relationships, but she also points to

> another, and longer-term, danger to Christian feminism in the *repression* of all forms of 'vulnerability', and in a concomitant failure to confront issues of

fragility, suffering or 'self-emptying' except in terms of victimology. And that is ultimately the failure to embrace a feminist reconceptualizing of the power of the cross and resurrection. Only . . . by facing – and giving new expression to – the paradoxes of 'losing one's life in order to save it', can feminists hope to construct a vision of the Christic 'self' that transcends the gender stereotypes we are seeking to up-end.[29]

Coakley suggests that this is to be sought through contemplation, understood as *askesis*: 'an ascetical commitment of some subtlety, a regular and willed *practice* of ceding and responding to the divine',[30] through the rhythms of sacramental worship and prayer. This invites openness to '"power-in-vulnerability", the willed effacement to a gentle omnipotence which, far from "complementing" masculinism, acts as its undoing'.[31] And this in turn entails respecting the importance of 'the narrative "gap", the *hiatus* of expectant waiting, that is, the precondition of our assimilation of Christ's "kenotic" cross and resurrection'.[32]

Coakley acknowledges that this patient and expectant practice of prayer is risky, but it is also

> profoundly transformative, 'empowering' in a mysterious 'Christic' sense; for it is a feature of the special self-effacement of this gentle space-making – this yielding to divine power which is no worldly power – that it marks one's willed engagement in the pattern of cross and resurrection, one's deeper rooting and grafting into the 'body of Christ'.[33]

From Coakley's perspective then, and indeed from Weil's perspective too, the surrender of the self in prayer is not a surrender to a God invested with masculine qualities of power, but a surrender to a God beyond patriarchy, a God who challenges patriarchy's ideologies and idolatries, by drawing the praying self into a space of vulnerability which, in Christ, becomes a space of strength and wholeness, not of diminishment and depletion.

But if prayer is to become the *modus vivendi* of the thinking self, then this requires the rediscovery of the classical theological relationship between reason, desire and knowledge – the nuptial relationship between philosophy and theology, according to Aquinas, even if a feminist reading might resist the sexual hierarchy implicit in this metaphor. Indeed, one could argue that only a marriage of equals permits a true dialogue between theology and theory or philosophy, for even if the theologian reads theory 'into' theology, she must also do so with a respect for the space of difference between the secular theorist and the confessing theologian. The task of non-violent persuasion and debate is only possible in a spirit of mutual respect and dialogue, and that is why the new Catholic feminists are unethical in their violent distortion and condemnation of feminist thought – even if feminist theorists manifest an equal violence in their silencing of feminist theological voices.

If a woman is to practise the kind of prayer described by Coakley, this entails coming to prayer as a reasoning feminist subject, even if that subjectivity is suspended in the contemplative state. To go beyond the kind of kenotic prayer that reinscribes a woman into patriarchal constructs of the self entails recognizing that desire for God is expressed not only in prayer but in our rational reflection on the material world and our place within it, informed by the philosophical and theoretical reflections of those who might not share our theological perspective. With this in mind, I want to explore more closely the relationship between desire, prayer and reason, as an epistemological resource which allows the feminist of faith to know the world in ways other than those offered by either feminist theorists or post-Enlightenment philosophers.

Desire and reason

We have seen the extent to which critics such as Parsons and Fulkerson question the unexamined relationship between power and knowledge in the writings of feminist theologians. Modernity brings about a transformation in epistemology, so that knowledge is no longer sought through the study of a natural world that reveals the will of the creator, but rather as the power of the human will to control and manipulate the natural world for its own ends. But Weil suggests that it is desire, not will, which draws us to the joy of learning, arguing that will power 'has practically no place in study', because 'The intelligence can only be led by desire.'[34] She goes on to say that

> It is the part played by joy in our studies that makes of them a preparation for spiritual life, for desire directed towards God is the only power capable of raising the soul. Or rather it is God alone who comes down and possesses the soul, but desire alone draws God down. He only comes to those who ask him to come; and he cannot refuse to come to those who implore him long, often and ardently.[35]

This understanding of the relationship between God and the soul in prayer is one that subverts models of domination and oppressive power. God is drawn to the soul by desire inspired by joy, and the divine response to desire has to be earnestly solicited, for it comes only by invitation and not by force. Prayer, understood as the quest for knowledge motivated by desire for God, thus invites philosophical reflection which begins, not with the autonomous, rational self, but with the self who is always already seen and desired by God, already constituted through a relationship to the other, and orientated towards the other as gift. But this involves exploring in more detail the relationship between desire and knowledge, and in order to do this I want to consider Pamela Sue Anderson's feminist critique of philosophy of religion.

Anderson argues for an expansion of philosophical concepts of rationality to take account of 'female desire, in the form of a "rational passion" named "yearning", as a vital reality of religion'.[36] Addressing herself to Anglo-American analytical philosophy of religion, she sets out to challenge the 'God's-eye view' which is implicit in the 'supposed objectivity of the rational, individual, male-neutral subject of western philosophy and theology',[37] through an appeal to feminist psycholinguistics, feminist standpoint epistemology, and Michèle Le Doeuff's idea of the philosophical imaginary. She identifies one of her central aims as being 'to study both feminist objectivity and female desire as essential concepts for achieving less partial and less biased beliefs than presently found in dominant forms of theism'.[38]

Anderson describes herself as a reformist, and she is committed to a modified Kantianism which seeks to uphold a rational model of enquiry into religious epistemology, while also questioning the boundaries which define rationality. Psycholinguistics and analysis of the philosophical imaginary allow for the scrutiny of what has been excluded in the validation of rationality, thereby widening the framework in order to take account of the role of female desire and yearning in the 'rational passion'[39] of religious belief and in the formation of concepts of justice.

Anderson's work is important for feminist theological reflection insofar as it draws attention to the significance of desire for women's spirituality, and it suggests ways in which one might explore the relationship between reason and desire. So, for example, my suggestion that prayer might be broadly understood as a form of thought that is focused on receptivity and interpretation rather than on objectivity and explanation could perhaps be described as a quest for a theological language of 'rational passion' – it is thought insofar as it reasons, and prayer insofar as it desires.

But I would question whether Anderson's modified Kantianism is capable of representing the situated female believer as a praying subject of religious yearning and desire. In her non-theological representation of religion, reason and desire, Anderson does not consider the significance of prayer as the language of desire in Christianity, although she does devote considerable space to the Hindu concept of *bhakti*, raising questions about the particularity and contextualization of religious knowledge which I cannot explore here.[40]

Anderson describes her project as follows:

> Unlike a feminist theology, my proposal for a feminist philosophy of religion is not to develop or defend any specific doctrine of belief in one particular religion, one God, or some particular goddess(es). Instead I contend that a feminist philosopher should be concerned with tools for critically assessing epistemological frameworks of belief, including tools for critically refiguring reason. To reinstate one crucial aspect of my ultimate goal, I intend to develop a philosophical framework which can generate less biased, less

partial, and so less false beliefs. But specific formulations of doctrinal beliefs are left to feminist theologians.[41]

From a theological perspective this passage is problematic, suggesting as it does that the task of philosophy is to 'generate' true belief, through the subjection of particular religious doctrines and beliefs to philosophical analysis. Thus philosophy claims an ultimate power over religion – its task is to generate, adjudicate and discriminate in matters of faith, while theologians are left with the secondary task of filling in the doctrinal details. So, despite her repeated appeals for an appreciation of the contextualization and situatedness of knowledge, Anderson's Kantianism entails a metaphysics in which reason, abstracted from every context and narrative, does indeed offer a philosophical 'God's-eye view'.

As an aside, it is interesting that Anderson gives no insight into her own religious positioning, adopting the position of the objective 'knower' who can evaluate and judge the desire of the other, from a perspective apparently unmarked by desire or religious yearning. This is despite her insistence on feminist standpoint epistemology, in which different modes of knowing are acquired through the endeavour to occupy different subjective contexts and perspectives, in order to arrive at a more contextualized and therefore comprehensive understanding of claims to truth and knowledge. But if the scholar claims access to different religious standpoints while her own standpoint remains masked, she is still exercising a form of objectivity which secures her own position beyond the critical scrutiny of her religious other.

Over and against this detached philosophical method of enquiry, I want to suggest that desire always entails particularity – we desire something or someone, and to categorize desire by evacuating it of all its referents may be to surrender female desire to the chaos of non-representability, a point that I shall return to in later chapters. We cannot understand women's religious desire unless we situate it in its particular contexts of language, devotion and faith. There cannot be a universal theory of desire, prior to its articulation in the grammar and practices of faith communities. It is in knowing who a woman prays to, how she prays, why she prays, who she prays with, and how this in turn shapes her understanding of who she is, that we might begin to understand the significance of desire for feminist reflection and the extent to which such desire is coherent in the context of a particular set of beliefs, visions and practices, and this cannot be achieved by a theory of religion in general.

The language of prayer as the open receptivity of the thinking heart may be a form of reason which proves highly resistant to the pursuit of objectifying Kantian rationality, however much one might modify this to take account of female desire. I am proposing a theological perspective which understands faith (I resist the word 'belief', for I am suggesting something more all-embracing than intellectual consent to a set of doctrinal propositions), not as something generated by philosophical reason, but as the response of reason to revelation, experienced as the awakening of desire for God or the transcendent Other. From this perspective, the task of philosophy is not to generate nor to justify faith, but to bring rational reflection to bear on the *a priori* truths of faith (*a priori* referring here not to a decontextualized understanding of universal truth, but to the fundamental observances or doctrines whose acceptance is necessary for identification with a particular faith community), in order to deepen understanding and coherence. Thus faith is not made subservient to the demands of reason but rather enters into a nuptial relationship with reason, so that in the intimacy and fecundity of faithful reasoning, a vision is nurtured that is within reason's sphere but beyond reason's grasp, but only insofar as reason is understood in the context of the particularity of faith.

To illustrate the difference between faith in the control of reason and reason in the service of faith, let me explore two accounts of women's religious desire – both of which employ oceanic metaphors. Anderson refers to Kant's metaphor of the 'stormy sea' as the realm of illusion:

> In the Kantian picture, the definite line separating the philosopher or seafarer from the sea represents the limits of ordered rationality and pure understanding. But if this line is drawn by men alone and represents the limits to their reasoning, can and should it be pushed back? According to certain feminists, human rationality should seek to grasp the contents of the marine waters whose turbulence evoke images of desire, birth, and love. By emphasizing these additional images, feminists offer a more comprehensive, however complex, account of reality.[42]

With her commitment to Kant, Anderson does not ask if knowledge motivated by women's desire for God might offer, not a 'more comprehensive ... account of reality', but an altogether different account of reality. Her epistemology is premised upon a modern understanding of knowledge as possession, even though much in her book might invite a different approach to knowledge through multiple situated rationalities. To know is to 'grasp' – but desire is not about grasping, unless it is a desire that seeks to control the object of desire. In theological terms, at least as far as some aspects of the Catholic tradition are concerned, desire for God is the expression of a desire which does not grasp but which rather immerses itself in the divine presence, experienced not as turbulence but as incomprehensible peace and union. Thus, Catherine of Siena, describing 'the light of most holy faith', writes:

> Truly, this light is a sea, for it nourishes the soul in you, peaceful sea, eternal Trinity . . . This water is a mirror in which you, eternal Trinity, grant me knowledge; for when I look into this mirror, holding it in the hand of love, it shows me myself, as your creation, in you, and you in me through the union you have brought about of the Godhead with our humanity.[43]

I am not convinced that Anderson's expanded rationality would better enable a philosopher of religion to understand Catherine's God, nor do I accept that such understanding could be arrived at prior to the formulation of doctrinal beliefs. For Catherine's knowledge of God and self is thoroughly shaped by her doctrinal context, centred as it is on a Trinitarian and incarnational theology. This language gives a context to God who remains Other beyond all human knowing, but who can nevertheless be spoken of in a shared language of worship and belief. The rationality in Catherine's prayer lies in its internal coherence – the vehicle for her desire is a language structured around the grammar of the Catholic faith, even if she pushes that language to the limits in seeking to express a passion that language cannot contain.

But it is not enough simply to cite Catherine as a response to Anderson's critique, as if the Catholic tradition offered sufficient resources for the construction of female subjectivities and the articulation of women's desire without the intervention of critical feminist analysis. If female mysticism and spirituality are shaped by a doctrinal tradition that has largely acted as an expression of masculine fantasies, fears and projections of the divine, to what extent does Catherine's highly orthodox, Trinitarian mysticism trap her within a way of being that will always wage war on the sexual female body? And Catherine's extreme asceticism cannot be ignored in asking this question. (Indeed, the same question would arise in the context of Weil's spirituality.) Is this not the problem for every woman who seeks to inhabit the *church* rather than the *house* of language – does she not always find herself already in the Father's house, constructed out of a language where Being speaks always and everywhere in the Father's tongue?

Consider Balthasar's claim that

> The 'metaphysics of the saints', in the sense of an aesthetic Christian transcendental reason, attains perhaps its purest and most exhaustive form in the *Dialogue* of Catherine of Siena (1378), where it becomes evident that the 'mystical' in her Christian experience is simply an elucidation of what is contained in every genuinely evangelical vision. The 'dialogue' that takes place here is the dialogue between infinite and finite reason, in Christian terms, between the triune God (whose voice resounds from the heights as the voice of God the Father) and the completely universalized soul, which has been broadened out to become the *anima ecclesiastica* . . . This prayer of passionate indifference is penetrated and imprinted by the expository, explanatory utterance of God the Father, who speaks in his Son and through the Son's words and deeds, and who with His Holy Spirit expounds the Son in men's hearts.[44]

If Balthasar is correct, then one might conclude that it is simply not possible for a woman to experience Being beyond the resounding voice from on high of God the Father, penetrating her being, speaking in a Son's words and deeds, colonizing and universalizing her desire in the name of an *anima ecclesiastica* which, as we shall see, in Balthasar's theology is a multi-gendered, collective hybrid from which female sexual embodiment is effectively banished. This suggests that women's religious desire may be poisoned by a tradition that allows it to speak only from a space of masochism and self-loathing – when Freud diagnosed the masochistic inclinations of the female psyche was he not, as Kristeva suggests, peering deeply into minds indelibly marked by the Christian tradition? We shall return to that question in some detail, but there is no assurance that Christian spirituality is capable of nurturing healthy, self-affirming desire in women, and there is much evidence to suggest that its fear and loathing of female sexuality has been internalized by women themselves.[45]

But Catherine tells us that God speaks in many tongues, as mother, friend, lover, Spirit, Trinity, in ways that elude the linguistic grids of patriarchal control. This is a God who plays 'a "lover's game"' with us, 'because I go away for love and I come back for love – no, not really I, for I am your unchanging and unchangeable God; what goes and comes back is the feeling my charity creates in the soul'.[46] This is a God who speaks, not in language that expounds, but in the language of a 'mad lover' who might render a woman speechless with desire:

> Why then are you so mad? Because you have fallen in love with what you have made! You are pleased and delighted with her within yourself, as if you were drunk [with desire] [sic] for her salvation. She runs away from you and you go looking for her. She strays and you draw closer to her. You clothed yourself in our humanity, and nearer than that you could not have come. And what shall I say? I will stutter, 'A-a,' because there is nothing else I know how to say.[47]

What has 'transcendental reason' to say to this madness of love with its ecstatic utterances? Might the resounding voice of the Father from on High fall silent for the sake of an 'unspeakable love' in whose name one might say, 'I beg you – I would force you even! – to have mercy on your creatures'?[48] And what mercy might still be revealed in the beings of womanly creatures who at last are bringing to thought and to speech – and therefore to Being – another way of being and a different awareness of Being, beyond even the 'metaphysics of the saints'?

For the unthinkable must be thought and the unspeakable must be spoken, even if our words ultimately fail before that presencing of Being that can speak only in the stuttered gasps and sighs of the body's *jouissance*. The future of God opens up in the coming towards us of sexual difference, and it is only in the thinking of God beyond the silencing of secularism and the abstractions of metaphysics, that we might begin to recognize this becoming God who is always and everywhere with us and among us, 'Never a slave to the law, making every text contradict itself, elusive in any formula adopted, escaping any prevailing cult, any idolatry.'[49]

Praying as a woman

How, then, might one begin to construct a feminist theology in which the use of reason, informed by feminist consciousness, allows a woman to enter into a space of kenotic openness to the divine Other, without surrendering herself to the patriarchal gods that masquerade as God in the language of Christian doctrine and devotion? This is ultimately an experiential question, for its response cannot be adequately discovered through theological reflection alone: in the end, only prayer itself might answer our questions about prayer.

Nevertheless, I believe that it is possible, through a feminist retrieval of the wisdom of the Catholic theological tradition, to begin a weaving together of spirituality and theology that might take us beyond modernity, to a renewed appreciation of the potential wholeness of our being in the world understood in terms of sacramentality. This entails recognizing that the tearing apart of knowledge and prayer, beginning perhaps with the rise of the universities in medieval Europe, created a milieu in which our understanding became premised upon oppositions which in our time we experience as destructive dualisms: oppositions between God and the world, between the individual and the community, between nature and reason, between male and female. By going before these dualisms we might also learn to go beyond them, even as we recognize that, in the history of Being, going beyond can never be a forgetting: it can only ever be a different way of remembering, in this case a remembering that might allow us to re-member the female body within the sacramental community of the Christian faith.

This is a task of both resistance and reclamation. If contemplative prayer draws us into the silent mystery of our desire for God – which is our response to God's desire for us – we must emerge from that silence into new ways of speaking about God, which might mean resisting some traditional forms of prayer and worship. It might mean praying as women, not through an experiential appeal to an essential womanly self, but through a mimetic appropriation of the language of femininity and motherhood, a parodic playing out of the roles to which we have been assigned. To quote Nicola Slee,

> We must pray with eyes wide open, refusing to see nothing of what is hidden, secret – blatant lies.
>
> We must pray with heads held high, refusing to bow in obsequiousness to prelate, priest or pope . . .
> We must pray with bodies known, bared: touching our own knowledge, knowing our instinctual wisdom, refusing to be violated or shamed.
> We must denounce false ways of praying, false names for God, false myths and images and stories.

> We must accuse our God of all that has abused us, crippled us,
> maimed us. We must drag deity to court, testify against him,
> lay the charge at his feet, bring forward many witnesses and see
> what he will answer. We must refuse all excuses, justifications,
> legitimations. We must insist on the charge, 'Guilty'.
> We must lament our lost history, liturgy, story. We must bewail
> our betrayed bodies, knowledge, beauty. We must reproach our
> abandoned altars, mourn our overturned tables, weep for the
> broken vessels: the sacred chalice scattered, scattered in a
> thousand pieces.[50]

This is the prayer of woman's resistance, a prayer whose righteousness may easily tilt into a form of self-righteousness, if it is not rooted in that contemplative silence before God in which the self recognizes its otherness, its vulnerability and its dependence, not as the dependence between the feminine creature and the masculine creator, but as a form of dependence upon the vulnerability and love of God beyond the constructs of patriarchy and gender, for only in the context of such dependence might a woman risk prayer.

But to pray as woman might also mean to pray as men have always prayed, to claim access to the language that 'man' has taken from woman, silencing 'her' desire in the name of an eroticized and feminized spirituality that can annihilate the body, but that can also restore to the body its rightful place of bodily desiring in the world. Throughout the Christian mystical tradition, there is a certain security to be gained for men who appropriate the language of female sexuality to express their relationship to Christ, by maintaining secure boundaries which separate language from the sexual body.[51] The repeated emphasis on bodily transcendence in the texts of Christian spirituality is in many ways a Butler-esque spiritual performance, unleashing a feminized language of desire which provides the scripts for man's longing for God, only to the extent that the female body remains inert and silent in the margins. But what might happen if a woman consciously incarnated in her own sexual self the kind of voluptuous feminized spirituality which one finds in the writings of male as well as female mystics?

Consider, for example, Gregory of Nyssa's lyrical reflection on the Song of Songs. In the following lengthy quotation, he is reflecting upon the phrase, 'My beloved put forth his hand through the hole of the door, and my belly was moved for him.' The *HarperCollins Study Bible* offers a translation of this verse which is perhaps more apposite here:

> My beloved thrust his hand into the opening,
> and my inmost being yearned for him.
>
> (Song of Solomon 5:4)

84 *The middle*

> 'Open,' says the Word to his bride, that he might give her the capacity to open the content of the divine names. The bride obeys the Word. (For she has become what she has heard: a sister, companion, dove, and perfect one.) . . . The bride opens the door after removing the veil from her heart; she opens the door, the veil of flesh; once the door has been flung wide open, the king of glory may enter. But the gate has a narrow aperture through which the bridegroom cannot fit, for he can scarcely get his hand inside. However, his hand reaches inside and rouses the bride's desire for seeing him. She considers as gain the knowledge of the hand of him whom she desired . . .
>
> [T]he human soul has two natures: the incorporeal, intellectual, and pure on the one hand; the bodily, material, and irrational on the other. When the soul is purged of the gross habits of earthly life, it looks up through virtue to what is connatural and divine; it does not cease to search out and seek the origin of created reality, the source of its beauty from which springs the power whose wisdom is manifested in it . . . Because the soul reaches from below to a knowledge of the transcendent and to a comprehension of God's wonderful works, it is unable to proceed further in curiously scrutinizing these works; rather, it marvels and worships him who alone is recognized by his works. The soul sees the heavenly beauty, the splendour of the luminaries, the swiftness of the earth turning on its axis, the good order of things, the harmony of the stars' course, and the yearly cycle with its four seasons. The earth is sustained by God who embraces it . . .
>
> When the soul looks at these wonders, it considers him who is recognized in his works. Similarly, in the age to come all limitations will yield to that life which is beyond anything seen, heard or understood . . . Meanwhile, our soul's limit of ineffable knowledge consists in appearances whose operation in creation we symbolically understand as the bridegroom's hands . . . Human nature is not able to contain the infinite, unbounded divine nature. 'My belly was moved (*throeo*) for him,' the bride says. The term 'wonder' (*throeosis*) signifies amazement and astonishment at the sight of this miracle. Every soul endowed with the faculty of reason is struck by the wonderful deeds of the divine hand which transcends our human capacity, for the divine nature effecting such wonders can neither be grasped nor contained. Every created being is the work of that hand which appeared through the aperture.[52]

If we subject this passage to the scrutiny of feminist analysis, then one could argue that it appears to reiterate the dualisms which have proved so destructive to female embodiment in the Christian tradition. The soul must transcend 'the bodily, material, and irrational' (and therefore the implicitly feminine), in order to attain to 'the incorporeal, intellectual, and pure' (the implicitly masculine). Only the soul that is 'purged of the gross habits of earthly life' can look up 'through virtue to what is connatural and divine'.

But Gregory's prose is more subtle than this, for the soul is feminized in both its rational and irrational aspects. The soul is like the bride whose desire is aroused by the bridegroom's hands, both in its incorporeality and in its materiality. Moreover, in its quest for 'the origin of created reality', the soul finds its gaze turned back from the impossible desire to see God, to the beauty of the material world as evidence of God's creative wisdom. It recognizes that it can know God only through its capacity to marvel at the handiwork of God, for 'The earth is sustained by God who embraces it.' Thus, a spirituality that seeks to transcend the body and creation in order to know God finds its attention returned to creation with a renewed sense of wonder at all that is. The soul, suffused with bridal desire, discovers itself to be embodied in a universe that pulses with the erotic manifestation of the divine life: 'Every created being is the work of that hand which appeared through the aperture.'

Aquinas's language lacks the lush sensuality of Gregory's prose, but both of them seek to express what we might call an epistemology of prayer, in which the material world is transcended only in order to be appreciated anew as that which we cannot possibly transcend in our yearning for God. The divine mystery is always just beyond the horizon of human knowing, receding infinitely further the more intimately close we become. But the gaze that allows itself to rest for a while on this far horizon is turned back to the world with a new vision and a new way of knowing and being in the world. For Catherine of Siena, this is also a new discovery of a self that is 'becoming divine',[53] for she recognizes God in herself and herself in God, through her awakening to the beauty of creation:

> For by the light of understanding within your light I have tasted and seen your depth, eternal Trinity, and the beauty of your creation. Then, when I considered myself in you, I saw that I am your image. You have gifted me with power from yourself, eternal Father, and my understanding with your wisdom – such wisdom as is proper to your only-begotten Son; and the Holy Spirit, who proceeds from you and from your Son, has given me a will, and so I am able to love.
>
> You, eternal Trinity, are the craftsman; and I your handiwork have come to know that you are in love with the beauty of what you have made, since you made of me a new creation in the blood of your Son.[54]

It would be anachronistic to hold up a medieval mystic as Catholicism's answer to feminism, yet beyond the limitations of Catherine's life and context, she does offer us, as Balthasar suggests, a possible glimpse of something universal, even if we must go beyond Balthasar to discern it. Like Catherine, feminist theologians today seek to recognize the image of God in themselves, to celebrate the beauty of creation, and to be empowered to will and to love differently.

But if pre-modern theology is a rich resource for the development of a feminist epistemology based on a prayerful, participatory way of being in the world, it also poses a question to those such as Fox who, in her secularized reading of Weil, suggests that this visionary epistemology can be evacuated of its references to prayer and to God, and still remain coherent. There is no way in which feminism could converse with Thomism without at least some openness to theological reflection, for, to quote Kerr, Aquinas's 'view of how our minds are related to the world is interwoven with his doctrine of God: no epistemology without theology'.[55]

The challenge for feminism, then, is to make the female body the site of a prayerful, graced way of knowing and being in the world, without yet knowing the extent of the difference that might be revealed in this process of coming to know. Sexual difference is the holy grail of the feminist quest – an elusive promise of an incarnate presence that is always just beyond where we find ourselves to be. It is perhaps not surprising that this difference provides the language for Christianity's most profound reflections on the relationship between God and the world, because the relationship between the sexual self and the sexual other is one that is acutely positioned on the cusp between intimacy and alienation. The challenge posed to feminist theology is that of fully inhabiting this gendered theological language for the first time, analysing its meanings and exposing its deceptions, 'in order to pry out of them what they have borrowed that is feminine, from the feminine, to make them "render up" and give back what they owe the feminine'.[56] That is the task of the second part of this book, in which I turn to the new Catholic feminism, with a particular focus on Balthasar, in order to pose a radical challenge to those who would seek once again to silence women through an appeal to this most modern and oppressive interpretation of so-called 'tradition'.

But this task entails thinking from that delicate space of encounter between the body and language, between the world and God, and between faith and reason. It means thinking gyroscopically, allowing thought to spin on a point of balance between the uncritical essentialisms of the new Catholic feminism, and the disembodied abstractions of postmodernist theory. It is a way of thinking that is premised upon Aquinas's Aristotelian insight that 'the soul is the form of the body', so that the mind's knowledge of the body denotes a particularly intimate participation between the 'thing' and the mind. If we are never reducible to our biological bodies, neither do we have any way of being in and knowing the world other than as bodily being and bodily knowing. Yet to know ourselves and the world in this way is to be led beyond knowledge, to ever more profound depths of mystery. As we move inwards from the world to the self and to God, we find our gaze turned outwards again to a world rendered luminous with the unknowable darkness of God, a dark unknowing that we have discovered at the very heart of our own way of being in the world. This new way of knowing as not-knowing requires a new way of speaking, a new way of discovering that we cannot always say what we mean or mean what we say, because language, like knowledge, falls short of desire.

I have positioned the feminist theological subject in a space of bodily receptivity to the revelation of God, without surrendering the significance of reason informed by feminist theory and philosophy, for enabling her to think through the position in which she finds herself, inevitably shaped as it is by the texts and traditions of patriarchal religion. Against the open horizon of the mystery of God, we can only question being from where we are. With this in mind, I turn now to the second part of this book, 'The end', in order to examine the ways in which new Catholic feminism positions woman in the world. This means assuming the role of Catholic woman, attempting to speak as she does, and to think theologically from the position assigned to her. As we shall see, this means the staging of a tragi-comic melodrama, a baroque extravaganza of sex and death with a hellish ending, as we seek to act out the woman's role in the script of Hans Urs von Balthasar's theo-drama.

Part II

The end

5 Incarnation, difference and God

Hans Urs von Balthasar might be viewed as the Catholic postmodern theologian par excellence, with a growing influence on Anglican as well as Roman Catholic theology.[1] By way of an all-encompassing vision expressed in a flamboyant theological poetics – Graham Ward describes him as 'a Dante composing a *divina commedia* for the late twentieth century'[2] – he seeks a post-Heideggerian return to the Christian faith beyond the wastelands of modernity, through a theology of glory that takes as a central concern Heidegger's challenge to rediscover the wonder of being in the world. He describes Heidegger's project as 'the most fertile one [in the modern period] from the point of view of a potential philosophy of glory',[3] arguing that 'If Christianity, failing to preserve a theology of glory, does not itself wish to fall victim to the new naturalism . . . , then it must make Heidegger's inheritance its own.'[4] Balthasar associates 'the waning of the category of glory' with a move in western thought 'from the atmosphere of prayer to that of concepts or intellectual speculation'[5] – a move that he traces back to Eckhart. He argues that Christianity is the only way beyond the predicament in which post-Christian humanity finds itself, on the far side of every attempt at meaning before and beyond the event of Christ. History is approaching

> a moment of decision: Christian man stands before the glory of the Christian God, which enables him to preserve something of the glory of creation; non-Christian man stands before the yawning abyss of reason and freedom, first opened up by Christians, and encounters there the self-glorifying Absolute.[6]

The only possible Christian response to this approaching crisis is 'self-surrender to the sign, in all its purity, of the glory of God's love revealed in Christ'.[7]

Balthasar's insistence on the absolute challenge of the Christian faith to the (post)modern subject is hardly likely to invite a sympathetic hearing from feminist theorists who, as we have already seen, are highly resistant to any theological perspective, let alone one which is as shot through with problematic sexual stereotypes as Balthasar's. Nevertheless there are good reasons for a feminist to take Balthasar seriously. Although he has been virtually ignored by feminist theologians, his influence on the so-called new feminism is profound, as it is on Pope John Paul II's theology of sexual difference. His vast theological corpus extends far beyond questions of sexuality and gender, and indeed there are few areas of thought, history, religion and culture that he does not seek to muster within his theological synthesis. However, sexual difference is the architectonics which structures his whole theology: 'everywhere in Balthasar's theology it is sexual difference – the difference between the sexes and the differencing of the sexes – that brings into view (engenders) the encounter between God and creature'.[8] It is this paradoxical and at times contradictory looping together of sexual difference and creaturely difference in an elliptical relationship that both holds together and threatens to unravel Balthasar's theological enterprise that constitutes the most problematic but also potentially the most fruitful aspect of his theology as far as feminism is concerned.

Balthasar and Irigaray: engendering difference

For Balthasar, as for Irigaray, sexual difference is pivotal to the attempt to rethink difference in the context of the challenge posed by Heidegger. Any attempt to seek human equality in a way that elides the significance of sexual difference can only deepen the forgetfulness of difference that has created a crisis at the heart of modern life, with a masculine-orientated, technological culture threatening to overwhelm the material, maternal dimension of being. By arguing that sexual embodiment is a crucial aspect of the rediscovery of the wonder of being, Irigaray and Balthasar take Heidegger's critique of technology into unexplored terrain. Balthasar argues that 'where positivistic, technology-oriented thinking succeeds in reigning supreme, the female element also vanishes from the attitude of the man. There is no longer anything that maternally embraces the human being's existence.'[9] Irigaray would appear to agree:

> The entire economy demonstrates a forgetting of life, a lack of recognition of debt to the mother, of maternal ancestry, of the women who do the work of producing and maintaining life. Tremendous vital resources are wasted for the sake of money. But what good is money if it is not used for life?[10]

The result of this masculine, technological ethos with its maternal forgetfulness is a homosexual culture. For Balthasar, 'Where the mystery of the marian character of the Church is obscured or abandoned, there Christianity must become unisexual (homo-sexual), that is to say all male.'[11] According to Irigaray, 'The law that orders our society is the exclusive valorization of men's

Incarnation, difference and God 93

needs/desires, of exchanges among men.' What the anthropologist calls the passage from nature to culture thus amounts to the institution of the reign of hom(m)o-sexuality.[12]

The solution to this hom(m)osexual culture must lie in the rediscovery of sexual difference. Irigaray writes,

> Women's exploitation is based upon sexual difference; its solution will come only through sexual difference. Certain modern tendencies, certain feminists of our time, make strident demands for sex to be neutralized. This neutralization, if it were possible, would mean the end of the human species.[13]

In a similar vein perhaps, Balthasar writes:

> the assault of 'feminism' is in a fatal predicament, because it is fighting for equal rights for women in a predominantly male-oriented, technological civilization. Thus it either takes up the front against this civilization as such . . . or claims its place within this civilization, which can scarcely be done without an unnatural masculinization of woman or a leveling of the difference between the sexes.[14]

In appealing for the rediscovery of the symbolic significance of sexual difference, both these Catholic thinkers apparently posit an irreducible difference between the sexes. According to Balthasar,

> The male body is male throughout, right down to each cell of which it consists, and the female body is utterly female; and this is also true of their whole empirical experience and ego-consciousness. At the same time both share an identical human nature, but at no point does it protrude, neutrally, beyond the sexual difference, as if to provide neutral ground for mutual understanding.[15]

According to Irigaray, 'I will never be in a man's place, never will a man be in mine. Whatever identifications are possible, one will never exactly occupy the place of the other – they are irreducible one to the other.'[16]

One could continue in this vein, harvesting the writings of each to show the extent of the apparent similarities between them. However, such comparisons mask a fundamental difference, because it is also possible to read much of Irigaray as an act of parodic feminist mimesis – and therefore to some extent an antithesis – of the kind of sexual difference represented by Balthasar. Through her quest for a morphology that symbolically incorporates the female body and sexual difference into language, Irigaray provides feminist readers with a psycholinguistic method – a mimetic feminine gaze perhaps – that lays bare the masculine subject that she discerns at the heart of every discourse, theory and philosophy. Read in this sense, she provides a site of textual/sexual difference from which to deconstruct some of the sexual stereotypes that Balthasar perpetuates, in order to expose the extent to which his theology constitutes woman, not as the authentically other, but as the other of the same.[17]

An Irigarayan reading of Balthasar would resist seeking to define or identify woman, but would concentrate instead on tracing 'her' disappearance behind the screens of sameness masquerading as difference:

> the issue is not one of elaborating a new theory of which woman would be the *subject* or the *object*, but of jamming the theoretical machinery itself, of suspending its pretension to the production of a truth and of a meaning that are excessively univocal. Which presupposes that women do not aspire simply to be men's equals in knowledge. That they do not claim to be rivalling men in constructing a logic of the feminine that would still take onto-theo-logic as its model, but that they are rather attempting to wrest this question away from the economy of the logos. They should not put it, then, in the form 'What is woman?' but rather, repeating/interpreting the way in which, within discourse, the feminine finds itself defined as lack, deficiency, or as imitation and negative image of the subject, they should signify that with respect to this logic a *disruptive excess* is possible on the feminine side.[18]

One could argue that, in expressing this 'disruptive excess', Irigaray is performing a baroque sexual comedy of mistaken identities, seductions and exposées worthy of a Shakespeare or a Mozart (not for nothing has she written an essay titled '*Cosí Fan Tutti*'), whereas Balthasar is scripting something more along the lines of a Victorian melodrama, with overblown romantic rhetoric, stylized sexual stereotypes, and a dark undercurrent of sexual repression, rape and violence.

But the picture is more complex than this, because the questions and challenges that Balthasar and Irigaray pose to one another multiply. While both seek to create new forms of theological and cultural discourse based on the interdependence of language and sexual embodiment, on the capacity of human sexuality to inspire new ways of speaking about God, and on the centrality of sexual difference for human identity and relationships, both in fact betray that commitment to difference. In Irigaray's work, the difference between God and creation is negated by way of a theological reductionism in which 'God' becomes a Feuerbachian projection of human subjectivity, or a space of transcendence too narrowly defined in terms of human sexuality. In Balthasar, sexual difference is denied, through a complex and often contradictory theological symbolics in which woman becomes a projection of man, and the particularity and revelatory potential of female sexual embodiment is denied. With these preliminary observations in mind, I begin by considering the significance of the body for Balthasar and Irigaray, and I then consider the denial of God's otherness in her work, and the denial of woman's otherness in his work.

Language and embodiment

Ostensibly, Balthasar and Irigaray share a profound awareness of the need to rediscover the significance of the body and the materiality/maternality of language, if thought is to move beyond metaphysics – and beyond Heidegger himself – to become incarnate in the time and space of sexuate human existence. For Irigaray, the philosophical forgetfulness of being, whose origins Heidegger traces back to Plato, is also a forgetting of the body: 'The affirmation of the body, and the love of the body, which are still spoken of in the Homeric epic, at the beginning of philosophy, will finally be forgotten in the metaphysical edifice.'[19] Going beyond metaphysics entails the recognition that 'Language, however formal it may be, feeds on blood, on flesh, on material elements.'[20]

O'Donnell claims that 'one of Balthasar's favourite words is "bodiliness"'.[21] Balthasar suggests that, even although we are creatures of culture and language who are never fully at home in the world, our sense of bodily belonging is a source of profound attachment:

> The I can in happy amazement experience how deep down into the organic and the physical its mysterious center is immersed – as heart, imagination, feeling, emotion, mood, eros – so much so that it would like never to be separated from this being-at-home in body and cosmos.[22]

Like Irigaray, Balthasar emphasizes the corporeality of language itself, although he also affirms its capacity to transcend the body in its forms of expression, since it is ultimately orientated towards the infinite freedom of God:

> Just as human beings as spirit indwell being in its totality, so through their bodies do they indwell the whole of nature, and can never be detached from it. They speak a corporeal organic language, one of natural sounds and gestures. This is what brings about the marvellous give-and-take and endless interplay between nature and spirit in our speech, the gradual transition from natural images to half-emancipated symbols and then to freely chosen signs.[23]

While Balthasar begins with the bodiliness of speech and moves to the transcendent capacity of language, Irigaray seeks the re-embodiment of language beyond its Derridean reduction to textuality alone,[24] through her extended exploration of the relationship between the sexual body and language. This leads to her idea of the 'sensible transcendental', which she describes in terms of 'beauty itself', referring to 'that which confounds the opposition between immanence and transcendence. As an always already sensible horizon on the basis of which everything would appear. But one would have to go back over everything to discover it in its enchantment.'[25] There are clear Heideggerian echoes in this description, but elsewhere Irigaray also refers to the sensible transcendental in specifically theological terms:

> In so far as he is alien to a sensible transcendental – the dimension of the divine par excellence – and of its grace, man would remain a little outside the religious world, unless he is initiated into it by women. And this happens in certain traditions. Even in our own, if one knows how to read certain texts: from the New Testament, from the Song of Songs, from the mystics, and so on.[26]

However, at this point Balthasar challenges Irigaray, for while she enables a feminist reader to expose the negation of the female body in his theology, he enables a Catholic reader to expose the evacuation of the sacramental body from Irigaray's feminized symbolics. Irigaray repeatedly appeals to Christian symbols and doctrines, as in the above quotation, but in doing so she abstracts them from their bodily significance in the context of a performative narrative of faith, through their insertion into the secularized discourses of feminist psycholinguistics where their effectiveness depends upon the refusal of their capacity to act as bodily ciphers. In presenting itself as a theory or a philosophy rather than a theology, Irigaray's prose thus remains locked in its Derridean captivity to the text in spite of itself, for she denies the incarnate, sacramental function of the Catholic symbolism to which she so often refers. Not surprisingly, perhaps, the intrusion of Irigaray's religious imagery into ostensibly secular feminist theory causes some consternation among her feminist readers.[27] Perhaps they, better than she, understand the threat that such language poses to the boundaries of the postmodern, linguistic self.

Irigaray and the otherness of God

Can Irigaray's 'God' bear the burden of difference between Being and beings, in a way that would allow us to speak of newness and transformation? Is her God truly other, or is 'he' or 'she' always another of the same, and if so, how can we possibly escape our entrapment within a closed world where meaning circulates, repeats itself, winds itself around us in a nihilistic vacuum with no opening through which grace might manifest itself?

In an essay titled 'Divine Women', Irigaray argues that the formation of women's subjectivity requires a Feuerbachian projection of a feminine divine as the grammar and horizon of women's becoming:

> We women, sexed according to our gender, lack a God to share, a word to share and to become. Defined as the often dark, even occult mother-substance of the word of men, we are in need of our *subject*, our *substantive*, our *word*, our *predicates*: our elementary sentence, our basic rhythm, our morphological identity, our generic incarnation, our genealogy.[28]

Although she refers to God as 'the other that we absolutely cannot be without',[29] it is quite clear in this essay that Irigaray's God functions, not as an absolute other, but as the 'other of the same', the one who safeguards feminine subjectivity in the same way that 'woman' safeguards masculine subjectivity, by becoming the bearer of the female subject's projections and imaginings concerning the divine. Thus God is the 'mirror' wherewith one becomes a woman,[30] the 'shadowy perception of achievement'[31] towards which a woman orientates herself: 'If she is to become woman, if she is to accomplish her female subjectivity, woman needs a god who is a figure for the perfection of *her* subjectivity.'[32]

There is also a suggestion that Irigaray's 'God' is contingent, that in resisting the Nietzschean death of God her concern is to keep open the possibility of certain linguistic constructs of the divine, even if these too ultimately become redundant: 'There comes a time for destruction. But before destruction is possible, God or the gods must exist.'[33] In the light of such theoretical manoeuvres, it is perhaps not surprising that Margaret Whitford argues that '"God", like other terms in Irigaray's discourse, is a symbolic category'.[34]

In a comparative study of Karl Barth and Irigaray, Serene Jones points to a negation of difference in both their work. Barth's insistence upon the radical otherness of God in relation to creation is limited by his adherence to a theological hierarchy in which 'God still occupies the position of master trope, the Law, the Logos, the central principle of identity'.[35] While Irigaray's feminine conceptualization of the divine challenges the kind of theological hierarchy perpetuated by Barth, in making God 'the idealized, projected other of women's emerging subjectivity',[36] she betrays her own commitment to otherness:

> To use Irigarayan language, it would seem that female desire has consumed God. Caught once again in the old game of symmetry, God is merely the screen necessary for self-knowledge, the mirror that reflects the narcissistic gaze of the subject, the hand that must touch the phallus (or her lips) for the purpose of self-identification . . . Although Irigaray maintains that Western thought must embrace an understanding of true, incommensurable sexual difference in order to allow true difference in human relations to flourish, her model of the God–human relation moves in the opposite direction . . . The consequences would seem to be the reinscription, at the theological level, of the very idealized 'logic of the same' that Irigaray correctly identifies as having repressive social consequences when it serves as the norm for the movement of thought in general.[37]

Jones suggests that Irigaray falls into this trap of eliminating theological difference because she idealizes both the subject and religion. Her understanding of subjectivity is 'seemingly immune to history and the social construction of identity', and her notion of religion is 'equally ideal and hence unable to admit the possibility of God as the real, incommensurable other'.[38] While Irigaray poses an inescapable challenge to the theological stereotypes that persist even in theology as radical as Barth's, Barth in his turn might challenge Irigaray to ask,

> if the difference between God and humanity cannot be affirmed, then how can difference between human persons be fully embraced? It seems that theology, truly to challenge its phallocentric moorings, at the very least must grant to God the same integrity and recognition of incommensurable difference that it grants to human persons.[39]

Perhaps Irigaray follows Heidegger too closely, in seeking a manifestation of Being among us that would retain difference and arouse wonder, while refusing any concessions to the Christian concept of divine otherness, rooted in the doctrine of creation.

Heidegger's error, according to Balthasar, is that, although his idea of Being is entirely dependent upon Christian biblical and theological concepts, he fails to recognize that, in negating the idea of subsistence in the Christian understanding of 'limitless subsisting Being',[40] he introduces necessity into the relationship between Being and beings, and thus difference itself becomes the absolute, but in a way that actually collapses the difference between Being and beings.[41] If Being has no existence other than as existents, then Being is dependent upon existents for its existence, as a result of which the Christian understanding of God's freedom in relation to creation, and the human response of wonder at the mystery of creation and his or her own creatureliness, is negated:

> man cannot perform the classical act of wonder in the face of the miraculous ordering of the world, nor the Christian act of a yet deeper wonder at the incomprehensibility of his own and of all earthly existence. Now he is himself a co-essential part of the mystery of Being which prevails necessarily as such . . . In the work of Heidegger, the true wonder at the fact that something exists rather than nothing does not run its full course, for it points to a freedom which he does not wish to perceive.[42]

Fergus Kerr writes that

> Heidegger's project to relieve the world of being 'created' depends on a radical misunderstanding of the Christian doctrine of creation *ex nihilo* as always already receiving the world as 'gift'. Where Heidegger sees the world

explained in terms of an effect of some cause as demeaningly losing its incomparable mystery, Balthasar's Thomas celebrates the world as a miracle of divine grace.[43]

Where Irigaray elides the difference between God and creation by reducing 'God' to the level of textuality, symbolism and projection, devoid of incarnate sexuality, sacramentality or otherness, Balthasar's vast oeuvre revolves around the dilemma of the representation of ontological difference: how to think the relationship between God and creation in a way that expresses the infinite distance and the intimate union between God and the human in Christ. He writes that 'God is not simply the "Other" (the "partner"); he is so high above all created things that he is just as much the "non-Other".'[44]

I shall return repeatedly to the questions this raises with regard to Balthasar's analogous association between the life of the Trinity and sexuality, but for now I want to suggest that, if Balthasar's theology challenges Irigaray's theory with regard to her representation of God, her theory challenges his theology with regard to his representation of woman. In what follows, I offer a brief summary of Balthasar's idea of theo-drama in the context of his understanding of human personhood, and I then consider his positioning of 'woman' within this unfolding drama.

Balthasar's theo-drama

Balthasar perceives the dilemma of the post-Christian subject to be one that focuses on the problem of freedom. O'Donnell writes that 'The plight of post-Christian people is that they are robbed of [the] sense of destiny' associated with paganism while being 'unable to re-establish the sacred harmony of pagan antiquity'.[45] As a result,

> they are left with the burden of carrying their own freedom which now has a weight they are unable to carry. Having been thrown into a world which is no longer sacred and having had thrust upon them the inescapable burden of freedom, they cannot help but live a daily alienation. Hence human existence is lived as an enigma from which only Christ can deliver it.[46]

Balthasar situates the question of freedom in the context of theo-drama, where the relation of the infinite to the finite makes acute the question of the relationship between human and divine freedom. How can finite human freedom resist being engulfed by the infinite freedom of God, if the two are brought into contact with one another at every point? The creation of finite human freedom by the infinite freedom of God constitutes 'the starting point of all theo-drama'.[47]

Balthasar's idea of theo-drama uses the theatre as a model for the playing out of the story of salvation, with its dramatic tensions and unresolved questions, on the stage of world history. Throughout his theology there is ostensibly a resistance to any move that would freeze the dynamism of theo-drama, or that would result in a static understanding of either God's relationship with the world or the world's response to God. The Church is called to 'an awareness of living in the unfolding *eschaton*',[48] as a player in a drama whose ending cannot be anticipated: 'We cannot know in advance what the stage will look like at the end of the play.'[49]

Theo-drama is the drama of the inner life of God, poured out and enacted on the stage of the world in the time and space of human existence, with the Church constituting the particular dramatic community within which Christians are called to manifest the love of Christ to the world: 'It is a case of the play within the play: our play "plays" in his play.'[50] Christian mission entails responding to God's initiative by playing out one's role in the life of the Church, in a way that incarnates Christ in the material realities and relationships of human existence. It is this dramatic, corporeal acting out of the Christian story that is lacking from Irigaray's theory, for all its creative refiguration of Christian symbols and doctrines.

According to Balthasar, the stage for theo-drama is the 'earth/heaven dichotomy', with these two having been created 'as distinct realms with a view to a drama in which each pole has its own proper, positive role to play'.[51] This is one of a series of dichotomies that constitute the enigma of human existence. There is the relationship between infinite and finite freedom, involving 'self-disclosure on the part of infinite freedom',[52] and arousing in the individual an awareness of his (or her?) orientation towards the infinite freedom of God. Most significantly for my purposes, there are three polarities that remain constant and that seem to entail a continuous movement of desire and lack between one and the other, for they cannot in this life be transcended. These three are spirit and body, man and woman, individual and community, and together they sustain the dynamic tensions which give the story of salvation its dramatic quality:

> When man thus eventually steps forth and becomes a question to himself, however, he takes himself along, together with all his constant attributes. For he is spirit and body, man and woman, individual and community. These constants are part of his nature, his essence, which does not mean that they solve his riddle; in fact, they render it more profound and more pressing. In all three dimensions, man seems to be built according to a polarity, obliged to engage in reciprocity, always seeking complementarity and peace in the other pole. And for that very reason he is pointed beyond his whole polar structure. He is always found crossing that boundary, and thus he is defined most exactly by that boundary with which death brutally confronts him, in all three areas, without taking account of his threefold transcendence.[53]

This dynamic movement of desire and difference means that Balthasar's human subject is not a fixed essence but an 'I' in the process of becoming, who awakens

Incarnation, difference and God 101

to self-consciousness in dialogue and encounter with the divine and human other as part of the inescapable drama of God's revelation:

> we are caught up in the drama, we cannot remove ourselves from it or even conceive ourselves apart from it. This means that, if we want to ask about man's 'essence', we can do so only in the midst of his dramatic performance of existence.[54]

To become a willing participant in this drama is to allow oneself to be awakened by grace to the self-revelation of God in Christ, so that one surrenders individual subjectivity in order to become a theological person, constituted by one's relationships to God and to others within the community of the Church. Thus the natural human subject comes to participate in the supernatural life of the Trinity and becomes a player in theo-drama: 'man is startled out of his spectator's seat and dragged onto the "stage"; the distinction between stage and auditorium becomes fluid, to say the least'.[55]

Balthasar and the otherness of woman

Ostensibly, men and women are equally called to personhood and mission in Christ, and Balthasar's key players in theo-drama include the Virgin Mary and women saints such as Catherine of Siena and Thérèse de Lisieux as well as male characters such as St John, St Peter and St Paul. However, a gendered analysis of Balthasar's texts in English is complicated by the fact that translators use 'man' in both an inclusive and an exclusive sense, whereas in German the term *Mensch* refers to the generic human being and would more accurately be translated as 'human', while man and woman are *Mann* and *Frau* respectively. When Balthasar is writing about the human subject or the human being, he uses the term *Mensch*, and when he is writing about the theological person he uses the word *Person*.[56] Only when he explicitly addresses the question of sexual difference does he use *Mann* and *Frau*.[57]

The most extensive and systematic development of Balthasar's theology of sexual difference is found in *Theo-drama III*, Part III, 'Theological Persons', under the heading 'Woman's Answer'.[58] But at this point a problem arises. Volumes II and III of *Theo-drama* address the questions of 'Man in God' (*Mensch*) and 'The Person in Christ' (*Person*) respectively. Apart from a discussion of sexual difference in Volume II when Balthasar is analysing the three polarities that position the human subject, there is no reference to the gendering of the subject or the person. One might therefore assume that everything that is said of the human being as subject before God or person in Christ applies equally to both sexes, so that sexual difference is not a fundamental characteristic of subjectivity or personhood. But this contradicts Balthasar's claim that the human experiences this as one of the inescapable and constant polarities of his (or her?) existence: 'the male/female polarity . . . pervades the entire living creation'.[59] He also argues that 'The man–woman relationship is . . . shown to be an ultimate one. All attempts to overcome it in the direction of an androgynous primal being or a sexless first man must be dismissed.'[60] If these claims are correct, then it should not be possible to say anything about the human being – nor indeed about any aspect of creation – except in language that expresses this pervasive sexual relationship, i.e. in language that is consistently gendered in a way that acknowledges sexual difference as intrinsic to every claim about human nature and nature in general. Yet the sexual differentiation of the human only becomes a central feature of Balthasar's theology when he addresses the question of the woman's role in theo-drama.

The suspicion therefore arises that, in Balthasar's theology, the question of the subject in God and the person in Christ is in fact the question of the male subject in God and the male person in Christ. Balthasar's *Mensch* is either an androgynous primal being, a sexless first man (a possibility which he explicitly denies), or he is a male who can be situated in the cosmos quite independently of the woman, and who therefore shows sexual difference, and woman herself, to be a non-essential aspect of what it means to be human. Sexual difference is not a genuine 'I–thou' relationship in which man and woman encounter one another face to face as mutual questions and mutual responses, because the woman is implicitly excluded from both subjectivity and personhood in her own right, in a way that sets up an irreconcilable tension in Balthasar's theology. To exist as the answer to another's question is to be denied one's own sense of questioning subjectivity, and thus Balthasar perpetuates the Catholic idea of sexual complementarity in such a way that the woman complements – and completes – the man's existence, but at the cost of her own personal identity in the drama of salvation.

Lucy Gardner and Graham Moss reach a similar conclusion in their complex analysis of Balthasar's representation of sexual difference. They point out that textually as well as existentially and ontologically, woman always comes second to man in his theology:

> Woman is . . . chronologically, temporally, historically, accidentally second: in the creation, woman, it would seem, happens on the earth after the man (*Mensch*); von Balthasar's text mirrors this 'fact' several times over. In the first account of sexual difference, it becomes clear in the consideration of the *Mensch* as man-and-woman that these two must be together, can only be together, and so must always in some sense be described in relation to each other. It is only right that woman should be described in her relation to man. But there is here at least an apparently unequal difference, for . . . the very same text introduces and considers the *Mensch* (man) without any reference to woman.[61]

Thus sexual difference becomes, not a creative and fluid polarity, but rather 'a vulgar difference or fixed distance between two unchanging, un-interchangeable points (man-first : woman-second) between which there can be no exchange'.[62]

Eve, Mary and the Church as woman

Balthasar develops his theology of sexual difference through a somewhat idiosyncratic reading of the creation stories in Genesis, basing his understanding of woman on the traditional Catholic identification of Mary as the New Eve, Bride as well as Mother of Christ, the New Adam. In *Theo-Drama II*, when analysing the polarities that position the human subject, he suggests a close relationship between sexual difference and the tension between the individual and community. In the Genesis story, God's verdict that 'It is not good for man to be alone' leads to the creation of a 'helpmate' or a 'counter-image' who must be 'both cosmic (sexual) and, to match Adam, metacosmic, in touch with the *theion*'.[63] The woman thus created, although she has been fashioned from his rib, can never be governed by the man, because she belongs to an entirely different category of human being, based on the fundamental difference between the sexes. Balthasar interprets this in terms of a mystery that cannot be clearly formulated:

> as a human being, man is always in communion with his counterimage, woman, and yet never reaches her. The converse is true of woman. If we take this man/woman relationship as a paradigm, it also means that the human 'I' is always searching for the 'thou' and actually finds it ('This at last . . . '), without ever being able to take possession of it in its otherness. Not only because the freedom of the 'thou' cannot be mastered by the 'I' using any superior transcendental grasp – since, in its proper context, all human freedom only opens up to absolute, divine freedom – but also because this impossibility is 'enfleshed' in the diverse and complementary constitution of the sexes.[64]

This quotation suggests a genuine reciprocity and mutual otherness between the sexes. Everything that is true of the man is also true of the woman. They remain free in relation to one another, with each unable to possess or fully know the other, because the horizon of their freedom is the infinite freedom of God and not some form of transcendental human freedom that can escape the corporeality of the sexual body in order to control or master both its poles. This quest for a theology of sexual difference that respects the otherness, mutuality and image of God in both sexes is one strand of Balthasar's thought. However, it is when he seeks a synthesis between the two creation stories in Genesis that the flaws in Balthasar's theology become apparent in terms of his representation of woman.

In the first account (Gen. 1:26ff.), Balthasar focuses on the reference to man and woman being made in the image of God and being called to fruitfulness – a recurring theme in his theology, particularly as far as woman is concerned. He proposes that the capacity to reproduce another human made in God's image renders human sexuality unique and elevates it above the reproductive function of other species: 'we should speak of human generative power, in its natural operation, extending into the divine creative power, which opens up and makes itself available in the creation of man'.[65] However, this theological insight from Genesis only becomes apparent with the coming of Christ: 'The real depth of this mystery only emerges when the child is seen no longer as "*res patris*" but as a personality in direct relationship with God: in Christianity.'[66] This idea that human procreation illuminates an aspect of God's creative power is important, as we shall see in later chapters, for it imputes to God a specifically masculine, sexual function in relation to creation.

Turning to the second account (Gen. 2:18–24), Balthasar draws out three implications from Adam's recognition of Eve as his own flesh, and as 'Wo-man' who 'was taken out of Man'.[67] This is a lengthy paragraph that I quote in full, since it is crucial for any subsequent analysis of Balthasar's theology:

> This implies three things: first, a primacy of the man, for in this original situation he is alone before God and with God; although potentially and unconsciously he bears the woman within him, he cannot give her to himself. Second, this loneliness is 'not good'. Again this banishes the idea of a primal, androgynous human being, supposedly originally at peace with himself and only subject to unsatisfied longing after being split into two sexes. But it also refutes the notion that the lonely human being (or man) can attain fulfilment by knowing and naming the world . . . Third and finally, it affirms that the woman comes from man. It is through being overpowered in a 'deep sleep and robbed of part of himself', near to his heart, that man is given fulfilment. In sum: the man retains a primacy while at the same time, at God's instigation, he steps down from it in a *kenosis*; this results in the God-given fulfilment whereby he recognizes himself in the gift of the 'other'.[68]

Balthasar goes on to argue that both creation accounts link up in that they 'give common witness to the dual existence of the human being'.[69] Nevertheless, for the full implications of this to be lived out,

> the archetypal image of Christ/Church must first radiate the fullness of light onto the creaturely copy. For, theologically speaking, the first Adam is created for the sake of, and with a view to, the Second, even if he appears first in chronological time (1 Cor. 15:45).[70]

Before considering how Balthasar explains the fulfilment of the Genesis story in the relationship between Christ and the Church/Mary, let me identify the problems with the foregoing interpretation of Genesis 2. First, there is agreement among modern biblical scholars that the original human creature referred to in Genesis 2 – *ha'adam* – is not gendered. It is a generic, non-sexed earthling which only becomes male (*is*) with the creation of the woman (*issa*).[71] In his catechesis on the Book of Genesis, John Paul II also gives a generic interpretation to the significance of the first human, arguing that *ha'adam* represents the original solitude of the human being before God, ontologically but not chronologically prior to the fulfilment of personhood through the encounter between the sexes.[72] If one adheres to this reading of Genesis 2, then Balthasar's whole theology of sexual difference and his insistence upon the primacy of the masculine in God and in creation is undermined.

But even setting aside this major difficulty, the foregoing account of Eve's creation cannot sustain any real difference between the sexes, for if the man 'bears the woman within him', if her creation means that he is kenotically 'robbed of part of himself', if she is '"taken" out of the [male] other', then she is not really other at all. Only if *ha'adam* is the non-sexed origination of both sexes is it possible to sustain the idea that human beings are united by a common human nature while being radically differentiated in terms of sex. Moreover, Balthasar's language implies that the creation of the woman is an act of divine violence against the man: he is 'overpowered' and 'robbed', so that he experiences his ostensible 'fulfilment' in her as an act of defeat and depletion. This is by no means an insignificant aside, for the suggestion that the woman constitutes a threat to the man's wholeness and autonomy before God is a subliminal theme that runs through Balthasar's sexual theology, as we shall see.

Tracing the evolution of Mariology from its patristic roots through to its medieval and modern developments, Balthasar argues that the relationship between Mary and Christ is the prototype for the relationship between the sexes, in a way that fulfils and explains the sexual relationship in the Genesis myth. Mary is the unique individual woman who responds to the man, Christ, in his human nature, and who is the '*Realsymbol* and epitome of the Church herself'.[73] In the relationship between Christ and Mary/Church, the original relationship between the man and the woman in Genesis is brought to its culmination through 'the creation of an absolute relationship between man and woman that is free of all entanglement in sin: here the woman is both Mother and Bride with regard to the same man, in a real but suprasexual way'.[74] Thus the temporal sexual relationship between man and woman is replaced by 'the original, "absolute", suprasexual relationship between the sexes'.[75]

As the preredeemed woman, Mary cooperates to bring Christ into the world, in such a way that her work 'is integrated into his. Both redemption and preredemption spring from the same Cross but in such a way that she who is preredeemed is used in the Church's coming-to-be'.[76] In handing her crucified Son over to the Church, Mary 'renounces her "I"' so that

> her unlimited mission comes to light . . . [H]er mission, in the feminine and creaturely mode, is to let things happen; as such it is perfectly congruent with the masculine and divine mission of the Son. Thus it is a concrete, realized prototype of the Church, and all other, particular missions in the Church will be integrated into it.[77]

We should bear in mind here the centrality of mission to Balthasar's understanding of theological personhood, based on his insistence on the bodily living out of the Christian truth:

> The *good* which God does to us can only be experienced as the *truth* if we share in *performing* it (Jn 7:17; 8:31f.); we must 'do the truth in love' (*aletheuein en agape* [Eph. 4:15]) not only in order to perceive the truth of the good but, equally, in order to embody it increasingly in the world.[78]

This description of Mary's mission as compared to that of Christ implies that Christian mission is itself gendered. The woman's mission is passive and creaturely, while the man's mission is divine and active.

In developing the idea of the Church's creation from the crucified body of Christ, Balthasar refers back to Eve's creation as a kenotic gesture on the part of Adam. As God, Christ is complete in himself and lacks nothing, but as man he is analogous to the first Adam. Thus, 'the Incarnate One possesses all "fullness" in himself (Col. 1:19, 2:9); out of his fullness he creates a vessel, then pours his fullness into it, fulfilling both it and – in a certain sense – himself through the realization of its possibilities (Eph. 1:23; cf. 4:13, 16).'[79] Through this kenotic process, the true meaning of the Genesis story is revealed:

> from the side of the sleeping Adam, the woman is drawn; now, from the (wounded) side of the sleeping Savior (on the Cross), the answering 'face' of the woman is taken and 'fashioned' (Eph. 5:27) – the woman who is essential to man's completeness. This is shown forth in the mystery of man and woman in the first creation, but the fullness of mystery is only attained in the mystery of Christ and his Church (Eph. 5:27, 33).[80]

But while Adam 'needs the feminine complement', Christ, as the Son of God, is 'far above all necessity'. This means that 'The Woman (the "Immaculata" of Ephesians 5:27) who comes forth from the Man as he slumbers on the Cross is not so much a gift to him in his need as the product of his own fullness.'[81]

The end of woman

But what actually happens to Mary when her subjectivity becomes one with that of the personhood of the Church on the cross? In *The Glory of the Lord*, Balthasar describes Mary's experience of being increasingly 'dispossessed of her Child'.[82] This means that

> the Mother must increasingly renounce everything vitally personal to her for the sake of the Church, in the end to be left like a plundered tree with nothing but her naked faith ('Behold, there is your son!'). Progressively, every shade of personal intimacy is taken from her, to be increasingly applied to the good of the Church and of Christians.[83]

In other words, Mary's unique and individual sense of personhood, identified with her maternity of Christ, is taken away from her and she becomes a collective entity, a 'woman' represented not by a woman's body but by the 'body' of the Church, which is in fact Christ's body, 'the product of his own fullness'. This becomes clear later in *The Glory of the Lord*, when Balthasar develops his idea of the Marian Church in relation to Genesis. Rejecting any attempt to make the Church an object of academic study, Balthasar argues that 'from the viewpoint of the Gospel . . . the Church has no other form than this relative form, whose function is to point to the supreme form of revelation'.[84] There can be no analogy in this case between human art, in which the work 'possesses an objective, autonomous form and a meaning quite independent of its creator',[85] and the Church as the work of Christ. This is because 'as the Church of Christ, she is created purely from the being of Christ himself'.[86] While Eve's creation from Adam's rib by God implies personal differentiation from Adam, the Church's creation from Christ allows for no such personal distinction between the two:

> since in the case of Adam God is the actual creator, Eve's personality does not derive from Adam but from God. Because, by contrast, Christ is at the same time God and man, the 'personality' of the Church as the new Eve can indeed derive from him, in so far as he is one with the Father in the Holy Spirit. It follows from this that the Church cannot claim for herself an autonomous form, even if she can be distinguished from Christ by analogy with the wife's distinction from her husband. When man and wife, however, are seen as two self-enclosed persons who stand over against one another and complement each other's natures, then the image cannot be applied to Christ and the Church. Whatever the Church may possess by way of 'personality' and 'nature' she has from Christ, whose 'fulness' [sic] she is because he has poured his own fullness into her, so that the Church is nothing other than 'Christ's own fulness' [sic] (Eph. 1:23).[87]

From such arguments, we begin to detect the hidden movement in Balthasar's thought, a dramatic unfolding of a story in which the female body is contingent, inessential and secondary to the man. The maternal feminine *persona* in theo-drama, 'woman', refers not to the sexual female body but primarily to the collective 'body' of the Church, and derivatively to the bodies of men who are women in relation to Christ – a point to which I shall return in the next chapter.

However, at this point we might ask what has happened to the repeated insistence by Balthasar, the new feminists and Pope John Paul II that an incarnational theology requires close attentiveness to the body's revelatory meaning, in a way that rejects the feminist problematization of the relationship between sex and gender. What indeed has happened to Aquinas's theology of knowledge, in which we come to an awareness of the revelation of God in creation through our prayerful and reasoned attentiveness to our sensory experiences? If the Church is woman, whose body does she feel with? Whose brain does she know with? Whose tongue does she speak with? Does she have breasts and a womb? Does she have a clitoris and a vagina? Who interprets what these bodily realities mean on her behalf, given that mother Church has no need of women as priests, preachers or members of the magisterium? These are questions that we must allow to develop over the next few chapters.

Balthasar does not attribute a single quality to the woman that is not derivative of or responsive to the man. She comes into being only to serve his ends and to fulfil his existence. In particular, her response to the man is understood in terms of fruitfulness and reproduction:

> Since it is woman's essential vocation to receive man's fruitfulness into her own fruitfulness, thus uniting in herself the fruitfulness of both, it follows that she is actually the fruit-bearing principle in the creaturely realm . . . In the most general terms, this means that the woman does not merely give back to man what she has received from him: she gives him something new, something that integrates the gift he gave her but that 'faces' him in a totally new and unexpected form . . . She responds through reproduction.[88]

This capacity of the woman to respond to the man in a way that bears fruit means that, 'whereas the man represents a single principle (word, seed), the woman represents a double principle: she is the "answer" and the common "fruit" of both of them'.[89] The significant difference between man and woman is therefore that the male is monadic, and the female is dyadic: 'She is bride and spouse to the man but mother to the child.'[90] This, then, is where Balthasar situates the fundamental difference between the sexes: masculine identity is (at least implicitly) a singular, static principle, while feminine identity is fluid, relational and dynamic.

This invites comparison with Irigaray's idea of the 'two lips', a morphological image that she uses to challenge the phallic singularity of the masculine subject. Questioning the Freudian 'scopic economy'[91] which represents woman as passive because her sex is perceived as a lack and an absence, Irigaray proposes a tactile, fluid form of subjectivity associated with female genitality:

> The *one* of form, of the individual, of the (male) sexual organ, of the proper name, of the proper meaning . . . supplants, while separating and dividing, that contact of *at least two* (lips) which keeps woman in touch with herself, but without any possibility of distinguishing what is touching from what is touched.
>
> Whence the mystery that woman represents in a culture claiming to count everything, to number everything by units, to inventory everything as individualities. *She is neither one nor two.*[92]

Balthasar's sexual anthropology is not, therefore, inherently inimical to at least some feminist refigurations of female subjectivity, and it may be that his idea of the dyadic female person is a resource for an Irigarayan feminist theology, with one important proviso to which I shall return: Balthasar's woman is dyadic because she is orientated towards the other – sexually to the man, and maternally to the child. Irigaray's woman is polymorphous within herself, prior to any encounter with the other. Later, I shall consider the implications of this for a feminist theological understanding of subjectivity. But returning to Balthasar, once again I want to ask just how different woman really is in his understanding of her dyadic fruitfulness.

Balthasar creates an analogy between the creature as 'originally the fruit of the primary, absolute, self-giving divine love' and 'the female principle in the world'.[93] This means that, 'if the creature is to be God's "image", it must be equipped with its own fruit-bearing principle, just like the woman (vis-à-vis the man).'[94] Thus

> every conscious creaturely being has a certain 'mission' at a natural level (by remote analogy to what we have described as the christological mission): to be ready and open to receive the seed of the divine Word, to bear it and give it its fully developed form.[95]

In other words, Balthasar's definition of feminine fruitfulness bears no necessary relationship to the female body in a way that would explain his insistence on an essential difference between the sexes. It is a spiritual quality of the human creature, which belongs as much to the male body as to the female body.

Nevertheless, Balthasar wants to insist that there is a 'christological position' particular to woman as an individual, represented by Mary, and he explains this as follows:

First, since the man Jesus Christ is an individual human being, his relationship to woman will be individual too; the woman to whom he relates is a particular person. On the other hand, insofar as he is the incarnate Word of God, carrying out in his earthly existence the Father's commission to reconcile God's entire creation with God (2 Cor. 5:19), there will necessarily be a social aspect to his 'helpmate', since she represents mankind (which, in relation to God, is female).[96]

Note again the sleight of hand by which the particular personhood of woman is affirmed and then elided in terms of sexual difference, for if men as well as women are female in relation to God, we have not yet established any significant locus of sexual difference.

Let me return then to my suggestion that Balthasar's 'woman' is not in fact a sexually differentiated person in her own right, but a mask, a *persona*, which enables the man to position himself as a creature in relation to God. If personhood is that form of human subjectivity which comes into being through our insertion into the eternal, intra-trinitarian relationships of the persons in God, then the female body is excluded for her existence is contingent, temporal and not of the divine.

The woman as body comes into being after the creation of Adam in Genesis, and her capacity to give bodily expression to a different form of sexual subjectivity ends on Calvary, when her individuality is violently stripped away (Mary is left 'like a plundered tree'), and she becomes the feminine, communal body of the masculine Christ, with no distinctive identity or personhood apart from this. Indeed, on closer examination we discover that at no point does 'woman' exist in Balthasar's theology except as a projection, a fantasy and the fulfilment of the man's existence, an idea which finds highly romanticized expression in a quotation he borrows from Przywara, referring to the Pauline epistles:

> It is true, on the one hand, that the man is the 'head' of the woman, the 'body'; but it is also true, on the other hand, that the woman, the 'body', is the man's 'fullness' and 'glory'. Thus she fulfils her origin: for she was created in man's 'ecstasy', as his 'dream'; she is the 'fullness' and 'glory' (1 Cor. 11:7; Eph. 1:23) into which he is 'incorporated' as into his 'house and household' (Gen. 2:22).[97]

An individual who exists as another's fullness, as his dream or his glory, is not a human subject in her own right, i.e. in God. She is not an 'I' but only a 'thou'. She has no essential significance of her own, but exists only as the other of the man – a projection, a necessary complement to his being, the space wherein his existence finds meaning without affording her any similar space of existence.

But while the female body has been effectively annihilated in the symbolic life of the Church, she continues to exist as a persistent question to the man, a question who finds no response, an 'I' whom he cannot see as a 'thou' because he sees her only as an extension and a projection of himself. And thus her otherness – a carnal, sexual, psychological and spiritual otherness – taunts him and unravels his careful theological arguments, setting up contradictions and continuing polarities through the persistence of difference where he longs for sameness, the persistence of fluidity where he longs for order and structure. In recognizing all this, but in being unable to accept its theological implications because of his commitment to an anachronistic model of sexual relationships that seeks to reaffirm the primacy of man over woman, Balthasar's theology declares war on the woman as body, because only through the violent eradication of her sex can he eliminate the threat she poses to his theological system. But before we explore the violence inherent in Balthasar's theological representation of woman and her associations with sex, sin and death, we must probe more deeply into the twists and turns of his theology of sexual difference, for if Balthasar eliminates the female body from the scene of salvation, this is not in order to let man be man, but in order to let man be woman.

To conclude this chapter, I have suggested that Balthasar and Irigaray can be read together as an exercise in critical intertextuality, in which we discover both commonalities and differences in their representations of God and sexual difference. Insofar as Irigaray affirms the radical otherness of woman in relation to man, she exposes the extent to which Balthasar's theology of sexual difference simply reiterates the same old sexual stereotypes in which the feminine is not a distinctive characteristic of the female body but a projection of the male, so that she remains the other of the same. On the other hand, by situating his theology in the context of theo-drama, Balthasar exposes Irigaray's failure to achieve a truly corporeal form of discourse, for in eliding the otherness of God and the performative sacramentality of the Christian story, her 'body' remains captive to the text in which it is inscribed. Only by recognizing the otherness of God and the otherness of the body in relation to the language which mediates the relationship between them, might Irigaray's psycholinguistic theory of sexual difference become an incarnate theology of fecundity and communion in the communicative encounter between bodily others.

The main focus of my concern in the next few chapters is Balthasar and the new feminism, and I shall return to Irigaray later. Continuing the quest for difference and otherness, I ask if Balthasar succeeds in allowing the mystery of the divine and sexual other to suffuse his theology. My suggestion is that he neither excludes nor accepts this mystery, but by allowing it some limited freedom to play through his language and ideas, he becomes trapped in a vicious and futile struggle to master the uncontrollable, elusive, mystery of the other which constantly threatens to disrupt and destabilize his theological enterprise.

6 Masculinity, femininity and God

In order to develop further this exploration of Balthasar's representation of sexual difference, we must consider the ways in which his understanding of the difference between the sexes provides an analogy by which he situates creation in relation to God. In this chapter, I argue that Balthasar's thought is consistent with pre-modern Catholic theology, insofar as its understanding of sexual difference is primarily concerned with gendered relationships rather than with biological essentialisms. Concepts of masculinity and femininity are used to position the human and the divine in relation to one another, and only secondarily do they acquire anthropological significance with regard to human sexual relationships. However, Balthasar imports into this pre-modern theological scenario a thoroughly modern understanding of a fundamental physical and psychological difference between the sexes.[1] This biological essentialism freezes the dramatic interplay of gendered relationships, resulting in a series of exclusions and occlusions with regard to female sexual embodiment which, as we shall see in later chapters, must be sustained with considerable violence if they are to resist the persistent presence of the female body, despite the fact that it has now been written out of the script of salvation.

In the first part of 'Woman's Answer', Balthasar asserts the following:

> The Word of God appears in the world as a man [*Mann*], as the 'Last Adam'. This cannot be a matter of indifference. But it is astonishing on two counts. For if the Logos proceeds eternally from the eternal Father, is he not at least quasi-feminine vis-à-vis the latter? And if he is the 'Second Adam', surely he is incomplete until God has formed the woman from his side? We can give a provisional answer to these two questions as follows: However the One who comes forth from the Father is designated, as a human being he must be a man if his mission is to represent the Origin, the Father, in the world. And just as, according to the second account of creation, Eve is fashioned from Adam (that is, he carried her within him, potentially), so the feminine, designed to complement the man Christ, must come forth from within him, as his 'fullness' (Eph. 1:23).[2]

Compacted into this short extract we discover all the theological and anthropological stereotypes which make Balthasar's theology problematic, particularly from a feminist perspective. Balthasar's Jesus is of necessity a biological male, because he represents God, who is 'the Origin, the Father'. Thus there is – at least implicitly – an identification of the divine fatherhood with masculine sexuality and the male body. But Christ is also 'quasi-feminine' because he proceeds from the Father. Later, Balthasar observes that 'the creature can only be secondary, responsive, "feminine" vis-à-vis God'.[3] Masculinity is the originating principle, and the feminine is the emanation of the masculine. The man is 'incomplete' without the feminine, which is a potential within the man and must emanate from him as his 'fullness', i.e. as woman. In other words, 'man can be primary and woman secondary, where the primary remains unfulfilled without the secondary'.[4] Thus sexual difference is not about two forms of human personhood – male and female – understood as co-equal but different in their capacity to image God. It is about the positioning of the human male as 'quasi-feminine' in relation to the transcendent masculinity of God, which represents the paternal origination of the world. The woman comes into being, not as a separate person, but as the man's complement and completion. But why is the woman necessary to complete the man? That is a question that this chapter seeks to explore.

Acting up: man as material girl[5]

It would seem that Balthasar's first (and last?) human is male, so that the woman who seeks her origins and her destiny becomes a ghostly remainder, an excess that remains unaccounted for, after the man has undergone his sexual metamorphoses to consummate his union with Christ. Woman surely in this scenario suffers the fate that Irigaray describes:

> Woman, for her part, remains in unrealized potentiality – unrealized, at least, for/by herself. *Is she, by nature, a being that exists for/by another?* And in her share of substance, not only is she secondary to man but she may just as well not be as be. Ontological status makes her incomplete and uncompletable. She can *never* achieve the *wholeness* of her form. Or perhaps her form has to be seen – paradoxically – as mere *privation*? But this question can never be decided since woman is never resolved by/in being, but remains the simultaneous co-existence of opposites. She is *both one and the other*.[6]

But here we must negotiate another twist in theo-drama, which becomes more and more like a Restoration comedy the more deeply we delve into its scripted performances. For Balthasar and the new Catholic feminists do not eliminate woman from creation: they eliminate man, and that is where the real issue lies. Balthasar's woman is 'by nature, a being that exists for/by another', who 'may just as well not be as be', because, while 'woman' has a role to play in this drama, her body is quite redundant to the performance, which is really 'his'. Thus we must turn this argument on its head, in order to see that Balthasar's theology does indeed posit a thoroughly sexed creation: a feminine creation, with the only masculine presence being the priest who represents the divinity of Christ, and therefore of God the Father as the (masculine) origin and source of life. Except that Balthasar forgets himself, and scripts the male subject into his theology at every turn.

Ostensibly, Balthasar's woman is secondary to man, as we have seen. But who in fact is 'incomplete and uncompletable' in Balthasar's scenario? Who is 'both one and the other', 'mere privation'? How can the first human be male, if all human creatures are woman in relation to God? Surely, it is Adam who comes to consciousness in Eden as a being that exists for/by another, incomplete and uncompletable, lacking wholeness? Adam, in Balthasar's logic, would in fact be 'woman' who does not know who 'he' is until 'she' appears. Only with Eve can he become who he is not – woman, bride, feminine other to the masculine God. Thus the male cannot have priority in creation, for there are no men in creation. Masculinity, according to this account, would make a brief epiphany in the incarnation – a flickering presence, almost effaced in the 'quasi-feminine' Jesus, and entirely poured out on the cross when, once again, the woman appears as 'his' fullness, 'his' body. A devouring woman perhaps, constantly threatening his divine transcendence, swallowing him whole as he struggles to deny his vulnerability, his bodiliness, as he strains towards that pole which is masculine, spirit, individual, and she lures him back to where he belongs, the only space available to him in creation – feminine, body, community. A consummate bliss to die for, perhaps? How can we conceive of such symbolic transformations?

It is worth returning here to Balthasar's idea of the tensions that position the human subject in the world – the polarities of spirit/body, individual/community and male/female. Ostensibly, these are three forms of difference in the midst of which every human being must find his or her way of living, but are they not all reducible simply to the man and his other, variously identified as woman, community, body? Balthasar's 'woman' is the body of Christ, while 'man' is the headship and divinity of Christ. 'She' is the community of the Church, while 'he' is the representative of the one and only true man, Jesus Christ. 'She' is the woman, identified with humanity, creation, derivation. 'He' is the man, identified with God, creator, origination. But he is not God, and in order to become other than God, in order to establish the diastasis that marks the separation between 'man' and God and to experience the desire that draws 'man' to God, he must become what he is not – he must become 'her'. She is his fulfilment and completion because only she allows him to know who he is in relation to God, i.e. he is not-God, and because she is not-man, and God is masculine, he must become 'she' in order to remind himself that he is not-God.

This dilemma of the male subject straining towards divinity while never being able to escape the 'femininity' of his body, his desires and his dependencies is not new. Tracing the emergence of concepts of divinity and sexual difference in the early Church, Virginia Burrus writes:

> If the horizon of human becoming is named in the terms of Father, Son, and Spirit, this does not in itself make of God a male idol – but it does, as a matter of fact, construct both an idealized masculinity and a masculinized transcendence. For the Fathers, femaleness is allied with the stubborn particularity of created matter, against which the unlimited realm of supposedly ungendered divinity may be defined by theologians who have risen above their gender as well.[7]

In Balthasar's God and in Balthasar's 'man', we are indeed confronted by a masculinized transcendence and by a theologian who appears to have risen above his gender, insofar as 'he' is not sexed until 'she' enters the scene of the text. But of the three fourth-century Fathers analysed by Burrus in her study – Athanasius of Alexandria, Gregory of Nyssa and Ambrose of Milan – it is Gregory whose theology most closely resembles that of Balthasar.[8]

Burrus introduces her chapter on Gregory of Nyssa with a quotation from Hélène Cixous which I repeat here, because it is also highly pertinent to a discussion of Balthasar:

> Is Tancredi a woman ending, or a man beginning to be a woman in order to be a man? But my God, I am only me, I am only a woman, how can I express what is more than me? I divine what is more than a woman, what is more than a man, but above me everything sparkles and dazzles me and merges into a single person with athletic aspirations, rather tall for a woman, yes, she seems to me to be a woman but set naturally in the bearing of a man, like my pearl in turquoise.[9]

Quoting Cixous again, Burrus writes that

> Gregory's masculinity is clearly a complicated affair. A 'character all the more man in that he is more woman', Gregory assumes a role that might, in a staging of his life, be most convincingly played by an actress, like the knight Tancredi of Rossini's opera.[10]

She continues,

> However much in awe of his sister Gregory may wish to seem to be, it is not women who are privileged as receptive lovers of Christ within the highly charged, sublimated homoeroticism of his soteriology, which catapults 'man' into the infinite pursuit of the transcendent Man, of transcendence, of Manhood itself . . . Is Gregory 'a woman ending, or a man beginning to be a woman in order to be a man?' It is difficult to place this writer, and difficult also to place myself, as 'woman,' in relation to . . . 'him'. Squinting hard against the dazzle of the performance, I look at a man and see someone alluringly like me, only taller. Coming closer, I perceive that the woman is 'set naturally in the bearing of a man'. Absorbed by this capacious masculinity, I sense my own 'ending', lurching abruptly into a 'beginning', the beginning for a man, for the man I am becoming – having been absorbed. If (as Nicole Loraux notes) in such dizzying transactions 'the man gains in complexity, while the woman loses substance', she is (I am) little more than a ghostly remainder, a spirit or an angel. Yet she also leaves her traces in his texts (not least as 'spirit' or 'angel'), footprints into which I may yet insinuate my soles.[11]

Burrus suggests something of the dizzying consequences of trying to read not just Gregory but also Balthasar as woman, where one's identity becomes caught up in the flux of the man's quest for meaning – for the transcendent Man/God – and the woman becomes ever more elusive and hard to locate. It is tempting to draw a number of parallels between Gregory and Balthasar, not just in the sexual instabilities that haunt their theology, but in their relationships to the women who leave their traces in these men's texts, so that one is not sure whether it is 'she' or 'he' who is speaking. Gregory's work on resurrection was inspired by the deathbed reflections of his sister, Macrina, whom he referred to as his teacher and revered for her philosophical and spiritual wisdom and for her life of faith.[12] Much of Balthasar's theology was inspired by the spiritual outpourings of Adrienne von Speyr, whom he met in 1940 and with whom he worked closely until her death in 1964, living in the home she shared with her husband, Werner Kaegi, for fifteen years. After her death, Balthasar wrote,

> On the whole I received far more from her, theologically, than she from me, though, of course, the exact proportion can never be calculated . . . Today, after her death, her work appears far more important to me than mine, and the publication of her still-unpublished writings takes precedence over all personal work of my own.[13]

As we shall see later, the relationship with Speyr may be a significant factor in explaining the violent sexual energy that drives Balthasar's theological rhetoric.

Sexual difference in eastern and western Christianity

Despite their apparent similarities, there are significant differences between Gregory and Balthasar, I want to open up a plurivocal conversation on the topic of gender and sexual difference in the Christian tradition, in order to ask what new potential might be revealed if we begin to explore the different ways in which tradition might be interpreted in response to contemporary questions about sexuality.

Gregory's Platonic theology employs a wide range of gendered metaphors and allegories to describe human and divine relationships. As we saw earlier (see Chapter 5), in his *Commentary on the Song of Songs* he represents the relationship between the soul and God and between Christ and the Church in nuptial imagery. But whereas Balthasar and the new feminists sometimes conflate the language of woman, femininity and bride so that they use them interchangeably, suggesting that the three are ontologically related (as are man, masculinity and bridegroom), Gregory's 'bride' is not woman, nor is she 'feminine' in the ways in which Balthasar uses that word. For Gregory, sexual difference has no ontological significance, and therefore his use of nuptial symbolism needs to be interpreted as a form of mystical language that transcends the body's sexual particularity. In his seventh homily on the Song of Songs, we read:

> No one can adequately grasp the terms pertaining to God. For example, 'mother' is mentioned (in the Song) in place of 'father'. Both terms mean the same, because there is neither male nor female in God (for how can anything transitory like that be attributed to God? But when we are one in Christ, we are divested of the signs of this difference along with the old man). Therefore, every name equally indicates God's ineffable nature; neither can 'male' nor 'female' defile God's pure nature . . . Neither does it make much difference whether one calls the Son of God the only begotten God, or the Son of his love. According to Paul, each name has the capacity to be a bridal escort which leads the bridegroom to dwell in us.[14]

The difference between Gregory and Balthasar is as much ideological as theological. Gregory may have been influenced by prevailing cultural stereotypes about men and women,[15] but his theology is not captive to a sexual ideology as Balthasar's is, and this allows him considerably more linguistic freedom in terms of analogy and symbolism,[16] because his gendered analogies do not constantly come crashing up against his sexual ontologies, with all the ensuing violence that results in Balthasar's theology. As a result, the gendering of Gregory's theology does not become a form of ontotheology in which sexual relationships are projected into the being of God. Rather, as with later women mystics such as Catherine of Siena and Teresa of Avila, his understanding of the soul as bride needs to be understood in the context of 'a profound apophatic sensibility about the divine "essence"',[17] by way of which the nuptial union goes beyond any difference that can be named or conceptualized, so that it opens into contemplation on the imponderable mystery of God.

To discover one's ending in one's beginning with Gregory is to go before and beyond sexual difference, to a creation and an eschaton in which humankind is sexless, and therefore 'woman' is arguably no more and no less significant than 'man'. Gregory reads the creation stories in Genesis 1 and Genesis 2 in terms of a double creation.[18] The first account of the human made in the image of God (Gen. 1:27) refers to a non-material creation, in which the human is a form of pre-sexual, angelic being. Sexual embodiment is a feature of a secondary, material creation in which God's foreknowledge of the fall makes sexuality contingent upon the coming of death into creation, but it is associated with animality and does not refer to the image of God in the human. At the resurrection this animal dimension will be stripped away so that we shall be restored to our original, pre-sexual condition in the image of God.

This brings us to a point of significant difference between eastern and western Christianity. The Orthodox Church has been influenced by the encratite theology of early Christian thinkers such as Origen, Gregory of Nyssa and Maximus the Confessor, in which the virginal body most perfectly symbolizes the redeemed, asexual human being.[19] The continuing influence of this tradition means that sexuality does not have ontological significance in Orthodox Christianity.[20] However, Roman Catholicism has followed a different route in its doctrine of creation, by adopting Augustine's understanding of a single creative act in which the will of God finds material expression in creation, so that everything that exists – including the sexual human body – is part of the originary and ultimate intention of God.[21] This means that, from an Augustinian perspective, sexual difference is to some extent ontological, even although the image of God is associated, not with the sexually differentiated body, but with the rational mind, which ostensibly transcends sexual difference in being common to both men and women.

Augustine is insistent that the female body is redeemed no less than the male body. Rejecting the encratite tradition, he refers to the verse from Matthew: 'For in the resurrection they will neither be married nor take wives, but they are like angels in heaven' (Matt. 22:30). But, to quote Børresen, 'Augustine stresses that in the resurrection there shall be no marriage, but the Lord did not say that there would be no women: "*Nuptias ergo Dominus futures esse negauit in resurrectione, non feminas*".'[22]

As we are created in the beginning, so we shall be in the end – before and beyond sexual embodiment according to Gregory, created and redeemed as sexual bodies according to Augustine. Augustine defends the resurrection of the female body in the following terms:

> a woman's sex is not a defect; it is natural. And in the resurrection it will be free of the necessity of intercourse and childbirth. However, the female

organs will not subserve their former use; they will be part of a new beauty, which will not excite the lust of the beholder – there will be no lust in that life – but will arouse the praises of God for his wisdom and compassion, in that he not only created out of nothing but freed from corruption that which he had created.[23]

This might be read as a theology of affirmation as far as female sexuality is concerned, although, as Børresen points out, 'Augustine's viewpoint is here decidedly androcentric, since he argues that the recreated beauty of female bodies will no longer divert resurrected human males, henceforth liberated from their sinful concupiscence.'[24] Nevertheless, insofar as this suggests the liberation of the female body from the sexualized male gaze, and asserts the value and beauty of female embodiment in its own right, as made for God and not for man, it is a significant text for feminist theology.

However, Augustine's vision of eschatological equality is tempered by his acceptance and justification of a created order in which woman and man are orientated towards one another in a hierarchical relationship that reflects the psychological relationship between the will and the passions. Just as the healthy mind is one in which (masculine) contemplative wisdom prevails over (feminine) everyday knowledge and emotion, so the healthy society is one in which men have authority over women. This is also bound up with Augustine's idea of the image of God being primarily reflected in the man and only secondarily in the woman. For example, he writes,

the woman together with her husband is the image of God, so that the whole substance is one image. But when she is assigned as a help-mate, a function that pertains to her alone, then she is not the image of God; but as far as the man is concerned, he is by himself alone the image of God, just as fully and completely as when he and the woman are joined together into one.[25]

So, although Augustine's affirmation of female bodily redemption is a potential resource for feminist theology, his hierarchical gendering of social and spiritual relationships reflects a deeply rooted androcentrism that to this day pervades the theology of Balthasar and the new feminists.

Ruether's influential 1974 essay, 'Misogynism and Virginal Feminism in the Fathers of the Church', offers a critical evaluation of the relative merits of Augustine and Gregory for feminist theology. She points to the difficulty that early Christian thinkers had in interpreting Genesis 1:27: 'God created man in His own image; in the image of God He created him; male and female He created them.' In an attempt to reconcile the transcendent, noncorporeality of God with the bisexuality implied in the second part of the verse, two different interpretations evolved, both of which privileged an androcentric perspective:

> For Greek thought it was axiomatic that spiritual reality was unitary . . . Duality appears only with matter. So God cannot be dual, nor can man's spiritual image be bisexual . . . The guiding view of the Fathers was not an androgyny that preserved bisexuality on a psychic level, but rather that monism which, alone, is appropriate to spirit. This could be stated by identifying maleness with monism, making femaleness secondary, or else by a nonsexual monism, but not by a true androgyny. Gregory Nyssa chose the latter course, and Augustine the former.[26]

Ruether traces the ways in which a profound hostility towards the body and sexuality developed in patristic theology, primarily associated with the female flesh. Although Gregory was more positive than Augustine about the compatibility of marriage with the spiritual life (he was probably married), there was nevertheless a widespread belief that the contemplative life was best served by virginal asceticism, and that the female body posed a particular threat to male asceticism. For Gregory, the sexual, animal accretions that come to be associated with humankind in the second stage of creation are weighted towards female bodily functions of procreation: 'The *dermatinoi chitones* are expressed as "intercourse, conception, childbirth, defilement, lactation, feeding, elimination of bodily waste, gradual growth, youth, old age, illness and death."'[27] Ruether quotes Augustine's advice regarding the love of women:

> A good Christian is found in one and the same woman to love the creature of God whom he desires to be transformed and renewed, but to hate in her the corruptible and mortal conjugal connection, sexual intercourse and all that pertains to her as a wife.[28]

It can therefore be seen that, while these two main trajectories of the Christian tradition offer different interpretations of the significance of the sexual body, both are deeply negative in their attitudes towards sexual embodiment, particularly female sexual embodiment, and neither invites a straightforward appropriation for the construction of a feminist theology. As Coakley suggests,

> if in the East we have detected at least a tendency to announce a spurious (and de-sexed) equality for female creatureliness, in the West a more explicit stereotype of subordinate female bodiliness has been the norm. From a Christian feminist standpoint clearly neither of these solutions is agreeable as a systematic view of female creatureliness.[29]

We shall return to these ideas, but let me now consider another reading of Augustine, which can also be constructively applied to Balthasar.

Sexual difference and the *imago Dei*

Penelope Deutscher points to the ambiguity in Augustine's thought, which on the one hand equates women and the body with distance from God, and on the other hand affirms that 'women as rational creatures are equally made in God's image'.[30] Deutscher argues that it is only by understanding the complex, interdependent relationships among the different terms – man, masculinity, woman, femininity – that it becomes possible to see how these concepts function as 'operative contradictions' in Augustine's texts, in terms of the relationship between man, woman and God. In particular, insofar as rationality is associated with the image of God, it is masculine. But man in this sense is not masculine, because he is bodily and material, while woman, insofar as she is rational, also has access to the masculine. Thus, while masculinity is always associated with reason and God, and femininity with the body and irrationality, it is the play of difference between masculinity and femininity, man and woman, that allows Augustine to express the differences between man, woman and God in multiple ways beyond binary gender dualisms:

> Augustine establishes a hierarchy according to which woman is secondary to and subject to man's will, while both are subject to God's will. As souls, man and woman are equal in the eyes of God. But as bodies, man is made in the image of God in a sense in which woman is not . . . While Augustine emphasises women's equality to man, he considers the spirituality of both to involve a transcendence of the feminine principle, the flesh. In the case of men, 'godliness' amounts to a series of symbolic connotations of keeping one's distance from women, who represent lust, and loss of will over the body. But for women, this signifies the more problematic understanding that women must transcend the flesh they themselves symbolically represent. Godliness would involve women keeping distance from 'themselves'. In the most extreme form of this position, the godliness of women involves them in a 'becoming male'.[31]

Deutscher goes on to explain how this gendering of relationships works in terms of helping the man to situate himself in relation to God. She points out that, 'Since Augustine associates women with nature and materiality, we may say that the material excess, by which man is constantly exceeding the masculine point which identifies him, is feminised.'[32] But it is not enough simply to say that man is like God in his masculine spirit and not like God in his feminine flesh, because that would collapse the essential difference between man and an implicitly masculine God:

> In effect, this means that the point of pure masculinity, which defines man and by which the feminine as 'not-man' is devalued, must be positioned as a

point inaccessible to man. Despite the fact that God has been defined as 'not-man', man is only truly masculine insofar as he approximates God. So for all that God is 'not-man', paradoxically it is God who is positioned as the ideal point with which man is identified. So the recession, while rendering an illusion of masculine identity as mind, or reason, does so by moving towards a point never arrived at. All that is progressively isolated from man and devalued as 'not-man' is displaced on to the feminine. Man is defined by a term he nevertheless is not, and is never at one with, defined by a term which is but a shifting recession to a point it never coincides with. So the feminine, being the extent to which man falls short of God, is thereby a term flexible enough to include *all that we typically define as masculine*: reason, mind, man.[33]

Just as with Balthasar, Deutscher shows how Augustine's man vanishes from creation, into the infinite distance between man and God. Insofar as he is not God, neither is he masculine, therefore he becomes thoroughly feminized, even in his masculine aspects.

The complex deconstructive strategies employed by Burrus and Deutscher in their readings of Gregory and Augustine respectively go beyond the more straightforward analyses of feminist critics such as Ruether and Børresen. Taken together, however, these diverse feminist voices pose significant questions to the classical theologies of East and West. Børresen argues that neither Augustine nor Gregory provides a viable resource for feminist theology. As far as Gregory is concerned,

> Gregory's theology can be labelled 'feminist' in the sense of defining maleness and femaleness as equally alien to divinity, and thereby correcting andromorphic God-language. Nevertheless, Gregory's correlated anthropology is particularly inapplicable from a modern feminist standpoint, since his definition of perfect humanity excludes both male and female gender. In fact, Gregory's double Adam and Eve are not properly human beings, but *hybrid* creatures, with angel-like, spiritual image quality and beast-like, sexually differentiated corporality.[34]

Augustine has a more 'holistic concept of humanity' than Gregory, but in defending the 'protological unity' between Adam and Eve/Christ and Mary through their mutual participation in the fall and the incarnation, his 'doctrinal sexology' collapses without a divinely ordained gender hierarchy to hold it in place:

> It is essential to note that Christocentric typology, even in Augustine's 'feminist' version, presupposes God-like Adam served by non-God-like Eve. Christ as new Adam is incarnated in perfect manhood, whereas the new Eve, Mary/church, re-enacts the first woman's ancillary role. A nuptial symbolism which

transposes creational androcentrism to the order of redemption, appears particularly anachronistic in post-patriarchal culture.[35]

She goes on to argue that

> genderfree God-likeness as introduced by Clement of Alexandria and enforced through Augustine, is in modern theological anthropology dismissed by a combined and inclusive holistic definition of *imago Dei*, where both women and men are fully God-like in their male or female humanity. It follows that asexual God-likeness in andromorphic disguise is now superseded.[36]

Ruether also argues for the full recognition of the *imago Dei* in both women and men, as a corrective to the 'patriarchal anthropology'[37] of the Christian tradition. She advocates the affirmation of 'a full and equivalent human nature and personhood, *as male and female*',[38] based on the awareness that

> The fullness of redeemed humanity, as image of God, is something only partially disclosed under the conditions of history. We seek it as a future self and world, still not fully achieved, still not fully revealed. But we also discover it as our true self and world, the foundation and ground of our being. When we experience glimpses of it, we recognize not an alien self but our own authentic self.[39]

Nevertheless, the affirmation of the *imago Dei* in both sexes as offered by Børresen and Ruether needs to be opened up to an analogical interpretation that is more attentive to the mystery of God in the human and the human in God, by asserting that, not only are man and woman equally made in the image of God, but that, as Mary McClintock Fulkerson argues, neither is capable of imaging God.

Fulkerson summarizes feminist arguments for the inclusion of women in the *imago Dei* as being based on the awareness that Christianity has focused on the maleness of Jesus 'to characterize authentic human being and to limit the implicit universal reach of *imago Dei*'.[40] The solution proposed by Ruether and others is to liberate women by recognizing that

> As a naming of subjects of God's saving care, the *imago Dei* entails no essential definition of the subject, characterized only by finitude and God-dependence . . . The doctrine's basic work is to say that being female is 'like God', too, even as it is God-dependent, and in so doing produce new insights about creation. As such, feminist theologians employ a traditional frame to focus on a particular subject, woman, and enhance the potential reach of that frame by inserting woman in the category of finitely good human subjects,

exposing the problematic character of the male-identified constructions of *imago Dei*.[41]

But Fulkerson argues that this inclusive approach to subjectivity, which entails an ever-widening use of the term 'woman' to include those currently excluded, fails to recognize that

> an identity is a function of a position within a system of differences. Subject identity does not depend on substance or natural essence, just as it does not depend on the sameness of the body. Rather it depends on the outside on which it rests.[42]

In Saussurean terms, language derives its meaning not from a referential relationship between signifier and signified, but from the synchronic structuring of relationships between words that constitute systems of meaning. Poststructuralism entails the recognition that 'these relations do not occur simply in structures that function as closed or self-contained producers of meaning. Rather they intersect with and unravel into endless processes of differentiation.'[43] Words derive their meanings from what is not said – from the excluded others that define them. So the word 'man' has significance only in relation to 'woman' – because to know what man is, one must know what he is not.

This problem of the excluded other is not overcome simply by adding more and more terms to a concept, because this will proliferate as many exclusions as it will meanings, since every meaning entails an outsider, a silenced negation of its other. Appealing to Butler, Fulkerson points out that

> the assumption that a view is a perspective and that what is excluded might be added, is to suggest that the categorical system man/woman of the heterosexual regime can accommodate the bodies and desires that fall outside. However, the Other, in these terms of difference, would be defined *in the categories of the dominant regime*, and virtually obliterated.[44]

Thus, to seek to include women as well as men in the *imago Dei* entails

> affirmation that the world is divided into two kinds of people, and what we want is respect for both kinds. But this implies that gender criticism is a kind of 'me, too' theory. Taking Butler's view, what is going on here is the deployment of the heterosexual binary. The continual affirming of man means that, minimally, what lurks behind the sign 'woman' in Ruether's formulation are certain constructions of heterosexual, male-desiring subjects who know their deep identities to be sexually female. For that is all that can be accommodated by the system of discourse that Ruether leaves in place.[45]

Within this system, Fulkerson argues that there will continue to be 'occlusions [which] support this binary, and we might fairly assume they are racial, too'.[46]

Fulkerson's commitment to poststructuralism is allied to a strong narrative perspective that allows her to go beyond linguistic analysis, to seek concrete strategies for the liberation of women. She argues that the Christian story of a God of justice provides a context in which all human discourse is relativized and called to account. The task of feminist theology is to retain a narrative dimension, by developing 'stories of a God of justice in light of poststructuralist destabilizations'.[47] This means that the feminist telling of God's story will be one that constantly draws attention to that which is outside its own discursive boundaries, so that its instability arises not from internal contradictions and multiplicities, but from an awareness of its own fragile and dependent positioning before the mystery of God's promise of redemption:

> A good feminist theological story will be an incomplete story of a God-loved creation, a creation for which the only requisite features of imaging God are finitude and dependence. That story must allow for the commitment to the particular situation to develop new sensibilities for the outside, defined as violations of the goodness of the finite, God-dependent creation. It must sponsor the capacity for total self-criticism, for commitment to the goodness of the partial, and for the possibility that all is redeemable. For the outside, as a place where the occlusions of a situation appear, is not a stable foundation. A theological story might name it as the lure of an eschatological future, but, by definition, it will require disruption of the present system. Therefore it will not look like God's eschatological future to many.[48]

To situate feminist theology in the context of the Christian story means, for Fulkerson, that God's justice is a limiting factor, allowing for the possibility of radical challenge and transformation, calling into question all human claims to knowledge and truth. Understood in this way, an awareness of the justice and unknowability of God might serve as a brake to the violence that feeds unequal and unjust power relations.

Fulkerson exposes the foundationalism inherent in critiques such as those offered by Børresen and Ruether in their readings of patristic theology. In seeking to go beyond both Augustine and Gregory, they appeal to the concept of 'woman' as a stable foundation for knowledge, from which it is possible to recognize exclusions and to construct a more inclusive and therefore just understanding of the *imago Dei*. But this fails to recognize the extent to which this heterosexual gendering of theological language simply shifts the boundaries of inclusion and exclusion, because in order to say that both man and woman image God, we have to say what does not image God, or the term becomes meaningless. As Fulkerson suggests, it is the destabilization of the whole concept of a two-sex anthropology, in the context of a Christian narrative of creaturely dependence and finitude in relation to God, that offers the hope of an ongoing process of disruption and transformation of systems of oppression.

Sexuality and sacramentality

However, here the plot thickens and the story becomes more complex, because we must bring into view the excluded other of Fulkerson's feminist story. Nancy Dallavalle writes:

> McClintock Fulkerson makes important arguments for restraint with regard to theological assertions about the subject 'woman' and the more complex 'women's experience', but surely these are shaped by her own Reformed tradition's position of 'iconoclasm' with regard to creation, now appropriated in a new way for McClintock Fulkerson's feminist insights. Such an 'iconoclasm' is foreign (not 'heresy') to both the Catholic tradition of finding biological sexuality to be theologically significant and the Catholic sacramental sensibility.[49]

In her quest for a liberating God of justice as part of the Christian story, Fulkerson does indeed offer a minimalist account from a Catholic sacramental perspective. While justice is essential to any human understanding of God and of personal and social relationships, God is not reducible to justice alone, for everything that we are is caught up in the divine life, so that our story about God has to include those aspects of ourselves that are more to do with desire, beauty, creativity and sensuality than with justice *per se*. The real challenge for Catholic feminist theology is to hold in tension the sacramental significance of gender in Catholic worship and devotion as expressions of human abundance before the abundance of God, with the need to remain attentive to ways in which this gendered language has the capacity either to affirm or to subvert social and sexual hierarchies with all the injustices and various forms of denigration and oppression that these can create for women.

Although Fulkerson is critical of the foundationalist approach that she associates with feminist theology, her own Christian story positions her in such a way that she does not have easy access to the kind of gendered discourse that prevails in some forms of pre-modern Catholicism, particularly in patristic theology and mysticism, and that allows us to talk of God in a cataphatic outpouring of love and abandonment. We have seen how both Burrus and Deutscher suggest ways in which a deconstructive reading of patristic texts opens into a polymorphous and constantly shifting use of gendered imagery, capable of challenging the dualisms and essentialisms of later theological models. Indeed, Burrus makes extravagant claims for the potential of patristic theology:

what is disavowed, suppressed, or dismissed as excessive in Christian discourse – seemingly so much 'nothing' – provides excellent material with which to create . . . The audacious act of situating desire and generativity in the realm of absolute divinity results in no mean inheritance; for a humanity said to be created in the image of God, ancient theology is a gift that keeps on giving.[50]

What was thoroughly disavowed by Protestantism was the sacramental, gendered imagery associated with Catholicism, including its sacramental priesthood, its potent devotion to the Virgin Mother of God, its organic, maternal ecclesiology, and its lavish devotional language of spiritual fecundity and desire. Protestant man and his Enlightenment successor were male through and through, with no explicit need of a feminine other to express their (homo)erotic desire for Christ. In a form of Christianity focused resolutely on the Word of God with every trace of divine presence and activity purged from the created world, in which taste, touch, smell and sight yielded to the sense of hearing alone, the sexual body became a site of moral rather than sacramental significance, ordered towards marriage but not orientated towards God in its abundant and unruly desire. Perhaps, in such a world, God is already sufficiently distant, sufficiently intangible, to remove the man's constant fear of being inappropriately seduced by his Man God through the constant stimulation of his senses by the revelation of God in the material world. From such a distance, one does not need to dress up in bridal veils and practise symbolic castration in order for human *eros* to reach out to God in sensuous passion. God chastises and sanctifies the Protestant soul, but on the whole 'he' does not seduce it.[51]

The challenge for Catholic sacramentality is to retain its sense of the revelatory significance of gender and sexuality, while acknowledging the equality in difference of the sexes as beings before God. This difference is not constituted by stable polarities of masculinity and femininity but by the dynamics of difference and desire which suggest to us something of the nature of our relationship to God.

One obvious solution would be the ordination of women, which would recognize the significance of both male and female bodies for the presencing of God in creation and worship, in the service of a dynamic sacramental analogy that would move restlessly, creatively, between the affirmation that God is both male and female and that God is neither male nor female. Irigaray's 'sensible transcendental' might then become a resource for a sacramental theology which acknowledges our experience of the divine in the bodily realities of human sexuality, desire and fecundity, while also recognizing that God is the infinitely Other, Being who transcends every possible way of being in the world while never abandoning the world or being separable from it. But in the next chapter, we shall see just how tortuous the arguments become, when the new Catholic feminists try to affirm the sacramental significance of the female body, while defending the exclusion of women from the sacramental priesthood on the basis of a nuptial ecclesiology that owes a great deal to Balthasar's influence.

7 *Cherchez la femme*: gender, Church and priesthood

If we would seek to go beyond Heidegger to shape our questions about being in the world through the lens of contemporary Catholic neo-orthodoxy, informed as it is by Balthasar's theology, we discover a paradox, for we find ourselves on the far side of sexual difference, in a thoroughly feminized creation inhabited by quite bizarre human forms. There are female bodies without personhood, male bodies who are women, and a divinized, transcendent masculinity that puts in an occasional appearance in the form of the male priest who represents God pouring himself out in the orgasmic *kenosis* of creation, incarnation and crucifixion. These claims will have to be explained and developed, but we have arrived at a drama of mimetic parodies that outstrips the sexual/textual antics of Irigaray and Butler, for this is a drama that inscribes itself sacramentally, sexually and ethically on the living bodies of women, children and men.

But is this really a different way of understanding God and the world, beyond Heidegger, beyond nihilism and beyond a certain kind of metaphysics? Are we not back in the same old world that Irigaray describes, where we come face to face with the masked face of 'the God of ontotheology . . . Father created by man in his idea or his image. According to a model that today is doomed to decline'?[1] The answer is only partly yes. Balthasar's Father God is indeed made in the image of the transcendent male, a phallic, inseminating God kenotically emptying himself into a feminine creation. But Balthasar's 'man', as part of that feminized creation, must also enact a *kenosis*, must empty himself of masculinity, pouring himself into the woman if he is to conceive/receive this God's love.

Irigaray, coming to Catholic theology by way of western philosophy, is too straight in her thinking, even when she seeks 'A gay science of the incarnation'[2] beyond Nietzsche. She fails to acknowledge the extent to which the masculine subject of ancient philosophy and culture was unsettled and called into question by the Catholic faith, as Burrus demonstrates in her study of patristic writers. To some extent, he was put back together again by Protestantism and the Enlightenment, both of which rejected the maternal feminine symbolism of the

Catholic faith. But from Gregory to Balthasar, western man in his ancient and modern incarnations never has been entirely at home in the Catholic Church (broadly constituted here as both Roman Catholicism and Orthodox Christianity, and to some extent by High Anglicanism as well). Thus Catholic man seeks his home – seeks to make 'her' his home, not only in order to crawl back inside her womb, but in order to become her, to evict her and colonize her body, the better to legitimate the forbidden love he feels for the bridegroom. This 'man' needs a dyadic Mary and a dyadic woman (as) Church, for he needs both a maternal body to enclose him and a bridal body to open himself to Christ.

Nancy Frankenberry sees a precedence for this in Israel's covenantal relationship with Yahweh:

> the dilemma of homoerotic desire is posed when men worship a male God in a culture based on heterosexual complementarity. Although the expression of divine–human intimacy is couched in the language of male–female complementarity, it is males, not females, who enter in to the covenantal marriage with the deity. Collectively, Israelite men were constituted discursively as 'she' and were said to be 'whoring' when they strayed from monotheism (monogamy) into idolatry (adultery) . . . When the dilemma of homoerotic desire is again posed for Christian men in relation to a male Christ's body, it, too, is avoided by speaking collectively of the Christian community as a woman.[3]

Catholic sacramentality is a love affair with a strong homoerotic component, but what becomes of the female body as these gay nuptials unfold? To ask this question, we must consider the ways in which sexuality and sacramentality inform one another in Catholic liturgy, with a particular emphasis on the priesthood and the Eucharist.

The nuptial significance of the priesthood

It is probably fair to say that only since the late twentieth century has the Church had to seriously contend with the question of women's ordination. While there is still debate as to whether or not women were ordained in the early Church, and what form that ordination might have taken,[4] it was the women's movement and the growing number of theologically educated women that first confronted the mainstream churches with a significant challenge to their exclusion of women from the ordained ministry and priesthood. The Vatican has issued a number of documents justifying the restriction of the ordained priesthood to men. The most significant of these was the 1976 declaration on the admission of women to the ministerial priesthood, *Inter Insigniores*, issued by the Congregation for the Doctrine of the Faith.[5] The declaration appeals to the tradition of the Church, the attitude of Christ and the practice of the apostles, and it goes on to explore the significance of the ordained priesthood in the context of the mystery of Christ as revealed in the nuptial relationship between the male Christ as Bridegroom and the feminine Church as Bride. Sara Butler makes the point that

> The existence of the bridegroom image is not proposed as the *reason* for excluding women from the ministerial priesthood. The reason is the unbroken tradition, in both East and West, of ordaining only males to the priesthood. This tradition is understood to express fidelity to the example of Jesus and the practice of the apostles, and therefore to be normative for the Church. There is a need to give a theological account of the normative tradition, to come to some understanding of its significance and its reasonableness, to illustrate its 'fittingness' or appropriateness.[6]

This is an important point, because it explains why conservative Catholic theologians are so preoccupied with sexual difference and with the nuptial symbolism of the relationship between Christ and the Church. For the first time, they have been challenged to find a 'fitting' theological explanation to justify the Church's tradition with regard to the male priesthood.

The idea of the Church as maternal body and Bride of Christ has always been present in Catholicism. It can be traced back both to the covenantal relationship between Yahweh and Israel in the Hebrew scriptures, and to New Testament writings such as the Letter to the Ephesians and the Book of Revelation. But never before has this nuptial and maternal symbolism been made to serve the kind of ideological purposes that it serves in the contemporary Church, and never has it been used doctrinally in the ways it is used today, when an implicit eroticism, most commonly found in devotional writings such as mystical reflections on the Song of Songs, has given way to an explicitly sexualized theological doctrine that describes the relationship between Christ and the Church in often floridly extravagant metaphors of sexuality and procreation.

Inter Insigniores explores the nuptial symbolism in the Old and New Testaments to describe Christ's role as Bridegroom and the Church as his Bride. Insisting on the biological maleness of the Bridegroom, it argues that

> we can never ignore the fact that Christ is a man. And therefore . . . in actions which demand the character of ordination and in which Christ himself, the author of the Covenant, the Bridegroom, the Head of the Church, is represented, exercising his ministry of salvation – which is in the

highest degree the case of the Eucharist – his role (this is the original sense of the word 'persona') must be taken by a man.[7]

The document considers the question of whether or not, since the priest acts in the name of the Church and not only in the person of Christ, a woman might also have this representative status. But it rejects this suggestion because, although 'the priest represents the Church, which is the Body of Christ', he does so 'precisely because he first represents Christ himself, who is the Head and the Shepherd of the Church'.[8] Thus *Inter Insigniores* establishes a position by which the exclusion of women from the ordained priesthood is justified (a) by an appeal to the enduring manliness of Christ, whose biological significance is inseparable from his role as Bridegroom and Head of the Church, and in the Eucharist, and (b) by a sexual hierarchy in which the essentially male Bridegroom has primacy over the inessentially female Bride.

These ideas are reiterated in Pope John Paul II's 1988 apostolic letter 'On the Dignity and Vocation of Women', *Mulieris Dignitatem*, which incorporates a number of themes from his catechesis on the Book of Genesis. In defending the essential masculinity of the priesthood, *Mulieris Dignitatem* also states that

> *all human beings – both women and men – are called* through the Church, *to be the 'Bride' of Christ, the Redeemer of the world.* In this way 'being the bride', and thus the 'feminine' element, becomes a symbol of all that is 'human', according to the words of Paul: 'There is neither male nor female; for you are *all one* in Christ Jesus' (Gal. 3:28).
>
> From a linguistic viewpoint we can say that the analogy of spousal love found in the Letter to the Ephesians links what is 'masculine' to what is 'feminine', since, as members of the Church, men too are included in the concept of 'Bride'.[9]

These two short paragraphs contain a remarkable proliferation of gendered identities, far in excess of individual masculine males and individual feminine females. All human beings of whichever sex constitute the singular, feminine Bride, a symbol that transcends bodily sexuality insofar as it is primarily a symbol, not of the female body but of a collective entity which includes 'all that is "human"'. Thus, as we saw with Balthasar's theology, bodily *sexual* difference is actually elided in favour of a *gender* difference, in which the differential principle applies not to male and female bodies but to human and divine bodies: human bodies of both sexes are feminine, individually and collectively, while the singular divine 'body' of Christ is exclusively masculine. Thus this is a one-way sex act as far as women are concerned: 'The Bridegroom – the Son consubstantial with the Father as God – became the son of Mary; he became the "son of man", true man, a male. *The symbol of the Bridegroom is masculine.*'[10] These are slippery arguments, for even as they affirm the significance of the sexual body, they introduce a perplexing array of gendered identities associated with the male body, including the masculine exclusivity of the priesthood, without ever identifying a unique and exclusive sacramental meaning associated with the female body. Might the picture become clearer if we turn to those who have sought to offer a theological justification for the reservation of the ordained priesthood to men? In asking this question, let me begin by considering Balthasar's idea of the Marian and Petrine Church.

The Marian and Petrine Church

We have already seen that Balthasar's theology revolves around a series of tensions or polarities which sustain the dynamism of the story of salvation and lend it its dramatic quality (see Chapter 5). This sense of dynamic polarity also informs his ecclesiology, in which the subjective, personalized faith and holiness of the Marian Church is set against the objective, institutionalized faith of the Petrine Church, which together constitute the 'irreducible, inner dramatic tension'[11] of the Church. The faith of the Marian Church is supremely personified by Mary herself, but also by other followers of Christ, particularly John, while the office of the Petrine Church is personified by Peter.

Balthasar insists that these subjective and objective dimensions of the Church's faith are inseparable, although the Marian dimension has priority:

> There is drama in the encounter between the believer's experiential knowledge, which comes from the fullness of Christ, and authority's official knowledge, which is imparted by Christ directly. These two modes of knowledge mutually presuppose each other. Thus Mary, the *(ecclesia) immaculata*, is on the scene prior to the call of the Apostles, yet the concrete community is built on the 'rock' of the apostolate.[12]

It is the nuptial relationship between faith and office that allows the male priesthood to make Christ materially present to the Bride throughout the history of the Church:

> The institution guarantees the perpetual presence of Christ the Bridegroom for the Church, his Bride. So it is entrusted to men who, though they belong to the overall feminine modality of the Church, are selected from her and remain in her to exercise their office; their function is to embody Christ, who comes to the Church to make her fruitful.[13]

However, Balthasar also insists that the Marian and Petrine dimensions of the Church are interdependent and complementary to one another, so that

All stark opposition is to be avoided: after all, the 'Bride' herself is nothing but the extension and product of the living reality of Christ, and the fact that she is rendered fruitful by the 'institution' simply guarantees the constant flow of life from him to her. Or, to put it differently: if the model for the 'Bride's' emergence from within the Bridegroom is the supralapsarian emergence of Eve from Adam, the mode for the 'Bride's' being made fruitful by the Bridegroom is the infralapsarian sexual relationship.[14]

Note once again the elision of the Bride's unique and distinctive sexual personhood – she is 'nothing but' the extension of Christ's life. While this might be appropriate in terms of ecclesiology, the sexual analogy has implications for the personhood of women which, as we have already seen, leads to the negation of female bodily personhood in Balthasar's theology because of his close identification of the Christian life with the corporate, organic life of the Church.

Balthasar identifies five related aspects of the Marian and Petrine Church as follows. First is 'the definitive incarnational tendency',[15] by which Christ's life is sacramentally imparted to the Bride through the office instituted by him, in such a way that the bodily living out of the Church's life is one and the same with Christ's own life, because 'where there is real, ongoing life, there is never any opposition between life and form'.[16] Second is the continual birthing of the Church from Christ, again based on the unity between life and form, assuring the faithful that, whatever the personal character of the office bearer, the 'ecclesial order of justice' (ibid.) is divinely ordained and the baptized person's mission in the Church is guaranteed as a participation in the righteousness of Christ. Next, the relationship between the objective holiness of the office-bearer and the subjective faith of the believer (including the office-bearer's own faith) expresses the inseparability of love and obedience. This is manifest in the relationship between Christ's intra-trinitarian intimacy with the Father, and his obedience to the will of the Father, objectified in the Holy Spirit, which became a 'pitiless rule'[17] in Christ's God-forsaken death. Fourth, the relationship between love and obedience, and between faith and office, expresses the relationship between Christian freedom and the discipline needed to follow Christ in the direction of the cross. This is reflected in Mary's own life, and therefore in the Marian life of the Church:

> Mary's Son made her undergo the hardest school of discipleship of the Cross; when she suffered rebuffs and alienation during his public ministry, she was none other than the prototype of the Church being submitted to the objectified 'rule' of the Spirit, the 'rod of iron' (Rev. 12: 5; 2:27; 19:15; Ps. 2:9).[18]

Finally, the Marian and Petrine dimensions of the Church express the tension between the 'Episcopal' and the 'prophetical' office . . . [T]he Episcopal office has to guard the authenticity of the 'prophetical' sense of faith that is alive in the whole people; it must evaluate it and keep it pure. On the other hand, the Episcopal office, for that very reason, has to pay attention to this 'prophetical' office of the whole Church, and when necessary it must learn from it.[19]

It is not my purpose here to offer a critical evaluation of Balthasar's ecclesiology, but rather to draw attention to the ways in which gender is implied throughout the foregoing summary. The Church is a person, a woman, in relation to the male Christ,[20] although in a telling phrase, Balthasar elsewhere writes of the Church that 'she is primarily an open womb'.[21] The relationship between Christ and the Church transcends but is analogous to the sexual relationship between husband and wife: it is a 'suprasexual' relationship.[22] Although institutional authority is vested in the objective holiness of the masculine Church, the feminine, Marian Church has priority, because Mary's 'yes' comes before any apostolic commission:

Being placed in the hands of Mary at his birth and after his death is more central than being placed in the hands of office, and is in fact the presupposition of the latter. Before male office makes its entrance in the Church, the Church as woman and helpmate is already on the scene.[23]

This priority of the Marian Church means, according to Edward Oakes, that 'the Church as a whole is feminine (1 Cor. 11:12), open and dependent on her Bridegroom, while the male hierarchy, by contrast, is only one part, whose vocation is to serve the feminine Marian whole'.[24] But this 'service' includes the objective, rule-making function of the institutional Church which commands obedience as well as love, so that the Marian Church is instructed, disciplined and governed by her masculine office-bearers. Thus the relationship between Christ and the Church functions in terms of a hierarchical understanding of marriage based on the husband's authority and the wife's submission, even as his authority is a form of service to her. But, unlike human marriage between two individuals, the Marian Church has no personhood or identity apart from Christ, for the life of the Church is the form of Christ's own life. So, from a feminist perspective, what kind of ecclesiology is implicit in this gendered symbolics of the Marian and Petrine Church?

Balthasar's understanding of the authority of the Petrine Church comes close to justifying a form of rigid masculine authoritarianism, which invites unquestioning obedience from the feminine Church. Christ disciplines the Church, as he disciplined Mary, with a 'rod of iron'. Christ's death is a form of obedience to the 'pitiless "rule"' of God. Even although the institutional Church is made up of individual human beings who are fallible and prone to error, it is possible for the official Church to make demands, according to the mind of Christ, that seem unintelligible and extreme to an individual or group; there is nothing strange in Christ leading us along the path of the Cross not only in person but also, most definitely, through the institution he himself has appointed.[25]

This calling to follow Christ along the path of the cross means that the Church cannot be evaluated simply as an ethical community, because Christ's main achievement lies not in his ethical teachings but in his '*allowing* something to happen, in *letting* himself be plundered and shared out in Passion and Eucharist'.[26] We should note here that, just as in Chapter 5 we saw that Mary is 'plundered' when she stands at the foot of the cross, so that she surrenders her individual personhood to become the Church, so here Christ is also 'plundered'. Christ's fruitfulness lies in this 'transethical'[27] surrendering of himself to the will of the Father, which means that his influence on the Church is hidden and is not susceptible to statistical or ethical scrutiny: 'every attempt to deduce it from the Church's visible, institutional forms, from the decisions of her official representatives and from the ascertainable cultic, ethical and political influences of signed-up members of the religion of Christ is doomed to fail'.[28]

Balthasar acknowledges that there are inevitably disputes in the Church and that the believer, with an informed conscience, might question as well as be guided by the teachings of the Petrine Church. Nevertheless, his theology lends support to a form of authoritarianism that advocates uncritical fidelity to the official Church, however 'unintelligible' or 'extreme' its demands, in a way that risks flying in the face of the traditional understanding of the relationship between faith and reason.

However, the Petrine Church is not only the bearer of an authority legitimated by Christ himself, it is also the locus of the Church's rebellion against Christ. Balthasar repeatedly describes the sins of the institutional Church in a flamboyant and highly sexualized polemics. In *Heart of the World*, his 'Christ' denounces the Church's priests and office-bearers for their acts of betrayal: 'No people is more torn asunder than yours, none so pervaded by discord down to the very foundations . . . Down the centuries you quarrel over the better places, forever tearing up and mangling my Body to the bone.'[29] In the institutional Church, the virginal holiness of the Marian Church is transmogrified into the *casta meretrix*, the chaste whore, behaving like 'a wanton courtesan'[30] in her betrayal of Christ.

Referring to the constellation of saints surrounding Christ, particularly to Mary and John, Oakes writes:

> what is significant in this constellation is the glaring absence of Peter, who represents the institutional Church *par excellence*. For he is not only the Rock on which Jesus will build his Church but also the man whose very absence at

the Cross represents the finite No that is entissued into the very fabric and body of the Church.[31]

In other words, Peter not only personifies the masculine office of the institutional Church, he also personifies the Church's sinful denial of Christ, her 'whoring' with the world. We will consider this claim in more detail in Chapter 9, but I now want to look more closely at other arguments used to defend the masculinity of the ordained priesthood, many of which are heavily dependent upon Balthasar, before I turn to the question of sexuality, sin and violence in Balthasar's theology.

Justifying the male priesthood

Sara Butler's work represents one of the more reasoned defences of the Church's position, and she writes as someone who was initially a supporter of women's ordination.[32] In an article in response to David N. Power's essay titled 'Representing Christ in Community and Sacrament',[33] she rejects Power's suggestion that the risen Christ has transcended Jesus's earthly maleness, so that 'the liturgical representation of Christ's headship requires only a common humanity, not gender correspondence'.[34] She points out that *Inter Insigniores* addresses the question of women's priesthood not in terms of their unsuitability but 'in terms of their ability to symbolize Christ. It must be addressed at the level of Christology.'[35] Summarizing the arguments of *Inter Insigniores*, she reaffirms its 'christological reasoning' which 'is related to a fact of history, the incarnation, and to the masculine symbolism for God enshrined in biblical revelation as a story of covenant love and made concrete in Jesus Christ'.[36] She surveys the ways in which the theological tradition has understood the headship of Christ as Bridegroom, and suggests that *Mulieris Dignitatem* 'modifies the idea of headship by placing it in the context of self-gift even to the point of sacrificing one's life'.[37] Nevertheless, while this modification offers a 'positive evaluation of the maleness of Christ', she acknowledges that it 'does not yet explain the link between the maleness of Christ and the priesthood'.[38] If 'the theological import of the incarnation is that the Word became *flesh*, became *human*', then 'Why – in what respect, or under what formality – does the maleness of Christ take on special symbolic significance in the exercise of the ministerial priesthood?'[39] The answer, she suggests, lies in 'the symbolic meaning of the sexes as mutually complementary'.[40] She explains this symbolic meaning as follows:

> In Christian symbolism, the Church is 'feminine,' the beloved bride of Christ. It receives the gift of salvation from Christ, and responds to this gift with answering love. The love of Christ (and of God, in relation to Israel) is symbolized as 'masculine'. There is a priority to divine love, an initiative which is creative and which actively seeks to bestow itself in love. This

priority in loving can be compared to a *masculine mode of loving*, of self-donation, when considered in light of the 'nuptial meaning of the body' and the active role of the husband in the marital embrace. Corresponding to this is a *feminine mode of loving* which is characterized by active receptivity, a welcoming love which meets, accepts, and responds to the husband's gift with its own gift of self.[41]

At this stage, we should note the pervasive influence of Balthasar's concepts of masculinity, femininity and sexuality, not least in the equation between the divine creative initiative identified as masculine, and the active receptivity of the human response defined as feminine. But once again, this difference between two sexes, male and female, mutates into something that looks different:

In the divine plan of salvation, all human beings are called to be 'the bride', for 'the feminine' is symbolic of all that is human. Likewise, all Christians are 'feminine' before Christ . . . Christ's love is likened to 'masculine love', and the Church's answering love is likened to 'feminine love'. The bridal Church is a collective subject: in it, women and men together welcome and reciprocate the love of Christ.[42]

Lest we begin to feel some unease about the sexual implications of this, Butler hastens to assure her readers that 'It is not that men are compared to the "superior" divine partner and women to the "inferior" human partner. Both men and women are compared to the "inferior" human partner!'[43] Well, that's all right, then. Men are just as inferior as women when it comes to our feminized humanity in relation to Christ's presumably superior masculinized divinity. And in actual marital relationships, presumably the wife remains 'inferior' in relation to her husband? Or are we to believe that the sacrament of marriage now surpasses the relationship between Christ and the Church in its respect for sexual equality?

It would be possible to go on rehearsing the arguments of theological conservatives and the new Catholic feminists, but the themes identified above form the focus of all these arguments when they move from the historical to the doctrinal justification of the male priesthood. Thus a tendency that has been present in the Catholic tradition from the beginning – for the man to attribute to himself qualities of divinity, transcendence, origination and initiative that he associates with masculinity, and to project onto the woman those rejected characteristics of his own humanity, immanence, receptivity and responsivity that he associates with femininity – has now become the hub around which Catholic doctrine revolves in its human and divine dimensions, because Balthasar's theology has become the hub around which Catholic neo-orthodoxy itself revolves. But if only the man can be priest, and if men as well as women represent the feminine, bridal Church, what is the sacramental significance of the female body. So far its sacramental function is entirely negative: a female body cannot be priest because the priest is male, but a male body can be bride because the bride is feminine but not necessarily female.

The sacrament of the body

Schumacher sets out to demonstrate 'the sacramental meaning of the female body, including the question of its influence upon woman's role and place in the church',[44] in order to refute feminist critics such as Susan Ross who claim that the Church is guilty of 'sacramental sex discrimination',[45] or Ruether who asks how 'we seem to have developed to a reversed view in modern Catholic teaching, in which women become equal in nature or creation (secular society), but unequal in grace (in Christ and in the Church)'.[46] Schumacher's main sources are John Paul II and Balthasar and, like them, her theological vision is rooted in the sacramental significance of the sexual human body, understood in the context of a nuptial ecclesiology. She describes the body as 'a sacrament of the person',[47] referring to John Paul II's description of the human body as 'a "primordial sacrament"':[48]

> The sacrament, as a visible sign, is constituted with man, as a body, by means of his visible masculinity and femininity. The body, and it alone, is capable of making visible what is invisible: the spiritual and the divine. It was created to transfer into the visible reality of the world the mystery hidden since time immemorial in God, and thus be a sign of it.[49]

In asserting the sacramental significance of the female body, Schumacher quotes Balthasar:

> If Eve was taken out of Adam . . . then Adam had Eve within him without knowing it. Of course, God created her and breathed his breath into her; but God took the material for her out of Adam's living flesh infused with the Spirit. There was something feminine in him, which he recognizes when God brings him the woman. And the Creator gives the man the power to be creative in this creaturely womb. But the woman is taken from the man; the substance from which she is made is masculine. She knows the man from the beginning. She is, together with him, feminine in relation to God, but she also has the actively responding power with him.[50]

She goes on to argue that there is

> in the mutual 'knowledge' of the marital union the coinciding of activity and receptivity: the man giving himself in a receiving sort of way; the woman

receiving the man in a giving sort of way; the man creating in woman's womb; the woman giving man 'the fully formed child that the seed can only indicate'. As his 'helpmate', she 'does all the work, which he only, as it were, proposes and stimulates'.[51]

These burlesque sexual parodies surely invite a certain sense of irony – but apparently, we are supposed to take them very seriously indeed. So what does all this mean, if we try to break it down into a two-sex anthropology in the context of Balthasar's theology, which Schumacher (like all new feminists) quotes without critical analysis or questioning, to support her argument?

Schumacher claims that 'The patristic witness to the full humanity of Christ – *quod non est assumptum, non est sanctum* (what is not assumed is not sanctified) should not . . . be understood as denying sanctifying grace to women whose femininity he did not assume.'[52] But Schumacher quotes Balthasar's claim that

> If the Church comes from Christ and, hence in everything which makes it the Church, lives from his substance, then the Son of God has this 'feminine' element in him at the deepest level, not because he is a creature, but because he is the Son of the Father. He knows simultaneously what it means to be God and to be begotten of the Father. In this double relationship he becomes the origin of the Church . . . What he gives is wholly his own, and, thus, he recognizes himself in us, as the Father also recognizes him in us. And we recognize ourselves in him, since we are his 'other' (his 'feminine completion') only through the communication of his substance.[53]

Christ therefore does, in some sense at least, assume femininity – 'Adam had Eve within him', 'the Son of God has this "feminine" element in him' – so the absence of femininity in him cannot be an argument against women's ordination. But Schumacher also claims that the woman, in being taken from the man, is made from 'masculine substance', although both are feminine in relation to God. But if the man as well as the woman is feminine in relation to God, where does this masculine substance come from? And if she shares his substance, wherein lies her difference?

As for the models of activity and receptivity that are implied in the sexual exchanges whereby the man gives himself 'in a receiving sort of way', and the woman receives the man 'in a giving sort of way', what does this mean? It makes just as much (or as little) sense to say that the woman gives herself 'in a receiving sort of way', and the man receives the woman 'in a giving sort of way'. The sex act has many configurations, even if we remain at the level of heterosexual genital intercourse for our metaphors and analogies. But let's use this kind of sexual rhetoric, and divest it of its coy references to 'marital embraces' and sexual knowing. We could say that the woman who opens her vagina to a man's penis (being penetrated by his love perhaps?) is giving herself in a receiving sort of way, just as we could say that the man who allows his penis to be enfolded in the vagina (being enfolded by her love perhaps?) is receiving in a giving sort of way. And by whose reckoning is the process of gestation and pregnancy 'work' in any meaningful sense? What kind of work are we talking about? What kind of transaction is going on when the man 'proposes and stimulates' (is this foreplay? isn't that sometimes work of a kind?) and the woman does all the work? These sexual economies add up to more or less than two sexes, whichever way one looks at it.

Schumacher has already, in an earlier essay, posited an 'essential connection between body and spirit',[54] and her whole argument in defence of the male priesthood is based on the theological significance of the sexual body. But in her uncritical appropriation of Balthasar to support her position, she perpetuates all the contradictions and inconsistencies of his thinking, so that it is almost impossible to pin down the sexual body in her texts. The logic of Balthasar's position entails that femininity is not difference but a form of parasitism on the masculinity of Christ. It is within him and 'lives from his substance'. Neither is it associated with being a female body, but with being the Father's Son, with being begotten. Femininity is begotten and masculinity begets. But what kind of femininity is this? What body does it refer to? Christ's masculinity is associated, not with his penis and his beard, but with his identification with the fatherhood of God who, we are repeatedly assured in the Catholic tradition, has neither a penis nor a beard. It may be that these are symbolic nuptial relationships insofar as they have the language of masculinity and femininity imposed upon them, with sexual generativity lurking somewhere in the background, but they are not bodily relationships in any meaningful sense. The 'we' who constitute the 'other', the 'feminine completion' of Christ, refers not to women but to the human community of the bridal Church. So what 'body' is a woman's spirit essentially connected to? Repeatedly, the answer seems to be the male body.

But perhaps it is time for a body count. How many sexes and how many bodies are involved in this nuptial relationship? There is the priest *in persona Christi* (a male body acting in a masculine way), and the priest *in persona Ecclesiae* (the same male body acting in a feminine way); there is the lay Christian as Bride of Christ (a male or female body acting in a feminine way) and the Church as Bride of Christ (a collective of male and female bodies acting in a feminine way); there is the actual husband (a male body acting in a masculine way) and the actual wife (a female body acting in a feminine way). In the material realm of sex and procreation, there is a female body – a wife. But in the realm that really counts – in the suprasexual nuptial relationship between Christ and the Church – there is only one body: the male. He is Bridegroom and Bride, masculine and feminine, priest and lay Christian. She is necessary only to show him what a bride looks like, what a feminine body is, the better to enable him to play his role and ensure that these gay nuptials at least have the symbolic appearance of heterosexuality. So we are no nearer to answering the question: what is the sacramental significance of the female body, so that she is essential to theo-drama?

Sacramentality and the female body

One possible response would be to say that only women can represent the Church, so that at the very minimum, for a Mass to be valid, there must be at least one woman in the congregation. According to Butler, 'Power hints that if Christ needs to be symbolized by a man, perhaps the congregation needs to be symbolized by a woman.'[55] But Power argues that neither is necessary, 'for the priest symbolizes Christ and the Church together, the *totus Christus* . . . A woman might hold this office as well as a man, since the priest symbolizes not one subject (Christ) but the communion itself.'[56] Butler rejects this proposition because, she argues, it is Christ, not the Church, which requires sacramental representation. Acknowledging that 'there is no corresponding *sacramental sign* of the Church as bride',[57] she claims that there is 'no need for a sign: we ourselves *are* the bride . . . It is Christ who must be represented *sacramentally*, for his active presence as true priest in the worshiping assembly is known only by faith.'[58]

Does this argument really hold up? Is Butler suggesting that, when an all-male community celebrates Mass, the men know themselves to be 'brides' by something other than faith? Do they not need a woman to look at now and again, to remind themselves of who they are? Or will the occasional statue do just as well, since it is not living women that are required, but simply a few props to furnish the concept of bridal femininity in order for the men to play their roles?

This idea that equates femininity with presence and masculinity with representation reinforces my suggestion in the last chapter, that it is masculinity, not femininity, which is absent from creation, for signification denotes absence, not presence. To the extent that woman is seen as immanent, totally one with creation and nature, she has no need of language or representation, for she simply is. Thus Speyr claims that

> Mary does not herself take part in the *revelation* of God because fundamentally revelation is no part of a woman's task. Her characteristics are silence and concealment, and they are the mark of all subsequent missions given to woman in the Church.[59]

To identify woman with immanence, nature and being in the way that Butler suggests – to deny her access to language and representation and to exclude her from any revelatory capacity (as Speyr does) – is to render her a mute animal, no different from all other non-human creatures. But to understand why the man's claim to bridal femininity as well as to masculine divinity entails the silencing and exclusion of the woman's voice, we need to turn to the argument put forward by Monica Migliorino Miller regarding the sacramental significance of the ordained male priesthood.

In seeking to account for male ecclesial authority, Miller sets out to explain 'how, according to the order of creation, the male body and sexuality serve as a symbol of God to the world', which makes it 'necessary to understand what there is about masculinity that reveals God that femininity does not'.[60] There follows a bizarre exposition of the representative significance of sexual difference, which includes quotations from Balthasar and from Walter Ong's book, *Fighting for Life*.

Explaining the difference between the representative capacities of the male and female bodies, Miller quotes Balthasar:

> While man, as sexual being, only represents what he is not and transmits what he does not actually possess, and so is . . . at the same time more and less than himself, *woman rests on herself, she is fully what she is, that is, the whole reality of a created being that faces God as a partner, receives his seed and spirit, preserves them, brings them to maturity and educates them* . . .
>
> Restored nature would bring to light – within the parity of nature and parity of value of the sexes – above all the fundamental difference, according to which woman does not represent, but is, while man has to represent and, therefore, is more and less than what he is.[61]

In the context of Miller's argument, this means that the man stands over and against nature and creation, just as God does. Woman, on the other hand, *is* nature, which is why she has no representational function or capacity. But this involves the man in an antagonistic struggle to become what he is not, because he is constantly threatened by the pervasive presence of femininity: 'Nature, creation, and mother are everywhere.'[62] Miller quotes Ong to explain the kind of masculine struggle for becoming that this entails:

> The adversary relationship with the environment, which has been seen to go back to the biological situation of the male embryo and fetus in the womb, would appear to serve as one basis for the male's tendency to fight. Human males tend to feel an environment, including other individuals of the species, as a kind of againstness, something to be fought with and altered. Environment is feminine, and women typically find they can rely on it as it is or comes to them. The received symbol for woman (♀), adopted by feminists apparently everywhere, signifies self-possession, gazing at oneself as projected into the outside world or environment and reflected back into the self from there, whole. The received symbol for man, Mar's [sic] spear (♂), signifies conflict, stress, dissection, division.[63]

144   *The end*

In appealing to such sociobiological arguments, Ong claims that a male priesthood may be necessary to set against the pervasive femininity of the Church, so that Catholic Christianity is credible and attractive for men as well as for women.[64] But even if these highly mythologized ideas could be shown to have some social currency, what does it mean to argue that this perception of engulfing femininity and male aggression should inform Christian sacramentality and liturgy, so that the priest stands over and against the rising tides of the feminine as a kind of Canute figure? Does the Church not then become the same kind of sexual battleground as the world, with the male priest representing God and man over and against nature and woman, not, here, in a reconciled love relationship, but in an adversarial relationship of 'conflict, stress, dissection, division'? Miller quotes further from Ong: 'Masculinity for human males and . . . even for infrahuman males engenders agonistic activity because it is something to be won, achieved . . . not at all simply something one is born with.'[65]

Miller goes on to offer a prolonged biological discussion of the process of insemination, to support the idea that 'in the act of procreation the male must deposit his life principle away from himself', but, because the man is 'the initiator of the procreative act and of conception . . . male sexuality also images God – who alone actively initiated all of creation'.[66] More importantly for my purposes than this lurid explanation of the meaning of sex, is Miller's attempt to relate this sexual function to the death of Christ:

> The death of Christ is essentially generative and marital in its order. In fact we should go so far as to say that His death is an essentially masculine death. It is the death of the man for the woman in which isolation is broken and a covenant formed. By dying the seed no longer remains alone. And it dies by falling into the feminine earth. The seed of the man will be absorbed into the woman, into her own life principle. The man will lose himself by being taken into her . . . In the lonely, heroic act of himself against the world the man is finally able to give something to the woman that is uniquely his own; something that she could not give to herself. This is the male sacrifice that Christ fulfilled for His bridal Church. He dies *for her*. Because of this initiatory act neither remains alone. They are one flesh.[67]

What are we to make of this? Miller's paganized account of the crucifixion accepts without challenge the common association between male orgasm and death. Consider, for example, Balthasar's question, 'What else is his eucharist but, at a higher level, an endless act of fruitful outpouring of his whole flesh, such as a man can only achieve for a moment with a limited organ of his own body?'[68]

(It is interesting that a woman uncritically reiterates this idea that equates orgasm with death: does Miller have no experience of female orgasm that might suggest a different possibility? After all, a woman's orgasm is a form of arousal rather than depletion. A man might expend himself in his first coming, but the second coming is a uniquely womanly affair. But let us be serious here, and keep to the subject. This is no place for a woman's clitoral parousia.)

If we try to trace what happens to sexual identities in the above passage, the picture begins to blur. We have already seen that the man's struggle for individuation against feminine nature relates to Balthasar's claim that he is 'more and less than himself': more than himself, because he represents God, less than himself because he cannot fully identify with nature in the way that ostensibly allows woman to experience a sense of immanence and wholeness in herself. But the picture seems to have shifted again, so that the sexual body once again has become other than what we thought it was. In the last chapter I suggested that, in order to remind himself that he is not-God, that he is in some sense alienated from God, man must identify himself as feminine. Now, according to Ong, man's identification with God leads to a sense of alienation from nature. But, if we follow Miller's logic, on the cross, the man ceases to exist and is totally absorbed into the feminine: he dies for her, and in the process he becomes 'one flesh' with her, but it is her flesh, not his. In this case, his 'lonely, heroic act' has come to naught, for that which the man must resist at all costs – the pervasive threat of femininity and nature – has triumphed. How, then, can it be an argument for a male priesthood that masculinity must continue to assert itself over and against feminine nature in the Church? Has masculinity itself not been vanquished by the feminine in the death of Christ? The more we try to follow these tortured sexual symbolics, the more we find that we are on the trail of the disappearing male, desperately defending his manliness against the rising tide of a castrating male God who renders him feminine, and a devouring feminine creation which absorbs him. So is this a question of *cherchez la femme*, or is it perhaps more a case of *cherchez l'homme*?

Miller claims that, in denying the symbolic significance of Christ's masculinity, feminists such as Ruether negate the need 'for any unique sign to represent Him to mark Him off from the community and creation – namely a male priesthood. The Church, for the sake of feminine authority or power, must completely absorb Christ.'[69] In other words, even beyond Christ's death and resurrection, masculinity (now represented exclusively by the ordained priesthood) must continue its agonistic struggle to separate itself from nature, the body and the feminine, now represented by the Church. The relation of the masculine priest to the feminine Church is not, then, the nuptial communion that is analogously represented by loving human sexuality. It is an ongoing battle between the sexes, a battle of the 'lonely, heroic' masculine subject against the all-consuming female flesh.

Cherchez l'homme: Balthasar's sexual paradoxes

In this strange world of sexual symbolics, nothing is quite what it seems. In Balthasar's ecclesiology, the authority of Christ is personified in the male hierarchy, but this is subservient to the Marian Church, which has primacy over the Petrine. Moreover, it is not the woman but the man who is represented as lack, insufficiency and incompleteness, so that there is a sense of absence and negation about masculinity. Brendan Leahy writes that

> von Balthasar sees the man-priest . . . as being simultaneously both more and less than himself in that as sexual being he only 'represents' what he is not (the Lord) and transmits what he does not really possess (the Lord's real presence and sacraments). Woman, on the other hand, reposes in herself and is entirely her own being, that is, the total reality of a created being before God as partner, receiving, bearing, maturing and nurturing his Word in the Spirit.[70]

From this perspective, as I suggested earlier, the male priesthood is a sign of absence rather than presence, a signifier which, in Derridean terms, represents the trace of the masculine God-Christ in creation, whereas the woman ostensibly has no need of signifiers, for she is presence, immanence, reality, 'being' itself. But that is not so either, because 'woman' is the signifier which situates man in the world, whether in the context of the Marian Church or the *casta meretrix*. But because she is a signifier, she functions most effectively when her body is absent from the scene of representation. His creaturely femininity signifies the fact that he is not-God and therefore not masculine. The female body is incidental to this whole performance: she is a wordless body that he plunders for signifiers to express his own lack of divinity and masculinity. And yet her body reminds him that he is not woman, so he is doubly absent from himself: he is neither the masculine God nor the feminine creature, both of whom exist as a form of 'being' beyond language.

For all his commitment to maintaining sexual hierarchies, Balthasar acknowledges that there is an inscrutable paradox at the heart of his ecclesiology. He claims that

> The Church's Marian dimension embraces the Petrine dimension, without claiming it as its own. Mary is 'Queen of the Apostles' without claiming apostolic powers for herself. She possesses something else and something more.[71]

He goes on to ask,

> Who has the precedence in the end? The man bearing office, inasmuch as he represents Christ in and before the community, or the woman, in whom the nature of the Church is embodied – so much so that every member of the Church, even the priest, must maintain a feminine receptivity to the Lord of the Church? This question is completely idle, for the difference ought only to serve the mutual love of all the members in a circulation over which God

gender, Church and priesthood 147

alone remains sublimely supreme: 'In the Lord, the woman is not independent of the man nor the man of the woman. For just as the woman [Eve] comes from the man, so also the man [including Christ] comes through the woman; but everything comes from God' (1 Cor. 11:11–12).[72]

Let me suggest that this question is far from 'completely idle', because, if Balthasar were to take it seriously, it would threaten the whole structure of his theology. In this dynamic circulation of love between woman, man and God lies the key to a much more mystical theology – a theology that Balthasar's thought simultaneously desires and resists – in which the sexual body might be liberated to express something of the paradoxical relationships which ebb and flow between gendered humans and God, in ways that unravel every system and every dualism, and which render redundant all forms of sexual hierarchy. It is Balthasar's inability to allow his theology this freedom that leads to the violent struggles and conflicts with which he must defend his essentialized vision of a masculine Christ and a masculine God against the ever-present encroachment of the female flesh, experienced as seduction, death and sin.

To go beyond the mute, passive female body and the castrated, alienated male body that constitute this violent Catholic melodrama, we must ask, with and beyond Irigaray, what would happen if woman's mission was indeed to speak and to reveal, to come out of silence and concealment in order to become revealed and revealing? What would this coming out entail? What nuptial love might then be possible? To ask these questions means reopening the passage between the body, language and God, and between the male and female person, in order to explore the sacramental meaning of the female body. But if this is to be a faithful quest, then we need to find a way of speaking the same language in a different way – the language of the Catholic faith, with its central symbols and sacraments of incarnation, Eucharist, sacrifice, redemption and resurrection, but also with its maternal, bridal and feminine imagery of birth, gestation, nurture and virginity. We need to 'make "visible", by an effect of playful repetition, what was supposed to remain invisible: the cover-up of a possible operation of the feminine in language'[73] For this, it is necessary to reopen 'the figures of [theological] discourse . . . in order to pry out of them what they have borrowed that is feminine, from the feminine, to make them "render up" and give back what they owe the feminine'.[74]

However, first it is necessary to unmask the violence that lies at the heart of Balthasar's theology with regard to the sexual female body, and in order to do that I turn to his understanding of the relationship between sex and death, and then to his representation of hell. I want to demonstrate that the elimination of the female body from the story of salvation is an unacknowledged impetus that drives Balthasar's theology towards a deadly conclusion, so that for the female body his theo-drama represents, not a story of redemption and resurrection, but a story of ruination and condemnation. Only by unmasking the murderous violence of Balthasar's womanly man towards his bodily, female sexual other might it be possible to go beyond his theo-drama in order for women to grace the world stage with the presence of Christ through their full participation in the sacramental performance of the story of salvation.

8   Desire, death and the female body

I have argued throughout this book that a sacramental approach to language holds the key to a feminist theological vision rooted neither in the post-Enlightenment, experiential subject of modernity nor in the fragmented, linguistic subject of postmodernity, but in the dynamic revelatory relationship between language and the body, mediated by grace. However, while this does not capitulate to a Derridean reductionism that would refuse to accord the body any extra-linguistic significance, it does entail the recognition that language itself provides the medium by which the body's performance is intentionally or unintentionally conformed to certain narratives of identity, meaning and truth, so that the linguistic representation of the body is of the utmost importance for the sacramental life of faith. I have also demonstrated that the female body has no position in the modern language of sacramentality as represented by Balthasar and the new Catholic feminists, being identified with a form of immanence that reduces it to the level of mute animality, while the male body appropriates 'her' language to determine 'his' identity as woman and Bride in relation to a masculine God, incarnate in a male Christ.

With this in mind I want to continue this gendered reading of Balthasar's theology, in order to ask how his unacknowledged exclusion of the female body from theo-drama leads to an identification of woman with sex, death and sin in a way that betrays a profoundly hostile attitude towards embodiment and sexuality. I have suggested that Balthasar's theology is riven with contradictions, insofar as its ostensible affirmation of the body, beauty, incarnation and sexuality goes hand in hand with a theological rhetoric that is preoccupied with violence, torture, death and sin. To point this out is not to deny that the Christian narrative itself confronts us with the brutality of crucifixion, betrayal and death as part of its redemptive vision, and later I shall ask how a feminist theology might reconcile this dimension of the story with its other dimension of birth, fecundity and life. But my point in the next two chapters is to demonstrate that, if one strips away the veneer from Balthasar's celebration of beauty and grace, there is in fact a logic at work in his theology of woman beyond its surface contradictions, for his whole theological vision of sex, sin and death amounts to a coherent account of the damnation of the female sex. To discover this subtext one has to read Balthasar against the grain, piecing together a story that forms the dark underside of his theo-drama, by resolutely taking up the position of the woman in order to explore the implications of his ideas for the female sex.

Balthasar's suprasexuality

Sex acquires eschatological significance for Balthasar primarily in terms of the dyadic nature of the woman, who is both bride and mother. Thus, in seeking to explain the relationship between Mary and Christ, Balthasar writes:

> the Second Adam comes from the second Eve, in contrast to the original relationship in paradise. But then this law of sexual derivation is transcended – it had already been breached insofar as Mary conceived while remaining a virgin – and replaced by the original, 'absolute', suprasexual relationship between the sexes, not without the difference proper to soteriological time . . . This return, through the unique relationship between Christ and Mary, to man's original state in the Garden of Eden cannot be submitted to biological analysis, nor can we imagine what man's original state may have been, in concrete terms. We simply have to posit such a state: if we follow man back to his origin, the vicious circle of sexuality and death is broken.[1]

Note here the relationship between sexuality, death and temporality, which invites closer consideration. Within historical time, sex and death are inseparable. It is only from the transcendent, ahistorical perspective of 'soteriological time' that it is possible to hypothesize about a non-deadly sexual relationship. After a lengthy discussion of the question of sex in Eden, Balthasar asks what kind of erotic relationship is represented in the paradise story, if it is not sexual. He responds that the question must be left open, 'even if it gapes like a wound'.[2] Aidan Nichols quaintly observes that

> Balthasar takes more seriously than many modern students the assertions of the Fathers that in their state of original righteousness the proto-parents would not have known sexual arousal and the woman defloration as we know them now . . . What form their union by eros would have taken he cannot say (he notes elsewhere it would be beyond the powers of lapsarian sexologists to describe), what he definitely affirms is that to dispose of patristic commentary on these matters as quasi-Manichaean is superficial and trivializing.[3]

I suspect that only in the Catholic Church would one find a celibate scholar who still thinks of women as being deflowered by sex.

Balthasar thinks that it is beyond our human capability to imagine paradisiacal sex between Adam and Eve. We can only posit such a relationship by projecting it onto Christ and Mary/the Church, and Balthasar makes clear that this projected, disembodied sexuality, which we participate in most fully not through human sexual love but through celibacy, is of a higher and better order than ordinary human sex:

> The suprasexual (and not sexless) relationship between the incarnate Word and his Church is a genuinely human one; human beings can be enabled to participate in it. Consequently the sexual man/woman fruitfulness need be no longer the exclusive model of human fruitfulness. On the contrary, this form of fruitfulness is seen to be the purely worldly metaphor of a unique fruitfulness that bursts through the cycle of successive generations and of which Christ says: 'He who is able to receive this, let him receive it' (Mt 19:12). This unique fruitfulness is signed with the sign of the Agape-death, which is the ultimate bodily form adopted by the spiritual Word of God. The natural process whereby a man 'leaves father and mother and cleaves to his wife' (Gen. 2:24; Eph. 5:3), which adds a new member to the sequence of generations, is changed; now a man steps out of the cycle of generation itself (Mk 10:29f.) in order to enter into the unique, supratemporal, sexual relationship between the New Adam and his 'Spouse' (Rev. 21:9). Thus man is enabled to transcend the sexual – as a function specific to earthly existence – in favor of a form of existence in which God's Agape, which also reveals its nuptial aspect (sealed in the death on the Cross), becomes the all-inclusive meaning of life.[4]

Balthasar's 'suprasex' is therefore an altogether transcendent, disembodied affair, which is analogously like sex between man and woman/husband and wife, and is therefore not at all like sex between man and woman/husband and wife.[5] (Given that this suprasex takes place between Mother and Son, we might perhaps be thankful for this.) Balthasar's suprasexuality is also closely bound up with the symbolism of death – the consummate moment is the cross, in which Christ achieves the remarkable feat of giving birth to a woman (the Church) by way of a death which, as we saw in the last chapter, is the equivalent of a cosmic male orgasm. Thus, 'The reciprocal fruitfulness of man and woman is surpassed by the ultimate priority of the "Second Adam", who, in suprasexual fruitfulness, brings a "companion", the Church, into being.'[6]

If we look more closely at the relationship between sex and death, we see that its temporal dimension is also bound up in the woman's role, as one in whom sexual difference is a question of temporality. I have already mentioned the

152   *The end*

relationship between woman and time,[7] but now I want to develop this discussion in the context of sex and death.

Woman, sex and time

In order to explain how the revelation of woman's personhood culminates in the coming into being of the Church, Balthasar offers a lengthy historical survey of the development of doctrine concerning Mary and the Church, focusing on 'the specifically dramatic dimension of Mariology/ecclesiology'.[8] The 'dyadic character of the woman' represented by Mary means that her role as Bride and Mother situates her in a different relation to time than the role of the man, represented by Christ. His is an absolute, transcendent role, while hers is time-bound and historical: 'she requires a certain span of time in order to develop from a receptive bride into a mother who gives birth to her child, nourishes it and brings it up.'[9] This temporal factor means that there is necessarily 'a certain amount of straightforward narration' in Mariology:

> whereas the Son's mission develops in a straight line in his masculine consciousness (however much he leaves 'the hour' up to the Father), Mary's falls into distinct periods. Prior to the Annunciation, her central mission is hidden, but from then on she allows her consent to be molded by the Son's will; her role is continually undergoing fundamental change, from the period of his youth to his public ministry, from the Cross to Pentecost, in step with the needs of him whose 'helpmate' she is.[10]

Once again, Irigaray might be invited to comment on this scenario. Irigaray's re-reading of Heidegger asks what difference it might make if Being were understood in terms of spatiality as well as temporality.[11] The denial of the significance of place represents a denial of the significance of the womb and the maternal body, insofar as these provide a place that is covered over in the unveiling of Being in language and time. In her reading of Plato's allegory of the cave, Irigaray suggests that representation is based upon a phallic trajectory, in which the space of origins (i.e. the cave as a metaphor for the maternal body) is denied. Thus, she describes Plato's prisoners as 'Heads forward, eyes front, genitals aligned, fixed in a straight direction and always straining forward, in a straight line. A phallic direction, a phallic line, a phallic time, backs turned on origin.'[12]

I have already suggested the extent to which Balthasar's representation of woman functions as a place for the man, not as her own place of becoming, and perhaps this gives some insight into why he sees temporality as a more fluctuating and complex process in relation to the woman than to the man. Mary provides the womb in which Christ begins the phallic trajectory of his mission, but this is not the real womb, the ultimate womb in which Christ's own seed will generate itself, for that is the womb of the Church. Balthasar cannot ask if, from the woman's perspective, the spatiality of her body might be more significant than temporality, for her mission must be absolutely dictated by Christ's progression from incarnation to death and resurrection (focused on the climactic significance of his 'hour'), and her relationship to time and space is bound by his. For this reason, prior to the Annunciation Mary has no identity worth speaking of. She becomes significant only when she is necessary for the man's becoming, whereas his mission is 'absolute' and not to be deflected from its linear trajectory. As a result, Balthasar finds the feminine 'elusive because of her twofold orientation toward the man and the child; this both constitutes her as a person through dialogue and makes her a principle of generation'.[13] He draws together this enigmatic dyad as follows:

> There is a twofold reason, therefore, why woman cannot be summed up in a neat definition. She is a process that oscillates (from the Virgin Bride to the Mother of the Church, from the answering Person to the Source of the race); it is the theorizing of men that attempts to make this flux and flow into a rigid principle.[14]

Let me suggest that the woman's identity fluctuates because she has no identity: the time of her becoming is contingent upon the absolute time of his becoming, for which she is the space. In other words, sexual difference hinges not upon two sexual persons each with their own unique relationships to time and space, but between his time and her as his space, whose time is therefore contingent upon his. As the space that opens up – the clearing, perhaps, in Heideggerian terms – to accommodate and reveal his being, the space that she represents must always be fashioned around the time of his being. The answering person has no bodily sex for 'she' is the eschatological promise of Mary/Church (and this, we shall see, presents considerable difficulties for Balthasar in acknowledging the material reality of the female sex and the earthly Church), and the Source of the race is the maternal body of the Church that hovers ambiguously between 'his' body and 'hers', again, because it is the maternal receptacle for his life, and she has no life of her own.

This becomes more apparent when we consider how Balthasar understands the relationship between Mary and the Church. When, in the Middle Ages, Mary became identified with the beloved woman in Song of Songs and therefore came to be seen as identical with the Church as Bride of Christ, the full implications of her virginal motherhood could be explored from an eschatological perspective. Mary's 'personal and unique' relationship with Christ makes her 'the concrete epitome of what we mean by "Church"' in such a way that her personal mission becomes universal:

> But since it is a woman's mission, it cannot be condensed into an abstract principle within ordinary time categories: being Mother and becoming a Bride (at the Cross, when the Church comes forth from Christ's side) are two different things; they can be seen as one within a heavenly perspective, such as the early Middle Ages adopted.[15]

This coming together of the 'christotypical' and 'ecclesiotypical'[16] dimensions of Mary's mission has two consequences: first, 'the man/woman problem is raised in a radical form: attention is directed to the absolute relationship between the sexes; woman is seen as a unity, as mother and bride'.[17] Second, 'this approach leads to the "helpmate" being promoted to equality of rank with man. This must have dire consequences in Mariology if the man/woman polarity is allowed to obscure the distance between God and the creature.'[18] Note here the anxiety that enters Balthasar's thought, as he contemplates the possibility that the death and resurrection of Christ elevate woman to a position of equality with man. It is a concern which reveals that Balthasar's understanding of difference is strictly hierarchical and therefore not difference at all, since distance and hierarchy do not in themselves constitute difference. We must begin to ask then if man is different from woman and God is different from creation because one has priority over the other, and one is temporal and contingent, while the other is eternal and absolute, in a way that threatens Balthasar's concept of absolute and irreducible difference both between God and creation and, analogously, between male and female.

As a result of the identification of Mary with the Church, Balthasar sees a number of distortions and excesses entering Mariology from the late Middle Ages, which the Second Vatican Council sought to rectify in its teaching on Mary in the Constitution on the Church, *Lumen Gentium*. However, Balthasar criticizes the Council's Mariology for emphasizing Mary's role as Christ's Mother but not as his 'associate', so that the example she provides is represented primarily in moral terms, without sufficient account being taken of the man–woman aspect of her relationship to Christ.[19] It is the quest to reclaim this neglected aspect of Mariology that leads him to propose a suprasexual relationship between Mary and the Church as Bride of Christ, in a way that illuminates the true meaning of the man–woman relationship in Genesis.

Finally, Balthasar moves from the mission and person of Mary to explore the relationship between the person of Christ and the person of his Bride, the Church. He holds in tension the idea that Christ as the Head and the Church as the Body can to some extent be seen as 'one person',[20] but only if the Church's mission as woman and Bride in relation to Christ is seen as a marker of difference. The Church is Christ's Body but she is also a 'we', constituted by the many individual persons who by the work of the Holy Spirit become incorporated into her personhood. This means that 'Christ gives and inaugurates what is his own; thus the Church, to that extent, is his "Body". He also sets it over against him, in dialogue, and to that extent the Church is his "Bride".'[21] As the Bride of Christ, the 'We' of the Church is 'an overarching feminine reality'.[22] But again, we must ask what has happened to sexual difference here. The woman is different from the man, not because she is an 'I' in relation to his 'I', but because she is a 'we' in relation to his 'I': just as we saw above that the difference between man and woman is a temporal difference (she is contingent, he is absolute), now we see that it is the difference between the one and the many. Balthasar's three polarities – the individual and the community, male and female, and matter and spirit – are beginning to blur into one another. Let me develop this suggestion further by considering a section in *Theo-drama II*, in which Balthasar considers the ambivalence of the sexual relationship, given the close association between reproduction and death, and the implications of this for an understanding of the supralapsarian significance of sex.

Sex, death and the polarities of human existence

Referring to Fichte, Augustine, Chrysostom, Hegel and Schopenhauer, Balthasar sees an ongoing problem associated with the relationship between the individual and the species, related to the process of birth and death. Reproduction is necessary to continue the species, because each individual dies, but this means that birth brings the individual into confrontation with the necessity of his (or her?) death. Balthasar quotes Fichte who writes that 'anyone who produces another human being in his place is also obliged to hand this place over to him at the proper time. Thus death and birth presuppose each other.'[23] He then discusses Aquinas's Aristotelian understanding of the relationship between corruptibility and incorruptibility in terms of the human constitution:

> Man, by his nature, is established, as it were, midway between corruptible and incorruptible creatures, his soul being naturally incorruptible, while his body is naturally corruptible. We must also observe that nature's purpose appears to be different with regard to corruptible and incorruptible things. For that seems to be the direct purpose of nature, which is invariable and perpetual, while what is only for a time is seemingly not the chief purpose of nature but, as it were, subordinate to something else; otherwise, when it ceased to exist, nature's purpose would become void. Therefore, since in things corruptible none is everlasting and permanent except the species, it follows that the chief purpose of nature is the good of the species, for the preservation of which natural generation is ordained. On the other hand, incorruptible substances survive not only in the species but also in the individual; and so even the individuals are included in the chief purpose of nature. Hence it pertains to man to beget offspring, on

> the part of the naturally corruptible body. But on the part of the soul, which is incorruptible, it is fitting that the multitude of individuals should be the direct purpose of nature, or rather of the Author of nature, who alone is the Creator of the human soul. Therefore, to provide for the multiplication of the human race, he established the begetting of offspring even in the state of innocence.[24]

If we analyse this passage closely in terms of sexual difference, then I think we begin to see more clearly the position that woman occupies in Balthasar's theology, in a way that suggests that all three of the polarities he identifies are in fact reducible to one age-old polarity – the polarity between the incorruptible male soul and the corruptible female body. The man is an 'I', because the incorruptible substance of the human species survives in him as an individual. The woman is a 'we' because she is part of the species, not incorruptible in herself but necessary for 'the begetting of offspring' in order that there might be 'a multitude of individuals' brought into being through 'the multiplication of the human race'. But of this multitude, only the men count. The 'direct purpose of nature' (i.e. of God) is to create men. Woman is secondary, and her existence is always orientated towards his. In terms of the polarities of the one and the many, matter and spirit, male and female, he is the one, the spirit, she is the many, matter. This is not the difference between sexual persons; it is the difference between culture as male, nature as female, soul as male, body as female, the absolute as male, the contingent as female. It is a difference that the agonistic, solitary male must sustain by constantly battling against the femininity of temporality, plurality and materiality, and by the antagonistic struggle between father and son as the son threatens to occupy the father's place. As Gerard Loughlin argues,

> Balthasar . . . does not really succeed in thinking difference-in-unity, and in particular the differentiated unity of man and woman. He fails to think sexual difference, not because he stresses unity at the expense of difference, but because the unity he does stress is finally, and only, male: a difference within the male.[25]

But, as Burrus and Deutscher point out, and as Loughlin also argues,[26] Christianity destabilizes this polarity, because if man is God in relation to woman, he is woman in relation to God. So in his struggle against woman, he is struggling against himself. In truth, he does not know who he is, and as a result his identity is constantly threatened, and he must fight to the death to assert himself in the face of the chaotic, carnal forces that threaten to consume him.

Balthasar's sexually charged theology is in fact the epic drama of the lonely hero, who must constantly resist the siren voices that seduce him and would lure him onto the rocks of body, sex and death. But this is a Sisyphean struggle,

Desire, death and the female body 157

because Balthasar's heroic man cannot ultimately be reconciled with the reconciling love of the risen Christ. He cannot accept the redemption that Christ offers, because he will not be reconciled to himself in her and to her in himself, and therefore this is a man whose rising and desiring is always also a falling and dying, a man for whom love is a devouring abyss that must be resisted and conquered if his manhood is to survive.

Balthasar's theology oozes sex, but despite his extravagant sexual rhetoric, and notwithstanding the ways in which the new feminists (including John Paul II) have subsequently interpreted this positively in terms of marital sexual relations, Balthasar never represents human sexuality in positive terms, as the coming together of bodies in mutual love. Sex is always a cipher for something else: for the eschatological desire of Christ's relationship with the Bride (which is represented in bodily, finite terms by virginity, not marriage), or for the dread of bodiliness, mortality and death. Despite his reputation as a theologian who celebrates the incarnate reality of the Christian faith and the beauty of creation, and despite his repeated appeal to sexual metaphors to describe theological relationships, Balthasar's work manifests a thinly veiled horror at the fact of the sexual origins of life. For example, in *Creator Spirit*, we read,

> For the individual, the thought of the appalling contingency of the sexual process to which he owes his origin remains a wholesome admonition; this thought can scarcely be borne, and if it were to indicate the total cause of his existence in the world, it could lead the being that is begotten and born to cynicism and the loss of all hope.[27]

He goes on to suggest:

> Between generation and spirit there yawns in Being something like a geological fault of dizzying height . . . This being that has been generated sexually is doomed from the outset to die; among purely natural beings, death must be accepted as the necessary counterpoint of birth, but what does dying mean for a spiritual person who has his being directly from God and is directly orientated to God – and yet who does not know himself in any other way than as a fellow citizen of the world of nature?[28]

Balthasar's attitude towards sex and death is trapped in the kind of necrophiliac stereotypes that feminist writers such as Grace Jantzen and Beverley Clack associate with the western philosophical imaginary (see Chapter 10). Sex is not the loving encounter of bodies in mutual desire (which is always also vulnerable to wounding and grief), but the unthinkable process to which man owes his existence. Sex is not the beginning of the fecundity and joy of life, but the terrible origination of the inevitability of death. Sex drags being away from its spiritual relationship to God, and condemns it to the carnality and mortality of human existence. Thus the whole orientation of life must be to struggle against this offensive carnality, in order once again to attain to the spirituality of being beyond sex and death. Life, then, becomes entirely enslaved to a post-mortem vision of its fulfilment. No wonder Balthasar has so little to say about the day-to-day realities of faith, life and love.

Nichols writes that 'Balthasar makes his own Heidegger's dictum in *Sein und Zeit* that death is the highest possibility existence affords, since only in relation to death can we decide the overall bearing of our life.'[29] Christ's life supremely expresses this defining quality of the hour of death, and it is only through the death of Christ that humankind can transcend the tragic inevitability of death.[30] O'Donnell describes as 'the centre of Balthasar's whole theology', the abandonment of Christ to the formless chaos of death:

> for Balthasar Jesus is the historical form of the transcendent God. In this sense he is the revelation of supreme beauty. But now we see that for the sake of love the beautiful one descends into the abyss of chaos, hate, ugliness. Hence, Jesus at the end reveals himself as without form.[31]

What becomes of the female body, so intimately associated with sex, birth and bodiliness, when this is the disposition of faith? As we shall see, she becomes the formless horror into which Christ dissolves, but before developing this claim I want to consider in more detail Balthasar's understanding of *kenosis*. If, as Miller and Ong suggest, the masculine psyche is shaped through an agonistic struggle to resist the consuming power of maternal femininity, what happens to Balthasar's essentially masculine God when he empties himself into the form of the human and into the formlessness of death, both associated with the femininity of the flesh? The answer is that he finds himself in a mortal and possibly unending battle to conquer and eliminate 'her'.

Kenosis, sex and death

We have seen that the idea of *kenosis* is central to Balthasar's theology, both in his understanding of relationships within God, and in his explanation of how creation becomes incorporated into those relationships. The intra-trinitarian life is made up of the constant self-emptying of the one to the other, and creation itself ultimately becomes taken up into this giving and receiving of love through Christ's incarnation, so that

> the world acquires an inward share in the divine exchange of life; as a result the world is able to take the divine things it has received from God, together with the gift of being created, and return them to God as a divine gift.[32]

Graham Ward points to the centrality of Hegel to Balthasar's thinking on *kenosis*, but argues that Hegel's idea of *kenosis* is 'one founded upon lack'[33] within God and within the human subject, in such a way that 'we are bound to God as God is to us',[34] so that God's freedom becomes subject to the necessity of creation, incarnation and crucifixion. As he does with Heidegger's Being, Balthasar ostensibly introduces the idea of absolute divine freedom and therefore of creation as gift into the Hegelian exchange. Moreover, 'the kenotic economy in Hegel is an erotic economy – force, desire, labour, the movement of the Spirit are correlations of each other'.[35] As a result, 'This subject of desire (where "of" is both subjective and objective genitive), pulls Hegel into the orbit of romantic erotics',[36] after which

> The erotic subject then plots its history through Schopenhauer, Nietzsche, Freud, Heidegger, Sartre and Lacan. The modern subject is the subject of desire, the acquiring, possessive subject, the capitalist subject. This subject is male and the female in this economy represents the unimaginable, the unpresentable, the enigmatic, the dark mysterious continent that must be conquered.[37]

Ward sees the primary difference between Hegel and Balthasar as focusing on the significance of difference in the concept of *kenosis*, so that Balthasar reasserts 'a theology of the hiatus, the *diastasis* between God and creation, theology and anthropology'[38] which is lacking in Hegel's thought. Here, Heidegger's ontological difference is significant for Balthasar's insistence upon the radical difference between God and the world, while Balthasar's understanding of the *analogia entis* 'introduces an ineliminable aporia, an irradicable secondariness' to the relationship between God and the human being made in the image of God: 'Hiatus fosters desire by opening the space for creativity, the stage for action, the yearning for unity; it fosters a spiritual *dunamos*, a theological *kinesis*, which is kenotic. There cannot be true kenosis without hiatus, without true difference.'[39]

There is, then, a close relationship in Balthasar's thought between difference (including sexual difference as an analogy for the relationship between God and creation and Christ and the Church), desire and *kenosis*, which pertains to relationships within the Trinity as well as between God and the world: 'Kenosis is the disposition of love within the Trinitarian community. It is a community constituted by differences which desire the other . . . All incarnation is kenotic; all Word becoming flesh, all acts of representation, are kenotic.'[40]

We have already seen the significance of sexual difference for Balthasar's understanding of *kenosis*: the primary kenotic initiative, the self-emptying which constitutes the origin of the world, is masculine: the originating Word is a male ejaculation. It is the *kenosis* of God the Father, and the *kenosis* of Christ insofar as he is God. The responsive *kenosis*, which receives, makes fruitful and returns the gift of the masculine initiative, is feminine. It is the *kenosis* of Mary and the

Church, of woman, of motherhood, of human discipleship, and of Christ himself insofar as he receives and abandons himself to the kenotic love of the Father in his feminized humanity. With regard to the life of Christ, there are two kenotic movements that are of supreme importance: the incarnation, when God empties himself into the form of the human Christ, and the cross, when Christ empties himself of life itself and of his relationship with God, to experience the formlessness, abandonment and desolation of death. But what happens when we allow these kenotic moments to become gendered? Let me consider the relationship between *kenosis* and desire more closely, again introducing a gendered perspective.

Balthasar's insistence that creation is incorporated into the divine life in Christ leads him to affirm the qualified significance of *eros* for theology. He claims that 'everything that, in modern times, sails under the flag of "Eros" . . . is in reality a secularization of Christian Agape'.[41] Referring to 'the glittering intermediate realm of *eros* which is found in Plato's *Symposium* and throughout all human history',[42] Balthasar rejects Anders Nygren's 'deep mistrust of the *eros* that seeks to arise from the creature to God'.[43] Instead, he argues that heavenly love can become incarnate in earthly love through the 'transformation and refashioning of *eros* by *agape*',[44] and this is what survives of earthly love beyond death. This finds paradoxical affirmation in the fact that 'manhood and womanhood cross the frontier of death, whereas sexuality – now superfluous – does not'.[45]

Significantly, however, Balthasar is careful to distance the positive dimension of human *eros* from marriage and sexual love, for once death no longer exists, there is no theological significance in human reproduction. The divine fruitfulness is rather found among '[t]he preliminary, earthly forms of . . . the Eucharist, which is an exchange of love between Christ the Bridegroom and the Church/Bride, and the life of virginity, which is a share in this suprasexual bridal life'.[46] Thus, contrary to the Catholic tradition, and certainly contrary to the romanticization of married sexuality and procreation found in the theology of John Paul II and the new feminists, Balthasar seems reluctant to attribute any sacramental significance to human sexual love and procreation. Marriage, like the female body, exists not as a good in itself but as a means to an end: 'the *communio sanctorum* . . . takes something of earthly marriage beyond itself, perfecting it in a final state that is free of all sexual cause and effect'.[47] Sex is deferred, transcended, idealized, but never incarnate in the coming together of human bodies. Desire circulates, not horizontally between human bodies but only vertically between human spirits and God, so that the less sexual we are in our humanity, the more fully we participate spiritually in the suprasexual life of the Trinity and the relationship between Christ and the Church. As we shall see, this involves the male (Balthasar/Christ) in a vicious struggle against the embodiment of desire in the female sex.

What really counts in this equation is not the difference between man and woman but the distance between man and God. Indeed, although Balthasar affirms the persistence of man and woman in heaven, it is hard to see how this relates to the female sexual body, since we have already seen that being a woman has nothing to do with being a female body: men in heaven might as effectively perform the roles of 'man' and 'woman' as they do in the Church. It is also worth mentioning here that, in the Roman Catholic tradition, the sacrament of marriage is the only sacrament which depends upon the presence of a female body for its enactment. Thus in eliding the sacramentality of marriage in favour of a revelatory *eros* situated in the Eucharist and the virginal life, Balthasar also effectively devalues the only sacramental space wherein a female body might have essential significance.

If, as Ward suggests, *kenosis* entails difference, and it is the kenotic movement of desire in the yearning for unity that creates the 'spiritual *dunamos*' of the Christian drama, then there must be a much more radical appreciation of the desirability of difference itself, for Balthasar's theology to succeed. As it is, the desire for union in his theology takes the form of destructive lust rather than life-giving desire, for it is orientated not towards consummation and love but towards consumption and obliteration: it is a desire which seeks not to let the other be, but to become the other. Contrary to what Ward claims, Balthasar's idea of *kenosis* does indeed entail a 'romantic erotics' for, as I shall show, in Balthasar's theology no less than in the modern thinkers listed by Ward, 'the female . . . represents the unimaginable, the unpresentable, the enigmatic, the dark mysterious continent that must be conquered'. This is because Balthasar's understanding of *kenosis* is not informed by an idea of the mutually kenotic desire of the sexes, nor by a possible kenotic imaginary founded upon metaphors of maternal embodiment and birth (although these are not lacking from his theology, as we shall see), but upon an understanding of *kenosis* as the willingness of the masculine God to be seduced into the female flesh and lured to his death.

Kenosis, masculinity and vulnerability

Coakley suggests that a narrative reading of Philippians 2 invites an understanding of the incarnation as Christ's revelation of God's perfection in human vulnerability. Thus, referring to 'Richard Swinburne's insistence that human and divine natures be kept somewhat "separate" in Christ . . . lest the divine nature permeate the human in such a way as to undermine its integrity',[48] she suggests that

> events like Gethsemane and Golgotha seem to show Jesus' humanity, according to Swinburne, as in some sense *defective* from its true, heavenly norm. But what, we may ask, if the frailty, vulnerability and 'self-effacement' of these narratives *is* what shows us 'perfect humanity'?[49]

Balthasar does not make the kenotic move that Coakley proposes, in which the vulnerability of Christ reveals God's own power in vulnerability (see Chapter 4).

Instead of the incarnation becoming the locus of an emptying out of our human constructs of an omnipotent, omniscient masculine God through the recognition of 'a gentle omnipotence which, far from "complementing" masculinism, acts as its undoing',[50] Balthasar freezes both sexuality and divinity in a way that actually affirms the patriarchal representation of God as standing over and against the vulnerability of the incarnation. His understanding of *kenosis* is therefore closer to that which Coakley identifies with fourth-century theological debates, when the dogmatic attribution of implicitly masculine characteristics such as omnipotence and omniscience to the divine nature led to considerable difficulties with regard to reconciling the incarnate suffering of Christ's humanity with the unchanging nature of his divinity. Referring to Cyril of Alexandria, Coakley writes,

> For Cyril, the word *kenōsis* signified no loss or abnegation, but simply the so-called 'abasements' in the taking of flesh. He was finally at a loss how to *explain* how this assumption of flesh could occur without detriment or change to the divine Logos.[51]

As I shall argue, for Balthasar the incarnation constitutes the feminized 'abasement' of masculine divinity, so that it represents a violent confrontation between God and 'his' greatest enemy – the female flesh experienced as weakness, corruption, seduction and death. While the second person of Balthasar's Trinity empties 'himself' in the incarnation, God the Father remains invulnerable and inviolate, and, as we shall see, the resurrection is represented as the Pyrrhic victory of masculinized divinity over the feminized flesh.

In this chapter, I have sought to demonstrate that the female body is a contingent player in theo-drama, making her entrance after Adam and her exit on Calvary when a new form of woman comes into being – a form that is entirely 'his' form, so that sexual difference is eliminated rather than affirmed in the death of Christ. This could be interpreted as a move beyond difference into a new nuptials in which male and female bodies together would inhabit a sacramental space of gendered fluidity, in which the sexed body becomes expressive rather than definitive of the love and desire of God for creation and of Christ for the Church. But before we can move to explore the possibilities for sacramental sex beyond Balthasar, we must first expose the fate of the female body when his drama reaches its climax in the death of Christ and its aftermath.

9   Sex, death and melodrama

In the last chapter, I argued that Balthasar does not allow the sexual body any positive significance in the form of human bodily love. His 'suprasexuality' is a projection into a transcendent sphere in which sexuality is both idealized and rendered remote from the ordinary interactions of human love and commitment. It is in the celibate's lonely struggle against sex that his fantasies of sexual fulfilment find expression in the risen life of Christ and the Church, but in order to indulge these fantasies he must guard himself vigorously against the seductions of the female flesh.

There is nothing new in this, but because of Balthasar's growing influence, and because of the almost universal failure of those who engage with him to problematize this aspect of his work with sufficient seriousness, it is vital for feminist theology to call attention to the poison at work in Balthasar's representation of sexuality in general and female sexuality in particular. In order to do this, it is necessary to bring his relationship with Adrienne von Speyr more fully into the picture, for the relationship between these two fuels his theology and represents theo-drama in action, insofar as they sought to become the living embodiment of the theology that they developed together. Speyr should stand as a caution to women who risk becoming caught up in this fantasy world of psycho-spiritual sex, for it is a deadly game as far as women are concerned, and Balthasar's theology risks luring a certain kind of theological imagination into the labyrinths of dread, repression and denial that have fuelled Christian misogyny for almost two thousand years.

Sexual role models? Hans Urs von Balthasar and Adrienne von Speyr

Johann Roten writes that 'von Balthasar's thinking and writings are in fact a theological biography, where it would be impossible to separate the spiritual from the theological, the existential from the intellectual'.[1] Roten describes the relationship between Speyr and Balthasar as 'a specific expression of the living and unswerving bond between God and the human person',[2] and he goes on to suggest that this relationship could be a potential model for gender roles within the Church:

> It seems that the example of Adrienne von Speyr and Hans Urs von Balthasar could usefully address the present discussion in the Church about gender roles . . . If feminist concerns are not merely a matter of hierarchic functional uniformity, then the example of Hans Urs von Balthasar and Adrienne von Speyr could be a challenging illustration – not necessarily to be copied as such! – of the best possibilities the Church has to offer to men and women, granted that both be shaped and permeated by the common fundamental Marian personality structure.[3]

This idea that Balthasar's life and theology are inseparable is often repeated. For example, in his almost hagiographical study, Angelo Scola writes of Balthasar that 'His theology . . . cannot be studied independently of the concrete experience of his existence as vocation . . . It is truly impossible in von Balthasar's case to separate this work of the theologian from the experience of the subject who produced it.'[4] Michelle Gonzalez, referring to Roten's article, writes:

> Balthasar and Speyr's relationship was, in their eyes, an embodiment of their theological views . . . Balthasar as priest and Speyr as mystic together were representational of God's intended humanity in its separate but united roles. The male and female each served a divine purpose that is fully realized in the unity of their relationship.[5]

Balthasar met Speyr in 1940, when they were both in their thirties. She was undergoing a crisis of faith associated with the death of her first husband, Emil Dürr, who had two sons by a previous marriage. Balthasar's account of her life suggests a highly intelligent and determined woman who overcame ill health to qualify as a doctor, and devoted herself passionately to social causes. It also seems that from an early age her spirituality was somewhat unusual, insofar as she claimed to have had frequent visions and supernatural experiences since early childhood. After meeting Balthasar she converted to Catholicism and he became her confessor and spiritual director until she died. For more than fifteen years he lived in the house she shared with her second husband, Werner Kaegi.

Roten divides their time together into three periods. The years 1940 to 1944 were 'mainly devoted to Adrienne's initiation and rooting in the Christological mysteries' and to '"being used" by God through countless visions, bilocations, emanations of light, ecstasies, and exterior stigmatisations'.[6] Speyr had suffered a debilitating heart attack in 1940, and this period of her life saw the beginning of a gradual decline in her health. (One can only ask what kind of Christian 'initiation' or spiritual direction this was that involved encouraging a seriously ill woman to enter states of psychosis rather than seeking psychiatric help.) The second period, from 1944 to 1948, saw them working towards the establishment of their secular institute, the Community of Saint John, together with Balthasar's growing realization (at Speyr's insistence) that he must leave the Jesuits in order to continue their work together. This was also a period that 'was marked by the so-called "great dictations", and represents a harvest of approximately thirty-five major writings dictated by Adrienne von Speyr'.[7]

Describing the onset of the mystical experiences of Christ's suffering that produced these dictations, Balthasar refers to Speyr being 'terrified' when 'she was asked for a consent that would extend itself blindly to everything that God might ordain for her'.[8] During the next four years, she was afflicted by stigmata which caused her great pain, and she experienced mystical insights into 'the interior sufferings of Jesus in all their fullness and diversity – whole maps of suffering were filled in precisely there where no more than a blank space or a vague idea seemed to exist'.[9] Eventually she became too exhausted to continue the dictations, and she appears to have spent the rest of her life until her death in 1964 in a state of slow and inexorable physical decline. Balthasar describes this experience as 'a vicarious dying which extended over decades and which, viewed physically, was inconceivably terrifying'.[10]

In Roten's study of their relationship, in which he is careful to absolve Speyr of any '"emprise" over Balthasar . . . much less any sensual dependence',[11] he refers to the 'objective intimacy'[12] of their relationship. Roten describes the supernatural dimensions of Speyr's experiences – visions of St Ignatius and Mary, transportations and bi-locations – without irony or any suspension of belief, and his account of their relationship draws on Speyr's descriptions of her Ignatian visions as if these could be taken entirely at face value. Referring to a mysterious wound that Speyr received below her left breast as a young woman, Roten writes:

> Concerning the wound Adrienne received at the age of fifteen and which she vicariously bears for Hans Urs von Balthasar, Ignatius observed that this was appropriate in a double mission. Since both were virginal, this was the way for the woman to be marked by the sign of the man. The very concrete symbolism of man and woman was retranslated into theological categories: to explain her mission with Hans Urs von Balthasar, Adrienne compared herself to the Church, which was given to Christ by God the Father (in the comparison, 'Christ' means von Balthasar), to be his companion on earth in order that he may have on earth a sign of the presence of the Father.[13]

To the best of my knowledge, this is a unique example of a male confessor appropriating to himself the place of Christ in a woman mystic's relationship to God. In the writings of all the great women mystics such as Teresa of Avila, Catherine of Siena and Thérèse of Lisieux, there is a direct nuptial relationship with Christ that is never mediated through their confessors or spiritual directors, and indeed, very often the struggle to realize a mystic's vision or calling is played out in the form of a conflict with the male priests and confessors who oppose her. I think this should be seen as evidence of the extent of Balthasar's control over Speyr, rather than as a model of Christian spirituality that could be supported by any appeal to tradition.

This virginal relationship, modelled on the nuptial relationship between Christ and the Church, was revealed by Ignatius to be 'a new basis for fecundity'[14] in which the 'child' was their shared mission in founding the Community of Saint John.[15] And if this relationship did not entail sexual intimacy, it apparently had a highly physical dimension, insofar as 'There are examples cited in Adrienne's diaries according to which she assumed personally von Balthasar's indispositions: "coughing, nausea, sore throat, and the like", to free her spiritual friend for his work'.[16] Roten sums up their double mission as being 'complementary in terms of their respective gender roles'.[17] He continues,

> The role of the woman (Adrienne von Speyr) was perceived as radically solitary and exclusive: the woman alone bears the fruit and brings it forth, she even has to bear the man's impossibility to participate in these acts . . . For Hans Urs von Balthasar and Adrienne von Speyr this common fruit was specifically the secular institute, christened the 'child' . . . This is, therefore, how Adrienne von Speyr and Hans Urs von Balthasar conceived the roles of man and woman in and for the kingdom of God – like two halves of the same moon – different and somehow terribly estranged from each other – making the other suffer because of it – and yet fruitful only together.[18]

What is the cost to the woman of this transaction? Is the fullness of life in Christ really discovered in the form of a sado-masochistic 'marriage' which condemns a woman to solitary hell so that a man's theology can bear fruit? A woman who even takes on his physical illnesses, despite herself being apparently at death's door? A woman whose body must be marked with a wound that is the sign of a man? Is this what the Catholic Church offers us, if we surrender ourselves to her ministry and teaching? Or should we rather recognize in Speyr's suffering and slow dying the extent to which there is, as Teresa Brennan argues in her study of Freud, a psychophysical dimension to these sexual stereotypes, so that Speyr became, quite literally, the embodiment of Balthasar's projected femininity?[19]

We should also bear in mind that this spiritual marriage with its virginal fecundity was being played out in Speyr's home, which she shared with her husband. Once again, there is a disjunction between the ostensibly incarnational nature of

Balthasar's theology, and its distance from any real human existence. This is a nuptial theology which, far from affirming the capacity of marriage to sanctify human sexuality, disrupts and even negates the claims of ordinary love and marriage, in aspiring for a spiritual marriage modelled on the 'suprasexual' relationship between Mary and Christ. But this metaphysical performance of a marriage is in fact an adultery and an infidelity – an act of spiritual fornication perhaps, redolent with the fears that Balthasar associates with female sexuality.

Hell and the female body

The female flesh represents an obstacle to Balthasar's feminized man in theodrama, and it is only through her elimination that the man can be freed from the bondage of human sexual embodiment with its intimations of mortality, vulnerability and death, to participate in the transcendence of the divine life. This seems like an extreme hypothesis, but to demonstrate its plausibility, let me consider the imagery of Balthasar's account of Christ's entry into hell on Holy Saturday, bearing in mind that this is an aspect of his theology which is heavily dependent on Speyr's visions.[20]

In his ambitious account of Christ in hell, Balthasar pushes the boundaries of theological language to its utmost. It is, as Graham Ward suggests, 'the strident darkness of clashing empty symbols'[21] (see Chapter 14), representing an attempt to explore the erasure of every sign and possibility of meaning, the utter abandonment and non-being of the state of death, as the prelude to the resurrection and the emergence of an altogether new form of presentation and representation on Easter Sunday.

Balthasar offers a dramatic refiguration of biblical and theological references to Sheol and hell, to justify his claim that Christ's 'going to the dead'[22] in hell (he deliberately avoids the word 'descent') signifies the utmost extreme of his solidarity with the dead. However, the epic style of Balthasar's account of Holy Saturday leads Ben Quash to argue that he

> tries to control the dazzling darkness with strategies that mitigate the drama . . . The irony of Balthasar's theology is that at the moment when it aims most concretely to concern itself with struggle, suffering and death, it also becomes most mythological. The Hell of Balthasar's theology of Holy Saturday is *outside* and *beyond* our own time: it is, in effect, 'totally remote'.[23]

Without disagreeing with Quash, I want to suggest that we must look more closely at the suggestion that Balthasar 'tries to control the dazzling darkness', and ask what that means for a gendered reading of his theology. If we look beyond its epic form, it can be read as the psychological struggle of the masculine religious imaginary against its feminine other, in ways which might also reflect Balthasar's personal situation. In this area where Speyr's influence on Balthasar is most apparent, do we see the dynamics of a relationship between the celibate man and the '*mystérique*', which invites an Irigarayan insight into his struggle?

This is the place where consciousness is no longer master, where, to its extreme confusion, it sinks into a dark night that is also fire and flames. This is the place where 'she' – and in some cases he, if he follows 'her' lead – speaks about the dazzling glare which comes from the source of light that has been logically repressed, about 'subject' and 'Other' flowing out into an embrace of fire that mingles one term into another, about contempt for form as such, about mistrust for understanding as an obstacle along the path of *jouissance* and mistrust for the dry desolation of reason; also about a 'burning glass'.

> [I]t is for/by woman that man dares to enter the place, to descend into it, condescend to it, even if he gets burned in the attempt. It is in order to speak woman, write to women, act as preacher and confessor to women, that man usually has gone to such excesses. That he has accepted the need to take the detour through metaphors that can scarcely be called figures. That he has given up his knowledge in order to attend to woman's madnesses. Falling – as Plato would say, no doubt,–into the trap of mimicking them, of claiming to find jouissance as 'she' does. To the point when he can no longer find himself as 'subject' anymore and goes where he had no wish to follow: to his loss in that a-typical, a-topical mysteria.[24]

Irigaray suggests that the female mystic represents to her male priest/confessor (Balthasar was both to Speyr) a source of irresistible but terrifying fascination, a place of chaos, madness and formlessness, which he enters only if he sacrifices his sense of subjectivity, coherence and meaning. In seeking to get inside the experience of Christ in hell (which is Speyr's experience), Balthasar finds himself drawn into the chaotic darkness of the female body: nowhere do we see more clearly the titanic struggle of the male subject who must resist what he desires most, in order to ensure that 'he' does not lose himself to 'her'.

Balthasar interprets Christ's 'going to the dead' as 'the efficacious outworking in the world beyond of what was accomplished in the temporality of history'.[25] Beyond the mythological interpretations that have accumulated around the idea of a divine descent into an underworld in Christianity as well as in other religions, Balthasar sees 'the idea of a *struggle* between the divinity which descends into the underworld, and the power hostile to God which is vanquished there and must yield up either the menaced or imprisoned divinity itself, or some other prey'.[26] Death is characterized in the New Testament by 'its lust to seize and hold (*krateisthai*): but God is stronger than death',[27] so that, in the resurrection, 'a voracious power is obliged to recognize its impotence to hold its prey'.[28] In hell, Christ in the state of death is powerless, and utterly dependent upon God's

Sex, death and melodrama 169

redemptive power. Being dead is 'a being in the abyss',[29] a condition of solidarity with the dead which is beyond all representation and signification: 'among the dead, there is no living communication'.[30] While Christ's suffering in the Passion was active, his suffering in hell is passive, not 'an active struggle against the "powers of Hell"'[31] but a becoming one with the reality of sin: 'In this amorphous condition, sin forms what one can call the second "chaos"'.[32] In entering hell, Christ does not enter a populated hell but 'the pure substantiality of "Hell" which is "sin in itself"'.[33] Balthasar goes on to search for images that might express something of the nature of this hell that is the very substance of sin:

> Plato and Plotinus created for this the expression *borboros* (mud, ordure) which the Church Fathers took up. Likewise, the image of chaos is a natural one here. In another image still, Eriugena says that, in our redemption, 'all the leprosy of human nature was thrown to the Devil'. And when the great harlot of Babylon, as quintessence of the sin of the world, 'has fallen', and 'has become a dwelling place of demons, a haunt of every foul spirit', when she has been abandoned on all sides to be 'burned with fire' in 'pestilence and mourning and famine' (Apocalypse 18, 2, 8), when men see, at first only from 'far off' the 'smoke of her burning' (18, 9 and 17), when she is 'thrown down' and is 'found no more' (v. 21), when the smoke arising from her 'goes up for ever and ever' (19, 3) we have beneath our eyes the ultimate image to which Scripture has recourse in the representation of pure evil's self-consumption. Of that self-consumption, A. Gügler, the disciple of Herder and Sailer, painted a great tableau, using the palette of the Romantic philosophy of nature. He describes Hell as the final 'residue and phlegm which it is absolutely impossible to restore to life' and where the 'hate which belongs to enemies is absolutely objectified'. For what is consumed can no longer be kindled again by contact with a Living One. It can no longer do anything more than consume itself eternally like a flame that is darkly self-enclosed, 'to engulf for ever in the empty abyss the final burnt out relics of all that can be burned'.[34]

Mud. Ordure. Chaos. Leprosy. Phlegm. But above all, 'quintessence of the sin of the world', 'the ultimate image', 'pure evil': the harlot. The sexual female body is not in hell, she is hell. She is that rapacious, consuming power against which Christ must pit his masculinity, his divinity and his transcendence. In all creation, she is the one thing that is not redeemed, for she is the space which does indeed consume him in the end, and only her total destruction will allow his release. She is that space which is, as Quash suggests, 'outside and beyond' time, that fluctuating, oscillating space/time enigma who interrupts the phallic trajectory of his being towards God by reminding him that he is being towards death. Briefly (if such a word makes any sense in this time out of time), she appears to triumph over him, dissolving his manly 'I' in the chaos of her non-being, so that he becomes her, at that furthest extreme from his being God. He/she is 'the pure substantiality of "Hell" which is "sin in itself"'.

Balthasar's struggle

If, as so many of his interpreters assure us, Balthasar's theology is one with his life, so that the relationship between the sexes in his work is mirrored in the relationship between Balthasar and Speyr, we might turn to his early work, *Heart of the World*, written in 1945, to gain a deeper insight into the tensions that inform his representation of hell. Andrew Louth suggests that *Heart of the World* is a striking foreshadowing of his more mature work, and 'an uncanny crystallization of the vision of Adrienne von Speyr'.[35] Peter Henrici describes it as 'the first thing to be written entirely under the influence of Adrienne's visions'.[36] In the Translator's Note, written in 1979, Erasmo Leiva waxes lyrical about the beauty of this book's style, referring to 'that happy union between beauty of expression and profundity of content that characterizes his [Balthasar's] theology'.[37] Leiva also sees this as a highly personal work, for 'in revealing to us the Heart of the World he could not do less than bare his own heart. The poetic form of the work, in particular, strikes us with its intimate tone.'[38] That is indeed a revealing insight, with regard to a work which I suspect would strike many modern readers as excessively self-indulgent and morose, but which suggests something of the spiritual and sexual struggle that Balthasar projects into so much of his theology, because he is a man torn between sex and death, desire and conquest, masculine aggression and feminine seduction. If this were nothing more than a psychological insight into the life of one Catholic priest and his mysterical female companion it would provide material for a slightly salacious biography and little more. But Balthasar's theology profoundly influences the ways in which some Catholic thinkers, including the new feminists, the last Pope and the new Pope, understand the significance of human sexuality, and it is important to ask what the implications of this might be for the Church's sacramental and ethical life.

Heart of the World is written as a series of dialogues which use different narrative voices to explore the relationship between Christ, the Church and the individual Christian, the latter speaking as one in the depths of sin and self-loathing, but also in a voice that is ambiguously situated between the sinner addressing Christ, and Christ addressing God the Father.[39]

Balthasar's 'man' describes himself in Pauline language as one 'imprisoned under the law of sin which reigns in my members'.[40] He speaks from a 'prison', a 'deep cavern of despair' within which, beneath his surface appearance of calm, 'there swarms a putrid rabble that hates the light; wasted opportunities, rejected graces, invincible dejection – the smell of putrefaction'.[41] This man's ego is in turmoil, for it feels itself being called out of its prison and yet, while he would gladly surrender his body, he cannot imagine himself without his soul. He tells God, 'You cannot exact the impossible feat that I should migrate out of myself.'[42] But God offers a fatherly response to this son's pleading, and perhaps we hear an anticipation of Balthasar's/Speyr's vision of hell here:

> I have tasted your prison; nothing of its bittersweet smell of decay was spared me. I have wandered through even the deepest chamber of all the prisons of all those who, in despair, have struggled against God's freedom. Down below in the lowest part of you, in the lightless disgrace of your impotence and your refusal, there have I chosen my abode.[43]

Nevertheless, despite this assurance, the tormented sinner believes that he has betrayed Christ's love so that he no longer belongs even among the 'communion of sinners' who, along with the communion of saints, are redeemed by the '*One* life of warm guilt and of warm remorse [which] throbs through them all'. But 'I have been expelled from this communion of sinners. Stiff and frozen, rolled up lump-like, I cower to the side: my sin is without comparison.'[44]

However, as we read on, it becomes clear that this abjection – which occupies an extremity beyond saint and sinner, beyond expression, where all is 'frozen' and 'lump-like' – is an attempt once again to articulate the condition even beyond death that constitutes the abyss of Holy Saturday, an abyss in which a glimmer appears as the first sign of resurrected life:

> What is this light glimmer that wavers and begins to take form in the endless void? It has neither content nor contour. A nameless thing, more solitary than God, it emerges out of pure emptiness. It is no one. It is anterior to everything. Is it the beginning? It is small and undefined as a drop. Perhaps it is water. But it does not flow. It is not water. It is thicker, more opaque, more viscous than water. It is also not blood, for blood is red, blood is alive, blood has a loud human speech. This is neither water nor blood. It is older than both, a chaotic drop. Slowly, slowly, unbelievably slowly the drop begins to quicken. We do not know whether this movement is infinite intrigue at death's extremity or the first beginning – of what? Quiet, quiet! Hold the breath of your thoughts! It's still much too early in the day to think of hope. The seed is still much too weak to start whispering about love. But look there: it is indeed moving, a weak, viscous flow. It's still much too early to speak of a wellspring. It trickles, lost in the chaos, directionless, without gravity. But more copiously now. A wellspring in the chaos. It leaps out of pure nothingness, it leaps out of itself.[45]

172 *The end*

Alleluia! Christ has come again!

But let us not be too hasty – let us have no premature ejaculations. 'The magic of Holy Saturday. The chaotic fountain remains directionless.'[46] This is not yet the Second Coming. Rather, it is the beginning of the new creation, and this trickle of life must struggle against the temporality and carnality of history, 'love trickling on in impotence, unconsciously, laboriously, towards a new creation that does not yet even exist'.[47] But still, it is growing stronger all the time, surging towards that ultimate fulfilment and triumph:

> The spring leaps up even more plenteously. To be sure, it flows out of a wound . . . But the wound no longer causes pain . . . Only the wound is there: gaping, the great open gate, the chaos, the nothingness out of which the wellspring leaps forth. Never again will this gate be shut. Just as the first creation arose ever anew out of sheer nothingness, so, too, this second world – still unborn, still caught up in its first rising – will have its sole origin in this wound, which is never to close again. In the future, all shape must arise out of this gaping void, all wholeness must draw its strength from the creating wound. High-vaulted triumphal Gate of Life! Armoured in gold, armies of graces stream out of you with fiery lances. Deep-dug Fountain of Life! Wave upon wave gushes out of you inexhaustible, ever-flowing, billows of water and blood baptizing the heathen hearts, comforting the yearning souls, rushing over the deserts of guilt, enriching over-abundantly, overflowing every heart that receives it, far surpassing every desire.[48]

Here, Balthasar's imagery becomes unstable. Is this a phallic triumph over the abysmal chaos of the female body, or is it an act of symbolic reclamation in which the 'gaping wound' of the female sex becomes instead the 'creating wound' from which 'all wholeness' draws strength? Is this a beginning or an ending – an ejaculation replete with its connotations of sex and death, or an act of giving birth that might open beyond this deadly masculine imaginary? Might it be an act of sacramental reconciliation that goes beyond such dualisms, to a fluidity of sexual imagery that begins to express something of the trans-gendering of desire and difference that circulates within God, between God and creation, and between human bodies, in the story of redemption? Louth, who quotes this passage, sees it as an intertwining of two themes:

> that in the God-forsakenness of the Son, the Chaos that stretches between the Father and the Son is the Holy Spirit, and that this provides the principle for the new life that is the fruit of the Trinity's embrace of the world in all its sinfulness and fallenness. But there is too, the exploitation of the mystery of the theme of the mystery of birth. The mystery of birth is central in Balthasar's understanding of the Trinity, of the creation and of the re-creation, as this passage makes clear.[49]

This suggestion will become of central significance in the next section, when I move towards a possible feminist refiguration of some of these themes. But at this stage, we must recognize with Irigaray the cost of this insight to the woman through whom the man has access to it:

> can life go on in such violence, however sweet it may be? Does one not die from dying, or die from not dying? . . . The bottom, the center, the most hidden, inner place, the heart of the crypt to which 'God' alone descends when he has renounced modes and attributes. For this most secret virginity of the 'soul' surrenders only to one who also freely offers the self in all its nakedness. This most private chamber opens only to one who is indebted to no possession for potency. It is wedded only in the abolition of all power, all having, all being, that is founded elsewhere and otherwise than in this embrace of fire whose end is past conception. Each becomes the other in consumption, the nothing of the other in consummation . . . But how to remember all this if the fire was so fierce, the current so strong as to remove all traces? If everything has become fire and water and nothing remains but a burning shimmer and flowing stream?[50]

Casta meretrix

Balthasar's Christ rises as a seminal flow or a maternal act of giving birth – which, or both? – from the matrix of hell, but this is not yet the eschaton. Eschatologically, the harlot sin has been consumed by fire and nothing remains of her, but between the resurrection and the eschaton stretches the life of the earthly Church: 'While I was feeble beyond all conceivable weakness, my Bride, the Church, was growing strong.'[51] This is not yet the Virgin Bride, for like Eve, the people within her succumb to the craving for glory and power: 'How sweet the song of the ancient serpent: "You will have knowledge and be like gods!"'[52] The dissolution and disintegration of Christ's death and the victory of his resurrection mean that his power now fills the universe, and everyone who lives is alive in him. But the world continues in its same old ways, full of 'hatred and lust . . . , frozen and seething' with hearts that 'turn to stone, rot and decompose'.[53] So, having gained absolute victory, Christ must still battle against the lustful, wayward flesh in order to fulfil what he has already achieved, and that means that Christ must conquer the Bride.

Towards the end of *Heart of the World* there is a chapter called 'The Conquest of the Bride'. Here, Balthasar writes as Christ in the first person, and he describes the battle between Christ and his Bride, the earthly Church. 'Christ' says to the Church, 'a slap in your face can elicit from you but an embarrassed smile. Disgrace covers the length of you, all the more poignantly as you try to deny it, pretending nothing is amiss.'[54] There follows a prolonged tirade in which 'Christ' berates the Church and celebrates his conquest over her:

174 *The end*

> It is with you, my Body, that I am forever fighting the great, apocalyptic battle . . . I, the strong God, have betrayed myself to you – my Body, my Church – and in the place where I did this I became weak: there alone could I be wounded to the death. In that place I yielded, I surrendered to the temptation of . . . delivering myself up to the obscure chaos of a body, of plunging below the shiny surface of the flesh; the temptation of passing over into this world – this simmering darkness, opposed to the Father's light . . . I dared to enter the body of my Church, the deadly body which *you* are . . . No wonder you realized your advantage over me and took my nakedness by storm! But I have defeated you through weakness and my Spirit has overpowered my unruly and recalcitrant flesh. (Never has woman made more desperate resistance!) . . . Our wrecked covenant – our blood-wedding, the red wedding of the Lamb – is already, here and now, the white bridal bed of divine love.[55]

Thus nuptial love between Christ and the Church is represented as a sado-masochistic 'blood-wedding', consummated in an act of rape during which the woman's body is conquered by the Bridegroom.

I am not suggesting that the language of passionate sexuality and eroticism has no place in Christian spirituality. I am arguing that Balthasar's imagery is pornographic, not erotic. Compare, for example, Catherine of Siena's mysticism, in which she repeatedly uses images of blood and fire. Referring to 'the sweet Lamb who bled to death with such burning love',[56] she writes that 'the sweet bride reclines on the bed of blood and fire, and the secret of the heart of God's Son is laid bare'.[57] Such language might strike modern ears as anachronistic and perhaps too visceral for comfort, but I would argue that it lacks that particular quality of sexual violence that is so shocking in Balthasar. Ultimately, Catherine's love for Christ is consummated in passionate tenderness, not in her rape by him.

One of Balthasar's most original contributions to modern theology (alongside that of Holy Saturday) is his retrieval of the medieval idea of the Church as *casta meretrix*, the chaste whore (sometimes translated as the chaste whore). Here he uncritically reiterates some of the most misogynistic and disturbing imagery in the scriptural and theological tradition, drawing selectively on a range of sources to put together a flamboyant rhetoric of depravity and sin associated with the prostitution of the Church, in which the full extent of his dread of the female body is exposed.

For example, he quotes extensively from the work of the Bishop of Paris, William of Auvergne (thirteenth century). William condemns the clergy who, in Balthasar's paraphrasing, 'prostitute Holy Church, because for squalid gain they invite all and sundry to shame her. And so her nipples are cracked and her breasts torn out, in a word.'[58] There follows a long quotation from William, in which the Church is described in the words of Jeremiah: 'You had a harlot's forehead; you would not blush' (Jer. 3:3), and in the words of Isaiah: 'Babylon, my beloved, has become an abomination to me' (Isa. 21:4). The following gives a flavour of what this lengthy diatribe amounts to:

> For God himself she has become an abomination. Is there anyone who would not be beside himself with horror at the sight of the Church with a donkey's head, the believer's soul with the teeth of a wolf, the snout of a pig, furrowed ashen cheeks, the neck of a bull, and in every other respect so bestial, so monstrous, that a person seeing it would freeze with terror . . . Heretics call the Church 'whore' and 'Babylon' because of the appalling scandal of the Church being overrun by the degenerate and carnal, a mob so large, riffraff so noisy, that the other members of the Church are hidden and cannot be seen . . . We are no longer dealing with a bride but with a monster of terrible deformity and ferocity.[59]

J. Cheryl Exum, in her analysis of what she calls the 'Prophetic Pornography' of the Old Testament prophets, offers a commentary that is particularly relevant here. She points to the complicity of modern biblical scholars in justifying the pornographic violence with which Yahweh describes the sins of his wife, Israel, and the punishments due to her. Exum refers to 'the ethical problems raised by passages in which a male deity is pictured as sexually abusing a female victim',[60] and she argues that this means considering questions of gender bias, not only in representation, but more particularly in interpretation. In other words, whatever these texts reveal about attitudes to female sexuality in ancient Israel, we also need to ask what their interpretation reveals about attitudes to female sexuality in contemporary biblical studies and theology. Analysing the interpretations of (predominantly male) Old Testament scholars, Exum offers a number of examples to support her argument that 'Typically these commentators either ignore the difficulties posed by this divine sexual abuse or reinscribe the gender ideology of the biblical texts; usually they do both in their ceaseless efforts to justify God.'[61] She goes on to suggest that

> Regardless of how we decide to respond to it, sexual violence of which God is the perpetrator and the nation personified as a woman is the object, along with its destructive implications for gender relations, is there. It cannot be dismissed by claiming that it is only 'metaphorical', as if metaphor were some kind of container from which meaning can be extracted, or as if gender relations inscribed on a metaphorical level are somehow less problematic than on a literal level.[62]

If one applies Exum's critique to Balthasar, then one might question not only why he reclaims with such apparent relish the idea of the *casta meretrix* and inscribes it into contemporary ecclesiology, but why none of his male translators and those who study him criticize this imagery. I have no doubt that many reading this book will by now be as nauseated as I am by these quotations, but I can find no evidence of such nausea among his devoted readers.

But there is a further point Exum picks up on, that is also relevant here. Exum refers to Robert Carroll's argument that women in the prophetic texts are 'metaphors, not persons',[63] and she goes on to explore the implications of acknowledging that 'The imagery of graphic sexual violation and abuse of a woman by a theologically justified abusive husband-deity is not addressed to women. It is, as Carroll recognizes, addressed to "essentially a male community".'[64] She continues,

> The way to insult a man is to call him a woman. You insult him more if you call him a filthy whore who is going to have her genitals exposed, which is what these prophetic accusations do. Already inscribed in the metaphors themselves is a whole range of negative views about women and about female behavior and female sexuality, as well as about power in gender relations: men dominate and women submit.[65]

The earthly Church is, as we have already seen, a community of men acting up as women, men in drag perhaps. It is the institutional, Petrine Church, personified in Peter's absence from the cross and his denial of Christ. So Balthasar's sexual tirade is actually a metaphorical assault on men, who suffer the ultimate indignity of being portrayed as a raped and ravaged female body, subdued and conquered by the male God. 'The Conquest of the Bride' is a fantasy of male rape, and the female flesh is the abyss, the non-being, upon which this fantasy is inscribed.

But again, this can only be partly true, because the woman is not absent from this scene, she is a formative influence behind the scenes. In *First Glance at Adrienne von Speyr*, there is a section titled 'Adrienne's Disposition in Confessing (*She is speaking under obedience*)'.[66] Balthasar writes of the necessity of 'an overall surrender' and goes on to say that 'during the confession itself, Adrienne frequently experiences that her surrender (in confession) changes into a being-taken by God'.[67] There follows a detailed explanation of Speyr's language and behaviour – her 'nakedness in confession', when

> the penitent is immersed in the slimy reality of universal sin. That is inherent in the atmosphere of the sacrament. For that reason, too, I must forgo the attempt to make myself naked: I am covered with slime up to my neck. And when you look at me, you see me covered with all these sins . . . Thus my being covered with the slime of sins acquires the character of a different nakedness. I was naked before in disclosing my sins; and more naked still when God uncovered more than I intended to uncover. But now I have to

Sex, death and melodrama 177

draw something out from this slime, call special attention to it, otherwise my relation to this slime will not be evident. I must expose that part of me that comes in contact with it . . . And in this nakedness even I see something of what I had not seen until now. It is as if I had a birthmark somewhere on my body where I could not see. God, however, can undress me and tell me, 'There is a spot which you must confess.'

It may also happen that you would like to reveal everything down to the last detail and the confessor says that it is sufficient to take off the left stocking, etc. That strikes me as an incomprehensible choice . . . You must learn that you cannot shape everything yourself, that confession is the very place where you are decidedly being shaped, and that a reversal of expectations may follow in its wake.[68]

This strange passage, written under obedience to Balthasar,[69] is redolent with sexual innuendo. The last paragraph is sexually provocative, implying that Speyr wants to reveal more of her nakedness than Balthasar can accept, thus creating a peculiar reversal between the confessor ('you' in this paragraph), and the one who confesses. The chapter ends by comparing the secrecy of the confessional to the secrecy of the sex act:

Just as a fruit, a pregnancy and birth, must follow the sexual act between husband and wife, which, of course, takes place and remains in secrecy, so an evident fruit must come forth from the secrecy of confession – which will be divulged no more than the secrecy of the sexual act.[70]

Speyr in the confessional represents, not the virginal Marian Church, but the *casta meretrix*, naked and immersed as she is in 'the slimy reality of universal sin', which is, as we have seen, the hell of the female sex. What does her confessor, Balthasar, 'Christ', see when he looks at her in this state? Does he see the 'abomination', the whore with whom he is 'forever fighting the great, apocalyptic battle'? Does this confessor, *in loco Christi*, experience in the woman before him 'the temptation of delivering myself up to the obscure chaos of a body'? The slimy sinfulness of the woman threatens the confessor priest, making him want to stop her in her advances. But this is an act of sexual consummation which takes away his advantage and refuses to allow him control, insisting on 'a reversal of expectations'. So he now begins to experience the helplessness of Christ, who rails at his Bride as she sexually overwhelms him.

Speyr bears a vicarious wound for Balthasar, just as the Church is engraved by Christ with the mark of his love. Balthasar loves Speyr, as Christ loves the Church. And therefore Balthasar must make her body his own, must ensure that no vestige of sexual femininity survives the absorption of her life into his: 'Live not from yourself; live solely in me and from me. Think of yourself no longer as of the one you used to be . . . Become obedient even to death.'[71]

Balthasar describes Speyr's increasing exhaustion, her 'sense of powerlessness', in the prolonged torment of her dying:

> From one year to the next the conviction grew — the absolute rock-bottom of human endurance had been reached. But always this point was lowered once again to new depths. Besides the increasingly severe pain — her body was like an organ on which all, and in fact constantly new and unsuspected, stops of suffering had been pulled out — there was the also increasing sense of powerlessness, of 'not being able to go on', of 'excessive demand': expressions which also repeatedly appear in her writings, and whose ultimate seriousness she now experienced . . . It was an inconceivably protracted diminuendo, which became ever softer and softer. A dying in the slowest of all slow motion.[72]

If Balthasar's theology is indeed autobiographical, if his theo-drama is a script to be performed in the living narrative of the individual and communal life of faith, then this slow and painful dying of the woman is not incidental to the plot, but an inevitable consequence of the role she must perform. Her sexual body is an encumbrance and a temptation to him, while her wounded body is a receptacle for his spirituality:

> The spiritual fecundity of the man will be put into the flesh of the woman, in order that it may be fruitful. In this sense, Hans Urs von Balthasar's fecundity was laid into the wound which Adrienne von Speyr had received for him.[73]

She exists to awaken him to his own maternal-femininity, his 'Marian personality structure'.[74] Speyr was, says Roten, 'the link between Mary and Hans Urs von Balthasar',[75] and indeed, 'Most of von Balthasar's specific and autonomous Marian writings were published after the death of Adrienne von Speyr.'[76]

Speyr is the living out of Balthasar's theology of woman. She is not a person in her own right, but a being who is given to the man in order that he can discover his own 'feminine' self even as he drains away her life. It is consistent with this that, upon the death of her body, he should ensure the continuation of her womanly voice as one indistinguishable from his own. I am not denying that Speyr was suffering from a number of physical ailments which eventually caused her death,[77] but I am arguing that the nature of her suffering can also be interpreted as a terrible mimesis of his dramatic representation of woman, a psychosomatic living out of his theology of woman. Summarizing her dying years (which in fact constituted more than half of the twenty-four years she spent with Balthasar), Roten writes, 'During the later years, from 1949 until Adrienne's death, there are but few salient events to be mentioned . . . Adrienne's theological mission after the years of the "great dictations" seemed to be largely accomplished.'[78] In other words, the beginning of Speyr's decline coincides with the end of her 'theological mission' and her usefulness to Balthasar.

The female sex as other

So far, I have focused exclusively on the question of female sexuality from the perspective of Balthasar's representation of hell, sin and embodiment. However, there is one last critical question I want to raise – and this may be the most challenging of all if one bears in mind the context in which he was writing. In the medieval Church, the idea of the fallen woman or the harlot was used to describe everything which was perceived to threaten the unity of the Church (*ecclesia*) or to resist the salvation that she offered. Balthasar develops his ideas about the *casta meretrix* under the title, 'The Eve Motif: Heresy as Harlotry',[79] explaining that the Fathers 'had the elemental feeling that heresy, the ruining of the ecclesial mind, is an intensely dangerous spiritual fornication'.[80] He quotes Paul's words in 2 Cor. 11:2–3:

> I feel a divine jealousy for you, for I betrothed you to Christ to present you as a pure bride to her one husband. But I am afraid that, as the serpent deceived Eve by his cunning, your minds will be corrupted and led astray from simplicity toward Christ.[81]

Balthasar goes on to explain that

> The unity of the Church is the 'simplicity [*haplotês*] of your spirit' toward the Bridegroom. Alien doctrine under the cloak of Christ, of the Spirit, of the gospel, means the ruination of this bridal simplicity and thus the disintegration of the ecclesial mind, the pursuit of an alien spirit, infidelity, adultery – this time in the image of the primal infidelity, the infidelity of Eve.[82]

With reference to patristic writers, particularly Origen, he explores an elaborate symbolic association between heresy, apostasy and fornication. The Christian life, although inspired and made holy by the Marian dimension of the Church, is nevertheless constantly threatened by the behaviour of Eve. The dialectic that runs through the individual Christian life and positions the Church in the world is therefore – at least implicitly – shown to be that between the virgin and the whore – the chaste, 'spiritual' woman, and the sexual, 'historical' woman – who between them represent 'the frontier between holiness and heresy' which 'runs through every member of the Church . . . ' True, the Church has her grounding

180   *The end*

in Mary, but in her members she constantly tends to lapse back into being Eve, or at best to strive upward from Eve to Mary.[83]

Balthasar refers to Origen's suggestion that

> Jesus addresses the synagogue not just as 'evil' but as an 'adulterous generation' (Mt 11:39). And so 'the Word of God abandons the synagogue of the Jews and goes off to take a "wife of harlotry", the people, that is to say, of the Gentiles, who were harlots when Zion was still a faithful city' (*Comm. in Matt.* 12:4).[84]

We have here an example of the intricate interweaving of the harlot and the bride imagery, insofar as the harlots are the gentiles, not the Jews. Balthasar is insistent that the harlot is not only external to the Church: more importantly, the tension between the bride and the harlot is inherent within every Christian individual and within the body of the Church. But, by the Middle Ages, the contrast between the harlot and the bride had come to symbolize, among other things, the relationship between *synagoga* and *ecclesia*, with *ecclesia* being represented as a crowned woman and *synagoga* being blindfold to signify moral or spiritual blindness, often with the broken tablets of the law in her hands and a fallen crown. The following two descriptions, taken from a website, make clear the anti-Judaism inherent in this imagery. The first refers to a wood carving on the choir benches of Erfurt Cathedral, Thuringia, Germany, dating from around 1400–10:

> Ecclesia on a horse is attacking the Synagogue with a lance. Her shield carries the Christian symbol of a fish. The Synagogue is symbolized as riding a pig. Her eyes are closed and with her left hand she holds on to a branch.

The second description is of a church window in St John's Church in Werben/Elbe River, Germany, and it dates from between 1414 and 1467:

> In the left section of the window the Church is riding a tetramorph (a creature with the heads of eagle, human, lion and bull, symbolizing the four Gospels). She holds the flag of the cross and the chalice in her hands. The divine hand from heaven places a crown on her head.
>
> In the right section the Synagogue is depicted as riding a donkey which is about to break down. In her right hand she holds the head of a he-goat. Her crown is falling. She is blindfolded. The staff of her flag is broken. But worst of all, the divine hand from heaven pierces her head and body with the sword of judgment.[85]

These images resonate with those of William of Auvergne, which Balthasar quotes with such relish in his description of the *casta meretrix*. Let us remember the context in which Balthasar invokes his images of harlotry, hell, apostasy, heresy and sin. He was writing in the heart of Europe after the Holocaust. Let us remember what happens to the harlot's body in Balthasar's hell, where she burns with fire and 'men see . . . the "smoke of her burning"', a burning which signifies 'her' total annihilation: 'what is consumed can no longer be kindled again by contact with a Living One'.

I am not suggesting a direct link between medieval anti-Jewish imagery and the Holocaust, although there are serious questions as to the relationship between the two.[86] I am questioning how it is possible for a Germanic Christian thinker to rehabilitate such language after the 1940s.[87] In a discussion of Balthasar's Christology in *Theo-drama II/2* and *III*, Donald MacKinnon acknowledges that he does not directly address the 'horrors' of the murder of six million Jews in the years 1933–45, but MacKinnon goes on to suggest that 'the nervous tension of the whole argument bears witness to the author's passionate concern to present the engagement of God with his world in a way that refuses to turn aside from the overwhelming, pervasive reality of evil'.[88] In an appendix written subsequently, after having had access to *Theodramatik V*, MacKinnon adds that Balthasar 'is one of those Christian theologians who never, as they treat of the mysteries of their God, allow their reader to forget that this century is marked indelibly in history as that of Auschwitz, Maidanek and Treblinka'.[89]

No matter how much truth there might be in this hypothesis, I am suggesting that the violent force of Balthasar's rhetoric and imagery raises profound questions about his psychological and spiritual health, and his historical and political awareness. I am inclined to sympathize more with Alan Ecclestone, who, commenting on Balthasar's work *Prayer*, argues that

> while von Balthasar insists that 'contemplation does not aim at remoteness from the earth', nor 'does it see earthly reality as a mere shadow, or maybe a screen shrouding the world of heaven', it is difficult to see where this earthly reality is seriously encountered. Conditions of work, war, sickness, politics, sex, racialism and deprivation do not enter into the discussion of how prayer is to be exercised. Yet these are the actual conditions in which the nature of love is perceived, in which men rise or fail to rise to its occasions. There is a timelessness which ignores the pressures of time and circumstance upon changing ageing human beings, so that the day to day dying which is so real a part of our lives gets little attention.[90]

Quash comes to a similar conclusion, referring to

> that recurrent epic tendency in Balthasar's thought, which is prepared to sacrifice some of the existential, unfinalizeable, dialogical seriousness of human self-determination. Attention is diverted from the struggles and suffering that characterize the social and material aspects of human history, and the structural and political aspects of sin are not considered.[91]

182 *The end*

Balthasar is lauded as the theologian who restored beauty to theology, but his theological vision is threaded through with themes of violence and tragedy. In his discussion of art and beauty, he argues for the necessity of art expressing ugliness as well as beauty, for 'right at the center of our existence in the world, there is the ugly, the grotesque, the demonic, the immoral and ultimately the sinful'.[92] He argues that 'The hideous form [*Ungestalt*] is part of the world's form [*Gestalt*], and so it must be included, essentially, among the themes and subject matter of artistic creation.'[93]

But Balthasar's treatment of suffering, tragedy and evil is a thoroughly metaphysical affair, concerned with philosophy, art and literature, but rarely touching on the fragility and vulnerability of ordinary human life in all its subtle chiaroscuro of joy and grief, hope and misery, redemption and despair. Seldom does his work communicate a sense of an ethical imagination capable of engaging with the actual events of his time, in a way that would make his theology relevant and meaningful to the realities of living as bodily, sexual and social beings in a muddled and complex world.

The indictment of theology

The real scandal of this theological vision, with its deep undercurrents of misogyny and sexual violence and its repellent ecclesiology, is its uncritical reiteration by a growing number of theologians, translators and interpreters, who appear either indifferent or oblivious to Balthasar's sexual violence. To give only one example, in a recent article in *Modern Theology*, Aristotle Papanikolaou offers a carefully developed reading of the idea of *kenosis* in the work of Daphne Hampson, Coakley and Balthasar, which he interprets in the context of recent writings about sexual abuse and violence against women. He acknowledges that theology has often been complicit in such violence, and he appears to offer a highly sympathetic reading of feminist arguments. Yet only in a footnote does he make any reference at all to the role of gender in Balthasar's theology, and the main thrust of his argument is to show that Balthasar's idea of *kenosis*, with its concept of the relational self, can be read in conjunction with Coakley – and against Hampson – to provide a non-abusive understanding of kenotic relationality. He claims that 'far from being meaningless in situations of abuse, Balthasar's understanding of *kenotic* personhood is the most adequate way to account for the healing of abused victims'.[94] This claim suggests a chilling insensitivity to the significance of language and metaphor for feminist theological analysis. I have tried to show that, far from being a healing experience, to read Balthasar as a woman, informed by feminist consciousness, is to experience a form of rhetorical sexual abuse that has profound consequences for the ways in which a woman as body might situate herself in the story of salvation. I wonder how many women readers have felt assailed in reading some of the quotations in this chapter? Even as I felt compelled to include them for the sake of strengthening my argument, I have felt myself recoiling in dismay from what felt like their pornographic assault on my own theological consciousness and on that of my readers.[95]

But this is not only about the denigration of female sexuality, for the female flesh symbolizes everything that is 'other' to the Church perceived as the Virgin Bride of Christ – heretic, harlot, apostate, Jew. From the beginning, the sexual body of Eve has been the negation against which Christianity has affirmed itself – 'death through Eve, life through Mary'.[96] In Balthasar's theology, Eve's expulsion is finally accomplished, through the imperative to lend justification to a theology which refuses sacramental significance to the female body. I cannot here develop the implications of this for Christian relationships with other religions, but to the extent that female sexuality is the unredeemed other of the Catholic faith, there will be no true peace and reconciliation in the Church until the men of the Church make peace with their own sexuality and with woman's incarnate capacity to be part of the sacramental revelation of God.

I referred in the Introduction to the instability inherent in Catholic theology, comparing it to Derrida's *pharmakon*. With this in mind, I now want to leave this dark scenario of woman's endings, in order to explore the possibility of new beginnings through a different reading of Balthasar. This does not rehabilitate his theology as far as feminism is concerned, but it does allow for a feminist reading of his work in order to discern the beginnings of a different story, a story of redemption that can indeed reach into the most profound areas of our human alienation, loss and desire, revealing what will one day be healed, allowing us to occupy that 'broken middle'[97] wherein we begin to discern the distant, fragile promise of the reconciliation of all things in Christ, beginning with the female body.

Let me end this chapter by quoting Irigaray. Although her words are addressed to Nietzsche, they are I believe an eloquent appeal to all men who, like Balthasar, seek to occupy the place of Christ in order to negate and appropriate the difference that woman represents:

> Endlessly, you turn back to that enigmatic question, but you never go on, you leave it still in the dark: who is she? who am I? How is that difference marked? Outside the struggle to the death with yourself-already-same. With the other you have already created for yourself as a possible adversary in your world.
>
> To begin, and again begin, each act with a duel, isn't this a dream of measuring your power? But in this face-to-face combat between likes, she whom you want to overcome has already disappeared. Your strength is already rated according to its power as mirage. Already you fight your visions, ghosts, and simulacra of every type. Already you forget the hatred that bends what you call the living to your will – to overcome life . . .
>
> So you become the Crucified One.[98]

Part III

The beginning

10 Being beyond death

From the post-apostolic Fathers of the Church to the theology of Balthasar, Christian men have for two thousand years been weaving a double narrative of sin and redemption, death and life, sexuality and virginity, temptation and obedience, around the figures of Eve and Mary. The old patristic motif, 'death through Eve, life through Mary', has given rise to a vast tradition of theology, art, literature, music and devotion focused on the association of the female body with sex, birth and death. Today, when the rich redemptive truths of the Christian faith have faded to watermarks on the edges of culture, Eve and Mary retain their subliminal power over women's lives as archetypes of the whore and the virgin, the bad mother and the good mother, the demonic and the godly, all revolving around the identification of sex with death, and the interruption of that deadly pairing through Mary's virginal motherhood.

I have explored the ways in which Balthasar develops this trend, with particular reference to his representation of sexual difference, his ecclesiology and his symbolic association of the sexual female body with death, sin and hell. In this final section of the book, I suggest the contours of a feminist theology beyond Balthasar, through the incorporation of the female body into language, representation and sacramental significance. This entails turning to different theoretical perspectives which might offer some insight into the ways in which gender functions in Balthasar's theology, in order to identify a process by which symbolic meanings might be turned around, and the silenced other of the Catholic faith might at last find words in which to reveal her role in the mystery of the drama of salvation. My intention is not to subject Balthasar's work to psychoanalytic scrutiny, nor to force his theology into a theoretical mould that would simply explain it away. Rather, by considering the ways in which feminist theorists analyse attitudes to women, maternity and embodiment embedded in western language and culture, I seek to identify certain resonances and resemblances which assist in a feminist critique of Balthasar. However, my purpose is not to dismiss his theology, but to ask how it is possible to transform his theo-drama, to allow his theology to become what perhaps it longs to be, by liberating it from its distorting and sometimes

188 The beginning

grotesque anxieties concerning the sexual female body and masculine identity. So, in what follows I seek a theological dialogue with various theoretical perspectives, keeping as my primary focus the problems that I have identified with Balthasar's theology, and asking how we might move from a theology of sexuality informed by conflict, violence and repression, to one in which male and female together might constitute the makings of a new sacramentality of being in the world.

I begin with the relationship between the mother and death, and the ways in which this feeds a culture of negativity and fear with regard to the sexual female body. This is the start of a complex interpretative task, for, unlike Protestant and post-Protestant theologies and philosophies, Balthasar's theology does not deny the significance of the maternal body in the making of culture and subjectivity. Indeed, insofar as Anglo-American feminist theory bears the distinctive marks of its evolution from Protestant and post-Protestant philosophy and theology, it affords a much less helpful resource for a critique of Catholic theology than French feminist perspectives.[1] But, notwithstanding its potentially rich maternal dimension, Balthasar's thought bears many of the hallmarks of a modern theological and cultural world view premised upon the denial of desire, embodiment, mortality and sexuality, and it is this denial which distorts his theology and makes it prey to the unacknowledged fears which haunt the male psyche with regard to the mother, the body and death.

Befriending death

The dualistic symbolics of the bad mother and the good mother, the devouring mother and the nurturing mother, is a common theme in the world's religions, and it is a significant feature in psychological theories, for example in the object relations theory of Melanie Klein,[2] as well as in the work of psycholinguists such as Irigaray and Kristeva who are more the focus of this particular study. It would seem to be part of our human condition to associate the mother with death as well as with life, in such a way that female sexuality too becomes charged with highly ambivalent meanings, often signifying death as well as delight for the man who yields to the woman's seductions. As Diane Jonte-Pace points out, 'Psychoanalysis did not invent or create the connection between woman and death; rather, it disclosed a persistent pattern.'[3]

Beverley Clack shows how this association between female sexuality and death predates the Christian tradition, so that in diverse ways both Greek and Christian thought are marked by a resistance to death which translates into a suspicion of sexuality in general and female sexuality in particular: 'Rather than see sexuality as something altogether different from death, linked with the processes of new life, an explicit connection has been made between human sexuality and the inevitability of death.'[4] With Christianity, this acquires added significance because of the association between the overcoming of death and the refusal of sex. For Augustine, 'the spiritual life involves resisting the sexual in order to conquer death'.[5] In seeking to go beyond these dichotomies, Clack argues that 'it is only by accepting that we are sexual and mortal beings that we shall be able to construct a truly meaningful life'.[6]

In common with some other feminist thinkers such as Jantzen and Ruether, Clack sees a connection between ideas of transcendence associated with the Christian hope of eternal life, and a negative attitude towards the physical world and sexual embodiment.[7] Over and against the models of transcendence that she associates with Plato and Augustine, Clack suggests that it is in Stoic thought represented by Seneca, and in the literary aspects of Freud's writings, that we might discover forms of transcendence within rather than outside physical life. Beyond both the Christian hope of immortality and modern culture's denial of death, she argues that, by philosophical reflection, by the communicative power of literature and in our relationships with one another, we can discover meaning through the decentring of the self and an acceptance of finitude and death: 'Rather than shoring up the self in the face of change and death, it becomes possible to throw ourselves unreservedly into life, finding in its very flux and change its meaning.'[8]

From the feminist perspective opened up by Clack, it is indeed possible to argue that Balthasar's theology reflects this orientation towards bodily transcendence and immortality, so that Christ's bodily encounter with death, symbolically represented by chaotic and devouring female sexuality, represents the ultimate humiliation of the male God. Nevertheless, I also want to suggest that the doctrine of the incarnation does not entail a choice between the Christian hope of immortality and a nihilistic acceptance of finitude and death. It invites us rather to weave a narrative of hope from within the bodily flux of our finite human lives, not through the deferral of meaning to some distant hereafter, but through the living expression of a faith which assures us that, in Christ, the very atoms and quarks of creation have become suffused with the divine life. Our bodies – finite, mortal and subject to decay – are nonetheless oriented towards eternity along with all of creation, and it is through our bodily senses that we encounter the eternal promise of God which suffuses the material world. This entails a prayerful gaze and a graced epistemology, which recognizes epiphanies of eternity in every act of knowing. In the words of Annie Dillard,

> It is a fault of infinity to be too small to find. It is a fault of eternity to be crowded out by time. Before our eyes we see an unbroken sheath of colors. We live over a bulk of things. We walk amid a congeries of colored things that part before our steps to reveal more colored things. Above us hurtle more things, which fill the universe. There is no crack.

Unbreakable seas lie flush on their beds. Under the Greenland icecap lies not so much as a bubble. Mountains and hills, lakes, deserts, forests, and plants fully occupy their continents. Where, then, is the gap through which eternity streams?[9]

From this perspective, death, for all its intimations of vulnerability, dependence and loss, is not a mortal enemy to be resisted but a presence to be befriended as life's constant companion. In the words of St Francis, she is 'sister death', and although Clack's analysis does indeed offer one way of befriending death, a theological perspective still says that, nonetheless, death is also a rebirth and a beginning. The death of Christ tells us that God, like us, is vulnerable to love's wounding and sorrow, but the resurrection of Christ whispers of a God whose dying is fecundity, rising again, and new life in the body.

Beyond necrophilia

There are similarities between Clack's feminist analysis of death and Jantzen's critique of 'necrophilia' in Christian theology and philosophy of religion, although Jantzen's analysis is more informed by psycholinguistic perspectives than that of Clack. In what follows, I explore Jantzen's ideas in engagement with the work of Lacan, since here we begin to discover profound resonances between psychoanalytic theory and Balthasar's theology.

Jantzen argues that, whether in the 'necrophilia' of religious perspectives with their quest to transcend the physicality and mortality of this life, or in the 'necrophobia' of contemporary culture which expresses itself in an evasion or denial of death,[10] there is a profoundly destructive obsession with death in western thought: 'the western intellectual tradition is obsessed with death and other worlds, a violent obsession that is interwoven with a masculinist drive for mastery'.[11] She demonstrates how, in both Freud and Lacan, there are complex and sometimes unacknowledged associations that link women, death and religion. Freud argues that the death-drive (*thanatos*),[12] which he associates with aggressive violence in men and with masochism in women, can be effectively sublimated through the civilizing influences of science, religion and art – although, in the age of scientific reason, religion is exposed as an anachronistic illusion and must yield to the more truthful knowledge of science. However, these different fields of endeavour are all primarily male pursuits, so that women, being less capable of sublimation, are more closely identified with self-sacrifice and death.[13] It is interesting in this connection to note the extent to which Balthasar's theology is indeed informed by the male-dominated aesthetics and ideas of western art, literature and philosophy: men achieve a sense of the transcendent presence of God through their artistic and intellectual endeavours, while women rest in being itself without creative initiative or revelatory potential, so that the female body becomes the antithesis of transcendence and beauty, for she becomes death.

Jantzen points out that 'Freud's account of death and of religion is more heavily gendered than he himself acknowledges.'[14] In his essay, 'The Future of an Illusion',[15] Freud depicts nature as a threatening and chaotic feminized force that civilization constantly struggles against. Individual human nature and nature as a whole have to be coerced and controlled in the interests of civilization: 'nature rises up against us, majestic, cruel and inexorable; she brings to our mind once more our weakness and helplessness, which we thought to escape through the work of civilization'.[16] It does not take a great leap of imagination to see in such ideas an implicit identification of nature with the devouring mother, and of civilization and individual subjectivity as a constant struggle to escape the mother's all-consuming presence. The resonances between Freud's depiction of man in nature and Balthasar's depiction of Christ in hell suggest the extent to which both these thinkers are situated in the context of a post-Enlightenment world view, in which the agonistic masculine individual must assert himself over and against the feminized forces of nature and the body which are bent on his destruction. For Balthasar, it is in the supreme God-man that the male spirit enters its last and deadly battle to conquer nature and the female flesh. In becoming flesh, the Word became feminine, sought to give shape and form to the feminine, but 'she' would not accept him. When her flesh devoured the Word, the Father intervened:

> The Word . . . came from above. It came from the fullness of the Father. In the Word there was no urge since it was itself the fullness. In him was light and life and love without lust, love which had compassion for the void, willing to fill up what was hollow. But it was the essence of the void itself to press on to fullness. It was a menacing void, a chasm fitted with teeth. The light came into the darkness, but the darkness had no eye for the light: it had only jaws.[17]

The Father God enables the Son, through an act of the most radical filial obedience to the Word, to achieve the ultimate victory by resuscitating him and releasing him from the desire of the flesh and the *vagina dentata* of hell: 'both Resurrection and Ascension are first described as a passive event: the active agent is God (the Father)'.[18] But this is an eschatological victory, and the Son's struggle against nature, the body and sex is written into the script of history for as long as the Church, the *casta meretrix*, remains on earth.

Freud attributes the development of religion to the emergence of the idea of strong father gods, eventually focusing on a single Father God, who provides protection against the elemental powers of nature in return for obedience to his law. From generation to generation people become psychologically invested in such a belief system, which Jantzen describes as 'a cosmic version of the Oedipal drama'.[19] Thus, argues Jantzen,

God/religion becomes the guarantor of civilization and its moral and legal system which keeps the death-drive in bounds. God, in such a system, must of course be firmly male, since civilization is built on the mastery of the 'female' chaos, nature, and death . . . Freud's understanding of civilization is wholeheartedly masculinist, and indeed *requires* the mastery of 'female' nature.[20]

In similar fashion, Balthasar's understanding of redemption *requires* Christ's 'mastery of "female" nature'.

Turning to Lacan, Jantzen points out that he, like Freud, represents religion in two different ways. On the one hand, it is associated with a deep longing identified as neurosis which should therefore be overcome, but on the other hand it serves to keep the death-drives in check and is therefore necessary to civilization.[21] Unlike Freud, the Lacanian emphasis is on social and linguistic constructs rather than on the opposition between civilization and nature, but for both thinkers, the death-drive is associated with the acquisition of language through the prohibition of maternal dependence and intimacy, in a way that sets up a close association between woman, religion and death: 'In Lacan it is even more obvious than in Freud that death is conceptually linked with the female, and attempts at mastery of death with mastery of the female.'[22] Let me trace these connections and associations, through a brief excursus into Lacan's thought.

The linguistic turn that Lacan brings about in his reading of Freud situates language and desire at the very heart of the psychoanalytic process, in protest against theorists such as Melanie Klein, whose focus on the mother–child relationship he sees as neglecting the centrality of desire and the castration complex to Freud's theory.[23] For Lacan, language comes about as a response to the social imperative to assume a unified but illusory subjective identity (which is always masculine), through entry into the symbolic order, as a way of masking the inchoateness of the pre-subjective or imaginary stage associated with the circulation of desire between mother and child. The acquisition of language is associated with what Lacan calls the mirror stage, because it begins with the infant's first external perception of itself as a separate individual, either through seeing its reflection in a mirror or through becoming aware of the way in which it is seen as separate by another, usually the mother.[24] Beyond the imaginary lies an even more primordial and inaccessible level of demand prior to any sense of differentiation or desire – the real – which is grounded in the primal sense of union with the mother.[25]

In Lacan's linguistic appropriation of Freud, the castration complex is associated, not with the biological penis but with the symbolic phallus. It is the one who is identified with possession of the phallus – an authoritarian father figure, who is not necessarily the paternal presence associated with the imaginary stage – who ruptures the relationship between mother and child, and who prevents the child from fulfilling its desire to be the exclusive object of the mother's desire for that which she lacks, the phallus.[26] The phallus thus marks the gap between the speaking subject and 'his' desire. It is a third term introduced into the mother–child relationship, representing the law that prohibits desire. But it is also a deception, insofar as the phallus itself *is* the object of desire. Although sexual difference is organized around the masculine subject who has the phallus and the feminine non-subject who lacks the phallus, nobody can in fact 'have' the phallus – it is not an organ or an object but a signifier, indeed *the* signifier, which holds in place the fragile illusion of masculine identity. Desire is focused on the infantile desire, not to *have* the phallus but to *be* the phallus, since that is the lack that constitutes the mother's desire. So the child's desire is not for the mother herself but to become the object of the mother's desire:

> Castration means first of all this – that the child's desire for the mother does not refer *to* her but *beyond* her, to an object, the phallus, whose status is first imaginary (the object presumed to satisfy her desire) and then symbolic (recognition that desire cannot be satisfied).[27]

Thus desire has as its ultimate focus, not the apparent object of desire but the unattainable (because illusory) object of the mother's desire – the phallus, associated with plenitude, union and satisfaction – and therefore desire is always deflected, never able to settle on its real object, moving restlessly from substitute to substitute. Lacan in his later work refers to the '*objet a*' or the '*objet petit a*', in order to suggest this process of deferral and displacement of desire through the operation of language.[28]

In his analysis of Lacan, Lee explains the linguistic function of the phallus as follows:

> the phallus is the ultimate *point de capiton*, the signifier that fixes the meaning of the signifying chains of every subject's discourse, by virtue of its being 'veiled' or repressed. The phallus is present beneath every signifier as the signifier that has been repressed, and as such every signifier in effect is a metaphor substituting for the phallus.
>
> As such a signifier, the phallus is not anything that any man or woman could possibly 'have' . . . Precisely because no one can *have* the phallus, it becomes that which all want to *be*. The phallus then serves to signify as well that fullness of being, that complete identity, the lack of which is the fact of our ineluctable want-of-being.[29]

Bearing in mind the preceding analysis of Balthasar's work in the context of theological constructs of masculinized divinity and feminized materiality, one can see why Irigaray suggests that the Lacanian Phallus has the same linguistic function as

'God': 'The god Phallus, indeed, because even though many people go around saying God is dead, few would question the fact that the Phallus is alive and well.'[30] The Phallus, like the Christian construct of a masculine God, is the symbol of a deferred masculinity. God, like the Phallus, both establishes and denies masculine identity. The man is and is not the possessor of that plenitude which it promises. He can neither 'have' God nor 'be' God. Like the woman, he too represents lack in relation to God/the Phallus, and the mark of identity thus also becomes the negation of identity. To paraphrase Lacan, in Balthasar's theology there is no such thing as The Man, except perhaps in the one and only man, Christ, a man whose masculinity also stands under the threat of erasure when he enters into the feminine flesh. Thus it becomes essential that masculinity survives, if not in the human nature of Christ, then in his divine nature. Christ, as the image of the Father God in creation, becomes the Phallus, and the priest, the one who has the phallus, is his representative/signifier on earth.

But if desire shifts restlessly from object to object because what it desires is always hidden, always unattainable, always beyond the immediate other, then perhaps we also see symptoms of such desire in Balthasar's 'Christ' and Speyr's 'Mary'. Adrienne and Hans desire God through consummate union with Christ. But Hans also desires Adrienne and Adrienne desires Hans. Yet the Phallus intervenes: Hans must not desire Adrienne. God forbids it. Deflected off the dazzling darkness of her mystical flesh, desire is projected onwards and upwards towards God. Having become his desire and its negation, she can desire only death, absorbing into herself his bodily suffering, his mortality and vulnerability, his aches and pains, his sore throats, his humanity. I do not want to elaborate upon these possibilities since I have neither the expertise nor the desire to psychoanalyse the relationship between Balthasar and Speyr, but I think it is important to draw attention to the way in which these dynamics of desire, denial and projection shape his theology. When this is a story about one man and one woman, it is a sad and cautionary tale. When it is a story that becomes emblematic of relationships between Catholic man and Catholic woman and between God and creation, it is a tragedy for the Church.

The linguistic function of the phallus explains the coming into being of sexual difference as a function of language: 'For Lacan, men and women are only ever in language.'[31] The child's realization of the mother's castration signals the onset of the awareness of sexual difference: prior to that, the child believes that the mother possesses the phallus (she is the phallic mother), and there is therefore no sense of sexual differentiation. The phallus functions as the masked signifier upon which sexual difference will henceforth depend: the one who has the phallus takes up the position of the masculine subject, while the desire to be the phallus constitutes the lack or absence that is the other of language – variously associated with femininity, the mother or God. Somewhat ingeniously (as many feminist critics have pointed out), Lacan claims that taking up the position of the man through possession of the phallus is a matter of choice, 'women being free to do so if they so choose. Everyone knows that there are phallic women and the phallic function does not prevent men from being homosexual.'[32]

Insofar as language constructs as its 'other' the unconscious – silenced repository for forbidden desire variously associated with the mother, woman, God and the phallus, all signifying the impossible longing for fusion or union – there is a lack at the heart of language, a silence and an absence whose presence is experienced through the exquisite haunting of unnameable desire which Lacan refers to as *jouissance*: 'as against the being upheld by philosophical tradition, that is, the being residing in thought and taken to be its correlate, I argue that we are played by *jouissance* . . . there is a *jouissance* of being.'[33]

Lacan's discussion of the significance of *jouissance* makes clear the association in his thought between God and the feminine, but it also reveals the extent to which neither of these can in any sense be truly other, since there can be no other outside language, and the other is therefore always reducible to a manifestation of the unconscious desire of the masculine subject. There is, Lacan claims, '*something of the One*'[34] which some of his readers have mistakenly interpreted as 'a certain Other who seemed remarkably like the good old God of all times'.[35] However, his intention is that of 'exorcising our good old God',[36] by showing that 'This Other, while it may be one alone, must have some relation to what appears of the other sex.'[37] The desire for the One is expressed, according to Lacan, in the superfluity of desire associated with *jouissance*, in such a way that the '*jouissance* of the supreme Being'[38] is nothing more than a fantasy of union associated with love, not of the other, but of the other of the self. Thus, in characteristically ironic fashion, Lacan claims that 'in loving God it is ourselves we love, and by first loving ourselves – a convenient charity as they say – we render to God the appropriate homage'.[39]

Similarly, in sexual relations, the man's desire for the woman is not a desire for an encounter or coupling with a sexual other, but rather a desire arising out of his own sense of lack associated with the intervention of the phallus in the oedipal process: 'short of castration, that is, short of something which says no to the phallic function, man has no chance of enjoying the body of the woman, in other words, of making love'.[40] Instead, the man 'takes on the woman',[41] as a fantasy of plenitude: 'what he takes on is the cause of his desire, the cause I have designated as the *objet a* . . . The act of love is the polymorphous perversion of the male, in the case of the speaking being.'[42]

As Jantzen argues, in Lacan's analysis, a man's love for woman and his love for God both express his insatiable desire for a sense of primal unity and wholeness, and they are both therefore a form of self-love. It is not surprising that women as a result tend to be identified as more religious and more spiritual than men. Insofar as psychoanalysis is concerned with the recognition of desires and illusions, in both the sexual and the religious case it will encourage the recognition that these ideals are impossible of fulfillment. There can be no actualizing of the imaginary ideal of the unified, autonomous, and rational subject, nor can either woman or God stand as its guarantor.[43]

However, Jantzen also identifies an ambiguity in Lacan's understanding of God, because God is both the One who guarantees masculine subjectivity, and the Other who, along with woman, signifies the object of desire that can never be attained by the masculine subject, so that 'both women and God are placeholders of the Other'.[44] There is, therefore, an inherent instability in the function that Lacan assigns to the idea of God. The Lacanian God, like the God of Feuerbach and Freud, is a masculine projection, but it is associated with a formless, unnameable desire that is feminine. God, like woman's *jouissance*, is 'something more',[45] because both are outside language and, as the Other of language, they are therefore unknowable: 'And why not interpret one face of the Other, the God face, as supported by feminine *jouissance*? . . . [O]ne can see that while this may not make for two Gods, nor does it make for one alone.'[46]

So far, then, Lacanian psychoanalysis suggests an economy of desire in which 'woman' signifies the excess of man's desire for the Other constituted by lack. This Other is God, femininity and the phallus itself, but it is ultimately an illusion, for there is nothing (no thing, no object) that can satisfy desire. Thus, as Rose points out, the orgasmic significance inherent in the term *jouissance* is used by Lacan 'to refer to something more than pleasure which can easily tip into its opposite'.[47] I shall come back to that suggestion, but at this point let us pause to consider the implications of the foregoing for Balthasar's theology.

We have seen that Balthasar insists upon the significance of difference for the dynamism of *kenosis* and desire which sustains the dramatic quality of the Christian story. However, this collapses into an economy of the same, because neither Balthasar's God nor Balthasar's woman is truly other: God is masculine, Father, Feuerbachian projection of thwarted male desires for invincibility, transcendence, power and control. Woman is his fantasy of plenitude, the desire he refuses and the *persona* he appropriates in order to be fucked by Christ, as an inadequate expression of the fusion he longs for because, no matter how hard he tries, he can become neither woman nor God. Beyond this symbolic coupling, there is wordlessness – the mute flesh of the female body, and the muteness of God beyond naming, language and knowing. But because Balthasar cannot let this other be other, because the infinite freedom of the person in God must not be allowed to rupture the grids of compulsory heterosexuality in the human and in God, his theology lurches towards a Lacanian nihilism. Beyond naming, there is abysmal nothingness, chaos, hell, a hell that is conquered by Christ but retains its seductive female power over him, so that neither he nor she is truly free, after all is said and done. And Balthasar's theo-drama goes nowhere, does not move, becomes a monumental edifice in which is contained all history, all becoming, even God.

Yet this also stands as a caution to feminist theorists who refuse the language of theology, including Jantzen. If God cannot be the other of creation and humankind – and indeed of theology itself – woman cannot be other than man. God and woman dissolve together into the space of man's desire, consuming one another in the wordless haunting of the mother's absence beyond the 'No' of the phallic God. If we would go beyond Balthasar we must also go beyond Lacan and feminist theory, to let God be God, manifest in everything and nothing, present everywhere and nowhere, an absence that is never nothing, a presence that is never something. This is close to the Irigarayan sensible transcendental. It is the potential inherent in Balthasar's idea of the encounter between infinite and finite freedom, creating a space in which there can be sexual consummation without consumption. I shall come back to this.

Lacan, Heidegger and death

In Lacan's interpretation of the Freudian death-drives, the fact that desire is focused on loss rather than satisfaction means that it is ultimately a desire for death. The relationship between language and the inaccessibility of the object of desire means that 'the symbol manifests itself first of all as the murder of the thing, and this death constitutes in the subject the eternalization of his desire'.[48] It is the constitution of subjectivity through the prohibition effected by language which infects the subject with the death wish from the beginning. Jantzen quotes Malcolm Bowie's succinct summary of this process:

> The subject comes into being 'barred' by the signifier and thereby injected with a sense of death. And this is poisoning rather than inoculation. The taste for death is not something that the subject acquires through experience, as one might say, or reaches towards as a last despairing manner of delectation, for it has been there from the start as a perilous gift from the signifier, and one that cannot be refused.[49]

Lacan claims that life 'has only one meaning, that in which desire is borne by death'.[50] Following Heidegger, he defines the human subject as 'Being-toward-death',[51] because the consciousness of temporality and finitude means that death is the ultimate limit towards which subjectivity is directed. Death is, according to Lee's interpretation of Lacan,

> an essential and revelatory future moment, not because it is a nonarbitrary end point of life, but because it is the one part of the subject's life that cannot be taken away from the subject: one's death is unavoidably one's own.[52]

Lee argues that 'Death and desire are . . . intimately related in Lacanian theory: indeed, the subject's assumption of his mortality is itself also the assumption of his desire.'[53] It is when the analysand becomes aware of his own desire and its effects upon him, that he is released from the alienation and illusory identity associated with the phallus, and is able to pursue an authentic existence based on a Heideggerian understanding of 'truth as essentially a state or process of disclosure'.[54] This process involves coming to terms with the real, through an acceptance of a temporal identity that is neither the imaginary identity of the mirror image, nor the symbolic identity of the socialized self:

> The authentic realization of temporality . . . would recognize the fundamental nothingness of temporality and, thus, the inescapable emptiness, *béance*, gap, or gulf around which the human subject builds a false identity.[55]

But, if Heidegger's understanding of truth and disclosure is, as we have seen, not marked by gender, the truth which discloses itself to the Lacanian subject is feminine, since it is an epiphany of the real beyond the constructs of both the mirror stage and the symbolic – a brief unveiling in which the signified manifests its dependence upon the signifier. Lee refers to the 'remarkable prosopopoeia of "The Freudian Thing", in which truth speaks of itself (or rather herself), announcing at the start that "I am the enigma of her who vanishes as soon as she appears."'[56]

Again, we should be aware that, although this might suggest the destabilization of the masculine subject through his acknowledgement and acceptance of his feminine other, the truth that reveals 'herself' is still a dimension of the masculine psyche. The real speaks as woman (or, to be more accurate, the real, like woman, cannot announce 'her' presence, so any fleeting consciousness of such a presence can only be an encounter with profound absence), and therefore the man's acceptance of the relationship between desire and death still hinges on the identification of the woman with these rather than with sexual difference. Woman is not a subjective other who announces her presence, but an absence who slips away as soon as her 'voice' registers. She therefore remains a mystery, an enigma and ultimately a lack, hence Lacan's elision of the definite object – The Woman:

> There is no such thing as *The* woman, where the definite article stands for the universal. There is no such thing as *The* woman since of her essence – having already risked the term, why think twice about it? – of her essence, she is not all.[57]

On such elisions and slippages Irigaray has constructed her extensive critique of Freudian and Lacanian psychoanalysis.

For both Heidegger and Lacan, the acceptance of temporality and mortality is also an acceptance – indeed, in Heidegger, a virile celebration – of the solitude and non-relationality of the human subject. For Lacan, it is based on the accommodation of the masculine psyche to its feminine non-identity, beyond sociability and subjectivity, and on the realization that there is nothing – no God, no Other, no Woman, no phallus – in the abyss that is constituted by desire. For Heidegger, death is the apotheosis of Dasein's potential: 'With death, Dasein stands before itself in its ownmost potentiality-for-Being.'[58] Authenticity entails a consciousness that is not simply 'falling' towards or evading death,[59] but that takes hold of the certainty of death and of the uniquely non-relational nature of that event, and realizes its existential truth as a form of anticipation – a consciousness of Being-toward-death. It is the inevitability of death that offers Dasein the opportunity to transform itself from the inauthentic existence of the 'they-self' – being constituted by and for its social relations – through the realization of its own individual potential:

> Death is Dasein's *ownmost* possibility. Being towards this possibility discloses to Dasein its *ownmost* potentiality-for-Being, in which its very Being is the issue. Here it can become manifest to Dasein that in this distinctive possibility of its own self, it has been wrenched away from the 'they'. This means that in anticipation any Dasein can have wrenched itself away from the 'they' already. But when one understands that this is something which Dasein 'can' have done, this only reveals its factical lostness in the everydayness of the they-self.[60]

Dasein's struggle for authentic existence through its anticipation of death does not immediately present the same associations with femininity and religion that we have seen in Freud and Lacan. However, Heidegger's Dasein is arguably more radically alone in its confrontation with death. Jantzen points out that, although Heidegger emphasizes 'being with' (*Mitsein*), so that '*Dasein* is always *Mitsein*, and the world is a shared world',[61] it is Being-towards-death rather than Being-with-others that constitutes authenticity. Jantzen quotes Seyla Benhabib:

> Although Heidegger, through his analysis of Dasein's worldliness as a form of Mitsein, made the experience of human plurality constitutive of the human condition, the fundamental categories of his existential analytic, rather than illuminating human plurality, testified to the progressing atomization, loneliness, and increasing worldlessness of the individual in the Weimer period in the 1920s.[62]

In Heidegger as in Lacan, the quest for authenticity is the acceptance of an abysmal truth – the thinking being must forge its identity in the face of the constant immanence of its own dissolution, because if Dasein is Being-there, Being-in-the-world, then 'Its death is the possibility of no-longer-being-able-to-be-there.'[63] This means that 'Death is the possibility of the absolute impossibility of Dasein.'[64]

Both Heidegger and Lacan are thinkers whose work is haunted by their Catholic heritage, but both resolutely reject the promises by which Catholicism seeks to offer consolation and hope in the face of death, in the pursuit of what they present as a more truthful and authentic form of existence based on an acceptance of the inevitability and finality of death. Their work, however, remains hostage to the obsession with death that Jantzen identifies among many of the great continental philosophers of the twentieth century, including Levinas and Derrida: 'for all their differences, [they] do not dispute the notion that it is death that confers meaning on life; they disagree only on exactly how this comes about'.[65]

It would be interesting to explore in greater depth the ways in which Freud's Judaism and Lacan's Catholicism influence their interpretations of psychoanalysis. While Freud delegates the mother to a position of marginal influence in the development of religion and in the oedipal process, Lacan's interpretation cannot avoid the ever-present enigma of the mother, who poses a constant distraction from the unashamedly patriarchal constructs of psychoanalytic theory. The Lacanian mother is a more pervasive and persistent presence than the Freudian mother, and her association with God involves a more complex process of negotiation, so that Lacan's God is and is not a thoroughly matriarchal absence – an absence and a deferral of desire which, although masked by the secular symbolic order, is a haunting refrain that echoes through the sacramental language of the Catholic faith, where the Mother is everywhere and nowhere.

However, my purpose here is not to psychoanalyse the psychoanalysts, but to ask how these philosophical and psychoanalytic insights might allow for a reading of Balthasar beyond Balthasar himself – and beyond the spectre of death, which is as much an obsession for him as it is for the male philosophers and theorists he draws upon. How might the Catholic faith enable us to befriend death, in order to create a space of fecundity wherein sexuality and God might come into being as promises of life, hope and being beyond death?

Christianity promises the reconciliation of all things in Christ. If the texts and practices of religion, philosophy and psychology are marked by sexual conflict and repressed desire perpetuated through the ongoing antagonisms that Balthasar identifies with the polarities of sexual difference, individual and community, and spirit and body, all of which combust in the event of death, one would expect the eschatological vision enacted in the sacraments to make present a reconciled and harmonious world, as a dramatic performance of the world to come. Liturgy and worship would thus feed an ethical vision and a life beyond the liturgical sphere, where one might look for epiphanies of heaven on earth in the values, relationships and practices of the Christian faith – an ethical community which would in many ways be close to that depicted by Jantzen in her pantheistic vision of an immanent divine. This would entail a capacity to think through and expose the masked violence that associates sex with death, a masking that René Girard suggests is fundamental to the perpetuation of sacrificial violence through the displacement of blame.[66]

René Girard: desire and violence

Girard, like Freud and Lacan, accords desire a central place in the formation of consciousness and the process of socialization, and in the continuum that links the development of individual subjectivity to the historical formation of social and religious structures and practices. However, Girard parts company with Freud insofar as his understanding of the dynamics of desire is more subtle and diffuse than is the case with the Freudian focus on sexual or libidinal desire. Girard sees an inconsistency in the development of Freud's theory of the Oedipus complex, for by placing all the emphasis on the mother as the object of sexual desire, Freud failed to explore the implications of his early insight that the child's desire for the mother was initially motivated by its desire to imitate the father. The primary factor in awakening desire, therefore, is not the object of sexual or libidinal desire, but the desire of the esteemed or revered other. The object of desire is desirable because another desires it: 'mimetic desire is rooted neither in the subject nor in the object, but in a third party whose desire is imitated by the subject'.[67] Although highly critical of Lacan – he refers to his 'linguistic fetishism'[68] – Girard cites Lacan's question as to why the father figure goes from being a figure of rivalry to being a figure of identification.[69] This Girard sees as a critical question that necessitates a new interpretation of the oedipal process, which can account for the father as a figure of both rivalry and mimesis.

Girard's theory revolves around the relationship between the model and the disciple, as the form of relationship that is central to all other relationships and that holds the key to understanding the dynamics of desire and violence within the social order. In the oedipal process, the child becomes the father's disciple because of the strong cultural conditioning that predisposes him to see the father as a model.[70] Still innocent of violence and envy, the child seeks to imitate all aspects of the father's desire, including his desire for the mother. It is the father who first awakens the child to the possibility of violence, by his subtle 'no' to the child's desire. This is what Girard refers to as the 'mimetic double bind' – the model prohibits the child from desiring what he himself desires:

> The model's very first no – however softly spoken or cautiously phrased – can easily be mistaken by the disciple for an irrevocable act of excommunication, a banishment to the realms of outer darkness. Because the child is incapable of meeting violence with violence and has in fact had no real experience with

violence, his first encounter with the mimetic double bind may well leave an indelible impression.[71]

Elsewhere, Girard describes the double bind as the affliction of the subject 'who is incapable of correctly interpreting the double imperative that comes from the other person: taken as model, imitate me; and as rival, do not imitate me'.[72]

Whereas Freud attributes murderous rivalry to the child with regard to the father, Girard argues that the origins of the oedipal trauma lie with the adult role (i.e. with the model rather than the disciple), and the result is a sense of guilt and shame that leads the child to deny itself and seek to venerate the father instead – an oedipal trauma that has cultural/religious as well as individual ramifications. It is worth quoting Girard at some length here, for this is a crucial insight for interpreting Balthasar:

> Faced with the model's anger, the disciple feels compelled to make some sort of choice between himself and the model; and it is perfectly clear that he will choose in favor of the model. The idol's wrath must be justified, and it can be justified only by some failure on the part of the disciple, some hidden weakness that obliges the god to forbid access to the holy of holies, to slam shut the gates of paradise. Far from reducing the divinity's prestige, this new attitude of vengeful spite serves to increase it. The disciple feels guilty – though of what, he cannot be sure – and unworthy of the object of his desire, which now appears more alluring than ever. Desire has now been redirected toward those particular objects protected by the *other's* violence. The link between desire and violence has been forged, and in all likelihood it will never be broken.[73]

Girard argues that this relationship between desire and violence is not based on a conscious awareness of the model as a rival – which is why he thinks Freud makes too direct a connection between the child's desire for the mother and its rivalry towards the father. Freud's hypothesizing of a conscious relationship between 'patricidal and incestuous desire',[74] however momentary that ego consciousness might be before it is repressed by the superego, is for Girard the central weakness in his theory – '[t]he mythical aspect of Freudianism'.[75]

Again, without wanting to over-simplify the picture, the foregoing surely invites comparison with the complex and violent struggles that Balthasar expresses in *Heart of the World*, during his early relationship with Speyr. Balthasar wants what Speyr wants: consummate union with Christ. But Balthasar also wants what Christ wants: consummate union with Speyr. Desire begins to flow restlessly from one to the other, nameless and abject. Does Christ say 'no' to Balthasar's desire for Speyr, because Speyr belongs first and foremost to Christ? Christ is both model and rival, but Speyr too is model and rival. She is the Marian person, the woman whom Christ desires. Balthasar must mimic her to be desirable to Christ, but he must also compete with her to become Christ. Balthasar speaks as a man who believes that, alone among sinners, he is unworthy of God, guilty of some vast, nameless guilt that sets him outside Christ's love, excommunicated and banished 'to the realms of outer darkness'. I have already quoted part of the following:

> There is a communion of saints, and there is also a communion of sinners. Perhaps they are both one and the same thing – this chain, this wave that rolls on through days and centuries, a bloody stream of guilt, the blunderers' course of those who drag themselves down and pull themselves up again. *One life of warm guilt and of warm remorse throbs through them all*, and amid this dark stream of good and evil suffering there flow also the redeeming drops of your blood, O Lord. You shall save them.
>
> I have been expelled from this communion of sinners. Stiff and frozen, rolled up lump-like, I cower to the side: my sin is without comparison.[76]

As we shall see, according to Girard, this 'bloody stream of guilt' rolling on through history, the 'dark stream of good and evil suffering' holds the social order together by violence and is transformed by the non-violent, reconciling love of Christ.

But Balthasar also becomes Christ in *Heart of the World*, speaks with Christ's voice, and vents Christ's vengeful sexual fury on the object of Christ's desire – the wanton flesh of his Bride. Balthasar's desire for Speyr/Christ becomes Christ's violent desire for the Church/the body. But Christ's violent rape of the Bride is masked by her sexual transgression: she was asking for it; she deserved it; it was for her own good. Let us bear in mind this masking of violence by sex in what follows.

It is his belief in the hidden nature of the relationship between mimetic desire, rivalry and violence, informed by his extensive readings of scriptures and myths as well as psychoanalytic and philosophical texts, that forms the core of Girard's theory of the scapegoat mechanism and the function of sacrificial violence as the masked foundation of the social order. Girard argues that socialization occurs through a continuous process of mimesis: we attach ourselves to role models and seek to imitate them, which includes the imitation of their desire. But as a result of our wanting what the model wants, he or she becomes an obstacle or a rival in the way of desire, and thus desire leads us to repeatedly destroy that which we originally admired.

This spiral of desire, frustration and antagonism produces a build-up of hostility and conflict, in which admiration turns to antagonism as the disciple begins to desire and compete for the object of the model's desire. Moreover, mimetic desire is a 'contagion'[77] which infects the model as well as the disciple,

204 *The beginning*

until desire becomes metaphysical: we desire that which we cannot destroy or possess. This is the model who would have absolute power, thus reinforcing a masochistic sense of shame and failure in the disciple as a corollary to the model's invincibility.[78] This insatiable quest for the invincible rival who would safeguard desire means that there is no end to the circulation of desire and its destructive rivalries, which include but are not reducible to sexual desire. Girard charges psychoanalysis with Platonism in its reification or essentialization of sexual drives, characteristics and instincts, and argues instead for the recognition of the transience and instability of desire which is always a consequence of rivalry for the object of desire.[79]

The roles of model and disciple become increasingly undifferentiated in the mutual rivalry that builds up between them, and the circulation of desire thus gives rise to the chaos of indiscriminate violence. These multitudinous examples of rivalrous desire build up within societies and communities, and if they are not to result in anarchic physical violence, they must have some controlled outlet. Girard argues that this is the function served by all forms of sanctioned violence involving ritual sacrifice or punishment of a universally condemned victim perceived to be outside the social group, which therefore protects the group members from unleashing their violence on one another, and also removes the threat of retaliation that might result if the victim had social claims upon the group.[80] The choice of the victim is arbitrary insofar as it can be any excluded individual or group which becomes the focus of the repressed violence circulating within the dominant group, but, because this act of violent scapegoating has to mask its true origins and function, it has to impute to the victim some crime or transgression that justifies the violence. Citing the example of Oedipus, Girard argues that this is often of a sexual nature, so that the allegation of sexual transgression projects blame onto the scapegoat, in a way that masks the random violence of the social order.[81] In the case of religious sacrifice, blame is removed from the group through the imputation of a divine command to sacrifice.[82] Because this cathartic violence temporarily restores a sense of peace and order to society, the scapegoat is often subsequently divinized as the one responsible for bringing about this positive transformation.

Girard and the peace of Christ

Girard's theory has had a significant impact on Catholic theology in recent years, and he himself has returned to the Catholic faith after becoming convinced that the story of Christ in the Gospels is the supreme exception that proves the rule of his scapegoating theory, even although Christian theology has yet to realize the significance of this: 'The Christ of the Gospels dies against sacrifice, and through his death, he reveals its nature and origin by making sacrifice unworkable, at least in the long run, and bringing sacrificial culture to an end.'[83] In the Hebrew and

Christian scriptures, but particularly in the Gospels and in the Suffering Servant imagery of the Book of Isaiah, Girard sees a revelation of the human origins of sacrificial violence, and an affirmation of the absolute innocence of the victim and of the non-sacrificial nature of God. In the passages that refer to God as the Father of Jesus, 'we are confronted with a God who is foreign to all forms of violence'.[84] From Mary's virginal conception through to the innocence of the crucified Christ, Girard sees a sustained refusal of the sacralized violence that marks the oedipal dramas of rape and murder found, for example, in the stories of Greek mythology. But in the inability of the social order to accommodate Christ's message of non-violence, Girard also sees the withdrawal of God from the violence done in God's name: 'A non-violent deity can only signal his existence to mankind by having himself driven out by violence — by demonstrating that he is not able to establish himself in the Kingdom of Violence.'[85]

In Christ's example of suffering love which refuses to retaliate, and which meets violence with forgiveness, Girard sees the invitation to a new form of discipleship, based on the mimesis of Christ's example as a way of forming communal bonds through love and forgiveness, rather than through the catharsis of sacrificial violence. Christ removes the obstacle to love that is the consequence of mimetic desire, by becoming a model who offers no rivalry and no threat:

> There is no acquisitive desire in him. As a consequence, any will that is really turned toward Jesus will not meet with the slightest of obstacles. His yoke is easy and his burden is light. With him, we run no risk of getting caught up in the evil opposition between doubles.[86]

Girard uses the example of the women at the empty tomb to symbolize this removal of the obstacle to love, and I quote him here to conclude this brief survey of his thought:

> Following Christ means giving up mimetic desire . . . If you look carefully at the text of the Gospels, you will see that throughout runs the theme of the obstacle that is dreaded by the faithful but is removed at the last moment — when all hope seems to be lost. The most striking case is that of the women on the morning of the Resurrection. They think only of corpses, embalming and tombs. They fret about the heavy stone that seals off the tomb and will prevent them from reaching the goal of all their efforts — the dead body of Jesus. Behind the obstacles, there are only dead bodies; every obstacle is a kind of tomb. When they finally arrive, nothing that they were expecting is to be found; there is no obstacle and no dead body any more:
>
> And when the Sabbath was past, Mary Magdalene, and Mary the mother of James, and Salome, bought spices, so that they might go and anoint him. And very early on the first day of the week they went to the tomb when the

sun had risen. And they were saying to one another, 'Who will roll away the stone for us from the door of the tomb?' And looking up, they saw that the stone was rolled back – it was very large (Mark 16:1–4).[87]

Perhaps a faithful reading of the Gospels through the centuries would have recognized the significance of the women who were present at all the key moments in Jesus's life and ministry, from his conception to his resurrection and ascension into heaven. Not only are women mentioned as being present, they are often named, as they are in this later addition to Mark's Gospel. Those who have been nameless, excluded witnesses to history become key witnesses, named persons, in the story of Christ. In John's Gospel, it is Mary of Magdala who becomes 'the apostle to the apostles', as she was known in the early Church – as witness to the risen Christ she becomes the first preacher of the Christian faith, a priestly initiation that the Church has yet to recognize.[88]

Christ restores the woman to her name and her place in history, and he gives her a voice so that she might become the bearer of revelation. But the men of the Church laughed and refused to listen, and still they refuse to listen. Girard refers to the women at the tomb. In the Orthodox Church's Easter liturgy, one of the most beautiful scenes is the repetition of this scene, when the women as myrrh-bearers come to the tomb. Three men play the role of the women, for women are not permitted to participate in the liturgy. Perhaps there is no more telling symbol of the argument that runs through this book than that image of three men posturing as the women who witnessed the resurrection, because the female body is deemed unworthy or impure – the men of the Church apparently knowing better than Christ himself who can and cannot enact the story of redemption.

The theoretical perspectives I have explored above do not mesh into a seamless argument, and they do not provide anywhere near a complete interpretative framework for understanding Balthasar's theology. There are significant differences among Freud, Lacan and Girard in the explanations they offer for the positioning of male and female bodies in relationships of violence and desire across the social spectrum. Nevertheless, from the perspective of feminist theological analysis, these differences pale into relative insignificance with regard to the overarching schema that links together sexuality, God, desire, sacrifice and death in the western imaginary – as Jantzen and Clack argue.

The rehabilitation of the mother in the Catholic faith has been achieved by way of an unacknowledged sacrifice – the sacrifice of the sexual female body, which has effectively covered over the early Church's recognition that death, not sex, was the great enemy of humankind, and that opposition to violence entailed opposition to certain forms of abusive and exploitative sexuality. This insight has been reversed, so that today we see a Church that is vehement and absolutist in its teachings with regard to sexuality and procreation, while it remains ambivalent with regard to violence and war. Only by exposing the violence that is concealed by sex might the redemption of female sexuality become intrinsic to the Catholic story of salvation, so that we might at last begin to see the emergence of a theology that is unashamedly on the side of peace and life. Until that happens, Catholicism will remain prey to every form of violence and misogyny lurking under cover of an unredeemed sexuality.

If theology is to go beyond Balthasar, theologians must learn from and go beyond critical theory and psycholinguistics, in order to develop a sacramental theology, enacted in liturgical performances, which might express the holistic and reconciling love of Christ for the world. This entails seeking to understand the complex ways in which maternity, sex and death interact in the human psyche, in order to ask how psychoanalysis in particular might provide the resources for a new appreciation of the vulnerability, interdependence and mortality of our bodily selves, as creatures who are born to die but whose finite lives are nevertheless filled with hope because we are positioned before the open horizon of God's infinite freedom and love, which is opaquely revealed in the world around us.

11 Maternal beginnings

So far, I have both implicitly affirmed and radically undermined Balthasar's claim that sexual difference permeates the entire created order. I have suggested that all the concepts by which we seek to give meaning to our most fundamental experiences of divinity, the body, sex and death are gendered, and I have sought to develop a more thoroughly gendered analysis of these than Balthasar offers, by showing the extent to which his understanding of sexual difference is a pervasive but deeply problematic aspect of his theology. For the gendering of creation and God in Balthasar's theo-drama does not entail difference, love and desire, but sameness, violence and conquest. Underneath his lavish rhetoric, we discover the same old stereotypes of man as presence, divinity, activity and revelation, and woman as absence, nature, passivity and silence.

However, unlike Protestant and post-Protestant theology and philosophy, Balthasar's sexual stereotypes are also radically undermined by a Catholic symbolics which is fluid and unstable in its understanding of gendered relationships, and which insinuates a powerful but problematic maternal presence into its symbolism and sacraments. In seeking to reconcile his commitment to a Catholic discourse of gender that constantly slips away from his grasp, with a rigid insistence upon a dualistic, heterosexual cosmic order, Balthasar is trapped in a theological space of violence and annihilation.

It is no coincidence that Lacanian psychoanalysis and its feminist critiques (Kristeva and Irigaray) provide such fertile resources for reading Balthasar. Lacan, Irigaray and Kristeva are shaped by Catholic Christianity. They translate Freudian psychoanalysis from its Jewish habitat into Catholic sacramental consciousness, and from there they explore questions of motherhood, sexuality and God that are profoundly embedded in that consciousness.[1] As Catholic Europeans, Lacan and Balthasar are almost classic examples of a particular kind of modern *homo religiosus* (or, to be more precise, *vir religiosus*), who is produced by the uneasy encounter between the modern masculine individual and the more deeply rooted psychological and spiritual claims of the Catholic tradition. Unlike the more rationalist Protestant fraternity across the channel – targets of feminist criticism by both Jantzen and Anderson – and perhaps unlike Freud himself, Lacan and

Balthasar do not quite fit the description of the modern masculine subject whose autonomy and rationalism are premised upon the denial of maternity and embodiment. Lacan and Balthasar are not entirely at home in the world of men, because they are sons of Holy Mother Church and feminine lovers of God, and therefore they cannot simply construct myths of identity, meaning and truth as if 'she' were not there. Rather, God, woman and the mother make claims upon them, demanding a place in their stories.

For Lacan, a nihilist, the solution is to analyse away God and woman as maternally induced projections of the masculine psyche – occupying the space of the desire that shadows language in the imaginary and that buries itself almost without trace in the Real. As a Catholic priest, Balthasar achieves a more complex double act. On the one hand, he projects woman and God out of the sphere of his own masculine psyche, onto the body of Speyr and the transcendent otherness of God, thus ostensibly preserving the difference of both and the polarities between them. But at the same time he internalizes these polarities so that they become a battleground within him – he wants to be the woman, and he also wants to be Christ. So when reading Lacan and Balthasar, we are on similar psychological and theological territory, even although they offer different narrative accounts of what this means. That is why I believe that to read Balthasar from the perspective of critical theorists who combine psychoanalysis and Catholicism is to begin to move towards a Catholic feminist theology that can go beyond politics and ideology, to address the most profound questions about the ways in which we receive and express the revelation of divine love as bodily, sexual beings made in the image of God.

But this leads to a question that goes to the heart of the sacramental tradition: why, in a maternal Church whose liturgical life is inspired by bodily images of birth, sexuality and death – all images that evoke profound associations with the maternal body – is the female body the one 'object' in all creation that is incapable of sacramental signification? Why, when Christ can be identified in bread and wine, in a range of images drawn from the animal world and the world of nature (the lamb, the harvest, the morning star, the sun), and of course in the male human body, is the female body absolutely banished from such symbolizing potential? I want to ask this question through a feminist sacramental reading of Kristeva and Girard, which I believe makes it possible to uncover that which has indeed been 'hidden since the foundation of the world',[2] but which Christ in our time might reveal as the sacrifice that brings peace, the death that gives life.

The maternal sacrifice

Although Girard rejects Freud's theory of the unconscious and the Oedipus complex, he sees a missed opportunity in Freud's interpretation of the *fort/da* game in *Beyond the Pleasure Principle*, which, argues Girard, Freud presents 'from a perspective that is both mimetic and sacrificial',[3] without recognizing the implications of this. In Freud's interpretation, the child's game of throwing away and retrieving a reel on a string is a way of gaining mastery over its anxiety at being left by its mother, and therefore of transforming that experience from one of distress into one of pleasure. But Girard points out that Freud expresses this in terms of the child's desire 'to revenge himself on his mother for going away from him'[4] through a process of substitution, which Girard interprets in terms of mimetic, ritualized behaviour as a foreshadowing of the scapegoat mechanism. While Freud dismisses the idea that the child's game might be imitative, Girard insists that it belongs to that same pattern of adult behaviour that is manifest in ritualized sacrifice. The child is expressing a form of mimetic desire for which the mother is both the model and the double, and in throwing away the object, it is expressing the violent rivalry it feels towards the mother.

Girard has been criticized by feminists for what some see as the androcentrism or even misogyny inherent in his theory.[5] Responding to such critics, he claims that 'If anything my hypothesis is pro-woman',[6] and he suggests that he is unfashionable among feminists because, unlike Freud, Derrida and Heidegger, he is not anti-Christian – a suggestion that my own reading of feminist theory and indeed of anti-Christian feminist prejudice leads me to sympathize with. Nevertheless, Girard's theory is vulnerable to feminist criticism, not least because his resistance to attributing sexual difference to the dynamics of mimetic desire introduces some inconsistency into his arguments. The fact that the *fort/da* game is directed primarily against the mother does not, for instance, elicit any speculation or comment from him as to the wider sexual implications of this primal rivalry. He claims that women's non-participation in sacrificial violence attests to 'their real moral superiority',[7] and he cites the example of the women around Jesus to demonstrate this claim:

> As important as the apostles are in the Gospels, the women around Jesus are just as important but in a different way: they are that part of humanity which has nothing to do with scapegoating him. They are the ones who stick with him through the crucifixion.[8]

But Girard's whole theory is undermined if 'moral superiority' alone is enough to account for women being more resistant to the scapegoating mechanism than men, and more willing to 'stick with' the scapegoat, particularly if, as he insists, mimetic desire is not in itself sexually differentiated. What particular moral faculty do women possess that men lack, which makes women less sacrificial than men? What is it that gives women this 'superiority', if it has nothing to do with any biological or genetic predisposition or any familial structure? What moral faculty (related to gender?) enables a person or a group (in this case, an entire sex) to recognize and resist what another group (the entire male sex?) cannot recognize, let alone resist? Girard claims that women are marginal to the sacrificial social order, but he offers no adequate explanation as to why this should be so. Citing the example of Bororo villagers in Brazil, he points out that the women 'played no role in the games of violence and the sacred, which is their superiority. Their marginality was inseparable from their nonparticipation in male violence.'[9] But why should resistance to sacred violence be a form of 'superiority', if it is a consequence of social marginalization? One does not acquire 'moral superiority' *de facto* simply by occupying the social position assigned to one: marginalization is not a moral quality, unless it comes about through an act of refusal or resistance, and this is clearly not the case when a sex, race or class is marginalized because it is the 'other' of the dominant group. One has to ask why women are marginal to societies whose social cohesion depends upon sacrificial violence. Is this marginalization in itself a form of scapegoating, collectively and possibly universally practised by men against women, and might this be related to what Irigaray describes as the original matricide, a murder so profound and so hidden that even Girard resists its implications? I shall come to Irigaray later, but in exploring the implications of this question, I want to begin by returning to Kristeva.

Martha Reineke introduces a gendered dimension into Girard's scapegoat theory, by reading him in engagement with Kristeva. Referring to Irigaray's theory that the sacrifice which underpins language and the social order is the sacrifice of the mother, Reineke suggests that Kristeva provides a more developed exploration than Irigaray of how this might be understood in terms of sacrifice and violence. Referring to Girard's argument that the primal murder is buried and concealed in language so that society does not recognize the sacrifice which it perpetuates, Reineke suggests that 'The one who Girard has said is barred from language, whose murder language conceals and ritual represents, is the mother whom Kristeva has said patriarchy denies: our linguistic and cultural codes are structured around the murder of the mother.'[10] In *Powers of Horror*, Kristeva explores what Diane Jonte-Pace refers to as 'a primal abhorrence of the mother',[11] an abhorrence which manifests itself at the boundary between language and the body, where the somatic drives threaten the coherence of the speaking subject, and the abjected relationship with the mother becomes the source of an overwhelming sense of horror associated with dissolution, madness and death.

In Kristeva's early work, she identifies the 'semiotic' as the dimension of the psyche wherein the bodily relationship with the mother still exercises a subliminal power over language, so that the coherence of the symbolic is pulverized by the repressed somatic desires and drives of the semiotic.[12] This subliminal experience of love and abjection, desire and mourning, which haunts the speaking subject of the symbolic order, finds expression in the language of the *chora*, based on Plato's concept in the *Timeaus* of 'an ancient, mobile, unstable receptacle, prior to the One, to the father, and even to the syllable, metaphorically suggesting something nourishing and maternal'.[13] One of the most significant differences between Kristeva and Lacan is that she does not entirely do away with the biological dimension of the Freudian drives, so that, whereas Lacan's psychoanalytic theory is entirely psycholinguistic, Kristeva's is more psychosomatic. In order to explore the implications of this for Catholic sacramentality, I want to consider her explanation of the development of the western psyche and its relationship to the maternal body through the various stages of the Hebrew and Christian scriptures.

Maternal abjection

Kristeva argues that the Judeo-Christian tradition represents the development of a religious and ethical world view that resonates with the psychological development of the individual, in its rejection of sacrificial religion and the establishment of religious identity through separation from the mother. In particular, she says of the Levitical codes that 'the object excluded by these rules, whatever form it may take in biblical narrative, is ultimately the mother'.[14] In delineating 'the precise limits of abjection', the Book of Leviticus has 'developed a true archaeology of the advent of the subject':[15]

> Indeed, this Book recounts the subject's delicate and painful detachment – moment by moment, layer by layer, step by step – as well as his journey from narcissistic fusion to an autonomy that is never really 'his own,' never 'clean,' never complete, and never securely guaranteed in the Other . . . The Bible is a text that thrusts its words into my losses. By enabling me to speak about my disappointments, though, it lets me stand in full awareness of them.[16]

Ideas of pollution and impurity are not, Kristeva argues (in agreement with Mary Douglas), qualities that inhere in forbidden substances, but in symbolic systems that have their own particular rules of classification regarding the clean and the unclean.[17] The dietary and pollution laws of the Levitical codes form the basis of Israel's identity over and against the surrounding cults, through the substitution of abomination for sacrificial killing. Kristeva relates this to Israel's gradual rejection of sacrifice, particularly after the Exile, and therefore of oedipal religious violence associated with the maternal cults. Thus, the dietary codes focus on the prohibition of carnivorous animals as forms of food, and the purity codes focus on substances associated with maternal femininity and death, so that Israel differentiates itself from the cults through its abomination of substances associated with sacrificial killing and the maternal body. Circumcision becomes the symbolic mark of male identity, an identity carved onto the male sexual organ that separates him from the impurity of the mother.[18] The integrity of the man's relationship to his God depends upon his resistance to the lure of idolatry represented by the maternal cults, so that

> it would be a matter of separating oneself from the phantasmatic power of the mother, that archaic Mother Goddess who actually haunted the imagination of a nation at war with the surrounding polytheism. A phantasmatic mother who also constitutes, in the specific history of each person, the abyss that must be established as an autonomous (and not encroaching) *place* and *distinct* object, meaning a *signifiable* one, so that such a person might learn to speak.[19]

Thus the development of the individual subject becomes enacted in religious and moral laws through the symbolic relationship with the material/maternal world, which is reflected in the psychological process of abjection and the establishment of psychic boundaries to separate the speaking subject from the consuming power of the maternal relationship. Kristeva claims that 'Far from being *one* of the semantic values of that tremendous project of separation constituted by the biblical text, the taboo of the mother seems to be its originating mytheme.'[20]

But the abjected is not abominable in itself – it is abjected because it is an abomination to Yahweh. In other words, it is the signifying power of language, expression of the divine law, that produces abomination, and it is the covenant between Yahweh and the people of Israel that makes this abomination binding upon them. But this means that the covenant, expressed through the semiotics of the law, carries the demoniacal within itself. It is God's Word that brings the impure as well as the pure into being, and thus there can be no clear distinction between them: the 'demoniacal force' is 'not at all autonomous but only intrinsic to and coiled within divine speech'.[21] This interdependence of the pure and the impure, the symbolic and the abject, means that the mother and death, although 'abominated, abjected, slyly build a victimizing and persecuting machine at the cost of which I become subject of the Symbolic as well as Other of the Abject'.[22]

Kristeva's psychoanalytic account of the development of Hebrew religion may not stand up to close historical scrutiny in some of its claims and arguments, but I summarize it here because it provides a highly relevant context for my own questions regarding the female priesthood and the Mass, if we go on to consider how she sees this symbolic world of the Hebrew scriptures being reinterpreted by Christianity. She argues that, with its abolition of the dietary codes and purity laws, Christianity brings about the psychological interiorization of the differences that Israel projected outwards in the context of its socio-religious relationships, so that the language of grace and sin takes the place of the language of purity and impurity. Deprived of its referents in the material world, the relationship between the pure and the impure becomes a feature of language alone, and the abjected other is driven deep within the speaking being where it becomes a permanent feature of the psyche. The New Testament transforms the Levitical codes by internalizing them through a process of 'oralization'.[23] Kristeva quotes a number of New Testament texts in support of this argument, for example, Jesus's saying in Matthew 15:11 that 'Not that which goeth into the mouth defileth a man; but that which cometh out of the mouth, this defileth a man.'[24] Kristeva suggests that this transition from external to internal, from a social to a psychological understanding of the clean and the unclean, potentially represents the symbolic rehabilitation of the pagan mother. She cites the story of the Syrophenician woman (Mark 7: 26–7), to illustrate her point that

> The nutritive opening up to the other, the full acceptance of archaic and gratifying relationship to the mother, pagan as it might be, and undoubtedly conveying paganistic connotations of a prolific and protective motherhood, is here the condition for another opening – the opening up to symbolic relations, true outcome of the Christic journey.[25]

This symbolic opening up to the maternal, however, does not bring about psychological integration between the subject and the abject: 'Maternal principle, reconciled with the subject, is not for that matter revalorized, rehabilitated. Of its nourishing as much as threatening heterogeneity, later texts, and even more so theological posterity, will keep only the idea of sinning flesh.'[26] Christ alone achieves perfect heterogeneity between 'the corporeal and the signifying',[27] and therefore he alone is 'a body without sin'.[28] After him, the subject experiences the ambiguity of the inter-dependent relationship between holiness and defilement in the form of sin, which comes to signify the state of separation that forms the unavoidable paradox of the human condition:

> Sin, even if its remission is always promised, remains the rock where one endures the human condition as separate: body and spirit, body jettisoned from the spirit; as a condition that is impossible, irreconcilable, and, by that very token, real.[29]

According to Reineke's reading of Kristeva,

> In its notion of sin, Christianity interiorizes Jewish abomination, absorbing abjection in speech through subjection to God of a speaking being who is divided within and who precisely through speech does not cease to purge himself or herself of impurities. Evil, displaced into the subject, torments but not as polluting substance. Instead, evil is met as an 'ineradicable repulsion of

divided and contradictory being': Christianity binges on and purges the mother.[30]

The ambiguous nature of sin means that it produces a system of morality and judgement – 'sin guides one along the straitest [sic] paths of superego spirituality',[31] but as its other side, sin is also 'the requisite of the Beautiful':[32]

> Neither debt nor want, sin, as the reverse side of love, is a state of fullness, of plenty. In that sense, it turns around into living beauty. Far from advocating solely a doctrine of limitation and conformity to divine speech, the Christian conception of sin also includes a recognition of an evil whose power is in direct ratio to the holiness that identifies it as such, and into which it can convert. Such a conversion into jouissance and beauty goes far beyond the retributive, legalistic tonality of sin as debt or iniquity. Thus it is that, by means of the beautiful, the demoniacal dimension of the pagan world can be tamed. And that the beautiful penetrates into Christianity to the extent of becoming not merely one of its component parts, but also probably what leads it beyond religion.[33]

At this point, let us note the resonances between Kristeva's understanding of the relationship between beauty and sin, and Balthasar's explanation of the relationship between beauty and ugliness in artistic expression as being part of the totality of Christian revelation. For Kristeva, as for Balthasar, Christianity's unique insight lies in its dialectic of sin and grace, in its recognition that holiness increases in direct proportion to the evil that it names and resists, not through expulsion but through conversion. Much of the dialectic of *Heart of the World* is precisely this playing out of the interdependence between sin and grace, flesh and Word and, as we shall see, for all its repellent violence, this theological reflection does indeed ultimately suggest a way beyond itself to an unrealized but promised peace.

The maternal subject

For Kristeva, the way beyond the present crisis in subjectivity and meaning is to go beyond sexual difference, to a greater understanding of the multiple differences which constitute every form of subjectivity and every social grouping. She argues that Freud exposes the extent to which the Enlightenment project, with its idea of the autonomous, coherent and unified subject, is achieved through a process of repression and alienation which makes us 'strangers to ourselves',[34] because the rationalized subject is unable to accommodate the 'uncanny strangeness'[35] associated with maternal femininity, death and the biological drives. This strangeness is projected onto others who become 'foreigners' when viewed from the perspective of the various forms of nationalism and patriotism which have gripped Europe since the seventeenth century. If we seek to build a culture of peace, suggests Kristeva, we must learn from Freud in order to recognize the foreignness, the uncanny, within ourselves. 'The foreigner is within me, hence we are all foreigners. If I am a foreigner, there are no foreigners.'[36]

An essay first published in 1979, titled 'Women's Time', gives a clear indication of concerns that have become central to Kristeva's subsequent work, particularly with regard to the nature of maternal subjectivity, and the possibility of a non-sacrificial social order. Kristeva raises a question about the social position of women which is germane to our present discussion:

> *What can be our place in the symbolic contract?* If the social contract, far from being that of equal men, is based on an essentially sacrificial relationship of separation and articulation of differences which in this way produces communicable meaning, what is our place in this order of sacrifice and/or of language?[37]

Kristeva appeals to different concepts of time which position women in relation to the symbolic order. Women have a close relationship to cyclical time, because of their bodily association with the cycles of fertility, reproduction and nature. But she also refers to two concepts of time that Nietzsche refers to as 'cursive time' which is 'the time of linear history', and 'monumental time', constituting 'the time of another history' which transcends linear time.[38] She argues that the women's movement, represented by suffragists and existential feminists, sought to gain women a place in linear time, through their participation in socio-political life. However, second-generation feminists situate 'feminist subversion . . . on the terrain of the inseparable conjunction of the sexual and the symbolic', one of the consequences of which was a radical a-topian feminism, 'a place outside the law, utopia's floodgate' that sought to 'make of the second sex a *counter-society*': 'Against the socio-symbolic contract, both sacrificial and frustrating, this counter-society is imagined as harmonious, without prohibitions, free and fulfilling.'[39] However, Kristeva argues that 'the very logic of counter-power and of counter-society necessarily generates, by its very structure, its essence as a simulacrum of the combated society or of power'.[40] In other words, women who situate themselves outside the social order risk unleashing forms of anachronistic violence that mirror those of the systems they oppose. In a Girardian insight, Kristeva suggests that

> Anthropology has shown that the social order is sacrificial, but sacrifice orders violence, binds it, tames it. Refusal of the social order exposes one to the risk that the so-called good substance, once it is unchained, will explode, without curbs, without law or right, to become an absolute arbitrariness.[41]

Kristeva suggests that women are vulnerable to this kind of anarchic violence because they already occupy a marginal status vis-à-vis the social order. But the myth of a non-violent, harmonious utopia embraced by some radical feminists is associated with 'the belief in the omnipotence of an archaic, full, total englobing mother with no frustration, no separation, with no break-producing symbolism',[42] and therefore with no mechanism for controlling violence. This means that 'we will never be able to defuse the violences mobilized through the counter-investment necessary to carrying out this phantasm, unless one challenges precisely this myth of the archaic mother'.[43]

Although she makes no explicit reference to Irigaray, the arguments in this essay explain why Kristeva resists Irigaray's appeal to a non-oedipal form of feminine subjectivity through the rehabilitation of the maternal relationship. For Kristeva, the oedipal process is a necessary stage in social development, and the abjection of the mother, with its legacy of yearning and loss, is the precondition for the individual's entry into the symbolic.

However, a persistent theme of Kristeva's work since the late 1970s has been the question of how the oedipal triangle might be rendered less violent, through the advent of an imaginary father figure capable of bringing about a less traumatic process of separation, and through the rediscovery of a maternal discourse of embodiment, mortality, desire and loss, that might provide an alternative to the rationalizing discourses of secular modernity, with their repression of the maternal voice.[44] This involves going beyond feminism's early opposition to motherhood, in order to bring about a more relational understanding of subjectivity based on women's own maternal experiences:

> Pregnancy seems to be experienced as the radical ordeal of the splitting of the subject: redoubling up of the body, separation and coexistence of the self and of an other, of nature and consciousness, of physiology and speech. This fundamental challenge to identity is then accompanied by a fantasy of totality – narcissistic completeness – a sort of instituted, socialized, natural psychosis. The arrival of the child, on the other hand, leads the mother into the labyrinths of an experience that, without the child, she would only rarely encounter: love for an other. Not for herself, not for an identical being, and still less for another person with whom 'I' fuse (love or sexual passion). But the slow, difficult and delightful apprenticeship in attentiveness, gentleness, forgetting oneself.[45]

This is, suggests Kristeva, a form of 'guiltless maternity' which depends upon the mother's capacity to retain her own sense of self as neither totally one with nor entirely separate from that of the child, making this maternal self a less individualistic, more inter-dependent concept than that of the modern subject.[46] The mother in this relationship is neither the archaic, pre-oedipal mother nor the disavowed and abjected mother of Freudian and Lacanian psychoanalysis. Rather, changes in the relationship between mother and child, from pregnancy through birth and beyond, represent subjectivity as a relational process rather than as the acquisition of a stable identity, and the discourse of maternal desire, with its somatic resonances and its intimations of love, mortality and loss, allows for the acceptance of the alienated and divided self, without the inevitability of violent conflict and repression. This means going beyond sexual difference, and beyond essentializing concepts such as 'Woman' – Kristeva reiterates Lacan's 'scandalous sentence "There is no such thing as Woman"', insisting that 'she does *not* exist with a capital "W", possessor of some mythical unity'.[47] Rather, difference must be acknowledged as something that operates within and among subjectivities, manifesting itself in multiple ways beyond the categorization of people in terms of sex, race and other differences. This entails 'the demassification of the problematic of *difference*, which would imply, in a first phase, an apparent de-dramatization of the "fight to the death" between rival groups and thus between the sexes'.[48] Ultimately, Kristeva argues, this opens the way for a radical process of social transformation, which she summarizes as

> an *interiorization of the founding separation of the socio-symbolic contract*, as an introduction of its cutting edge into the very interior of every identity whether subjective, sexual, ideological, or so forth. This in such a way that the habitual and increasingly explicit attempt to fabricate a scapegoat victim as foundress of a society or a counter-society may be replaced by the analysis of the potentialities of *victim/executioner* which characterize each identity, each subjectivity, each sex.[49]

Ultimately, then, Kristeva agrees with Girard that desire and violence need not be gendered, and she suggests that a social order in which these differences were recognized as struggles within the subject rather than projected out into society might enable a transition to a non-sacrificial social order. However, whereas Girard simply denies that sexual difference has any significance for his theory, Kristeva recognizes that these socially constructed differences perpetuate the sacrificial social order, through the primal sacrifice of the mother and the repressed violence that ensues and manifests itself against the body and against the other. To quote Reineke again,

> Kristeva would emphasize that violence is writ large in society but it is not born there. Tracing its lineage to the pre-Oedipal drama, Kristeva would invite Girard to stay at the ridge between nature and culture to glimpse the subject at the moment of its bloody birth.[50]

Many of the themes that Kristeva analyses in 'Women's Time' are explored in her lyrical reflection on motherhood titled '*Stabat Mater*', in which she seeks to give voice to a form of maternal discourse that subverts and calls into question the Marian theological tradition, without denying its religious potency as a sublimated form of maternal discourse. The essay, which constitutes a maternal dialogue with Marina Warner's study of the cult of Mary in *Alone of All Her Sex*,[51] is written in two columns. The right-hand column, representing the symbolic, offers an academic survey of the cult of Mary and its influences, while the left-hand column, representing the semiotic, maternal voice, is in heavy print and signifies a persistent bodily presence that disrupts, questions – and is occasionally silenced by – the symbolic. This is the voice that speaks when 'the speaking being finds a refuge when his/her symbolic shell cracks and a crest emerges where speech causes biology to show through: I am thinking of the time of illness, of sexual–intellectual–physical passion, of death.'[52] This rediscovery of a form of language that can express the relationship between the body and the social order, between the mother and the subject, opens the way to 'an heretical ethics separated from morality, an *herethics*, [which] is perhaps no more than that which in life makes bonds, thoughts, and therefore the thought of death, bearable'.[53]

However, if the rehabilitation of a pre-oedipal maternal imaginary constitutes one aspect of this potential socio-symbolic transformation, the other aspect is the recovery of the pre-oedipal father figure, as a benign paternal presence who is the third part of this oedipal triangle. Whereas the Freudian and Lacanian father is a figure who prohibits desire and bars access to the mother, Kristeva's imaginary father is more a figure of mimetic desire, along the lines suggested by Girard:

> The loving mother, different from the caring and clinging mother, is someone who has an object of desire; beyond that, she has an Other with relation to whom the child will serve as go-between. She will love her child with respect to that Other, and it is through a discourse aimed at that Third Party that the child will be set up as 'loved' for the mother.[54]

By introducing the imaginary father into the scenario – the Freudian 'father of individual prehistory'[55] – Kristeva brings a relational dimension into the oedipal process that potentially lessens some of its violence, while still recognizing the unavoidability of maternal abjection and the trauma associated with it. The emptiness that the child experiences through its first perception of itself as separate from the mother, is compensated for by the presence of the imaginary father who, like the imaginary mother, needs to be recognized as a dimension of the pre-oedipal psyche. At the moment of rupture that sets in motion the process of subjectivity, Kristeva displaces the focus from the Lacanian object of desire to the parental relationship. The void that lies at the heart of desire is compensated for by a love that points to the presence of the Other. Thus, to quote Reineke,

> In this love story, at the very splitting that establishes the psyche, the subject uncovers an open space and is supported in being between the One and an Other. Because love promises that for the One there is an Other, love promises being in difference. In theological terms, it promises God.[56]

This openness to the Other also leads beyond Freud's association of love with narcissism, based on the theory that the ego perceives difference as a threat, and therefore it seeks to love that which is the same as itself.[57] The Third Party represented by the imaginary father allows for a love of difference, by introducing a personal relationship beyond the object of the mother's desire, and therefore beyond the psychic emptiness that opens up in the formation of identity. In the absence of this sense of an Other or God in modernity, Kristeva suggests that narcissistic tendencies associated with the Christian love of the self are 'transmuted into a narcissistic intolerance of otherness: knowledge as self-loving contemplation goes over into knowledge as subjugation of otherness and difference'.[58]

The incineration of meaning

I shall return to the figure of the father in the next chapter, but let me recap and bring out some of the questions that now need to be asked in this search for a sacramentality beyond sacrifice. Both Girard and Kristeva agree that the social order is sacrificial, and that there are resources in the Christian tradition that offer a non-sacrificial alternative. For Girard, the key to this lies in a deepened Christian fidelity to the Gospels beyond historical Christianity, in order to recognize the full implications of their revelation of the scapegoat mechanism as requiring a Christian refusal of all forms of violence. Kristeva poses a challenge to Girard insofar as she suggests that it is psychoanalysis rather than Christianity which can ultimately reveal the origins of sacrifice, in the primal sacrifice of the mother. For many centuries, Christianity effectively sublimated the worst effects of the oedipal process, through its symbolization of the parental relationship in the form of a loving Father God and a potent but non-sexual virgin mother: 'Christ's incarnation, that is, the body-and-soul Passion of Man-God, gave momentum to the psychic dynamic that has been nurturing the inner life of Christian humanity for two thousand years.'[59] The Christian faith thus provided a structured context for psychic fantasies and desires in its celebration of divine, incarnate love. Modernity is in crisis because these positive influences of the Christian tradition have been lost, but nothing has yet been found to take their place. The western subject has lost 'his' soul, and Kristeva offers a vivid description of what this means:

> We have neither the time nor the space needed to create a soul for ourselves, and the mere hint of such activity seems frivolous and ill-advised. Held back

by his aloofness, modern man is a narcissist – a narcissist who may suffer, but who feels no remorse . . . When he is not depressed, he becomes swept away by insignificant and valueless objects that offer a perverse pleasure, but no satisfaction. Living in a piecemeal and accelerated space and time, he often has trouble acknowledging his own physiognomy; left without a sexual, subjective, or moral identity, this amphibian is a being of boundaries, a borderline, or a 'false self' – a body that acts, often without even the joys of such performative drunkenness. Modern man is losing his soul, but he does not know it, for the psychic apparatus is what registers representations and their meaningful value for the subject. Unfortunately, that darkroom needs repair.[60]

For Kristeva, the 'repair' must be effected not by a revitalized faith but by a psychoanalytic approach that incorporates and goes beyond Catholic Christianity:

By laying bare the splendors of the Virgin Mary, Christianity, after having relied on a neo-testamentary discretion toward this subject, has unintentionally revealed what lies behind faith. In contrast to Freud, it could be maintained that the presence of the Virgin throughout Christianity is less a return to paganism than an acknowledgement of the hidden side of the sacred mechanism (of any sacred mechanism), which draws us into its soothing and grinding motion in order to leave us with a single path to salvation: having faith in the Father.

Psychoanalysis does not fall short of this, but goes even further: it is 'post-Catholic' by X-raying *meaning* as a *fantasy*, and then going on to take various phantasmatic functions to be an original fantasy in the form of the object-*abject of maternal love* and a cause of eternal return. Finally, it is 'post-Catholic' in that it includes *its own process* within this same course of eternal return. Through this three-way loop, the experience of psychoanalysis results in a sort of combustion.

Let us say then that everything ends up as fire – the fire of Heraclitus, the fire of the burning bush, the fire that burned Isaiah's tongue, or the fire that bedazzled heads with Pentecostal tongues. The truth of the matter is that I envisage the fate of meaning during an analytic session in a similar fashion – as a meaning that is multifaceted, indefinable, set ablaze, yet One Meaning that exerts its influence everywhere. We can admit that this meaning requires the analyst to cling to the Bible's rigor, logic and love, so that this fire might *be* and not die down right away.[61]

'Everything ends up as fire.' With Kristeva, as with Balthasar, we must pass through the incineration of meaning, the dazzling darkness wherein representation loses itself in abjection, in order that language might be 'set ablaze' by that

'One Meaning' — that maternal sacrifice — that founds all meaning. The Bible retains its revelatory capacity, even from the secularized perspective of psychoanalysis, because it expresses rather than conceals the long historical and psychological journey from the pagan maternal cults to the divided consciousness of the (post)Christian subject. For Girard, the biblical exposure of the scapegoat mechanism reveals something of God that is hidden from human consciousness — the Bible retains its divine revelatory potential. For Kristeva, the biblical exposure of the abjected and re-absorbed mother reveals something of the psyche that is hidden from modern consciousness — the Bible retains its revelatory potential, but only in psychological terms.

But is Kristeva herself not a victim of modernity's violent conceits, when she promotes psychoanalysis as the modern alternative to faith? Psychoanalysis is an individualistic and intensive therapy available only to the wealthy few. It has no communal, social dimension, and it can offer acceptance but not hope to those whose suffering it lays bare. It explains away the language of eternity, of redemption, of transcendence, of divine love, by repositioning all these within the wounded psyche even if, in its Kristevan version at least, it does so with the utmost respect and even reverence for the ancient discourses that it appropriates and refigures. For Kristeva, religion remains an illusion, as it was for Freud, but 'the function of the psychoanalyst is to reawaken the imagination and to permit illusions to exist'.[62] Psychoanalysis is 'narrative fiction'[63] that has something in common with religion insofar as it allows for the recovery of illusion.

In writing off the relevance of faith for contemporary culture, Kristeva also writes off the beliefs and practices of many millions of the world's people. Indeed, one could suggest that she sacrifices these bodily, semiotic practices to a therapeutic regime which is highly discursive and disembodied in its approach. As Crownfield points out, 'Christianity has long provided a public, interpersonal semiotic of identity and desire that has sustained and continues to sustain many lives.'[64] One might then invert the relationship between psychoanalysis and faith. If Kristeva argues for the necessity of psychoanalysis retaining the insights of the Christian tradition, one might ask if Christianity might enfold within itself the insights of psychoanalysis, without losing its narrative of truth, hope and redemption. How far can Catholicism allow itself to be interrogated by psychoanalysis, and to what extent can it incorporate into its practices, structures and teachings the rich insights that psychoanalysis offers into its own language of love and desire, fear and abjection? To quote Crownfield again, this depends

> on how the discourse of desire, of identity, of emptiness plays out across and with and through the discourse of God and Jesus and the church. It depends on whether the ancient battles of orthodoxy against heresy can be reinscribed

as a defense of triadic openness against narcissistic alternatives. It depends on whether acknowledgment of the fictive and erotic dynamics of faith renews or dissolves the power of this semiotic to sustain not just individual lives but communities of moral and social practice.[65]

But, says Crownfield, it also depends on the alternatives:

> If the only alternatives are narcissistic symbolic systems founded either on mystic fusion or on a will to domination, or else abjective icons of terror and rage, nihilistic, addictive, and violent, it is premature to dismantle a historic and social semiotics that is rooted in the inseparability of personal identity from the acknowledgment of the third party, and that is still tacitly imagined in the basic textures of our secular discourses of identity and coexistence and value.

Is there, then, a future for an imaginary, erotic, open, optional Christianity?[66]

The Catholic Church is a paradox. How can one speak of such a vision, when a conclave of ageing cardinals appoints a seventy-eight-year-old celibate man, noted in the past for his authoritarianism, as the new face of Christ's presence in the world? How can we speak of an 'erotic, open, optional Christianity' in a Church whose most intense energy continues to be focused on the control of sexuality, even if it means denying the use of condoms to protect oneself against AIDS?

But in the Introduction, I suggested that the paradoxical nature of the Catholic tradition makes it resistant to the controlling logic of the modern world, and indeed to the controlling manoeuvres of the Catholic hierarchy. For the life of the Church is embodied not in the College of Cardinals but in the hopes and visions, fears and sorrows, of those millions around the world whose faith finds expression in carnivalesque rituals of festivity and mourning, in day-to-day gestures of devotion and doubt, in muddled expressions of desire and denial where the body of Christ mingles with the touch and tingle, with the blood and semen, milk and mucus, of our ordinary human couplings and encounters in a Eucharistic community that scrambles our tidy boundaries of nation, kin and class, of morals, laws and creeds. The pontificating of cardinals and feminist theologians alike barely impinges upon this other Catholicism, a Catholicism whose fecundity lies not in bearing babies for the Pope but in the stubborn persistence of Christ's maternal love for the world. There always has been an 'erotic, optional, open Christianity', but until the Church can transcend the violent dualisms that this creates in the struggle between the whore and the virgin, the pure and the impure, this Christianity will remain masked by the headline-grabbing politics and scandals of the men who only think they rule the Church.

Can a renewed feminism encounter a revitalized Catholicism, in order to open a clearing wherein a voice of difference might come into being, a voice that burns with things hidden since the foundation of the world, a voice that might reignite the stagnant imagination of the Church with a blazing promise of peace? Let us keep that question in mind, as we continue this task of bringing to birth a new way of speaking in order to nurture a new way of being in the world.

12 Redeeming fatherhood

In this chapter, I move towards the refiguration of the divine fatherhood through a closer analysis of the ways in which concepts of paternity and masculinity inform the understanding of God, both in Balthasar's theology and in critical theorists. Given the extent to which discourses of fatherhood shape Christian theology and worship, one must go beyond a feminist critique of Christian patriarchy to a new understanding of fatherhood, through the deconstruction of dominant theological motifs.[1] If male and female bodies, and maternal and paternal relationships, are to find a space of peaceful co-habitation within the Christian story, then we must go beyond Oedipus to the paternal and maternal *agape* of God for the world. This entails considering more closely the ways in which sacrifice is represented in Catholic theology and literature.

God, suffering and sacrifice

We have already seen how Balthasar's understanding of the fatherhood of God is closely tied to Greek philosophical concepts of paternal origins, undergirded by an essentialist theology of sexual difference. The concept of *kenosis* which is central to his theology is implicitly (and sometimes explicitly) associated with male ejaculation, so that the *kenosis* of God in the act of creation and in the incarnation, and the *kenosis* of Christ on the cross, take on the aspects of male sexuality. We have also seen that the most challenging issue that arises in a feminist reading of Balthasar is not sex but violence: it is not the sexuality of his rhetoric *per se* that creates problems, but its inexorable association with death, violence, sin and hell, frequently represented in the rhetoric of female sexual embodiment. To explore the implications of this more closely in association with Girard is to open up possibilities for readings of Balthasar beyond violence, particularly as far as the maternal representation of God is concerned (see Chapter 13).

Balthasar describes Girard's theory as 'the most dramatic project to be undertaken today in the field of soteriology and in theology generally'.[2] However, he has several objections to Girard, accusing him of producing a 'closed system' which makes all religion 'the invention of Satan'.[3] His main concern centres on the relationship between God and the sacrifice of Christ. He argues that, in Girard, 'The dramatic tension between the world and God is so overstretched that the link breaks, rendering impossible a drama that involves the two sides.'[4] In particular, by neglecting the concepts of justice and sin in favour of concepts of 'hostility', 'power' and 'violence',[5] Girard offers a psychological explanation for the cross that renders God powerless:

> What takes place on the Cross, according to this theory, if . . . the power-less Father-God demands nothing in the nature of an 'atoning sacrifice'? To put it more concretely: the Church regards the Eucharistic celebration as a representation of the 'sacrifice of the Cross', in which Christ has effectively offered himself for mankind; how then can she present and offer Christ's self-surrender to the divine Father if the latter, who is no longer an Old Testament God, has 'no pleasure' in it, since he did not *want* the Cross, and even less *commanded* his Son to accept it?[6]

Later, referring to Raymund Schwager's interpretation of Girard, Balthasar claims that

> God's forgiveness and the Cross (that is, the bearing of sin) cannot be left in mutual isolation: they are related. In this case, therefore, it will not be enough to follow Girard and Schwager in demythologizing the Old Testament picture of God so that he changes from a violent, wrathful God and becomes a powerless God who does not engage in retribution.[7]

Ultimately, for Balthasar, Christ's death must be seen as an act of obedience that implies the involvement of the Father and of the Holy Spirit:

> in his obedient death, Jesus dies of the sin that murders him but . . . he also dies because God forsakes him . . . [I]t is the human expression of a shared love-death in a supereminently trinitarian sense: the One who forsakes is just as much affected (in his eternal life) as the One who is forsaken, and just as much as the forsaking and forsaken love that is One in the Holy Spirit.[8]

Balthasar's objection to Girard, therefore, pivots around the distance between the Father and the Son in the death of Christ, which entails the abandonment of the Son by the Father and the expression of the Spirit's love as a form of forsakenness. Related to this is his insistence that the Father God must not be rendered powerless in the event of the crucifixion: the image of a 'violent, wrathful God' must be reinterpreted but not rejected altogether, if the Christian doctrine of atonement is to retain its truth, particularly with regard to the Eucharistic expression of the sacrifice of Christ. For Balthasar, it would appear that one must choose between a violent retributive God and a powerless God. There is, as Coakley suggests, no sense of a God whose power is revealed in the vulnerability of Christ. The more vulnerable Christ becomes in the passivity of his dying, the more distant from God he becomes, and the more masculine qualities of power, violence, wrath and retribution must be asserted within the fatherhood of God.

But what kind of God and what kind of worship are at stake here? Not only does Balthasar refuse to accept that the cross might challenge the patriarchal image of God as a wrathful, powerful father figure, he also insists upon the sacrificial character of the Eucharist. Once again, if we ask what this means, we discover that Balthasar's theology depends on sacrificial violence. To take Girard seriously would begin to call into question some of Balthasar's most fundamental theological claims, not least the claim that Speyr's years of torture were a privileged form of revelation through participation in Christ's suffering. We might have to ask who exactly willed this suffering – Christ, or Balthasar? Whose 'desire' did she embody, and what forms of violent mimesis circulating as a contagion between these two demanded her masochistic sacrifice in order that he might take her place?

There is, as MacKinnon suggests, a sense of 'the overwhelming, pervasive reality of evil'[9] in much of Balthasar's theology (see Chapter 9), but the problem is that Balthasar seems at times to revel in the apocalyptic violence of Christ's struggle, rather than protesting against the needless suffering of his fellow human beings. The early Christian vision of Christ's cosmic victory over the power of death is translated by Balthasar into a rhetoric of visceral savagery, so that Christ seems to be the perpetrator as well as the victim of the violence that he unleashes. We have already seen the sexual violence that informs Balthasar's understanding of the relationship between Christ and the earthly Church, but his Christ is sometimes portrayed as a warrior figure, to such an extent that to participate in the Mass is to be called to participate in a slaughter.

Consider, for example, the following quotation from a section of *Theo-drama II* titled 'Liturgy and Slaughter'.[10] Here, Balthasar develops his idea of Christ as the dramatic hero, the one in whom the Word finds particular and unique expression but also acquires universal significance through having to be 'shattered so that the universality which was contained in concentrated form in his mission may be manifested'.[11] This manifestation of 'absolute Goodness and Beauty' in 'an ultimate, definitive shape, a definitively incarnate Word'[12] demands an active response:

> In the face of this definitive figure and its victorious ruination, no one who witnesses it can remain unmoved (or moved) on his spectator's seat: he is

228 *The beginning*

provoked to step onto the stage and offer his services. 'One has died for all; therefore all have died' (2 Cor. 5:14).[13]

What does it mean to respond, to 'step onto the stage and offer [one's] services'? Taking his imagery from the reference in the Book of Revelation to the stream of life which comes from the throne of 'the Lamb slain from the foundation of the world' (see Rev. 13:8), Balthasar describes existence in the face of the Absolute as 'simultaneously a liturgy of worship and a battlefield':[14]

> The Lamb, 'as though it had been slain', rides into battle like a warrior, his garment drenched in blood, together with his 'called, chosen and faithful ones', to fight against the powers and forces of the world; there seems to be no end to the cries of woe, the slaughter and annihilation. Can this darkness, this wrath that is unleashed from above and from below, these cries of anguish in the face of ever-intensifying plagues, this elegy on the (almost wanton) ruin of all that the world holds precious and enjoyable, be reconciled with the serene, ceaseless hymns of worship before the throne, on the Sea of Glass, beneath the light of the Seven Lamps of the Spirit? How does this carnage fit with the extolling of him who was, and is, and is to come, and who – when the drama is at its climax – 'has begun to reign'?[15]

This constitutes 'the mysterious, apocalyptic simultaneity of liturgy and drama'.[16] In the Book of Revelation, the 'holy war' of the Lamb shows that 'there is no hiatus between worship and service and above all no hiatus between the powerlessness of being slain and the power of conquest – the latter comes by virtue of the former'.[17]

What are we to make of this imagery? In a (post)modern world that seems to stand on the brink of apocalyptic violence, there can be no act of worship that is not open to the suffering of our times, and the Christian language of peace and reconciliation is hollow unless it takes with the utmost seriousness the extent to which human lives are daily destroyed by every kind of violence, oppression and abuse – what the Church today refers to as 'the structures of sin'. But Balthasar's language, for all its apparent bloodiness and bodiliness, is abstract in the extreme. It has much more in common with Tolkien's *Lord of the Rings* than with the grim human realities of war and violence. His apocalyptic prose surrenders humanity to the inevitability of violence and slaughter as some cosmic epic in which the political and ethical choices of individual lives fade into insignificance. All we can do is to choose which side to fight on, in a spiritual battle that has little if anything to do with the concrete realities of life and death, justice and oppression, peace and violence, which form the fabric of our engagement with the world. And, despite MacKinnon's defence, it is hard to see how anyone who was living and writing theology in the dark years of the 1940s can claim that there is 'no hiatus between the powerlessness of being slain and the power of conquest' (see Chapter 9) unless, that is, they had the kind of insight that Girard has. For Girard might indeed say this: that Christ conquers violence with non-violence, and that his powerlessness thus reveals the power of forgiving, non-retaliatory love. But that would entail an entirely different theology of the cross than that which Balthasar offers.

Masculinity and violence

The Second Vatican Council signalled a shift away from the exclusive focus on the Mass as sacrifice to a more pluralistic interpretation of its potential meanings. However, the reactionary spirit within some sections of the Church in recent years has seen a reassertion of magisterial authority, as well as a reaffirmation of the sacrificial significance of the Mass, sometimes expressed in lurid language. Consider, for example, the following extract from a document titled 'The Eucharist: Source and Summit of the Life and Mission of the Church', produced by the Synod of Bishops in 2004:

> St John Chrysostom looks at the Eucharist from the perspective of baptismal initiation, as the food of a life which is received and sustained in the struggle against Satan. His words of explanation are particularly helpful in understanding the eschatological aspect of the Sacrament: 'For when you see the Lord sacrificed, laid upon the altar, and the priest standing and praying over the victim, and all the worshippers empurpled with that precious blood, can you then think that you are still among men, and standing upon the earth? Are you not, on the contrary, straightway translated to heaven, and casting out every carnal thought from the soul, do you not, with disembodied spirit and pure reason, contemplate the things which are in heaven?'[18]

As one woman correspondent commented to me on reading the above passage, 'I am translated to a macabre ritualistic sexualized fantasy of celibate men!'[19]

Yet at this stage we might pause to ask why, perhaps alone of all modern institutions, the Catholic Church still has what appears to be a deeply rooted psychological appeal based on its cultic, sacrificial mysteries. For it is often pointed out that the liberalizing and democratizing tendencies of the Second Vatican Council produced a radical decline in church attendance and religious observance among Catholics, while the more conservative forms of Catholicism would appear to be vigorous and thriving. The growing influence of Balthasar is one manifestation of this trend. In order to explore this question, I want to return to Walter Ong, to whom I have already referred in terms of Monica Migliorinio Miller's highly selective and one-sided reading of his book, *Fighting for Life*.

One of the main points of Ong's argument is that western thought from the time of the ancient Greeks has developed through forms of academic confrontation that reflect the agonistic struggles of men to separate from their natural, maternal environments and assert their individuality and independence. The transition from exclusively male universities to more inclusive student bodies has created a crisis in knowledge, because women students challenge the assumptions inherent in this aggressively antagonistic culture of learning. In particular, Ong argues that the Catholic Church has proved most resistant to these changes, because of its investment in these 'agonistic patterns' that have shaped western consciousness more generally. From the biblical era on, Ong argues that the Catholic tradition is rooted in models of

> spiritual struggle or warfare carried on paradigmatically by male against male . . . Preaching Jesus' gospel of faith, hope, and divine love, the Church has from the beginning been very much at home in the agonistic male world, and nowhere more than when engaged in intellectual activity.[20]

Ong associates this particularly with the use of Learned Latin, 'the extrafamilial, sex-linked, distinctively male language that carried with it the old agonistic mindset and thought forms'.[21] Writing less than twenty years after the Second Vatican Council, he points out that 'the discontinuation of Latin and the collapse of agonistic theology are not yet two decades old'.[22] He suggests that, as a consequence of Vatican II, 'the agonistic . . . has moved from the center to the periphery',[23] so that 'the intensely agonistic stage of consciousness has been superseded by another stage, and existence is no longer defined so utterly by polemic'.[24] Perhaps, then, we might read Balthasar's theology as the last furious assertion of this masculine power struggle, as it faces its immanent collapse beneath the combined pressures of feminism and liberalism in the postconciliar Church.

Nevertheless, I have already suggested that a theological vision premised on the values of liberal feminism is an impoverished one which substitutes a political ideology for the profound psychological and spiritual resonances of the Catholic tradition, with its mystical, transcendent beauty, its incarnate sacramentality, and its visceral bodiliness – all of which have as their shadow side the kind of theology and spirituality that I have been exploring in the last few chapters. The question is, can feminist theology find the resources to challenge the sacrificial violence that is inherent in this necrophilia of one side of the Catholic tradition, without also sacrificing that tradition's compelling truthfulness in its capacity to express the interweaving of hope and anguish, peace and conflict, love and desolation, beauty and ugliness, that make up the light and shade of our being in the world? In order to ask this question, it is not enough simply to invent a rhetoric of political correctness to glaze the issues. We need to try to understand why the Church is as it is, and this is where psychoanalysis is an indispensable resource.

Christ the dragon-slayer

Ong describes Christianity as 'a gold mine for depth psychologists', rooted as it is 'in memory and thereby in the history of consciousness'.[25] Whereas feminist theology tends to represent Christianity as a thoroughly patriarchal institution, Ong suggests that the reason for the ongoing struggle of assertive masculinity in the Church has much to do with its being a thoroughly feminized and maternal institution. Ong argues that 'Roman Catholic doctrine is inexorably psychosomatic and in this sense essentially hospitable to neobiological insights, despite recurrent Manichean or Cartesian drives that occasionally inhibit recognition of this fact.'[26] Because of this 'psychosomatic' emphasis, 'The Church's teaching is structured permanently in the deep feminine–masculine polarities that shift dialectically through time.'[27] In our own time, this dialectic has produced 'the needed and welcome ascendancy of the feminine in consciousness signaled most conspicuously by women's liberation movements and also perhaps even more by worldwide ecological concern, which regards the whole universe as a house, a home'.[28] However, this feminization of the Church presents a challenge to masculinity, since the 'overwhelming femininity of the Roman Catholic Church' from the human side suggests that a male clergy is basically not a characterizing feature of the Church so much as a countervailing feature.[29]

Although he is careful to admit that his argument 'does not resolve the question of the ordination of women',[30] Ong claims that this 'overwhelming femininity' of the Church explains why

> Despite the masculine clergy, in macho cultures (of which there are many), where the male labors under more than the usual male insecurity, open association of males with Church services is relatively rare, so great is the threat of being swamped there in the feminine. In such cultures even an all-male clergy is likely to be regarded by other males as somewhat feminine because of the close alliance with the feminine Church.[31]

Ong then seeks to defend the masculinity of Christ, by reinterpreting his agonistic struggle in terms of a non-violent but active acceptance of the violence of his enemies and his own death:

> This free quietness, related to Jesus' nonviolence, differentiates his struggle from the purely male, aggressive, violent *agōn* through which so much has been effected in biological evolution but which in a human bespeaks some sort of insecurity and weakness. The masculine in Jesus' redemptive action is

> complemented by this feminine strength-in-quietness – which is not passivity at all but a free and active choice. Such free choice, free response, is what makes woman in her 'quietness' appealing to man – not passivity, which is infrahuman – and what makes woman 'always conquer,' according to the Chinese proverb. For this quietness bespeaks power.[32]

Ong goes on to compare Jesus to the epic hero as archetypal dragon-slayer:

> Jesus is like the mythological dragon slayer, the masculine ego . . . in that he wins from captivity his bride, the Church. But he is quite unlike the dragon slayer in that he conquers by his free obedience to his Father in freely submitting to death.[33]

But even if Jesus, as 'a personal friend, related to each individual human being, male or female . . . is not entirely like the dragon slayer',[34] Ong still argues that the solitude of his final hours makes him a figure of 'the male fighter. He had to go it alone.'[35]

I have already suggested that Ong's sexual essentialisms need to be read as cultural constructs and therefore open to negotiation, so that his suggestion that Jesus is masculine in his 'redemptive struggle' and feminine in his 'strength-in-quietness' must be challenged. But even as feminists question such cultural assumptions, it is important to recognize their power to shape human behaviour, and this is where I think Ong is persuasive, particularly as far as masculine behaviour is concerned.

Feminists might argue that the internalization of feminine ideals that are primarily masculine projections has a profoundly oppressive effect on women, but if these ideals are damaging, they are first and foremost damaging to women themselves because they are fundamentally masochistic. The passive, obedient woman is not a threat to others, except insofar as her own daughters might pattern their behaviour on hers, or except insofar as she colludes in the violence and aggression of the men around her. But, as Freud points out, if women's psyches are shaped by the masochistic internalization of the death-drives, in men these are externalized in the form of aggression. So the man whose identity is formed by the kind of agonistic values that Ong describes is a profound threat to others, and in a world torn apart by violence of every kind, it is still true that men are predominantly if not exclusively responsible for that violence, including terrorism and the war on terrorism, the international sex trade, the arms trade, the implicit violence of global economic policies, and the ongoing violence of rape and assault played out daily on the bodies of women and children in city streets, family homes and on the world-wide web. In recent years, studies of masculinity have begun to address the problem of male violence, but we have yet to reach a stage when church leaders, politicians and policy-makers fully acknowledge its destructive significance.

Peace and martyrdom

One of the problems with liberal feminism is that it offers a vision of Church in which we would all be terribly nice to one another and work together for a better world – nice men are included in this offer – in a way that sidelines the roots of sexual and social conflict deep within our own psyches, and our need for something beyond the imperative of justice. As Balthasar so well recognizes, we need beauty, aesthetics, art, literature, and that means that we need a theological vision that can express darkness as well as light, struggle as well as creativity, conflict as well as harmony.

If we can go beyond Ong's sexual stereotypes, I believe he suggests a way forward that might bring us to a Girardian spirituality of non-violence, in which we are not simply tamed and pacified but energized and activated through a radical, activist, pacifist Church – a Church militant, in the sense of the early Christians, who recognized that the rhetoric of spiritual warfare was utterly inconsistent with the shedding of blood. But we cannot use that language at this point in history, when Christians still go out to bomb, kill and maim their fellow human beings in the name of some greater good, and when the language of struggle has become so infected with the fear of sexuality, as we have seen in Balthasar's theology. We need a different idiom, but an idiom that still allows us to express the fullness of the Christian faith and its demands upon us.

Ong suggests that 'For the followers of Jesus, female and male, faith is also a high-risk undertaking, involving struggle.'[36] He points to the example of the martyrs,

> the supreme witnesses, men and women who contest death in quietness, who go freely to their deaths because they will not desist from proclaiming the Gospel, the Good News, from telling what Jesus did and said, what he means to them . . . Like Jesus, the martyr, male or female, is a nonviolent agonistic figure, struggling to stand upright in obedient love against attack. Though martyrdom is agonistic, a struggle, a contest, it is totally nonaggressive . . . Martyrdom is the sublimation of all aggression but a contest for all that. And it is one to which all Christians, male and female, in principle may be called.[37]

Let us note that Ong's sexual dualisms have disappeared at this point, even although he has previously made so much of them. If the martyr, male or female, is 'a nonviolent agonistic figure', is this not a model of Christian discipleship that transcends gender, so that every man and woman must find within herself or himself that 'strength in quietness' that produces 'redemptive action'? If, in the non-Christian world, non-violence and aggression, passivity and strength, are gendered as feminine and masculine respectively, then the transformation of Christian personhood – the transformation of the human subject into the

Christian person, to use Balthasar's image – is most conspicuous through its resistance to the definitions and stereotypes that position men and women in relationships of masculine aggression and feminine passivity, masculine initiative and feminine receptivity. It is the integrated person who incorporates within herself or himself the strengths associated with both sexes, and who addresses the destructive internalization of gendered stereotypes that corrode her or his ability to manifest the fullness of life in Christ, to become a new person in Christ. To say this is not to render the sexual body insignificant: it is to incorporate the body into a new symbolics so that the meanings it reveals are interpreted through the rich texturing and gendering of a language that can express the encounter between human *eros* and divine *agape* that plays among and between us in the liturgy and in the Christian community.

This means moving beyond a theological and ecclesial environment which, as Ong suggests, perpetuates a conflictual relationship between the masculine psyche and the maternal Church. In the antagonistic sexual milieu of modernity, with its individualistic masculine subject and its passive feminine other, we have seen in Balthasar's theology that this risks giving free rein to an anachronistic masculine religious imaginary to indulge its most vivid and sometimes macabre fantasies of sex and death, in a way that is increasingly likely to alienate women. I cannot believe that any non-Catholic feminist who has persevered with this work so far would have been attracted to Catholicism by Balthasar. On the contrary, women are increasingly likely to be driven away from a Church whose beliefs and practices are informed by such theology.

The challenge is to find a way beyond this situation that capitulates neither to liberal modernity nor to reactionary conservatism, but that might genuinely open up a space of liturgical and sacramental significance capable of expressing the most profound truths, hopes, desires and fears of our human condition, while healing some of the violent traumas and disjunctions of our modern subjectivities and societies. This means asking how Christianity became fixated on an idea of a sacrificial, masculine Father God, invested with characteristics and attributes that so often seem to run counter to the Gospel relationship between Christ and his heavenly Father.

God's origins

Throughout his work, Balthasar resists the suggestion that the Christian understanding of God might be seen in terms of an originating maternal principle. His argument is summarized in the following quotation, which refers to 'Woman, as *synagogue-Mary-Church*':

> As the active power of receiving all that heaven gives, she is the epitome of creaturely power and dignity; she is what God presupposes as the Creator in

order to give the seed of his Word to the world. In no religion (not even in those of matriarchal cultures) and in no philosophy can woman be the original principle, since her fruitfulness, which appears more active and explicit in the sexual sphere than the fruitfulness of man, is always ordered to insemination.[38]

Exploring the implications of this in relation to the masculinity of Christ, he writes that God

> as the Creator, bears in himself the archetype of man and woman but . . . is to be revered as 'Father', since he always has priority in generating. At most one can say that the eternal Son in whom the Father created all things is, as 'wisdom', in a certain way 'feminine' in relation to the Father, but he must represent the Father in the world by his Incarnation, and this he can do only as a man.[39]

There is a dangerous literalism at work in these theological ideas, for it is hard to see how Balthasar can avoid the charge that, despite his denials to the contrary, he is guilty of importing an implicitly pagan understanding of divine sexuality into the Christian theology of creation, in a way that finds little support in the Bible. With regard to Genesis, Paul Ricoeur makes the point that 'God is not designated as father and . . . a specific verb – *bara* – is used to tell about the creative act; any trace of begetting is thus eliminated.'[40] With regard to Mary's conception of Christ, while there has been a widespread tendency to describe this in erotic terms in devotional writings, the Church Fathers went to great pains to dissociate this from any possible confusion with the mythical sexual couplings of women and gods. Justin Martyr (d. c. 165) refers to the Spirit which, 'when it came upon the virgin and overshadowed her, caused her to conceive, not by intercourse, but by power'.[41] Of course, I am not suggesting that Balthasar ignores these insights and he is careful to insist that he does not posit an explicitly sexual function to creation or to the conception of Christ, but his theology of masculine divinity owes considerably more to Greek philosophical ideas of origination than to the Bible.

Nevertheless, in Balthasar we have already seen that nothing is ever quite as straightforward (nor indeed as 'straight') as it appears to be. So let me begin, with Irigaray's help, by teasing out some of the implications of this insistence on a philosophical concept of divine masculine origination.

The association between divine generativity, the fatherhood of God and feminine passivity or receptivity entered Catholic theology through the influence of Greek philosophy, particularly the neo-Platonism of Plotinus (via patristic theology, including Augustine) and Aristotle (via Aquinas). Irigaray's *Speculum of the Other Woman* seeks to trace the occlusion of maternal originations back through the western philosophical tradition, from Freud to Plato. Like Kristeva, Irigaray locates the sacrificial social order in the originating sacrifice of the mother. In her reading of Plato's allegory of the cave, she explores the ways in which his theory of the Forms leads to the denigration of nature, the body and maternal origins, through its privileging of an originating source of knowledge by which the philosopher comes to understand that the material world is made up of shadowy imitations of transcendent Ideals. Behind the metaphor of the cave Irigaray posits a more ancient place of origination – the mother's body – a source that has been forgotten, denied and abandoned, along with nature and the material world, in the masculine thrust towards transcendence and God. In this inverted universe,

> It is God-the-Father who created the heaven, and the stars, and these convert you to his idea. To his image. This world is 'true' only insofar as it is engendered by Him alone, and related to Him alone. This is fairly evidently the case for everything that dominates and stands above the earth, treading her under foot, under its erection . . . Engendering the real is the father's task, engendering the fictive is the task of the mother – that 'receptacle' for turning out more or less good copies of reality.[42]

In seeking to 'unearth' the maternal body buried beneath the metaphor of the cave, Irigaray exploits the philosophical association between matter and the mother, an association that is particularly evident in her reading of Plotinus elsewhere in *Speculum*, in which she devotes a chapter to selected extracts from the Sixth Tractate of his Third Ennead. Through an act of mimetic appropriation of Plotinus's texts, she positions the philosopher's voice within her own text to reveal the freezing out of maternal origins in the development of a metaphysics of paternal origination that has dominated Christian theology and the western intellectual tradition. The chapter is titled '*Une Mère de Glace*', representing a play on the sounds *mer/mère* (sea/mother), and on the meaning of '*glace*' as both ice and mirror.

As a neo-Platonist, Plotinus depicts Matter as an inert, non-corporeal receptacle that acquires shape in the form of visible objects when it is penetrated and acted upon by an Ideal Principle. Plotinus describes Matter as being 'like a mirror showing things as in itself when they are really elsewhere, filled in appearance but actually empty, containing nothing, pretending everything'.[43] In relation to this deceptive matter, the visible object is 'Feeble in itself, a false thing and projected upon a falsity, like an image in a dream or against water or on a mirror.'[44] Central to the thesis of maternal exclusion that informs all Irigaray's work is Plotinus's metaphorical association of inert Matter with the mother, and of the Ideal Principle with phallic masculinity. Using the metaphors of water and the mirror, Irigaray asks again and again what it means to represent the maternal body as a surface of reflecting images, so that 'she' can reflect only images of the paternal ideal, without ever having access to forms of representation capable of expressing her bodily difference and maternal significance.

Here is Plotinus, quoted by Irigaray:

> The Ideal Principles entering into Matter as to a Mother affect it neither for better nor for worse . . . This, I think, is why the doctors of old, teaching through symbols and mystic representations, exhibit the ancient Hermes with the generative organs always in active posture; this is to convey that the generator of things of sense is the Intellectual Reason-Principle: the sterility of Matter, eternally unmoved, is indicated by the eunuchs surrounding it in its representation as the All-Mother . . . [T]here is no intention of suggesting a complete parallel with motherhood to those not satisfied with a surface impression but needing a precisely true presentment; by a remote symbolism, the nearest they could find, they indicate that Matter is sterile, not female to full effect, female in receptivity only, not in pregnancy: this they accomplish by exhibiting Matter as approached by what is neither female nor effectively male but castrated of that impregnating power which belongs only to the unchangeably masculine.[45]

For Irigaray, this association of the mother with inert, castrated matter is more than an ancient philosophical metaphor. It is an act of symbolic matricide that finds repeated expression in the texts of western philosophy and in the Freudian theory of the Oedipus complex, and it provides the dominant symbolics of Christian theology. It explains how language – the system of representation and meaning – comes to be constructed exclusively around masculine and paternal values, abstracted from the body, nature and the maternal relationship.

We have seen that, in Lacanian psycholinguistics, language is a substitute for the mother's body. The acquisition of language is associated with the child's awareness of separation from the mother, and with the incest taboo, which means that it must repress its desire for the maternal body when it becomes a speaking subject. In Lacan's linguistic interpretation of Freud, it is not the Law of the Father but the Name of the Father that forbids access to the mother, by asserting the father's prior claim to her body associated with possession of the symbolic phallus. (Lacan plays on the similarity between 'nom' and 'non' – the name of the father is also the father's prohibition of infant desire.) But for Irigaray, this psycholinguistic insight can be traced back to a more original sacrifice than that of the primal father which forms the basis of the Oedipus complex in Freud's later work:

> Does the father replace the womb with the matrix of his language? But the exclusivity of his law refuses all representation to that first body, that first home, that first love. These are sacrificed and provide matter for an empire of language that so privileges the male sex as to confuse it with the human

race . . . The social order, our culture, psychoanalysis itself, are all insistent that the mother must remain silent, outlawed. The father forbids any *corps-à-corps* with the mother . . . The problem is that when the father refuses to allow the mother her power of giving birth and seeks to be the sole creator, then according to our culture he superimposes upon our ancient world of flesh and blood a universe of language and symbols that has no roots in the flesh and drills a hole through the female womb and through the place of female identity.[46]

The challenge that Irigaray poses is to discover a form of language that expresses rather than represses the relationship to the maternal body and the desires associated with it:

We . . . . need to find, rediscover, invent the words, the sentences that speak of the most ancient and most current relationship we know – the relationship to the mother's body, to our body – sentences that translate the bond between our body, her body, the body of our daughter. We need to discover a language that is not a substitute for the experience of *corps-à-corps* as the paternal language seeks to be, but which accompanies that bodily experience, clothing it in words that do not erase the body but speak the body.[47]

This does not mean substituting matriarchy for patriarchy, but rather reconnecting paternal and maternal origins, reopening the passage between Plato's cave and the sky, between the body and language, between immanence and transcendence, so that both sexes have access to a form of gendered language that allows them to express their sexual subjectivity in relation to one another and to God.

We have already explored at some length the ways in which Balthasar's theological superstructure is deeply vulnerable to the kind of critique offered by Irigaray. Indeed, it is tempting to parody his womanly men in the Church as a latter-day equivalent of 'the eunuchs surrounding . . . the All-Mother', with God's erect phallus as the hidden Lacanian signifier that holds the structure in place, and a castrated feminized creation. In the next chapter, I consider the linguistic and sacramental rehabilitation of the maternal body, but now I want to explore possibilities for going beyond Balthasar's idea of the patriarchal Father God, to ask if it is possible to redeem the fatherhood of God beyond patriarch.

Insofar as a deconstructive approach to language seeks to liberate rather than annihilate meaning, it is not enough simply to posit a maternal discourse about God over and against or alongside the existing paternal discourse. The meanings inherent in the word 'father' must be destabilized and called into question, if 'mother' is to find a space of signification beyond the binary dualisms that will always entail a level of rhetorical violence in the struggle for meaning. The relationship between maternal and paternal images of God needs to be understood not in terms of oppositional or hierarchical meanings, but in terms of the unfolding of revelation in the space where our ordinary human relationships open out into promise and hope. In other words, beyond the disappointments and struggles of every human relationship, however loving, beyond the sometimes violent failure of mothers and fathers to reflect the tenderness and compassion of God, we need to retain a vision of the potential of such relational language to communicate something truthful about God's love for the world. If, as Ruether and others suggest, patriarchy itself is an originating cause of injustice, oppression and suffering in the world, then our idea of fatherhood stands in need of redemption, not abandonment.

The compassion of the father

Paul Ricoeur describes the father figure as

> a problematic figure, incomplete and in suspense. It is a *designation* that is susceptible of traversing a diversity of semantic levels, from the phantasm of the father as castrator, who must be killed, to the symbol of the father who dies of compassion.[48]

In his essay, 'Fatherhood: From Phantasm to Symbol', Ricoeur explores the significance and transformative potential of the father figure from the perspectives of Freudian psychoanalysis, Hegelian phenomenology and biblical hermeneutics. In particular, what concerns me here is Ricoeur's argument that the Bible represents a shift away from the oedipal father gods common to all religions, to a new understanding of fatherhood through a return of the repressed. Ricoeur points to the sparsity of references to God as father in the Old Testament, and to the fact that the creation story in Genesis omits any reference to either a father or a son. He traces the biblical development of the father figure as one which involves a transition from the phantasm of the ancestral oedipal father, to the father as a symbol and a name who is beyond kinship, and who encompasses both maternal and paternal qualities. This transformative process culminates in the father becoming a figure of invocation in the New Testament, in such a way that 'Fatherhood is . . . placed in the realm of a theology of hope.'[49] The fatherhood of God that enters the scene anew in the Gospels, particularly in John's Gospel, is therefore not 'a relapse into archaism'.[50] Rather,

> it is rare, difficult, and audacious, because it is prophetic, directed toward fulfillment rather than toward origins. It does not look backward, toward a great ancestor, but forward, in the direction of a new intimacy on the model of the knowledge of the son.[51]

Through the idea of the 'Just Sufferer' or the 'Suffering Servant', epitomized in Christ, death is inscribed into the father figure in a way that converts the murderous killing of the primal father in the Freudian oedipal complex, to the compassionate death of the father for others: 'A *dying for* would come to take the place of a being *killed by*':[52]

> The Just One is killed, certainly, and thereby the aggressive impulse against the father is satisfied by means of the offspring of the archaic paternal image; but at the same time, and this is the essential point, the meaning of the death is reversed: by becoming 'dead for another', the death of the Just One achieves the metamorphosis of the paternal image in the direction of a figure of kindness and compassion. The death of Christ stands at the end of this development . . . Here is completed the conversion of death as murder into death as offering.[53]

Ricoeur makes clear that Christianity has failed to realize this transformation in its theology, which 'abounds in purely punitive and penal interpretations of the sacrifice of Christ'.[54] Nevertheless, he shows how a biblically faithful and psychoanalytically informed reading can redeem the fatherhood of God, so that a figure that many feminists associate with sacrifice, torture and oppression, becomes instead a figure of self-sacrificing compassion and love – an image that is culturally and theologically more often associated with motherhood than with fatherhood. From this perspective, the *kenosis* of the father would entail an emptying out of the patriarchal privileges of primacy, superiority and hierarchical power, in order to make space for a new creation of the word 'father'.

Kristeva offers a different psycholinguistic approach to the reconstitution of fatherhood, through a retrieval of the pre-oedipal, pre-sexual father associated with love and desire rather than with prohibition and taboo.[55] While Irigaray seeks to go beyond the necessity of the Oedipus complex through the transformation of sexual subjectivity, Kristeva seeks the modification of the oedipal process through a renegotiation of both the maternal and paternal roles. In Lacanian psychoanalysis and in object relations theory, the pre-oedipal mother (in Lacanian terms, the phallic mother) represents an all-engulfing, pre-linguistic and therefore pre-subjective totality in terms of the infantile relationship. The separation effected by the symbolic or oedipal father, with the accompanying threat of castration, constitutes a violent rupture between this phallic mother and child. However, Kristeva appeals to Freud's idea of the 'father of individual prehistory',[56] to explore the influence of the imaginary father as a loving third party (not necessarily to be identified with the biological father), who forms an alternative focus of the mother's attention and thus enables the child to develop a sense of separation from her. This pre-oedipal father is a seducer rather than a legislator, insofar as he attracts the desire of both mother and child, and also enables the separation that allows for love between mother and child. It is the child's awareness of the mother's desire for another, and its own relationship of desire and identification in regard to the imaginary father, that offers protection against abjection, against the devouring mother and the primal emptiness associated with her. The relationship to the imaginary father is a precursor to the subject's incorporation into the symbolic order. More separate than the mother but more loving than the symbolic father, the imaginary father is associated with a form of loving that allows the child to emerge from the oedipal process with a capacity to love others and to find appropriate forms for the expression of love and desire.

Kristeva undertakes a complex reinterpretation of the Freudian father figure in arriving at her theory of this loving, imaginary father, but the main interest here is that she associates this figure with the agapaic love of the Christian understanding of the fatherhood of God. *Agape*, unlike *eros*, is not a love that rises up towards the desired object, but a love that '*comes down*; it is gift, welcome, and favor . . . [A]gape is disinterested, less a choice than benevolent generosity, a fatherhood that isn't stern but familial and enlightening.'[57] Moreover, because this love entails 'the sacrifice of a body'[58] but also its resurrection, it allows for an unleashing of the death drive towards a greater transcendence, a subjectivity based on idealized identification with the Name of the Father, through adoption with the Son. Because this is a temporary sacrifice, allowing for the recovery of a resurrected body beyond the erotic and lustful body, it goes beyond masochistic self-destruction to reveal the meaning that is to be found in a sense of identification with the Other:

> The Christly passion and, by homology, any passion that ends up in death, is thus only evidence of love and not a sacrifice stemming out of the law of social contract. Sacrifice is an offering that, out of a substance, creates meaning for the Other and, consequently, for the social group that is dependent on it. Conversely, passionate love is a gift that assumes total suffering and loss, not in order to make of it a metaphorical assumption toward the Other but to allow a Meaning, always already there, anterior and coming from above, to manifest itself to the members of the community that share it.

It is difficult to unravel the dense psychoanalytic entanglements in Kristeva's text, but if I read her correctly, she is suggesting that the Christian narrative turns upon the sublimation of narcissism and of the masochism of the Freudian death drives, through the acceptance that linguistic identification with the father entails death – i.e. in psycholinguistic terms, the negotiation and possible negation of pre-oedipal desire associated with the bodily relationship to the mother, through the acquisition of language associated with the Name of the Father. But because this is a death that culminates in resurrection and that brings with it adoption as 'sons', it invites an understanding of subjectivity in which the narcissistic love of self associated with the ego yields to a love of self established in the knowledge of being loved by God in a community of agapaic love of others.[59] Thus, although for Kristeva the subject remains masculine, and language is always associated with the father, both subjectivity and fatherhood are refigured in terms of *agape*, and this also has implications for the relationship to the mother. The Eucharistic meal constitutes a reconciliation, by allowing the father as third party to intervene and deflect the fear of being devoured by or wanting to devour the archaic mother:

> Turning love into an identification with the ideal father and having that identification based on an absorption, an oral assimilation of his body, introduces into Christianity a relief of oral sadism directed at the archaic maternal body. The mother will not eat you, do not eat her; look for the sign of the father within her, do not let it scare you, but liken yourself to that crossroads that is both body and name, desire and meaning. You will become sensible, that is, enamored of yourselves, Him, others. Christianity, by thus inserting a Third Party between the Self and its destructive hunger, by setting up a distance between that same self and its nurse, offers to destructive avidity – a Word. Language.[60]

There is a great deal more attentive reading and interpretation that could be brought to Kristeva's psycholinguistic reading of Christian ideas of love and fatherhood, but the foregoing is intended to outline some of the possibilities that open up when one approaches the question of the fatherhood of God from outside the parameters of Greek philosophy that have so dominated the Christian tradition, but still in fidelity to the biblical story. The quotation above suggests a necessary interdependence between the maternal and paternal, between profound intimations of desire and loss associated with the mother's body, and the expression of those desires in the language of the speaking subject constituted not by the Law but by the agapaic love of a father figure more intimate and compassionate than the father of philosophy and patriarchy.

There are clearly a number of questions that arise from the perspective of feminist theology, with regard to the adoption of women into the Father–Son relationship described by Kristeva, however compassionate and giving that relationship might be. Nevertheless, let me sketch here a number of suggestive possibilities that might be open to further development, if we allow some of the foregoing ideas to resonate with one another.

The community of the father

In the next chapter, we shall see that Balthasar associates the maternal awakening of love in the child with prevenient or created grace, and he suggests that this is a universal experience associated with religious consciousness. We come to our first awareness of the relationality of our existence and our openness to the love of the other through the mother, and this loving relationality is intrinsic to our natural human personhood and to our capacity to respond to revelation. But there is also a specifically Christian form of personhood, which comes into being when the natural subject or person responds to the grace of God in Christ and becomes incorporated into the life of Christ through the community of the maternal Church. This means that, with Christ, we acquire the right to call God 'father' – a designation that is unique to Christianity, insofar as no other religion describes the relationship between the human and the divine so consistently in terms of fatherhood. Christianity thus offers 'a Word. Language', that constitutes a form of paternal intervention between maternal abjection and the subject. But, according to Ricoeur, this paternal appellation constitutes not the perpetuation but the disruption of patriarchal kinship systems and religions based on oedipal father figures, through the institution of a new form of fatherhood that both Ricoeur and Kristeva associate with compassion and gift rather than law and sacrifice.

For Kristeva, the loving intervention of the father provides a necessary rupture in the maternal relationship, a fragile mark of delineation associated with desire, which allows for the containment of the abject. For Ricoeur, 'the history of the divine names belongs to the adventures of the libido'.[61] Thus, in both interpretations the psychoanalytic understanding of the dynamics of desire contributes towards a deepened appreciation of the liberating potential of Christianity's paternal God. Whereas the oedipal process makes the father a figure of murderous envy and punitive prohibition associated with the child's desire for the mother, the death of Christ and his identification of that death with the fatherhood of God acknowledges and goes beyond the murderous psyche with its death drives, allowing death to be willingly incorporated into the subject and into God as the means to the realization of new life and love.

For Kristeva, it is through the encounter with death as abjection that we experience 'a resurrection that has gone through death (of the ego). It is an alchemy that transforms death drive into a start of life, of new significance.'[62] Comparing Freud with Hegel, Ricoeur suggests that Hegel's idea of the 'unhappy consciousness' associated with the death of God shares with Freud an insight into the transfiguration that comes about through 'the death of separated transcendence'.[63] Ricoeur proposes a possible analogy between psychoanalysis, philosophy of spirit, and philosophy of religion through

> a theology of the weakness of God, like that which Bonhoeffer envisaged when he said: 'Only a weak God can bring help' . . . The final theme, for each of these three disciplines, would be the inclusion of the death of the father in the final constitution of the symbol of fatherhood. And this death would no longer be a murder but the most extreme abandonment of self.[64]

Clearly, this opens the door to a theological undertaking of far greater magnitude than anything I can offer here, and I do not intend to introduce a Hegelian perspective into what is already becoming a very dense interweaving of themes. However, I think it is possible to gesture towards a feminist theological route through some of these ideas, but not without difficulty, and not without perhaps raising more questions than I can answer.

Christianity entails a willingness to enter into a community wherein one becomes known by the Name of the Father – it is insofar as a person is willing to be incorporated into the fatherhood of God with Christ that one becomes a player in theo-drama. But this also brings about a conversion, because, if Balthasar is correct in associating the mother with the awakening to religious consciousness, the response of that consciousness to Christian revelation creates a sense of separation from the natural maternal ambience of culture, religion and kinship, with their violent oedipal relationships and repressed desires. It means a dying to the self associated with conventional family relationships and social structures and values, and baptismal rebirth within an agapaic community gathered together by bonds of sacramentality and language that is brought into being and sustained by the transfiguration of desire, death, motherhood, fatherhood, sexuality and subjectivity: 'And [Jesus] replied, "Who are my mother and my brothers?" And looking at those who sat around him, he said, "Here are my mother and my brothers! Whoever does the will of God is my brother and sister and mother"' (Mk 3:34).

This is not simply a postmodern symbolic parody – although it shares many of the same characteristics in terms of its subversion of socialized identities and family relationships. Kristeva suggests that it is a narrative that can reach into or arise out of the marrow of our being, at that primal frontier where body and language encounter one another as love and abjection, as sin and grace, as thunder and silence, as lack and desire, in a visceral struggle where the self experiences the unnameable abyss between identity and otherness:

> The love of God and for God resides in a gap: the broken space made explicit by sin on the one side, the beyond on the other. Discontinuity, lack, and arbitrariness: topography of the sign, of the symbolic relation that posits my otherness as impossible. Love, here, is only for the impossible.[65]

If Christianity is to create a space for this impossible love, then it needs to go beyond the kind of phallic theology of origination and sacrifice represented by Balthasar and the new feminists in their defence of the fatherhood of God. Instead, theology can learn from the biblical and psychoanalytic insights offered by thinkers such as Ricoeur and Kristeva, to develop a new understanding of divine fatherhood, based on what Ruether rightly refers to as 'the kenosis of patriarchy'. Thus fatherhood is potentially transformed and redeemed rather than reinforced and absolutized in the Christian story. Although the dominant theological motif in the Christian tradition has been the patriarchal model of divine fatherhood that has been widely challenged by feminists, this symbolic refiguration is a process of retrieval as well as of renewal, for there have always been alternative images of God's fatherly tenderness, particularly in devotional language. Consider, for example, the representation of fatherhood in the following quotation from the writings of St Peter Chrysologus:

> As God sees the world tottering to ruin because of fear, he acts unceasingly to bring it back by love, invite it by grace, to hold it by charity and clasp it firmly with affection. Hence, he washes the earth grown old in evil with the avenging flood. He calls Noah the father of a new world, speaks to him gently and gives him kindly confidence. He gives him fatherly instruction about the present and consoles him with good hope for the future. He did not give orders but instead shared in the work of enclosing together in the ark all living creatures on the earth. In this way the love of being together was to banish the fear born of slavery. What had been saved by a shared work was to be preserved by a community of love.[66]

This kind of imagery challenges patriarchal authoritarianism by representing God as the father who comforts and encourages humankind, not in a hierarchical relationship of command and obedience, but in a shared endeavour of redeeming love. Through attentiveness to such alternative imagery, it is possible to construct a theology of divine and human fatherhood that remains faithful to the Christian vision, liberating it from its captivity to patriarchal values through an appeal to the core Christian values of mercy, forgiveness and love. This brings us back to Coakley's suggestion that the *kenosis* of Christ needs to be read, not as a conflict between masculine divine power and human vulnerability, but as a revelation of a God whose strength is made perfect in weakness, a God who reveals that the perfection of our Godlike human nature lies in our capacity for power-in-vulnerability, which might also be read in terms of Ong's association of the Christian life with the non-violent martyrdom of the saints.

But, if the fatherhood of God might find expression through the gathering together of a loving community of sisters and brothers in Christ in a new creation, beyond death, violence and patriarchy, how does the motherhood of God express itself in this new creation? For if the mother does not become enfolded as a sacramental presence within the love between the father and son, then patriarchy is not redeemed but sanctified and given absolute value – as indeed it has been in Protestant Christianity. So how might the maternal Church be reinterpreted, in order to go beyond hierarchical structures to a harmony of loving relationships held together by love, not law, experienced not beyond but through the body's hunger, desire and vulnerability?

13 Redeeming motherhood

Much of the foregoing has been an exposé of the deeply problematic nature of Balthasar's theology for feminism. However, I now want to turn to an aspect of his thought that is ripe for feminist interpretation, and that is his understanding of the maternal activity of God. Nowhere do the self-contradictions in Balthasar's theology become more apparent than in his attempt to keep God tethered to masculine generativity, because the motherhood of God is an irrepressible theme that recurs again and again in his writings.

We have seen how psycholinguistic theory allows for a feminist analysis of the relationship between the forbidden mother, death and sex that shapes the western philosophical and theological imaginary. This suggests that the route to a new, non-sacrificial understanding of love and desire must be via the maternal body. If the female body is to be permitted a space of non-violent, sacramental being in the world, then the primal antagonisms, denials and repressions that constitute the maternal relationship need to be refigured in new relationships of bodily mediations and communications, in which we can position ourselves as desiring mortals in the space between the maternal body and language, through the rehabilitation of maternal and paternal relationships beyond oedipal violence and religious sacrifice. This invites a subversive reading of Balthasar in order to effect an opening in 'God' to motherhood and fatherhood as mutual principles of divine origination which encounter one another at that confluence where representation opens into mystery through the analogous meeting of opposites.

God and the status quo

In seeking to demonstrate the relevance of Balthasar for contemporary questions about gender, David Schindler argues that Balthasar's idea of femininity as 'active receptivity' enables him to retain the philosophical association between femininity and receptivity, while avoiding the association of femininity with mere potency and therefore imperfection. He quotes Balthasar:

> Receiving (*Empfangen*) and letting be (*Geschehenlassen*) are as essential for the concept of absolute love as giving (*Geben*) which, without the receptive letting be – and everything else which belongs to love: the grateful owing of oneself and the turning back of oneself to the giver – would have no capacity to give at all.[1]

This quotation suggests the inseparability of God's giving and creation's receiving of life. If it makes any sense to speak of this in terms of masculinity and femininity, then the interdependence of the two is clear: God can only be actively masculine insofar as creation is actively feminine. If the creature withholds 'her' giving of self, God's giving is also frustrated. Referring to the classical tradition, Schindler argues that

> Balthasar . . . retains the link there between the feminine and receptivity. But in so doing he nonetheless transforms the meaning of this link: above all, receptivity is now seen as an essential ingredient of what is meant primitively by act (*esse*), that is, as distinct from what is merely 'potential,' and receptivity is thereby seen from the beginning as a perfection.[2]

This perfection of feminine receptivity as well as masculine generativity allows Balthasar to achieve a balance between God's relation to the world and God's immanence within the world, by way of his understanding of the supra-sexual dimension of the Trinity. According to Schindler, both relatedness and immanence

> follow from the receptive – i.e., feminine – dimension inherent in God as a Trinity. That is, God, precisely in the 'masculine' activity whereby he creates the world, allows himself to be 'affected by' the world . . . ; and he remains present within the world which he creates. It is for this reason that Balthasar says that 'God's relation to the world is not only masculine, as *Deus Faber*, but womb-like and feminine, achieving the redemption of the entire universe through pain.'[3]

Nevertheless, however maternal some aspects of God's Trinitarian life might be, 'Balthasar insists on the primacy of the (supra-)masculine character of God's relation to the cosmos.'[4] Somewhat ominously from a feminist point of view, Schindler argues that

> as the originating source of the being and redemption of the cosmos, God remains properly a transcendent Father. Indeed, because the principles require affirmation of some truly analogous sense of (supra-)gender in God, they permit a deepening of the traditional position – which insists on the

> importance of calling God Father, even as it has nonetheless often insisted simultaneously on God's being simply without gender. Recognizing the important truth to be protected in insisting on the genderless character of God (namely, that he is beyond gender in the limited, embodied form of which we have direct experience), we must nevertheless recall as well that, from a Catholic perspective, a biblical positivism never suffices: the centrality of God-as-Father in the New Testament does not reflect what is merely an empty symbol but on the contrary says something important *about the way things ultimately are*.[5]

This quotation makes clear that, however many concessions are apparently made by these neo-orthodox theologians with regard to motherhood and femininity, the patriarchal metaphysics of Catholic theology are not only reaffirmed but actually taken beyond some of their earlier restraints. The apophaticism that ultimately removes God from any such sexual projections is overridden by the qualification that God's 'genderless character' is not absolute, for there is 'some truly analogous sense of (supra-)gender in God', and the lack of biblical authority for projecting philosophical principles of generativity onto the fatherhood of God is dismissed by an appeal to 'a Catholic perspective', notwithstanding the fact that, as I suggested in the last chapter, the fatherhood of God can be seen as referring primarily to relationality rather than generativity.

If we read on, it becomes clear that there is more at stake here than the theology of the Trinity, for a whole set of socio-sexual stereotypes is once again reinforced by this securing of fatherhood in God. Thus it is not surprising to discover that '[W]omen, whether physically mothers or not, and insofar as they act in capacities not directly related to physical motherhood, nonetheless remain (ought to remain) for all that is properly maternal domestic.'[6] Moreover, 'the future of western civilization'[7] depends upon the Church playing by the rules:

> the mission of the Church is to give the world – indeed the cosmos in its entirety – a Marian-feminine form: to give all of human civilization the maternal disposition which alone will permit it to give birth to Christ . . . Here, then, is why the Church can never relinquish the image of Bridegroom and Bride as descriptive of the relation between Christ and the Church. Here is why she must continue to limit the specialized (albeit indispensable) function of the ministerial priesthood to men. Here, finally, is why she must continue to oppose the confusion of genders evident today in the description of homosexuality as an 'alternative lifestyle', and in the dominant feminist drift toward androgyny.[8]

Once again, it is clear how deeply Balthasar's theology is implicated in the politics of gender by which conservative Catholics oppose women's ordination, feminism and homosexuality. Thus an ancient association between Plotinus's masculine Ideal Principle and maternal Matter continues to prove an effective support system for a theology motivated at least to some extent by a resistance to feminism and its causes.

Nevertheless, I have already suggested several times that the violence in Balthasar's theology arises in no small measure from its orientation towards a much more radical understanding of gender, which he strenuously resists because of his commitment to the patriarchal sexual stereotypes of a certain understanding of Catholicism viewed through the lens of modern European romanticism. Yet if his sexual theology strains against the leash in this respect, his theology of the motherhood of God is remarkable for its lack of violence and its implicit openness to a new understanding of the significance of maternal symbols and relationships for theology. As Schindler acknowledges, God's relationship to the world is not only masculine, according to Balthasar, it is also 'womb-like and feminine'. What are the implications of this for taking his theology into new terrain?

Balthasar's motherly God

Despite his insistence on the fatherhood of God as the origin of creation, Balthasar repeatedly refers to God's activity in creating and sustaining life in maternal terms, which poses a fundamental question to the whole logic of his argument regarding the essential masculinity of Christ and the priesthood. In *Theo-Drama II* he refers to the creature 'being born, together with the Son, from the generative primal womb of the Father'.[9] Developing the idea of the Trinity in the last section of *Theo-Drama III*, he writes:

> if he-who-is-sent has essentially to reveal the love of him-who-sends, and if he is identical with his divine mission, he must (as the personal bearer of this mission of love), be the divine, that is, eternal Offspring of him-who-sends, whom he himself calls 'Father' in a sense that bursts all analogies.[10]

He goes on to suggest that 'such "fatherhood" can only mean the giving away of everything the Father is' in 'a giving-away that, in the Father's act of generation – which lasts for all eternity – leaves the latter's womb "empty"'.[11] This image of the empty womb is a very different way of symbolizing *kenosis* from that which appears in Balthasar's more explicitly sexual accounts of creation, associating it with childbirth rather than male ejaculation. A few pages later, he refers to 'the simultaneous personalizing and socializing of the man who is the recipient of grace' who receives in Christ 'the grace of new divine sonship, of being born with Christ from the Father's womb'.[12]

But if such language can be used of God, then one has to ask what Balthasar means when, in an argument against women priests, he writes,

> insofar as Christ is a man, he . . . represents the origin, the Father, for the fruitfulness of the woman is always dependent on an original fructification. Neither of these points is to be relativized, nor is the resultant representation of the origin by the Church's office.[13]

If Christ and creation come from the womb of God, then one could legitimately ask, who fructifies God's womb? Beyond the maternal God in whose womb Christ originates, this would require another paternal, inseminating God. I say this in order to make clear that the logic of Balthasar's sexual literalism translates into theological nonsense. Only if he really can 'burst all analogies', including those of human sexuality and reproduction, can he liberate his theology from a biological stranglehold and give full and free expression to the range of maternal and paternal language that is necessary in order to speak of God.

But the quotation above points to the anxiety that prevents this from happening, because such recognition would undermine his insistence on the essential masculinity of the sacramental priesthood. If it is indeed possible to speak of God's originating relationship to Christ and to creation in the language of the maternal body, then there should be no reason why a woman priest cannot represent this dimension of the divine mystery (even if we accept the debatable claim that the role of the priest is inseparable from the symbolization of divine origination). To recognize this would allow Balthasar's theology to contribute to a sacramental understanding of a maternal priesthood that might bring a rich new perspective to Catholic worship in its capacity to express and celebrate the relationship between God and the world in Christ. This is especially so given the extent to which Balthasar discusses the relationship between mother and child in terms of the fundamental relationality of the human being, in a way that has both theological and anthropological significance.

Personhood for Balthasar can only be interpreted in terms of relationality, or the 'I–thou' relationship. This is understood with reference to the Trinitarian relationships within the Godhead, to the human subject's responsive relationship to God in Christ and his or her incorporation into the body of the Church, and also with regard to the primal sense of being loved by another that is awakened by the first encounter with the mother: 'The interpretation of the mother's smiling and of her whole gift of self is the answer, awakened by her, of love to love, when the "I" is addressed by the "Thou".'[14] This first experience of the mother, and the sense of openness to the other that it engenders, constitutes the spiritual nature that all humans have in common. To be human is to be a creature whose being is almost totally implicated in the material contingencies of natural existence, and yet it is also to be a spirit whose prior orientation towards God was awakened and is to some extent, however rudimentarily, sustained by the experience of maternal love, which translates into an expectation of its ultimate fulfilment in the absolute. The first encounter with the mother's love constitutes an awakening to self-consciousness which gives the child 'a genuine promise of absolute grace and love'.[15]

Balthasar suggests that this is the starting point for 'The dialectic of the idea of God'[16] that is found in all mythologies, philosophies and religions. One can, he argues, 'start from the foundation of human personal existence in the call made by love and the answer made to love to formulate something like an a priori postulate for the form of religion'.[17] However, unlike the mother–child relationship, God and the human have no common nature as the basis for their love and knowledge, and this for Balthasar raises the question of the relationship between nature and grace.

Although 'person' is reserved 'for the supernatural uniqueness of the man who has been called into a relationship of intimacy with God; every human being can share this distinction to some degree'.[18] Balthasar suggests that this might entail distinguishing between 'two forms or grades of personhood'.[19] The first experience of the mother's love is a sign of the prevenient grace that prepares the subject to recognize and respond to the revelation of God, given that only grace makes possible such recognition. The mother's smile is the first means of grace, by which the subject is awakened to his or her potential for the fullness of personhood in Christ.

With regard to the mother–child relationship, mutual recognition in the sphere of nature arises out of the knowledge that the mother is the source of the child. However, this natural bond also translates into the mother's encounter with mystery as she stands before her child: 'she has indeed received a seed and borne it to birth, but how is she to be responsible for the spirit-endowed, eternal person who looks out at her from the eyes of the new being?'[20] He goes on, through a series of bold brushstrokes, to make this encounter between an analogy for the coming into being of the person before God:

> Just as a space of time intervenes between the birth of the child and its first act as spirit (in which it returns thanks and answers the mother's smile with its own smile of recognition), there is likewise a space between man's being created by God and his awareness that he is the object of God's gracious address; in this space, he is indeed already in a relationship to God (for he is God's creature) but does not yet possess the fulfilled relationship for which he was created and born.[21]

Extending this maternal imagery, he continues,

> Man is brought forth into the world from God's creative womb; not, of course, in one single act of sending forth, like a human birth, for God must continually accompany the finite being and hold it in existence, but nevertheless in an act that establishes man in his existence in the world and frees him for this.[22]

Again, the symbolism that expresses our human awareness of origins in God derives, not from the masculine inseminating power of God, but from a sense of being conceived in the womb of God and sustained by the motherly attentiveness of God. Moreover, from this perspective the sustaining power of being in the world is a continuous maternal act: there is something rather than nothing, because God unceasingly mothers creation.

Balthasar develops the idea of the maternal origin of grace in terms of the difference between the grace that originally orientates the human being towards God, and the awakening that enables a personal response to God. While the human remains sensitive to 'his origin in the eternal womb',[23] the knowledge of God must be negotiated in the face of its own frustration and disappointment, just as nothing in our subsequent experience can equal that first joyous experience of being totally loved by the mother. The primal human relationship to God is vulnerable to the distortions and neglects of 'a nonparadisal world order',[24] in the same way that the mother cannot fulfil the promise of absolute love that her smile initially communicates to the child. Even the greatest human experiences of love can only approximate to the memory and expectation of that originating totality of love. The spirit 'bears along in its wake, in its memory, the origin that has become inaccessible and carries out its act of evaluation with a view to an ultimate goal that corresponds to this origin and cannot be objectified'.[25] This apprehension of the absolute in the face of contingency, suffering and finitude, constitutes the natural knowledge of God posited by Aquinas.

At this point, a number of perspectives come into view. Balthasar's idea of an original bliss associated with the mother resonates with psychoanalytic theory, but instead of this constituting a relationship of love and desire that must be repressed, it becomes the matrix wherein faith is nurtured in the face of life's realities. Moreover, this 'natural knowledge of God' is a form of knowledge associated with the maternal relationship, not with the lonely subject's struggle for transcendent truth. It positions us from the beginning as relational, dependent beings whose memory of the mother becomes an opening into God.

Yet it is also worth noting here a certain realism as regards the maternal relationship. This is not the romantic ideal that one so often finds in Catholic texts, nor is it the child-centred perspective of maternal insufficiency that informs the work of object relations theorists such as D. W. Winnicott. Rather, it allows space for the real mother whose love will never be sufficient for the child's hunger, but in this very frustration of desire she remains the primary model for the maturing of faith. Instead of an individual, masculine subjectivity modelled upon the Father in which the maternal relationship is abandoned, this is a form of relational subjectivity in which the child's struggle to adjust to the limitation and imperfection of the maternal relationship becomes a form of spiritual development. Thus the person in Christ is a person whose relationship to a maternal God is mediated through his or her relationship to the mother, in a way that invites a different narrative of subjective becoming than that afforded by philosophy and psychoanalysis.

However, theological language still refers beyond itself to a God who is truly known only in absence and not-knowing, so that maternal as well as paternal language must ultimately yield to the silence of that which is beyond human experience. From this perspective, a maternal God is no more accessible, tangible and bodily than a paternal God, for we remain at the level of symbolic representations. But the quest for the maternal is also a quest for the body, as we have already seen with Irigaray and Kristeva, and therefore the primal sense of loss and separation that Lacanian psychoanalysis associates both with the Mother and with God seeks consolation in bodily representations associated with the maternal presence.

Maternity and natality

Over and against the symbolic significance of the transcendent, abstract (and hence absent) father, feminist theorists posit the immanence, relationality and embodiment of the mother. This language of corporeality is intended to challenge dominant western concepts of both subjectivity and divinity. For example, Christine Battersby argues that the female subject-position is bound up with maternity and 'fleshiness'[26] in a way that problematizes dominant models of subjectivity, inviting recognition of the 'ontological significance'[27] of birth, and not only of death. She writes, 'becoming a woman involves a privileged relationship to a bodily morphology',[28] arguing that 'the "female" subject-position is one that points to embodiment – and to what women share with animals – in ways that differentiate it from the "feminine", and also from the "male"'.[29] Referring to 'the normality of a body that can birth', Battersby argues that

> natality troubles the notion of identity as a fixed, permanent or pre-given 'thing' or 'substance'. Natality considered as an abstract category allows us to think identities as emerging from a play of bodily relationships: an emergence that is not sudden, but that occurs over time.[30]

Whereas first-wave feminists such as de Beauvoir sought to minimize the significance of motherhood for female subjectivity, Battersby represents a new generation of feminists who, influenced by psycholinguistic theory, seek not to overcome but to transform the traditional association between women and mothering. This involves asking how the marginal discursive space to which the maternal body has been consigned might become the site of a new form of subjectivity constructed around a female morphology that takes into account the relationship between female embodiment and maternity.

Jantzen proposes the idea of an 'embodied, earthed, female divine',[31] an Irigarayan projection of feminized divinity which constitutes a pantheistic alternative to the binary dualisms that structure modern western thought. This is a religious imaginary that appeals to symbols of natality and flourishing, as opposed to the 'necrophilia' that Jantzen identifies with western religion, Protestant Christianity in particular, in its preoccupation with salvation and eternal life. Appealing particularly to Hannah Arendt's idea of 'natality' and to Irigaray's idea of 'becoming divine',[32] Jantzen argues for a this-worldly religion in which 'the masculinist symbolic of the west' is disrupted by recognition of the fact that

> We are all natals, whether or not we are mothers . . . We have all begun as part of somebody else; we have all been utterly dependent, nurtured well or badly into being who we are both physically and spiritually. And we are all still deeply dependent on the web of relationships with other natals and with the earth that supports us.[33]

Jantzen argues that the Christian emphasis on salvation 'both reflects and reinforces the necrophilic imaginary and its obsession with domination, mastery, and escape',[34] whereas 'An imaginary of natality, expressed in an idiom of flourishing, would lead in quite different directions, opening the way to a divine horizon which celebrates alterities and furthers the aim of the divine incarnation of every woman and man.'[35] This 'transformed imaginary'[36] has the potential to create new communities whose flourishing would be manifest in relationships of trust and interdependence in which diversity is celebrated and the divine is reverenced in nature, materiality and embodiment, leading to 'patterns of thought and action' which 'would foster respect rather than domination, mutuality in place of mastery'.[37] This would include an acceptance of finitude and mortality as part of the human condition, and a rejection of the idea of a disembodied and omnipotent God which upholds the present symbolic order: 'the masculinist symbolic of the west is undergirded by a concept of God as Divine Father, a God who is also Word, and who in his eternal disembodiment, omnipotence, and omniscience is the epitome of value'.[38]

Although such an approach is pantheistic, it does not seek to set transcendence over and against immanence, but rather to reconcile the two through an appeal to

Irigaray's idea of the sensible transcendental. Jantzen proposes that the opposition between transcendence and immanence is a consequence of, not an argument for, the presupposed 'separation of the divine and the material'.[39] The reintegration of the two entails the recognition that transcendence is necessary for an understanding of both the human and the divine, insofar as meaning is not entirely reducible to the physical, but at the same time there is no part of us that is not bodily:

> It is indeed true that if the divine is to serve as the horizon of our becoming, then the divine must be transcendent, ever beyond present actuality, and certainly not reducible to the set of physical particulars of the material universe . . . But from this it does not follow that the divine must be a separate entity, an 'other' being, somewhere else, at least in principle, any more than the requirement that human personhood be understood as irreducible to physicalism requires there be a 'soul-piece' somehow lodged in the body but in principle detachable from it.[40]

It may be that this rather crude concept of God and the human soul has been implicit in much Christian theology as well as philosophy of religion, but I have already suggested that, in its post-Heideggerian return to Aquinas, much Catholic theology today is formulated in terms that come close to Irigaray's idea of the sensible transcendental. Indeed, there is very little difference between Aquinas's understanding of revelation and Jantzen's theory about the bodiliness of our experience of transcendence. So, although Jantzen offers an incisive critique of Christian ideas of salvation, and she is persuasive in her argument that a religious preoccupation with death has fuelled a culture of war and violence, if her philosophical approach is to inform a feminist critique of Catholic ecclesiology, it needs to be more closely focused. Although she repeatedly appeals for the contextualization of knowledge, and despite her stated intention to 'develop a gendered genealogy of religion',[41] Jantzen offers little by way of historical or contextual analysis in terms of the development of different models of Christianity, nor does she explore the implications of this for the kind of religious imaginary that she is proposing. In a philosophical reflection on the symbolic potential of maternity and natality, it is surely important to acknowledge that perhaps the most conspicuous difference between Protestantism and Catholicism lies in these areas. The Marian dimension of Catholic Christianity stands in need of feminist deconstruction and reclamation, but this entails a very different approach from that needed to challenge the austere masculinism of much mainstream Protestantism, particularly as this is expressed in Anglo-American philosophy of religion.

Moreover, if Jantzen's philosophy is to find embodiment in ethical communities such as those she imagines, then it will have to become more theological, because it is only as theology that philosophy of religion can make the transition from theory to practice, by informing the material practices of religious communities. The way beyond philosophy of religion with its rationalizing tendencies and its Protestant denials of desire, embodiment and maternity entail a recovery of the past as well as a vision of the future. A sacramental, maternal ecclesiology, reinvigorated and transformed by the kind of religious imaginary that Jantzen proposes, might offer her ideas a space of flourishing without doing violence to the existing beliefs and practices of many millions of people whose faith lies far outside the boundaries of influence of philosophy of religion as she defines it.

The maternal Church

We have already seen how Irigaray's critique of western culture is premised upon the claim that a denial of the significance of the maternal body lies deep at the heart of its philosophical traditions and its linguistic structures. From the time that Plato's philosopher turned his back on the cave/womb to seek truth in the world of Forms and Ideas, western values and beliefs have followed a phallic trajectory that leads away from the earth, the body and the mother, to seek truth in the transcendent realm of paternal ideals: 'Heads forward, eyes front, genitals aligned, fixed in a straight direction and always straining forward, in a straight line. A phallic direction, a phallic line, a phallic time, backs turned on origin.'[42] There is, suggests Irigaray, no going back, particularly not to that first body which, because it is unthought and unsymbolized, retains its dark inchoate power:

> It is essential that relations of man and body should be in the service of the Beautiful and the Good. That their aim – *telos* – should be to rise up toward the Father. And that precludes them from keeping company in a place that in any way revives the maternal realm, since the dream of a mortal birth has not yet been totally banished . . . All this arouses many a fantasy bewitching to a gaze, to a soul that is still sensible, but the philosophy tutor – who is a pederast in fact – will rid the child of such things. He delivers him from the repulsive naturalness of that womb, to the point where he spurns it underfoot, under his erection. Moreover, he blocks out all nostalgia, any longing to go back to something that might have existed beforehand, apparently by occupying his rear. The order of progression must be rigorously observed at present, or there is a risk of straying down other paths.[43]

Contemporary Catholicism is not short of pederasts, and there is much about the Catholic tradition that is vulnerable to Irigaray's bitingly witty analysis. Yet she is too one-sided in her critique, because for much of its history the western tradition did stray down another path, taking the philosophical tradition with it, to be sure, but 'keeping company' in a place that did indeed revive 'the maternal realm'. For the Catholic community believed itself to have been formed and nurtured in a mother's womb wherein the gaze was drawn, not only upwards and forwards to the Father's light, but inwards and earthwards to the Son's incarnation, in a way that caused considerable consternation to the protagonists of Greek philosophy. This set in motion a dynamic set of analogies linking the maternal body, the Virgin Mary, Eve, and the Church. I have discussed these in some detail elsewhere,[44] but my concern here is to explore the implications of this in terms of the symbolic representation of the maternal body. If the maternal feminine symbols that form the living heart of the Catholic tradition have been evacuated of any sense of female 'fleshiness' through the exclusive privileging of the male body in terms of sacramentality and liturgy, the question is how to pour meaning back into these symbols, through the morphology of a feminized sacramentality, bodily enacted by women as well as by men.

De Lubac offers a 'paradoxical image' to describe the motherhood of the Church:

> whereas, in the physical order, the child leaves the womb of his mother, and, withdrawing from her, becomes increasingly independent of her protective guardianship as he grows, becomes stronger and advances in years, the Church brings us forth to the new life she bears by receiving us into her womb, and the more our divine education progresses, the more we become intimately bound to her.[45]

Irigaray represents the making of the western subject and culture as a process of denial and repression of the maternal relationship, but de Lubac suggests that it is through a symbolic return to the womb and ever closer intimacy with the 'mother' that the Christian experiences new life and personal transformation: 'it is in deepening [the] childlike spirit that the Christian advances to adulthood, penetrating ever deeper, if we can put it this way, into the womb of his mother'.[46] This is surely a 'conversion' that invites greater feminist attention, for it suggests that Catholicism – the repressed 'other' of Protestantism, modernity and indeed of feminism itself – is a potential site of difference for those seeking more relational and corporeal figurations of subjectivity through an appeal to the maternal body.

As we have already seen, this is a highly fluid symbolics in which the Church is also the Bride of Christ, so that her maternal 'body' is 'one flesh' with his, and through her sacraments Christ nurtures the people with his own body and blood. Thus Ambrose writes, 'he is a virgin who bore us in his womb; he is a virgin who brought us forth; he is a virgin who nursed us with his own milk'.[47] These maternal metaphors express a range of meanings by which Christians have sought to express what it means to be baptismally reborn in Christ, to be eucharistically nourished by his body and blood, and to experience characteristics associated with both motherhood and fatherhood in the relationship between God and humankind incarnate in Christ and the Church. If a deconstructive approach to language entails interrogation of the repressed or negated 'other' that gives a dominant term its significance, the gendered language of the early Church often achieves its purpose through the invocation of these interdependent terms, so that meanings become encoded within relationships that defer to one another. So, for example, Tertullian writes,

> The title of the Father expresses veneration and power. At the same time, the Son is invoked in the Father . . . But mother Church is not forgotten either. In the Father and the Son, one recognizes the Mother, by whom the name of the Father like that of the Son is guaranteed.[48]

Thus if the Mother is recognized in the relationship between the Father and the Son, they are recognizable as Father and Son only in the context that 'she' provides: the naming of the Father and the Son depends upon the Mother's guarantee.[49] She in turn is made recognizable in the context of the relationship between the Father and the Son. These are, then, profoundly relational and interdependent symbols, each acknowledging rather than masking the fact that its meaning depends on its position within a chain of signifiers.

I have already referred to Miller's polemical assault on feminism in *Sexuality and Authority in the Catholic Church*, but in drawing on a rich range of resources in the Catholic tradition, Miller unintentionally offers the resources for the construction of a sacramental ecclesiology informed by feminist insights. She argues that Christian identity is formed when a person becomes incorporated into the fatherhood of God and the motherhood of the Church through the sacrament of baptism: 'the Christian life of grace is the result of being born of God through our Mother the Church. It is not only the action of the Father – but also the action of the Mother that is vital.'[50] In the womb of the Church, the Christian is nurtured by the body and blood of Christ, and feminine authority derives from this maternal power to give and nurture life. She quotes Augustine:

> Let us love our Lord God, let us love His Church: Him as a Father, Her as a Mother: Him as a Lord, Her His Handmaid, as we are ourselves the Handmaid's sons. But this marriage is held together by a bond of great love: no man offends the one and wins the favour of the other . . . *Your Father is God; the Church is your Mother. Far otherwise will you be generated by them than when you were begotten by your physical parents*. No labor, no misery, no weeping, no death will attend these parturitions, but only ease, blessing, joy, and life. Generation through human instruments was full of sorrow; through these, it is desirable. They, in giving us life, generated us into eternal punishment because of the longstanding guilt; these, in regenerating us, bring it about that neither fault nor punishment remain.[51]

Explaining what this means, Miller points out that

> It is, of course, Christ, and not the Father, who is the spouse of the Church. Nonetheless, when St Augustine teaches that Father God and Mother Church enjoy a marital unity, his thought illustrates an important point, namely, the covenantal unity of God and the Church.[52]

Augustine's notorious understanding of original sin might make the above quotation about 'eternal punishment' problematic from a feminist perspective, but what if we give it a different slant? Feminists agree with Augustine that all is not well with the human being's place in the world, and parental relationships are part of the problem. The marriage between the fatherhood of God and the motherhood of the Church provides the locus for a new form of human identity, displacing the oedipal family structure by way of a sensible transcendental in which the love of the father finds bodily expression in the maternal Church. The fatherhood of God is first and foremost a fatherhood of relationality and interdependence, understood only in the context of the incarnation and life of Christ, which is made manifest in the sacramental life of the maternal Church.

But we should note once again how subtly this language confounds the arguments of those who would use it to support a stable sexual hierarchy based on binary couplings. The Church's spouse is, 'of course', says Miller, Christ and not God the Father. But why 'of course', as if there is some obvious logic at work here? This is an area where theology frequently strays into poetic language that knows or cares little about the incest taboos and kinship groupings that hold the social order in place.[53] Mother Church, it would seem, is somewhat incestuous in her promiscuity, being the Bride of the Father and the Son, not to mention the Holy Spirit, who also sometimes puts in a spousal appearance. Even as Miller tries to fix her position, there is something about gender and God that refuses to stand still.

The oedipal process is disrupted by these volatile couplings. Far from prohibiting the Son access to the Mother, the Father shares 'his' Bride with the Son. But this process of the Father opening rather than closing access to the Mother's body also describes the individual believer's relationship to God in the Church. God the Father does not sever the maternal relationship but restores the baptismal 'child' to the Mother's womb. The Father's Name (the Lacanian *Nom*) is not associated with the 'non' of the incest taboo, but with the Mother's 'yes'. God becomes Father because 'she' agrees to become Mother – in Mary the Mother of Christ, and in the Church the Mother of the 'children' of God.

Like psycholinguistics, ecclesiology in this context involves a narrative of human becoming that is focused on the symbolic significance of the parental relationship. In psycholinguistics, our subjectivity is constituted around lack and repressed desire associated with the role of the phallus-bearing Father in prohibiting access to the Mother's body. In Catholic ecclesiology, we are recreated as persons when the 'sorrow' and 'punishment' of the actual parental relationship is transformed by the desire and joy brought about by the symbolic reconciliation of Mother, Father and child in Christ and the Church, in a virginal scenario from which the phallus has been banished. Baptismal rebirth is a restoration of what has been sacrificed in the process of becoming a socialized (masculine) subject, and, as we have already seen, it is a transformation that takes place at the level of gender: the masculine subject becomes a feminized, Marian person in relation to Christ and the Christian community, constituted by maternal as well as nuptial relationships: 'If . . . the Church is mother, each Christian also is or should be a mother.'[54]

At the heart of these images there is a necessary paradox, for we are dealing with forms of language that seek to express rather than repress mystery. The inability of language to control meaning is a strength, not a weakness, in this context, for only that limitation makes it possible to speak theologically. All these linguistic endeavours are focused on a quest to express what it means to encounter God in the material relationships and devotional practices of the Church, in the awareness that it is only to the extent that God reveals herself and himself in creation that we can speak of God at all. In this context, the Church is a new creation in which created realities acquire sacramental significance, through their capacity to mediate the presence of God in Christ through the maternal body of the Church and the consecration of the elements of the natural world – fruit of the earth, fruit of the vine, water, oil, the body itself, made holy by the power of God and the work of human hands.

But we must ask then how a revitalized ecclesiology might create openings for the expression of this transformation of human subjectivity, beyond repression and violence, so that the maternal Church's sacramental and ethical life might truly constitute an alternative to the sterile masculinities that shape our modern world.

The cosmic mother

Vatican II brought about a symbolic transformation in ecclesiology. Its focus on the Church as the Pilgrim People of God represented a significant shift away from the idea of the maternal Church that had prevailed since the apostolic era, and ushered in a more modern understanding of the Church's role in the world. Consider, for example, the opening lines of two documents that are only a few years apart. Pope John XXIII's 1961 encyclical, *Mater et Magistra*, begins with the words:

> Mother and teacher of all nations – such is the Catholic Church in the mind of her founder, Jesus Christ . . . To her was entrusted by her holy founder the twofold task of giving life to her children and of teaching them and guiding them – both as individuals and as nations – with maternal care.[55]

Redeeming motherhood   261

Four years later, the Vatican II Pastoral Constitution on the Church and the Modern World, *Gaudium et Spes*, begins with,

> the joy and hope, the grief and anguish of the people of our time, especially of those who are poor or afflicted in any way, are the joy and hope, the grief and anguish of the followers of Christ as well. Nothing that is genuinely human fails to find an echo in their hearts. For theirs is a community composed of men, of men who, united in Christ and guided by the holy Spirit, press onwards towards the kingdom of the Father and are bearers of a message of salvation intended for all men.[56]

Balthasar sees this symbolic change as a disaster for ecclesiology. The loss of the maternal, Marian perspective has resulted in the masculinization of the postconciliar Church, so that it has since the Council

> to a large extent put off its mystical characteristics; it has become a Church of permanent conversations, organizations, advisory commissions, congresses, synods, commissions, academics, parties, pressure groups, functions, structures and restructurings, sociological experiments, statistics: that is to say, more than ever a male Church, if perhaps one should not say a sexless entity, in which woman may gain for herself a place to the extent that she is ready herself to become such an entity . . . What can one say of 'political theology' and of 'critical Catholicism'? They are outlines for discussion for professors of theology and anti-repressive students, but scarcely for a congregation which still consists of children, women, old men, and the sick . . . May the reason for the domination of such typically male and abstract notions be because of the abandonment of the deep femininity of the marian character of the Church?[57]

It should by this stage come as no surprise to note that Balthasar's hyperbolic lament for the Marian Church is presented as a warning against women priests, nor that he groups women with children, old men, and the sick, over and against professors of theology. (Professors of theology include an abundance of old men and even a few women.) But if women are cautioned against becoming part of the male hierarchy in this thoroughly functional Church, might there be space for women priests in a less hierarchical, less masculine Church? Might the presence of women within the priesthood constitute a challenge to this thorough-going masculinity of the postconciliar Church, particularly if those women come bearing the values of relationality, nurture and 'feminine genius' that we are assured are the special prerogatives of women?

Balthasar's evaluation of the postconciliar Church has some credibility, and his critique of the politicization and functionality of the contemporary Church poses a challenge to liberal feminist theology. But he finds an unlikely ally (at least up to a point) in a radical feminist not in the past noted for her allegiance to Catholic tradition.

Charlene Spretnak's book, *Missing Mary*, also criticizes the decline in Marian devotion among Catholic liberals or so-called 'progressives' after the Second Vatican Council. She argues that 'it was a mistake for the Church to have deleted official recognition of Mary's cosmological spiritual presence forty years ago and disallowed her grand symbolization as the Maternal Matrix in order to shrink her down to more "rational" proportions'.[58] This was, she suggests, partly attributable to a misguided ecumenism that sought to make Catholicism more acceptable to Protestants, by adopting a reductive biblical approach to Mary – what she refers to as a 'biblical*only*' approach.[59] Spretnak argues instead for a 'biblical*plus*' perception of Mary,[60] one which is closer to Catholic tradition in recognizing Mary as 'a spiritual figure who was more than human but less than divine, a conduit of Christ's grace, a compassionate maternal power, and a loving presence on Earth as well as in heaven'.[61] Observing that 'The Roman Catholic Church is a container and guardian of mysteries far greater than itself',[62] Spretnak describes the destructive influence of rationalizing modernity on Catholic devotion to Mary in language that resonates with that of Balthasar – even although she does not engage directly with him:

> When, forty years ago, the Roman Catholic Church deemphasized and banished an essential cluster of (Marian) spiritual mysteries, as well as the evocative expression of ritual and symbol that had grown around them, a profound loss ensued. Today, the theology and liturgy of the Catholic Church is less 'cluttered', less mystical, and less comprehensive in its spiritual scope. Its tight, clear focus is far more 'rational' but far less whole. We who once partook of a vast spiritual banquet with boundaries beyond our ken are now allotted spare rations, culled by the blades of a 'rationalized' agenda more acceptable to the modern mindset.[63]

However, although she shares Balthasar's critical view of the destructive impact of rationalizing modernity on Catholic culture and devotion, Spretnak has no investment in maintaining the Church's sexual or political status quo. She argues that a rediscovered Marian cosmology in Catholic theology, liturgy and devotion is consistent with the political and ethical concerns of progressive Catholics, including feminists, particularly from the perspective of postmodern cosmology and ecology.[64] As our perceptions of reality change from 'the old, mechanistic worldview of modernity'[65] to a view informed by quantum physics and an awareness of the dynamic and organic nature of the cosmos, traditional Catholic beliefs associated with Mary as Queen of the Universe and all-embracing Mother acquire profound contemporary relevance, contributing to a 'deepened and enlarged sense of sacrament and the "sacramental imagination" – that is, sensitivity to the sacramentality of every moment'.[66] This does not constitute a break with tradition, but a rediscovery of Aquinas's understanding of 'the extraordinary diversity of the Creation as an analogous mode through which we may perceive divine magnificence'.[67]

Sarah Jane Boss's work on Mary also seeks to demonstrate the extent to which pre-modern Mariology is a resource for the development of an ecological theology that challenges the rationalizing and mechanistic approaches of modernity, with all their destructive influences on culture, women and the environment. Her book, *Empress and Handmaid*, appeals to the theoretical perspectives of the Frankfurt School to trace the ways in which changing attitudes towards nature and the female body have been reflected in changing images of Mary. The kind of docile femininity that informs modern Catholic views of Mary is, argues Boss, far removed from the creation-centred sacrality of medieval representations of the Mother of God: 'Western Christians' perception of Mother Nature finds constant reverberations in representations of Mother Mary, from the glorious queen of Romanesque art to the dutiful servant of contemporary devotional texts.'[68] Modern Christianity shares the wider culture's alienation from nature and the body as bearers of sacred significance, so that

> Western Christianity has moved away from a culture in which a maternal body, carrying several layers of meaning, could be incorporated into religious devotion . . . [T]he medieval representations of the Virgin as physical mother and bearer of God have been gradually supplanted in Catholic devotion by images of a prayerful young woman whose body had no ostensible association with maternal functions.[69]

In a more recent book, Boss identifies Mary with the primal Chaos out of which God creates the cosmos, seeing in her maternal virginity a powerful symbol of nature as both fertile and untamed. To gain insight into the relationship between God and the cosmos that is materially revealed in Mary is to begin to ask far-reaching and urgent questions about the relationality of all nature and all beings, and about the consequences for human relationships with one another and with nature if this sacred dimension of the cosmos in Mary is overlooked or denied. I shall return to this idea of Chaos in the next chapter.[70]

Boss and Spretnak focus primarily on Mary as the great maternal presence in the Catholic faith, and they say relatively little about the motherhood of the Church. However, the cosmic dimension of Mary's motherhood needs to be incarnate in the life of the Church, which in her sacramental and liturgical life enacts the promise of the world to come, not beyond but through the consecration of the material world. While patristic theologians likened Mary's virginal body to the earth of paradise, they also saw the Church as the new paradise. It is through the matrix of the Church that we become bodily players in the drama of salvation, weaving together history and the eschaton in an unfolding drama that leads us from the paradisal memory of our beginnings to the promised fulfilment of our ending.

This would mean that perhaps the Church rather than Mary needs to be seen as the Goddess figure of the Christian religion, so that the relationship between the Church and Mary is analogous to the relationship between God and Christ. Mary is the Church incarnate, just as Christ is God incarnate. After the resurrection and the assumption, the one flesh union of Mary and Christ is expressed in the Motherhood of the Church, making immanent, sensual and earthly what is now also transcendent, spiritual and heavenly. Related to this, Spretnak argues that, rather than suppressing any association with goddess figures, Catholicism should celebrate Mary's syncretistic capacity to accommodate within Christianity the religious and spiritual perspectives associated with the great goddess religions: 'Christianity from the very outset was a convergence of the earth-honoring Motherline with the cult of the sky-god Father. The new Father–Son religion was immeasurably enriched by the compassionate and cosmological attributes of the Blessed Virgin Mary.'[71] To affirm this of the Church, as the fulfilment and universalization of Mary's syncretistic capacity, is to open up questions of the Church's relationship to other religions – not just the goddess religions of old, but the religions that encounter one another in our postmodern cultures.

In language that resonates with Spretnak's description of Mary, de Lubac discusses Tertullian's claim that 'the Church, true mother of the living', came from the wound in Christ's side:

> Thus the image of the *Magna Mater* which dominated the Hellenistic paganism is found transposed into the Christian climate . . . The totality of the cosmos was included in this universal mother; everything living left her womb in order to return to it. In the same way – but with everything changed, everything renewed, everything turned inside out, 'converted' – the totality of the new cosmos is included in the Church.[72]

It is in the Church that the cosmos is redeemed, and it is in the Church that we discover the cosmic maternal vision proposed by Boss and Spretnak – a maternity that is inseparable from God's creative and sustaining love for the world. This is a vision that can only be expressed analogically, which means recognizing that it is difference itself that draws us to God, and it is in the space of encounter within difference that we discover the silence of God beyond words. But this also means going beyond Balthasar's concept of difference and desire played out between conflicting and violent polarities, to inhabit what Gillian Rose calls 'the broken middle', in which we find ourselves positioned within the 'three in one, one in three of singular, individual, universal; they represent the middle; broken between morality and legality, autonomy and heteronomy, cognition and norm, activity and passivity'.[73] This is the condition in which we experience both freedom and unfreedom, as free individuals subject to institutions and laws, but, argues Rose, 'Because the middle is broken – because these institutions are systematically flawed – does not mean they should be eliminated or mended.'[74] It is in the broken middle that we encounter the New Eve, the Church as historical institution and cosmic mother, symbolizing the 'now' and 'not yet' of our redemption, fallible and becoming perfect beyond the ugly rhetoric of the whore and the virgin.

The Church as Eve

We have already seen in Balthasar that an emphasis on the transcendent, Marian perfection of the Church sets up as its opposite the highly negative image of the fallible, institutional Church as the *casta meretrix*, identified with Eve. If a cosmic, maternal ecclesiology is to find carnal expression without such dualisms, then the figure of Eve needs to be revitalized as well as that of Mary. This entails bearing in mind the early Christian understanding of the Church as New Eve, in a way that was analogous to but not identical with Mary's relationship to Christ as the New Eve – what Balthasar describes as the relationship between 'genus and species'.[75] As the New Eve, the Church is 'mother of the living', and therefore she is the realization of Adam's naming of Eve in Genesis 3:20. In the Church as Eve, Catholics labour with the world in its birthing pains, sharing the human condition, seeking to shape a maternal ethos of compassion and care out of the unruly and sometimes violent desires of our wayward humanity. This is the historical, pilgrim Church described by Vatican II, a nomadic mother called to journey alongside humankind as part of the institutions and laws of history, mindful that she too is journeying between paradise and promise and therefore shares the human condition in its experiences of hope and distress, persecution and tyranny, success and defeat, vulnerability and power. This is the Church that needs ethical and political visions (including 'political theology' and 'critical Catholicism'), and it is also a Church that is implicated in the violence and destructiveness of the human story. The Church as Eve stands alongside all people of good will in striving for justice, peace and integrity, because she shares the suffering of a fallen world. But she also shares the imperfection and struggle of humankind, and therefore she also has a capacity to stand over and against people of good will, on the side of injustice, war and violence.

But in her sacramental life, the Church's worship is a foretaste of heaven on earth. Here, we gather at the heavenly wedding feast in the mystical presence of the risen Christ and the Queen of Heaven, who provide maternal nurture for the pilgrim people of God and a glimpse of the world to come. Rather than the kind of dualistic imagery inherent in Balthasar's ecclesiology, we need to see the relationship between history and liturgy in terms of an eternal process of becoming perfect. Referring to Gregory of Nyssa's idea of perfection, Sarah Coakley writes:

> Famously re-defining 'perfection' as 'never arriving' – a daring move for a Platonist – he similarly understands the partaking of Eucharist in this life as an already-anticipated reception of heavenly food. We are on a continuum . . . from this 'body' to our 'angelic' future 'bodies', and death need not be a *dramatic* shift in the case of a holy ascetical body.[76]

From this perspective, the Marian Church with all the instabilities of gender inherent in this also being the maternal body of the male Christ, is not an already accomplished perfection set over and against the sinful, earthly Church. It is rather a dynamic coming into being in the liturgy of a mystical way of being in and beyond the world that we are moving towards, through a continuous process of transformation.

Mother Church roots the incarnation in the soil of creation. Her life is marked by the seasons and the cycles of the year. Her time is cyclical, linear and monumental, spiralling towards eternity from Christmas to Christmas, and rotating around that axial moment when the full moon shines on the birth of the risen Christ from the womb of the earth, keeping rhythm with women's fertile, lunar cycles, when Mary Magdalene runs to tell the good news to the world:

> Jesus said to her, 'Do not hold on to me, because I have not yet ascended to the Father. But go to my brothers and say to them, "I am ascending to my Father and your Father, to my God and your God."' Mary Magdalene went and announced to the disciples, 'I have seen the Lord'; and she told them that he had said these things to her.
>
> (Jn 20:17–18)

The Church Fathers saw all the women of the Bible as types of the Church, in whom Eve is redeemed. That is why Peter Chrysologus, referring to Mary Magdalene's encounter with the risen Christ, can say,

> Christ had care of woman first, since the tempter infected her first. He banishes perfidy from woman, and restores faith to woman, that she who had wrought perdition might be also the ministress of salvation; and at length, through God she might be mother of the living, who so long, through the devil, had been mother of the dead . . . Let Mary come, let her come who bears the name of the Mother, that man may know that Christ dwelt in the secret of her virginal womb, to the end that the dead might go forth from hell, that the dead might go out from the sepulchres.[77]

A woman encounters the risen Christ in a garden, and in that meeting place between nature and culture where woman once lost her voice, her personhood and her dignity before God, Christ gives her a name, a voice and a message to tell the world.

Christ goes back to the beginning of the human story, and there, where a woman is held responsible for the primal sin which establishes an abyss between humankind and God, which alienates the human from the natural environment, and which brings *thanatos* instead of *eros* into the relationship between the sexes,[78] Christ begins his work of healing and redemption. Christ's entry into the womb of Mary is also his entry into death, but he does this in order to break death's hold on woman and to set her free to be a symbol of life instead of death. She is to become the 'ministress of salvation'. Any theology that perpetuates the relationship between the female flesh and death has therefore failed to recognize the significance of the incarnation and the resurrection for the female sex. This means that most of what has been written about Eve, certainly since the late Middle Ages, has been a distortion of the Christian story.

In order for the full significance of this aspect of the story of redemption to emerge, we must bring about a reversal of Balthasar's hell. Eve, like Mary, is both the speaking person who is redeemed in Christ, and the maternal body who gives birth to Christ. If Christ is the 'work of creation', and if Mary gives birth to the infant Christ, it is Eve who gives birth to the risen Christ. It is the earthy chaos of her sex that becomes 'mother of the living' in the birthing of Christ from the tomb, and in the sacramental fecundity of the Church on earth, the New Eve. In this great act of reconciliation, the harlot flesh has been healed and redeemed, brought back from the darkness to which man has consigned her with his lust and his fear and his power, and been reconciled to the virginal fecundity of life in Christ. This means recognizing that 'his' flesh is also 'her' flesh, and that the body redeemed on Calvary is a body that incorporates every meaning, not in order to consume but in order to consummate the goodness of the male and female body made in the image of God.

Nevertheless, however many analogies and metaphors we invoke to affirm the maternal body of the Church, we have seen that, in Balthasar's theology, a lavish celebration of the mother does not allow female sexuality to 'go forth from hell'. It is not enough to speak of maternal redemption, if our language remains at the level of a symbolics evacuated of the flesh, blood and mucus of the actual maternal, sexual female body, and if these remain hostage to a theology that can use them only as metaphors of filth, damnation and sin.

Mary is not simply the animality of maternal flesh, for she is also the woman who freely co-operates with God to bring Christ into being. Mary's 'fiat' is the Heideggerian clearing. Her 'yes' opens a space – a space within herself, a space within the world – in which Being might clothe itself in flesh and be seen for the first time in the everyday worldliness of beings. This 'yes' which creates a space for Christ, in turn allows Christ to create a space for her. The body that births and bleeds is restored to speech, and Eve, banished, silenced and forgotten, rises and is reformed from death by this second birth from heaven. Mary is 'Eve's Advocate'. In the words of one early Christian writer, 'she bears the person of Eve'.[79] We must therefore look more closely at what has been left unsaid in the Church's discourses of maternal femininity, if we are to recognize the sexual as well as the maternal body as a bearer of meaning and revelation. If Eve is to speak as one who questions being and not simply as the mute answer to man's question of being, we need to recover her body from the fiery depths of Balthasar's hell, and restore her to her place in language and culture where she might begin to express the redeemed dignity of her personhood in Christ. Only then can we truly say that Christ has risen so that 'the dead might go forth from hell, that the dead might go out from the sepulchres'.

14 Redeeming language

The relation to the mother is, suggests Irigaray, 'a mad desire, because it is the "dark continent" par excellence. It remains in the shadow of our culture, it is night and hell.'[1] I have repeatedly alluded to the relationship between the maternal body and chaos, and in Balthasar's representation of hell we have seen that relationship pushed to its limits. But the story of Christ's death and descent into hell need not be read as one which gives free rein to the necrophilia of a masculine imaginary obsessed with sex and death. Chaos is a space of beginnings as well as endings, where we find ourselves back where we started and, in the words of T.S. Eliot, 'know the place for the first time' ('Little Gidding', *Four Quartets*), and if we shake the kaleidoscope through which we view these ideas, then language rearranges itself into new patterns of meaning.

The silenced sex

Seeking to explain the role of 'feminine authority' in the Church, Miller explains that

> Feminine authority exists as women exemplify the Church as mother. The authority of woman as *Mater Ecclesia* is so prerational, so close to us, and perhaps most importantly by its own nature, unenshrined by sacramental office, that it easily goes unnoticed and is misunderstood.[2]

The maternal body, 'unenshrined by sacramental office', thus becomes a mute, 'prerational' force, a 'phallic mother' invested with all the wordless potency of the unconscious which, according to Irigaray, constitutes a silent, deadly threat of annihilation as far as the masculine subject is concerned:

> the opening of the mother, the opening to the mother, appear as threats of contagion, contamination, falling into sickness, madness, death . . . Some men and women would prefer to identify maternal power, the phallic

mother, as an ensnaring net. But such attribution occurs only as a defensive mesh that the man-father or his sons casts over the chasms of a silent and threatening womb. Threatening because it is silent, perhaps?[3]

If, in its symbolization of the maternal body, the Catholic tradition undermines Irigaray's theory about the matricidal foundations of western culture, it remains the case that this maternal symbolism is dissociated from female sexuality and the female body. The 'silence', therefore, refers to a language in which the nuanced dialectic between sexual and maternal embodiment has given way to a violent dualism in which the sexual female body is a silent and deadly threat to the virginal purity of the maternal Church. The female body does not inhabit the house of language, because although, unlike the western philosophical tradition, it is a house shaped around the maternal body, the female sex has been evicted in order to serve the purposes of a trans-gendered masculine imaginary, in which the fear of castration or consumption is an ever-present threat because of the pervasive presence of the maternal presence in the Church and in creation. As Irigaray suggests, this translates into a fear of female sexuality:

> The womb is never thought of as the primal place in which we become body. Therefore for many men it is variously phantasized as a devouring mouth, as a sewer in which anal and urethral waste is poured, as a threat to the phallus or, at best, as a reproductive organ. And the womb is mistaken for all the female sexual organs since no valid representations of female sexuality exist.[4]

Mother Church is indeed a body with a womb and breasts, but with no labia, clitoris or vagina. And, lest her virginal motherhood be contaminated, real women with real sex organs are denied sacramental significance, while 'brides' with penises pretend to be men (and therefore God) in order to exercise their priestly role. But the other side of this sexual exclusion is the inclusion of female sexuality as sin, seduction, whore, hell. Therefore the redemption of the female sex entails a journey to hell and beyond, in order to bring back what has been appropriated, silenced, conquered, raped and defeated in the struggle for representation.

But we must remember that this is a symbolic journey that must weave its way through language itself in order to discover the silenced 'other' of language. What is lacking is not the sexual body but the symbolic and sacramental meanings by which female sexuality – and therefore male sexuality as well – can be inscribed within the story of redemption as a good and holy aspect of God's creation, beyond the too-narrow focus of the Church's teachings on marriage and procreation, and beyond the 'supra-sexual' couplings that take place between a Church with a womb and no vagina, and a Christ with a vicarious penis in the body of the male priest who, being celibate, has no sexual need of it. (Although, unlike the clitoris, the penis is a multi-tool. Only the female body has been designed by God with an organ dedicated to exquisite sexual pleasure alone.)[5]

In Balthasar's account of the cross and the descent into hell, Ward argues that

> Representation experiences its crisis. And a new word appears, 'his utmost word', on the far side of the death's profound *passio*. Only in and through the cross, the death of God, is there redemption and an ability to 'see the form'.[6]

Ward likens Balthasar's hell to 'the strident darkness of clashing empty symbols' which theology itself becomes '[w]ithout faith as kenotic, self-abandoning love': 'This is the hell Christ descended into on Holy Saturday and from which the redemption of form and representation will issue on Easter Sunday.'[7]

In seeking to explore the significance of this 'redemption of form and representation' for theology beyond modernity, Ward draws out a number of parallels between Kristeva's psycholinguistics and Balthasar's theology. Quoting Kristeva, he refers to her description of psychoanalysis as '"an imaginary discourse that serves as truth", for assisting modernity's *ego* in its search for a lost soul, for facilitating a transposition from necrophilia to resurrection life'.[8] He suggests that

> Kristeva provides Balthasar with an anthropological account of transcorporality; Balthasar provides Kristeva with the Catholic theology which acts in the silent white margins of her own texts. The human *eros* is made part of a wider economy of desire – the desires of other people which propel my desire and the divine *eros* drawing me out in love, worship and obedience, pouring me into a Trinitarian kenosis. Kristeva demonstrates how language is motivated by and abides within desire. Discourse, then, is always an amatory discourse proceeding through a never-to-be-entangled interplay of human and divine desire. It is a desire which both affirms and requires representation and yet denies and puts representation into crisis. Its enfleshment, its incarnation, is both its prison and its possibility of freedom.[9]

Ward describes transcorporality as follows:

> *en Christō* it is by our sign-giving and receiving, by our wording and reading, that we are redeemed . . . Our knowledge of God is, then, both active and passive, a knowing as a being known; a form of incorporation coupled with the realization that we are incorporated. The kenotic economy is the

narrative of transcorporality. It narrates a story of coming to know through coming to love – love given, love endured.[10]

There is, however, a problem with Ward's comparison, and this lies in his failure to acknowledge the different ways in which Balthasar and Kristeva interpret the significance of sexual difference and the representational potential of the maternal body. For Kristeva, the move beyond violence and sacrifice to the unveiling of love and desire requires the psychological integration of difference, and therefore a move beyond the signifying duality of sexual difference. Balthasar's God remains the patriarchal, sacrificial Father God, and sexual difference is emphasized as the *sine qua non* of human and divine relationships. Ultimately, Balthasar cannot yield to several alternative possibilities that struggle to manifest themselves in his theology: the possibility that God is maternal as well as paternal; the possibility that sexual difference is an analogy that liberates the female body as well as the male body to play its role in the drama of salvation through a plurality of gendered roles; the possibility that the female sexual body has sacramental significance. Balthasar's resistance to these 'desires' in his own theology takes the form of a violent struggle that manifests itself particularly strongly in his representations of sex and death. There is no 'transcorporality' in Balthasar as far as the female body is concerned, and therefore there can be no true *eros* when only one 'body' has the kind of dynamic fluidity that is suggested by Ward's 'amatory discourse', for Balthasar's *eros* is engulfed in the narcissism of the man as woman who desires to be desired by God. Moreover, if 'representation experiences its crisis' in Christ's death and descent into hell, we have seen that this crisis is resolved through the burning away of every trace of female sexual embodiment, leaving the signifiers associated with that body free for the man to colonize in his relationship to Christ and the Church. If, as Ward suggests, we are redeemed 'by our sign-giving and receiving, by our wording and reading', then the female sex is not yet redeemed.

But stripped of her signifiers, the female body refuses to die. She is not incinerated by Christ in hell, but persists as a disruptive silence, a chaotic presence on the margins of 'his' ordered world. 'He' projects onto 'her' his hysterical femininity, his sexual carnality, his deadly fantasies, and in an act of perfect mimesis she accepts this burden, becomes the mysterical body that lures him into the hellish depths of her mystical madness, so that he can take her language and fold it back into his own, leaving her mute, blind, bedridden, dying. If Catholicism is psychosomatic in its symbolism, then the relationship between Balthasar and Speyr is the most eloquent possible bodying forth of those symbols, and it stands as a warning to all who would follow in their footsteps in seeking to live to such an extreme this particular theological vision.

At the furthest edge of modernity, Balthasar at last completes the symbolic annihilation of the female body which has been threatening the Christian theological vision for much of its history. Balthasar completes it because, for the first time, the position of women in the Church has become an urgent question that demands a theological response. In the past, sexual hierarchies have been sustained by an unchallenged theology of male authority and female subordination, which gradually in the development of the Catholic tradition has gathered around itself a proliferating discourse of masculinity and femininity, maternity and paternity. In Balthasar, perhaps more than in any other modern theologian, we see an attempt to give theological legitimation to these various cultural constructs, by projecting them even into the intra-trinitarian life of God – rendering them eternal and ontological.

But might it be possible to allow this sexual coupling to go beyond 'a love within sameness',[11] to a love of otherness, a love for the other? Might this open the way to a life-giving encounter in which, instead of sex, death and hell, there could be mutual fecundity and desire – a space of transcorporality where activity and passivity, giving and receiving, revelation and silence, were not 'his' and 'hers' but ours and God's, allowing God to dance among us in language and gesture, in silence and music, in all the eloquent means by which we sacramentally embody meaning on this near side of the far horizons of love?

The body that speaks

In *Theo-Drama V*, Balthasar's reflections on the 'Final Act' of Christ's passion are a dense interweaving of themes of light and dark, separation and intimacy, but also, significantly, of Speyr's voice and his own. Quoting Speyr, Balthasar writes,

> 'Every individual sin is expiated individually on the Cross, each one goes through the totality of his wounds; . . . he takes on every sin with his entire body.' . . . The Son, as it were, actively gathers unto himself sins, but also the world's pains, and particularly the sufferings of the Old Covenant, which, far from having no significance for redemption, 'attain their fulfilment through the Cross'. Thus for the Son, as for us, the Cross grows until it exceeds our grasp. Although it is the overcoming of the chaos of sin, it becomes a 'pathless', a 'wordless' suffering, unveiling the world itself as chaos.[12]

But Balthasar/Speyr go on to insist that

> when the kingdom of the Prince of this world is being finally established and the Lord's defeat is 'so shattering that no one – not even the believers – will be able to avoid accepting its reality'; at that very moment 'everything is reversed.'
>
> This reversal is not the result of a divine decision coming 'from outside'; it is made possible by the fact that the Son's God-forsakenness is drawn into the love relationship within the Trinity. The Son 'takes the estrangement into himself and creates proximity'.[13]

Thus, in this Trinitarian reversal, Christ takes the abject into his own body – 'sins', 'the world's pains', 'the sufferings of the Old Covenant' – and this pathless, wordless chaos becomes the path beyond chaos, the overcoming of sin, so that the greatest possible alienation becomes the closest intimacy of Trinitarian love, a divine reconciliation that does not come from outside but is generated from within God by the *kenosis* and desire, the abjection and love, which is the life that flows among the persons of the Trinity and between God and creation. To quote Kristeva, 'The time of abjection is double: a time of oblivion and thunder, of veiled infinity and the moment when revelation bursts forth.'[14]

But Kristeva argues that the 'sufferings of the Old Covenant' are the sufferings of an identity which must be forged through maternal abjection and separation, in response to the divine law. If, as Kristeva and Balthasar suggest, the genius of Christianity lies in its capacity to reconcile but go beyond the religion of the pagans and the law of the Hebrews, where might we look for the healing of the divided body that would allow this to manifest itself in the Church, beyond 'the idea of sinning flesh' that 'theological posterity' has preserved (see Chapter 11) – in Balthasar's writings as much as in any other?

Kristeva writes that 'Christ's Passion brings into play even more primitive layers of the psyche'[15] than Freud's interpretation which sees it as 'an avowal of the oedipal murder that every human being unconsciously desires'.[16] The Passion, according to Kristeva,

> reveals a fundamental depression (a narcissistic wound or reversed hatred) that conditions access to human language. The sadness of young children just prior to their acquisition of language has often been observed; this is when they must renounce forever the maternal paradise in which every demand is immediately gratified. The child must abandon its mother and be abandoned by her in order to be accepted by the father and begin talking . . . The 'scandal of the cross', the *logos tou savron* or language of the cross, which some, according to Saint Paul, would call 'foolishness' (1 Cor. 1:18 and 1:23; Gal. 5:11) and which is indeed inconceivable for a god as the ancients understood the term, is embodied, I think not only in the psychic and physical suffering that irrigates our lives (*qui irrigue notre existence*) but even more profoundly in the essential alienation that conditions our access to language, in the mourning that accompanies the dawn of psychic life.[17]

Thus one could extrapolate from Kristeva, to suggest that the 'reversal' or 'reversed hatred' of the cross puts us in touch with that primordial sense of loss, site of original sin perhaps, where the speaking subject is cut off from the maternal paradise and set adrift in the wilderness of language and culture, where the intimate presence of God in paradise becomes the absent, unnameable God of history, law and covenant. But the cross symbolizes the healing of that primal separation: it promises, not alienation but reconciliation, not condemnation but redemption, and paradise regained in communion with God and the sexual other in the heavenly wedding feast. From this perspective, the cross as described by Balthasar/Speyr is a psychic path before and beyond language: a journey to the far side of meaning, into the abjection of 'pathless, wordless suffering' – but this dying is also a rebirth into a new way of speaking, where the autonomous, masculine subject learns to speak anew as a womanly person constituted in relation to Christ and the maternal Church.

This invites us to revisit Balthasar's idea that Mary surrenders her identity to Christ on Calvary, in a nuptial union in which she becomes 'one flesh' with him in the motherhood of the Church. Rather than seeing this as the loss of the woman's identity, might we interpret it as the coming into being of a new form of subjectivity such as that proposed by both feminist theorists and Balthasar's idea of personhood – the relational subject, constituted through the symbolization of the maternal body, a bodily self who is more than one but less than two? Too daringly for many modern Catholics perhaps, in the words of John Paul II, 'At the root of the Eucharist . . . there is the virginal and maternal life of Mary.'[18] He says of Mary on Calvary that

> she offered him and she offered herself to the Father. Every Eucharist is a memorial of that Sacrifice and that Passover that restored life to the world; every Mass puts us into intimate communion with her, the Mother, whose sacrifice 'becomes present' just as the sacrifice of her Son 'becomes present' at the words of consecration of the bread and wine pronounced by the priest.[19]

To insist on Mary's maternal presence in the self-giving of Christ is to introduce fecundity as well as sacrifice into the symbolic significance of the cross. If, as Irigaray suggests, sacrifice is associated with patriarchal religions and fecundity with matriarchal religions, and if matricide constitutes the founding sacrifice of the social order, then this is a sublime reconciliation of maternal and paternal divinity, through the restoration of the sacrificed mother to language and meaning. The vulnerable God of the Christian faith is revealed to be other than the oedipal Father God who is appeased through sacrifice, for this is a God whose outpouring of love on Calvary materializes in a maternal body that gives birth to and nourishes the Church. The mother's flesh is no longer shunned and reviled, but is redeemed in Christ and restored to her rightful place.

Thus the maternal body becomes a site of linguistic coming into being that challenges the masculine subject of the Freudian and Lacanian scenario. Beyond the mourning of Christ's passion and death, there must be a return to the womb and a reclamation of what has been covered over and silenced in bringing the subject to speech. Beyond the speaking masculine subject and the silence of his feminine other, a form of personhood emerges from this death and rebirth – this baptism in the birthing fluids of water and blood that flow from the open wound of Christ – in which the self and the other become one flesh. This sets in motion a form of dynamic personal becoming brought about by the movement of desire and lack, love and abjection, within as well as between subjects whose existence unfolds in the space of difference that constantly threatens the stable subject, the secure identity, the 'I', through an acceptance of the fundamental relationality and interdependence of human and divine persons, and of word and flesh. In Christ, the monadic, masculine individual becomes dyadic. (S)he learns to speak with the 'two lips' of the female sex. He becomes woman. But until he can be 'woman' with her rather than over and against her, his speech will always be premised upon the sealing of her lips, in order to close up that devouring abyss which would draw him away from the Father's transcendence into the chaos of nature, sex and death.

Ward suggests that Christ's descent into hell and his resurrection constitute the unmaking and remaking of language. On the far side of hell, the resurrection brings a new transparency to language – it allows us to 'see the form'. Postmodernism reminds us, beyond modernity's literalisms, that our language of the body is metaphoric, but Christians must nonetheless speak as if the body speaks, in analogy beyond metaphor, in anticipation of that final coming together of the Word and the world when we will no longer 'see in a mirror dimly, but . . . face to face': 'Now I know only in part; then I will know fully, even as I have been fully known' (1 Cor. 13:12).

Psycholinguistics tells us that the body which struggles to speak through us is the maternal body, a body swollen with desire and fear, the dark and sensual lining to the subject's smooth discourse. According to Kristeva, this is a body which was abjected in the long making of Israel's covenant history with God, which was fully assimilated and rehabilitated by Christ through its incorporation into the speaking subject, but which was later abjected from Christian consciousness just as it had once been abjected by Israel's law and ritual, so that 'only the idea of sinning flesh remained'.

Balthasar's depiction of hell is, as we have seen, redolent with the language of female sexuality. In that abyss beyond every possibility of representation, Christ is consumed by the body of the harlot, but God the Father conquers the devouring female flesh and delivers Christ up to life. After the incineration of language in hell, there are no longer words for her body, her sex, because she does not signify: 'revelation is no part of a woman's task'.[20]

But woman does speak: Speyr speaks from the depths of hell. It is the woman's voice, not the man's, which shapes language in that space of horror. So Balthasar's risen Christ cannot rest in his battle to defeat her, for she is not as silent as she pretends to be. In fact, she speaks endlessly, repetitively, with a deadly vision that keeps him spellbound or earthbound. She represents the last vestiges of sin in this Christ's perfect world, contaminating his suprasexual incestuous marriage with the body that he has rejected and condemned. Christ remains locked in sacrifice, in bloodshed, in repeated acts of rape by which he seeks to tame and subdue his wilful Bride: 'Never has a woman made more desperate resistance!' And, by implication, Christ's representatives on earth – priests, popes, bishops – are themselves locked in battle against sex and the female body, believing that only this resistance proves the Church's unworldliness.

But what if we interpret Balthasar/Speyr differently, if the female body looks to his sources and her visions for the form and representation of her becoming in Christ, rather than for the signs of silence and exclusion? Might this at last bring respite, peace from the battle, love without rape, desire without violence, fecundity without control? To ask these questions, we might once again find unexpected resonances if we read Balthasar and Kristeva together.

Redeeming the nightmare

In his study of the origins of the idea of hell, Balthasar compares early Christian writings with representations of Sheol in the Hebrew scriptures. He suggests that the idea of Sheol as a place gradually changes in Christianity to the idea of hell as a condition – a change in meaning that can also be identified in some earlier Hebrew texts:

> The Old Testament descriptions are so existential in their tenor that the accent falls much more on the condition of the dead than on the place where they find themselves. It is not, then, a matter for surprise that, in Christian theology, the theme of places (*receptacula, promptuaria*) and that of conditions are set side by side with little or no reciprocal influence, and that the second can sometimes appear without the former.[21]

Balthasar refers to Augustine's *Literal Commentary on Genesis*, in which he 'admitted the purely spiritual character of Hell'.[22] But this means that 'Hell' has an imaginary quality:

> If the soul is spiritual, it can nevertheless experience the play of mental images, conjuring up the reality of bodies, and by them (for example in dreams) be either tormented or rendered blessed. 'Hell' would be the condition where one is so affected in the intensest way possible.[23]

Balthasar suggests that 'Though a de-mythologisation so radical as this is not common, it opens the way to a psychic solidarity between the dead Christ and those who dwell in the Hades of the spirit.'[24]

The Christian hell, then, constitutes the transformation of 'place' into psychic condition, but this condition is such that, 'in dreams' perhaps, one can imagine it as bodies, where there is an unsurpassable intensity of torment and blessing. Hell, then, is populated by the imagination: there is no body in hell, apart from the bodies that our dreams and nightmares are made of. The maternal – harbinger of life and death, of heaven and hell – passes from body to language, and is reconstituted within the psyche in the form of the dead Christ, who becomes sin, chaos, harlot flesh. But it is the genius of the Christian psyche to find words for this unspeakable abyss within itself, holding madness at bay at the borderline of speech. It is only the psychotic, the truly abject, who crosses the border beyond all desire, beyond all representation:

> The *symptom*: a language that gives up, a structure within the body, a non-assimilable alien, a monster, a tumor, a cancer that the listening devices of the unconscious do not hear, for its strayed subject is huddled outside the paths of desire. *Sublimation*, on the contrary, is nothing else than the possibility of naming the pre-nominal, the pre-objectal, which are in fact only a trans-nominal, a trans-objectal. In the symptom, the abject permeates me, I become abject. Through sublimation, I keep it under control. The abject is edged with the sublime.[25]

Christianity dreams of bodies, and finds words for the unspeakable. Religion, says Kristeva, stands at the intersection of sublimation and perversion, where the self stands divided between abjection and the sacred.[26] But Balthasar's dead Christ (revealed in Speyr's visions) goes beyond sublimation to become 'the symptom', experiencing 'the second death', beyond Calvary, beyond the crossroads between life and death, fecundity and sacrifice, the abject and the sublime:

> the second death which, itself, is one with sheer sin as such, no longer sin as attaching to a particular human being, sin incarnate in living existences, but abstracted from that individuation, contemplated in its bare reality as such (for sin *is* a reality!). In this amorphous condition, sin forms what one can call the second 'chaos'.[27]

In this no place and no time, Christ becomes sin and hell, 'huddled outside the paths of desire'. But it is Balthasar who must speak as Christ, finding words for this death beyond death, in that time out of time to which Speyr has taken him so that he speaks as the abject – 'I have been expelled from this communion of sinners. Stiff and frozen, rolled up lump-like, I cower to the side: my sin is without comparison'[28] (see Chapters 9 and 10).

In speaking of this second chaos we are indeed on the edge of the sublime. Speyr's hell takes Balthasar beyond the ego, beyond coherence, to that point at which meaning threatens to tilt into oblivion, and from that precipice of human consciousness on the brink of everything and nothing, Balthasar peers into the

Redeeming language 279

darkness and attempts to speak of the corpse of Christ. Here, Balthasar's theo-drama enacts an encounter with abjection as described by Kristeva:

> as in true theatre, without makeup or masks, refuse and corpses *show me* what I permanently thrust aside in order to live. These body fluids, this defilement, this shit are what life withstands, hardly and with difficulty, on the part of death. There, I am at the border of my condition as a living being . . . If dung signifies the other side of the border, the place where I am not and which permits me to be, the corpse, the most sickening of wastes, is a border that has encroached upon everything. It is no longer I who expel, 'I' is expelled . . . In that compelling, raw, insolent thing in the morgue's full sunlight, in that thing that no longer matches and therefore no longer signifies anything, I behold the breaking down of a world that has erased its borders: fainting away. The corpse, seen without God and outside of science, is the utmost of abjection. It is death infecting life. Abject . . . Imaginary uncanniness and real threat, it beckons to us and ends up engulfing us.
>
> It is thus not lack of cleanliness or health that causes abjection but what disturbs identity, system, order.[29]

This is the brink to which Speyr leads Balthasar, when she tumbles into the mystical madness of her visions in order to lure him into the presence of the dead Christ who threatens to infect and engulf him. He allows her to take him there, recognizing his own resistance to the Christ who speaks through her:

> I do not long to go outside of myself! What would be the good of an ecstasy of 'coalescing' with nature or with a loved person, if I could no longer experience them? How could I make you a gift of my love or offer you my ego in love if I no longer have this ego, if I am dispossessed of myself?[30]

Balthasar goes nearly all the way with Speyr, but, after visiting hell with her, at the border of the dissolution of the self, he must withdraw and redraw the boundaries, insisting on the 'identity, system, order' which Christ secures when God the Father raises him up from the chaos of sex and death, making him henceforth a marker of transcendent masculinity in a creation that would otherwise be entirely surrendered to the 'feminine' and therefore to death. The Phallus will hold this chaos at bay, and the male priest will be the anchor which prevents Holy Mother Church from swirling out of control, as he battles in God's name against her wayward flesh till Kingdom Come.

The language of Kristeva's abjection resonates with the same imagery as Balthasar's hell, but whereas she seeks a way beyond the destructive projections that lead to the entanglement of sex, desire and death through the masculine subject's repression of the bodily, maternal other, Balthasar reinforces this destructive potency by affirming rather than questioning the identification of the female sex with the corruption of death and hell. When Balthasar searches for words on the far side of language, he discovers that he is in the abjected darkness of the female sex, a darkness that must be burned away if his male Christ is to conquer the Bride by way of a suprasexual love that rises above the chaos of the body. Projecting his terror back onto the 'body' of the Church, 'she' becomes not only his unattainable dream of virginal perfection, 'she' also becomes the personification of the sin of a corrupt institution which is represented in its sacraments and institutions by celibate men.

Only when the sins of the Church are recognized as male sins – including the sin of demonizing the female sex – will men and women be able to move towards mutual understanding as bodies called to occupy the space of encounter between language and body that constitutes our sacramental being in the world. In Balthasar's rehabilitation of the medieval idea of the *casta meretrix*, and in the failure of the male theological establishment to question this imagery, we are reminded that the contemporary community of priests and scholars still functions in a world of moral and existential blindness as far as the gendering of sin is concerned: men's sins, like their love for Christ, are an essentially feminine affair. But while the female body is evicted from the positive sphere of this feminization, it remains thoroughly identified with the negative sphere. 'Woman' is a male body in her sacramental love for the Bridegroom, and a female body in the sin that alienates her from the Bridegroom. Collectively, the male hierarchy is guilty of the sin of whoredom and harlotry, even if individually they are brides of Christ, but the female body is individually and collectively banished from the sphere of representation. Only when men find a language of the sin of the Church that is capable of identifying and analysing the sins of men, and the ways in which they sin as men, will the Church be free from the pernicious grip of an authoritarian masculinity hedged round with repression, fear and alienation.

But psychoanalysis cautions us against a liberalism that would seek justice through a rhetoric of political activism alone. It enables us to read the texts of Catholic theology in a way that reveals the primal darkness at its heart. If we are to address the ways in which these visceral dimensions of the Catholic psyche distort the Church's understanding of sexuality and play out in an ongoing resistance to the sacramentality of the female body, it is not enough simply to ignore the hell in which these fears originate. We must find a way to refigure this language and make it speak of redemption rather than damnation, so that we break the vicious association between female sexuality, death and hell which is rooted in the depths of the Church's psycho-theological vision. Let me turn to Sarah Boss's reclamation of chaos, as a possible resource for this feminist refiguration of language beyond death.

The elemental matrix

Boss brings an intriguing interpretation of Ramon Lull's (1232–1316) representation of Chaos in his *Liber Chaos* to her reflections on Mary. Boss points out that Lull's concern is not that of modern science, but that 'people should come to know and love God by means of knowing and loving God's creation'.[31] This leads Lull to prayerful reflection on the nature of prime matter, the 'all-pervasive substance of the material world'[32] out of which all created forms emerge. But prime matter is itself already present in Chaos, according to Lull, since Chaos is the primal state of all that is, 'made by God *ex nihilo* – "out of nothing". It is the foundation of all corporeal beings, and all that constitutes corporeal beings is initially present *potentially* in Chaos . . . Difference, says Lull, is everywhere present in Chaos.'[33] Boss suggests that '*Chaos is that in virtue of which bodily things as such participate in one another by identity.*'[34] This means that every earthly creature has some participation in Chaos and therefore in the identity of every other, but, because of the incarnation, Mary is uniquely identified with Chaos:

> the purpose of the incarnation of God in her body was precisely the union of God with the whole cosmos; so the participation of Mary in the fabric of the universe is not just a necessary aspect of her humanity, but is essential to the world's redemption and to the fulfillment of its purpose.[35]

For this reason, Boss argues,

> the Blessed Virgin Mary shares an identity with the elemental matrix, or *chaos*, of which the world is created. If we start by imagining the cosmos as fabric whose thread and weave are ever changing, then Mary is in some sense the same as the entire assembly of the most minute, invisible particles of the fibres of which the world is spun and woven. She is present in all physical things as their foundation; yet at the same time, she shows the glory to which all things are called by their Creator.[36]

But Boss also points to the 'twofold status'[37] of Llull's understanding of Chaos. As the primal, undifferentiated form of creation, containing within itself all other form and matter, it is both 'that in creation which, in its basic state, is farthest from perfection; yet . . . it comes immediately from the hand of God, and has Godlike aspects that are proper to it alone'.[38] Chaos, then, according to this interpretation, is the most original feature of creation, and its meaning cannot be established or understood, for it is both the closest to and the furthest from God of all that is.

Boss develops this idea in a rich Trinitarian reflection on the traditional association of both Mary and Christ with the figure of Wisdom. Referring to the Christian doctrine that 'the world is created *by* God the Father, *through* God the Son, *in the power of* the Holy Spirit',[39] Boss writes, at Christ's conception, God the Son becomes himself the new creation through the agency of the Blessed Virgin Mary: she is not only the matter of which the new creation is formed, but also the moral agent by whom it takes life in the created world. So the original creation, God's first creation, is made through Christ, who is Wisdom, in eternity. But in the *new* creation, Christ is himself the work of creation. And this new creation in Christ is formed *through* his mother Mary. So it is now she who takes on the mantle of Holy Wisdom, *through whom* God does the work of creation. As the first creation was wrought *through* Holy Wisdom in the person of Christ, so the new creation, Jesus himself, is wrought *through* Holy Wisdom in the person of Mary. So in Mary, who is both the substance of the cosmos and a unique co-operator in the work of redemption, Wisdom is one with the material foundation of the universe. Not only is the relationship between Mary and her son cast in the image of that which exists between the first and second Persons of the Trinity, but it is also cast in the likeness of the relationship between the second Person of the Trinity and the order of creation.[40]

Here, we begin to see that Christ, in the incarnation, takes the mother's flesh upon himself, passing through and uniting himself with the mother's body, which is also the matter of the cosmos. Thus the long process of separation and abjection is reversed, and what is furthest from the God of Israel but also from the Greek philosophical idea of divine transcendence – the maternal flesh – becomes inseparable from God in Christ.

But this goes far beyond anthropocentrism, for it constitutes a rediscovery of the cosmic nature of salvation. According to Balthasar, Christ goes beyond even the tomb of death, into the very womb of Chaos itself. The symbolization of Christ and Mary as the New Adam and the New Eve situates the story of the incarnation at that point in creation where the human comes into being, but Boss and Balthasar suggest that Christ does not only go back to the beginning of the human story in death, because he also experiences 'the second death', in which he enters the wordless abyss of all that is, 'in the beginning' when 'the earth was a formless void and darkness covered the face of the deep' (Gen. 1:1). Therefore Christ goes beyond every human condition, including that of death, to become one with that which is furthest from and closest to God – 'the abject edged with the sublime'. Beyond even the haunted longings of our maternal beginnings, Christ enters that abyss which is both everything that ever can be, and nothing that has ever yet been. Call it the Real if you will – for here, names and words have no matter/*mater*.

Thus beyond the healing of the psychic wound, before any individual separates itself from the primordial matter of creation, transgressing the boundary of the abject, Christ becomes abjection. Beyond death itself, he becomes Chaos. Reunited with the maternal body that birthed him, he goes beyond the body's identity to that realm of undifferentiated differences, of form and representation waiting in Chaos for their coming into being, and there, Christ heals the cosmos, atom by atom and quark by quark, creating anew everything that is by his dissolution and union with the matrix of being:

> When God makes the new creation in Christ from his mother Mary, he does this by returning to the foundations of the universe, to the pure, untarnished Chaos that comes immediately from his own being, as the stuff out of which the new creation will arise. And Mary as Chaos, as creation's righteous beginning, is Mary in whom there has never been sin.[41]

In Christ's non-violent acceptance of the violence that is done to him, he takes upon himself the sin of the world. He becomes the sacrifice to end all sacrifice. In hell, he goes to heal what has been destroyed by violence: the bodies of the dead, the earth which cries out with the blood of Abel, the world in its origins.

But what does it mean to say that he becomes sin? In Paul's Letter to the Romans we read that 'Apart from the law sin lies dead' (Rom. 7:8). Balthasar insists that 'sin *is* a reality',[42] but there are others who would agree with Catherine of Siena that 'sin is a nothing'.[43] For Catherine, those who sin suffer because their desire is compulsively directed towards nothingness, but God tells Catherine that 'from this nothingness of sin, a thorn that pierces the soul, I pluck this rose to provide for their salvation'.[44] Indeed, in words that would be a fitting eulogy to the nihilism of our postmodern age, Catherine writes that 'They who wanted to rule the world find themselves ruled by nothingness, that is, by sin – for sin is the opposite of being, and they have become servants and slaves of sin.'[45]

There is no law and no sin in hell, for there is no language and no being in hell: hell is the most profound non-being. But paradoxically, then, hell is at one and the same time sin and sin's unspeaking. Sin is real, and sin is a nothing. Sin is the Real, the no thing that occupies the darkest darkness, the most profound silence, out of which surges some primeval impulse to destroy being, a death-drive that would return to non-being all that is. But we do not see sin as such: we see only the violence that it feeds, and therefore we never see sin except in its human form. Yet part of that violence is to project back onto sin itself the human form, the other, so that we make of the nothingness a body to hate and to murder. If, as Balthasar suggests, hell is a psychic condition populated by bodies of the imagination, we have seen that this imaginary hell is also the female sex. Kristeva points us again and again towards the maternal body that feeds this murderous desire, so that the undoing of violence must be the undoing of a certain way of speaking or not speaking about the mother. This means that we must recognize Balthasar's personification of hell as the dark dreams of an unhealed psyche, in which sin takes the form of the sexual other as the greatest terror, the greatest threat. We might recognize and accept this as a psychological phenomenon that is widespread in Catholic spirituality, as the first step in the move towards healing, but we should not baptize it as Christian theology.

Eve is the one who forms the borderline of Christian consciousness, symbolizing that point of exit and entry, beyond which all is flesh, sin, pagan, heretic, Jew, other, hell. When Eve's flesh comes into speech, she brings the other with her, so that only in the redemption of the female sex might the Catholic Church welcome the other within herself, the uncanny stranger that disrupts her virginal fantasies and dreams of wholeness with bodiliness, difference and desire. The Second Vatican Council created a rational, discursive space in which dialogue with otherness is possible but, as Balthasar suggests, it did so at the expense of the dark and visceral beauty of the Church's mystical life, creating structures and systems and institutions capable of briefly accommodating the other on our own terms. The challenge now is to go further, to an ecclesiology in which the necessary structures of a social institution are held together, not by men in drag pretending to be women pretending to be men, who must reassert their masculine authority with defiant power when the feminized other comes too close, but by men and women together living in the imitation of Christ through the maternal Church.

Difference beyond death

Balthasar's hell may be read in a way that is analogous to Irigaray's reading of Plato's cave. For Irigaray, the cave serves as a screen upon which images are reflected, but the cave itself remains unthought and unrepresented. It is the maternal body that underlies all representation, but which is in itself incapable of representation. It is what has been sacrificed and covered over in the making of a language and a culture which turns its back on the body of the Mother to seek truth in the Father's transcendent light. When that light is brought back into contact with the body through a morphology that seeks to bend and shape it to the contours of the female sex, it is refracted and reflected along curved surfaces that shatter its meanings and set fire to its forms and representations.

But Balthasar is neither a Greek philosopher nor a post-Enlightenment man of reason. Balthasar is a Catholic whose language of the Father is also, always and everywhere, a language of the Mother. His eyes have been trained to see in the dark, and he thinks that he can see beyond the shadows to the screen itself – remembering that it is a woman, Speyr, who teaches him how to look. But what does Speyr reveal to Balthasar through her visions? Does he view the Chaos she shows him only through the screen of her body, so that he sees superimposed upon it his own terror of female sexuality – of the body that she is, the Other Mother, Eve, the sexual, carnal body that consumes the Father's light?

Balthasar asks how Christ can bring about the emptying of hell, so that even those who die outside of Christ are not absolutely dead because 'a heavenly shimmer of light, of faith, love, hope, has ever illuminated the "abyss"'.[46] In the second death, Christ goes beyond the condition of the dead in hell, to become the condition of hell itself, but in so doing he 'sets the limits to the extension of damnation . . . forms the boundary stone marking the place where the lowest pitch is reached and the reverse movement set into operation'.[47] Thus, Christ extends the boundaries of consciousness, creating space in the human imagination for that which has been abjected, transforming what it means to be human by inserting the praying subject into the space of self and otherness, word and flesh, male and female, life and death, where identity is constituted by difference, by lack, by the realization that 'I' am the not yet of God's promise calling me into the fullness of being through the encounter with death. 'Hell is a *product* of the Redemption,'[48] claims Balthasar. At the furthermost limits of the psyche, where the self dissolves in the abyss of the other within itself, we are also at the primal moment of the new creation, at the turning point where redemption begins: 'Abjection is a resurrection that has gone through death (of the ego). It is an alchemy that transforms death-drive into a start of life, of new significance.'[49]

If Christ and woman are to live beyond Balthasar, then we must recognize his hell for what it is – the hell of the human mind, projecting language into the darkness and forms into the formlessness. But this is not the rebirth of language beyond the resurrection, for it is still the language of sacrifice and violence. Boss's description of Chaos provides a more life-giving, more theologically coherent account of the ways in which Christ redeems the cosmos with and through the cosmic Mother. But she also reminds us that Christ takes us to the very outermost edges of creation – to the continual creating of something out of nothing that holds the world in being – beyond which, even in our wildest visions and imaginings, we cannot go. We have arrived at that point in our journey where we started, that point at which we cannot say what God is, but only what God is not. God is not anything that we have said or could say, but God is in everything that is.

If we revisit Balthasar's hell with these interpretative possibilities in mind, a different reading opens up. The 'sacrifice' reveals the violence that men do in the name of God, to the body of God. It reveals God's refusal of that violence, so that all the sacred signifiers dissolve and nothing is left beyond the death of God but the love of God. This love descends into the tomb and into the heart of the earth, and there it makes peace. It heals what was sacrificed in the making of worlds; it brings back what was abjected in the making of difference. It becomes the primal chaos, and befriends death. The dead body of Christ becomes a maternal body, a body that gives birth to itself in the motherhood of the Church. The man on the cross and the mother at the foot of the cross make visible the difference that Christ incarnates – they are one flesh, but they are not the same. Within and between them, they embody difference, and thus in the spaces between their bodily differences we discover all the meaning that there is. It is a meaning that resists every hierarchy, every system, every dualism, a meaning that shines within and between words that slip away, refusing the grid, the logic, the necessity of saying what they mean and meaning what they say. To follow such language one cannot march to the rhythms of society's orderly ranks. One must dance, make merry, and join the carnival:

> To you, my Church, have I entrusted this fountainhead. Out of you, who are my Body, out of your open side does it flow forth to refresh all peoples. Just as you, as the new Eve, have sprung forth from my sleep, so do I, who am divine life itself, spring forth from you. Your hands distribute me as the Bread of the World. For, to be sure, the woman derives from the man, but the man is then born of the woman. Everything, however, derives from God. Being God, I am the Source and am before every being, and for this reason the man is the glory of God and the source of the woman, and God-become-human is the man, while the Church is a woman, since the woman is the glory of the man. But, because I became the Son of Man, I have been born from human beings and am your child, O Church. For everyone who does the will of my Father is not only my brother and my sister, but my mother as well. You have sprung forth from my Heart and I have rested under your heart. You, to whom I gave birth with much suffering at the Cross, will be prostrate in painful labor with me until the end of the world. Your image mysteriously blurs to merge with the image of my virginal Mother. She is an individual woman, but in you she becomes the cosmic Mother. For in you my individual Heart, too, widens to become the Heart of the World. You yourself are the holy heart of nations, holy because of me, but unifying the world for me, making my Blood circulate throughout the body of history. In you my redemption ripens, I myself grow to my full stature, until I, two-in-one with you, and in the bond of the two-in-one flesh – you, my Bride and my Body – will place at the feet of the Father the Kingdom which we are. The bond of our love is the meaning of the world. In it all things reach fulfillment. For the meaning of the world is love.[50]

The cosmic Mother and the holy heart. The body of history that depends on the circulation (not the spilling) of blood, an image that might be more placental than sacrificial. This language is too voluptuous for our modern, sanitized world. Too voluptuous perhaps for Balthasar, who struggles to retain the hierarchies and structures that are slipping away, dissolving, looping back on themselves, opening language up to difference within difference, to bodies that mutate, blur, mingle, resist the duality that would keep them apart – he and she, mother and son, man and woman, first and second, source and derivation. Here is the transcorporality, the remaking of language and of worlds struggling to be born, if only Balthasar had allowed himself to go all the way. We are much closer here to Judith Butler than to the new Catholic feminism.

Theology beyond feminism

With her rich psychoanalytic insights, Kristeva offers a guiding light through the labyrinths of the Catholic soul and offers a language for its healing and redemption. She reveals to us the hidden recesses of minds uniquely shaped by a tradition which is not yet an anachronism, but which has reached an unprecedented crisis of imagination and meaning. For Kristeva, the future is post-Catholic, and the promise of peace becomes a secularized vision in which psychoanalysis goes through and beyond religion to recover what religion has sacrificed, while remaining dependent upon religion's resources.

But we need not go willingly to this sacrifice of religion. Kristeva's vision of wounded healing directs us towards a mature spirituality of everyday life. It shows us how we might reconcile ourselves to mourning without sacrifice, to separation without alienation, to difference without division. This invites a reappropriation of Catholic theology and spirituality after its appropriation by a certain kind of psycholinguistics. It means rediscovering the ways in which theology can be enriched and revitalized by the insights of secular theory and philosophy, in the nuptial relationship between the two. If this process did not and could not meet every feminist demand, it would go some way towards recognizing that personal and social transformation go hand in hand, and that the slow and painful work of healing the Catholic psyche of its long sacrificial history is a patient and prayerful task, focused on the fears and desires associated with the female body.

But Kristeva is also a pragmatist. Unlike Irigaray, her language is neither utopian nor eschatological. It seeks a way of enabling us to live without violence in the world as it is, through an acceptance of the inevitability of suffering, loss and separation. If Catholicism is to go beyond the necrophilia that Jantzen describes, Kristeva suggests that the solution lies not in a new dualism that opposes fecundity and sacrifice or natality and mortality as Jantzen does, but in a courageous willingness to acknowledge that violence, death and sacrifice are within each one of us, coiled within our desire. Men have more successfully projected their deadly desires into the social order than women, so that women have remained largely marginal to or victimized by societies held together by violence. But as women gain access to ever more institutional power, Kristeva shows us what is at stake: do we seek an equal place within society through an acceptance of its institutionalized violence, or do we risk an even more explosive sacrifice by rejecting these orderly conduits through which blood flows under every economic, political and military guise, opening the way to a deadly and more bloody anarchy? Kristeva asked these questions in the 1970s, but at the beginning of the twenty-first century, the clash between societies of institutionalized violence and cultures of anarchic terror has never seemed so acute or so deadly, and it remains to be seen where women will ultimately position themselves in relation to these. For if women do not take up a fully conscious, committed and informed stand for peace, then we are likely always to remain the most silent of victims or the most suicidal of martyrs.

Augustine wrote that 'The peace of all things is the tranquillity of order.'[51] Feminists today might resist his interpretation of this as a hierarchically ordered society in which everyone – including women – knows their place, but in a world of so much suffering and violence, we should never underestimate what women have to gain by the tranquillity of order. This is not the illusory peace that feeds on sacrifice, but the peace of God that is beyond all understanding and that resists all sacrifice. This is a peace that begins deep within every human spirit, when we plumb the depths in trust because Christ has been further still, beyond death, beyond the worst hell that the human mind can imagine. Thus we can say with the psalmist:

> Where can I go from your spirit?
> Or where can I flee from your presence?
> If I ascend to heaven, you are there;
> if I make my bed in Sheol, you are there.
> If I take the wings of the morning
> and settle at the farthest limits of the sea,
> even there your hand shall lead me,
> and your right hand shall hold me fast.
> If I say, 'Surely the darkness shall cover me,
> and the light around me become night,'
> even the darkness is not dark to you;
> the night is as bright as the day,
> for darkness is as light to you.
>
> (Psalm 139)

But in order to say this, we have to continue with the psalmist's words, and acknowledge the body in which we have our beginnings, before any word came to be:

> For it was you who formed my inward parts;
> you knit me together in my mother's womb.
> I praise you, for I am fearfully and wonderfully made.

In turning to the psalms, we have arrived at that point where liturgy and life encounter one another. For centuries, the psalms have marked out the rhythms of Catholic daily life, repeated through the years in the hours and the seasons of time as it spirals towards its fulfilment. This is a marking of time that is cyclical, linear and monumental. The liturgy turns on the cycles of nature and travels in the direction of history, but it also embodies the transcendent in the here and now, cultivating a sacramental vision which learns, with the poet,

> To see a world in a grain of sand,
> And a heaven in a wild flower,
> Hold infinity in the palm of your hand,
> And eternity in an hour.
>
> (William Blake)

Within the time and space of human existence, the liturgy seeks an encounter between heaven and earth, between time and eternity, reminding us that we are bodies at play against the backdrop of heaven.

The Christian life is both liturgical and ethical, eschatological and historical, organic and institutional. It is a life whose idiom requires different registers, for as well as its social, political and cultural expressions, it needs a language of prayer, devotion and worship wherein we turn to face the eschaton and seek to glimpse the glory of God shining through the sacramental life of the Church, in speech refulgent with mystery and hope.

If Irigaray's lavish sexual prose is too utopian for the ethical challenge of everyday life, if, as Kristeva suggests, it trails in its wake the possibility of greater rather than lesser violence through its unleashing of uncontrollable power, then let me suggest that it is in liturgy that we might abandon ourselves to the parodies and carnivals of difference that Irigaray proposes. Floating free of any communal context, cut adrift from its religious moorings, her language may indeed suggest a dangerous utopia. But embodied and embedded within the sacramental life of the Church, might it help us to recognize anew what heaven might be, if our eschatological vision could see beyond sacrifice, to the fecundity of love incarnate among us?

In the liturgy, Irigaray's psycholinguistic drama of sexual difference and encounter allows us to come out of ourselves, into a space of gendered sacramentality where we become brides and grooms, lovers and mothers, parents and children, friends and companions in the ever-present wedding feast of God with creation. In order to discover the potency of this sacramental vision, we need to situate ourselves in a space of risk and transformation, surrendering all ways of being in our play before God, allowing new figurations to emerge from the coming together of silence and speech, of body and language, of man and woman, of strangers and aliens, of angels and mortals, in a heavenly space where all things are possible. Here, we experience our coming to be in the God who comes to us through and beyond gender, embodiment and speech. Here, we celebrate our becoming perfect in our orientation towards that open horizon beyond which an eternity of perfect becoming comes towards us. Here, we come at last.

15 Redeeming sacramentality

> Now the apostles were in the place Chritir with Mary. And Bartholomew came to Peter and Andrew and John, and said to them: Let us ask Mary, her who is highly favoured, how she conceived the incomprehensible or how she carried him who cannot be carried or how she bore so much greatness . . . But Mary answered: Do not ask me concerning this mystery. If I begin to tell you, fire will come out of my mouth and consume the whole earth.[1]

We are playing with fire. From Balthasar's hell to Kristeva's incandescent discourse of the unconscious, we are brought into the presence of a mystical mother who knows that her sex/her words have the power to 'consume the whole earth'. When the blazing light of the Father's glory meets the combustible matter of the mother's body, must the result be annihilation? 'A burning glass is the soul who in her cave joins with the source of light to set everything ablaze that approaches her hearth. Leaving only ashes there, only a hole: fathomless in her incendiary blaze.'[2]

What is at stake in the postmodern incineration of language, which is being brought about not least by the igniting of voices of otherness which melt the frozen structures of reason and dissolve the white western man's monopoly on 'Truth'? Does postmodernism risk a conflagration of meaning more extreme and final than any we have seen in history, for it is enacted in an era in which humankind is capable of the ultimate sacrifice? Girard writes,

> Condemning humanity to nonsense and nothingness at the very moment when they have achieved the means of annihilating everything in a blink of the eye, entrusting the future of the human habitat to individuals who now have nothing to guide them but their desires and their 'death instincts' – all of this is not a reassuring prospect, and it speaks volumes about the incapacity of modern science and ideology to master the forces that they have placed in our hands.[3]

It is against the spectre of annihilation that we have to ask our questions about language, meaning and truth, ever attentive to the ways in which the body can be branded as well as graced by the words we use. While we western academics act out our stylized sexual politics, our technological cultures are manufacturing increasingly effective ways to deliver their incendiary messages, cautioning us that such explosive words are not simply the tropes and *topoi* of a disenchanted elite. That is why we must heed Girard's caution about postmodernism's unleashing of desire and the death-drives, if we are not to participate in a sacrifice more extreme than any that has gone before.

Kristeva offers a bodily understanding of being that resists the severance between word and flesh, while remaining attentive to the potent ways in which the fragile incarnation of love and desire is ever threatened by the violence of the body's horror and hunger. She suggests an ethical transformation in the here and now, mindful of the limitations of our human condition, through seeking to live with vulnerability instead of violence, sorrow instead of sacrifice. Along with Girard, she invites Catholic Christianity to enter more deeply into its own psychological and cultural inheritance, in order to discover anew its revelatory potential in the midst of the world as we find it, and as the Church has helped to make it. Together, these two thinkers suggest ways in which a pacifist Church, reconciled to its own shortcomings and failures, courageous enough to confront its own repressions and fears, might offer an ethical alternative in a world depleted by violence and hungry to discover anew the body's truth.

But the Church's ethical vision is fed by her liturgical life, and this invites the exploration of a form of language that is orientated towards a future of plenitude and wholeness, because it is a performative expression of the Christian hope that heaven and earth will one day be reconciled at the heavenly wedding feast. As an anticipatory enactment of this promise in the here and now, how might the sacramentality of the liturgy become a space of mystery and grace, where male and female bodies together can express their faith in the peace of the risen Christ? What new symbolic and sacramental possibilities might be revealed, if the female body at last acquires priestly, sacramental significance? As always, in asking such questions, the task is for Catholic theology to read the signs of the times, to learn from but go beyond the philosophical and theoretical insights of secularism, in order to incarnate the Christian story as a dynamic, unfolding drama in the midst of history and culture.

Today, theology's questions are positioned against a spiritual and intellectual backdrop in which all its metaphysical claims have been undermined by the fragmentation of meaning in an era of proliferating discourses and competing truth claims, when the meta-narratives of the western mind have yielded before the no less powerful meta-narratives of globalization, with its radical opportunities for both destruction and creativity on an unprecedented historical scale. How can the liturgy become a credible performance of the Church's unchanging hope, on a world stage of multiple narratives, plots, themes and possible endings, in which the drama fluctuates scene by scene between comedy and tragedy? One cannot ask this question without acknowledging the extent to which the postmodern crisis in meaning has as one of its core themes the question of gender. If we are uncertain about the nature of the play we are called to enact on the stage of history, not least of this uncertainty revolves around the sexual identities, responsibilities and relationships of ourselves as players.

The fire and the rose

Carl Raschke reads Umberto Eco's *The Name of the Rose* as an allegory in which 'the end of the book' signifies the end of metaphysics:

> The saying of the unsaid, the reaching towards the unreachable, the naming of the unnamed name – all signified by the rose – is literally 'the end of the book'. *The Name of the Rose* concludes with a fire that burns down the monastery and its enormous library. We may read into the fire an eschatological event – the apocalyptic capsizing of a metaphysical era in which God's secrets have remained closeted in forbidden books. From a philosophical point of view, the 'naming' of the rose is at the same time its dissolution; it is the semantic displacement of the signified by the act of signification. Signification is seen as disruption, a violation of context, a transgression.[4]

As the female body raises the question of being for the first time from her space of being in the world, is she already too late to search for her signifiers, to seek her own naming in God? Does she risk crowding the space of signification with ever more violence and ever more conflict, as she squeezes herself into the gaps and seeks a silence out of which she too might speak her desire? With a forked tongue? With tongues of fire?

Postmodernism would have us believe that the symbol is 'the murder of the thing',[5] the signifier means death to the signified. In the act of naming the thing, we acknowledge the no thing, the nothingness. But the Christian story tells us that it is life, not death, which comes into being in the encounter between language and matter. Language is the emergence of meaning from a graced creation. This is a world illumined from within, so that, for those who have eyes to see, there is an incandescent shimmer of grace in all being. The sacrament breathes life where the symbol brings death. Here, word–flesh once again discover their mutuality – their nuptiality. Here we might discover anew

> the fruit of the covenant between word and nature, between *logos* and *cosmos*. A marriage that has never been consummated and that the spirit, in Mary,

would renew?

The spirit? Not, this time, the product of the love between Father and son, but the universe already made flesh or capable of becoming flesh, and remaining in excess to the existing world.

Grace that speaks silently through and beyond the word?[6]

Raschke concludes his article on Eco by referring to T.S. Eliot's *Four Quartets*:

> *Four Quartets* is 'postmodern' because it is a sweeping poesis disclosing not jewels in the lotus but 'sapphires in the mud', a genuine Heideggerian 'worlding of the world' through the movements of signification that suddenly appear like a 'thousand points of light' (Wordsworth) across the craggy terrain of 'mass culture'. The closure of the poem, however, is not about the 'naming' that takes place through discourse, but about fire. The discourse of the world is set aflame. As we discover at the conclusion of *The Name of the Rose*, the end of the book is also the end of the world. The presentation of the metaphysical aeon burns up. For 'our God is a consuming fire'.[7]

Eliot's poem, quoting Julian of Norwich, concludes that 'All manner of thing shall be well/When the tongues of flame are in-folded/Into the crowned knot of fire/And the fire and the rose are one.'[8]

The rose, symbol of love and fertility, of mysticism and the Virgin Mary, is also a symbol of the female genitals.[9] Might the fire of Balthasar's hell yet become the fire by which Christ lights up the female sex, not this time in a consuming holocaust but in 'a fire always burning but never consuming',[10] so that this does indeed become a 'burning bush' (let us pun a little now, for we are playing words as well as with fire) which suggests the presence of God? And in a world where our minds have become closed to the enchantment of being, where we no longer sense the presence of angels among us, what might kindle this revelatory fire which makes visible the female sex?

> Mysteriously, the rose's bloom recalls something of blood and of the angel. It is reborn ceaselessly, causelessly, because it must bloom, having no care for the world. The flower is like a pure apparition of natural generation, the angel is like a pure vector of spiritual spatiality, rapt purity before any conception occurs, any meeting of fixed dimensions or directions.[11]

The knowledge of angels

Angels are incorporeal beings, weaving meaning between God and the material world. Irigaray suggests that we need angelic mediations if we are to weave the female body into meaning. Angels lubricate the membranes between the human and the divine, the body and language, so that like mucus they enable couplings and consummations without violence and rupture:

> The angel is that which unceasingly *passes through the envelope(s)* or *container(s)*, goes from one side to the other, reworking every deadline, changing every decision, thwarting all repetition. Angels destroy the monstrous, that which hampers the possibility of a new age; they come to herald the arrival of a new birth, a new morning . . . They represent and tell of another incarnation, another parousia of the body. Irreducible to philosophy, theology, morality, angels appear as the messengers of ethics evoked by art – sculpture, painting, or music – without its being possible to say anything more than the gesture that represents them.[12]

Angels are part of the 'carnivality' of postmodern popular culture, appearing everywhere except in the Church, which has become far too rational to take them seriously. We name them in our worship, joining 'the angels and saints' when we proclaim God's glory, but we no longer inhabit an enchanted liturgical space populated by 'countless hosts of angels':

> Source of life and goodness, you have created all things, to fill your creatures with every blessing and lead all people to the joyful vision of your light. Countless hosts of angels stand before you to do your will; they look upon your splendour and praise you, night and day.
>
> (Eucharistic Prayer IV)

What are these strange beings, and might they indeed – as Irigaray suggests – become the bearers of good news, messengers of annunciations that open the way to a new birthing of God among us, incarnate at last in the divinization of the female body? Would such an incarnation allow for the rediscovery of a lost enchantment, a new mysticism of the earthy, sexual being before God?

> What is Mary listening to in the message of the angel? Only the Word of the Father? Or is she heedful of the universe that bears her, of a heaven and an earth that have always been and are still virgin of culture? And that, going beyond and falling short of the word, make its engendering possible.[13]

For pre-modern Christians, the angelic ether provided the medium through which meaning was communicated between a graced creation and God-like human reason. Modernity closed down that space of mediation, sealing off the human mind from its natural communion with God. For postmodern Christians, the recovery of sacramentality requires a conscious linguistic act, for only through the medium of language might we liberate creation from its (post)modern captivity to

Redeeming sacramentality   295

language, and speak an opening into the silence of the rupture between faith and reason. This means, as Schumacher suggests (see Chapter 2), resisting the dissolution of nature into culture through the celebration of a graced creation, but it also means a move beyond the frozen essentialisms of the new feminists into a space of carnivalesque encounter between the body and language. Naming thus becomes an act of consecration, an invitation to the angels who have migrated from their home in the Church to populate the postmodern marketplace, recognizing perhaps that they are more welcome in that world of fantasy, creativity and imagination than in the constipated rituals of the Christian Church. The language of the angels might once again allow us to gather the world up in speech, making human words and gestures the bearers of divine grace by uttering a 'fiat' through which nature itself is transformed and sanctified.

The angels are, Aquinas tells us, incorporeal bodies gifted with the fullness of the knowledge of God, more knowable to the finite human mind than God, mediating between the worlds of heaven and earth, but inaccessible to our ordinary, sensory ways of knowing. For Aquinas, the created mind cannot know the essence of God in this life for its knowledge is always derivative of what can be perceived by the senses, nor can any created being know God by its own natural powers, but only insofar as God endows it with that ability (see Chapter 3). Angels are gifted with this knowledge of God, and therefore they mediate between the finite, sensory knowledge of the human intellect, and the fullness of God's being:

> the created intellect cannot see the essence of God, unless God by His grace unites Himself to the created intellect, as an object made intelligible to it. This mode of knowing God is natural to an angel – namely, to know Him by His own likeness refulgent in the angel himself.[14]

Angels, then, are refulgent with the likeness of God, and yet knowable to some extent by human consciousness. Traditionally, they have been understood to be beyond gender. Moreover, angelic beings occupy a state of indeterminacy with regard to the significance of corporeality in relation to God:

> Incorporeal substances rank between God and corporeal creatures. Now the medium compared to one extreme appears to be the other extreme, as what is tepid compared to heat seems to be cold; and thus it is said that angels, compared to God, are material and corporeal, not, however, as if anything corporeal existed in them.[15]

Angels inhabit the cusp between language and the body, space of turbulence and uncanny knowing where consciousness encounters its other. It is, suggests Irigaray, the angel who lubricates the passage between the two, allowing the body's entry into language by sculpting language around the body's grace:

> As if the angel were a representation of a sexuality that has never been incarnated. A light, divine gesture (or tale) of flesh that has not yet acted or flourished. Always fallen and still awaiting parousia . . . A sexual or carnal ethics would require that both angel and body be found together.[16]

Neither male nor female, neither material nor immaterial, angels invite new conceptions of the divine among us and between us. But if this transformation in our ways of knowing is to bring about the marriage of language and the body in the way that Irigaray envisages, then language must be permitted to make a claim upon us. We have to 'hear the word of God and do it' (Luke 8:19), not as an intellectual exercise in textual deconstruction, but as a corporeal commitment to embody new ways of being in the world. This is where an incarnational theology goes beyond Irigaray because, despite her insistence that a sexual ethics requires that 'both angel and body be found together', Irigaray's angels never escape the printed page. If the body is indeed to become suffused with the divine life, then it needs to open itself to the other through sacramental encounters and commitments, and this entails vulnerability, risk and faith.

David Power writes that

> rituals may be considered as disclosures of human vulnerability and incompleteness. Bodily rites, in their very intensity of rhythm, bring to the surface the modes of being in time and space, together with the tensions inherent to this condition of being human.[17]

Power describes sacramental ritual as a 'language-event'[18] that traverses social and cultural boundaries, creating encounters with otherness, and disrupting the smooth, coherent surfaces of our narratives. After modernity, Power points to the significance of narrative in the formation of identity and meaning, but also to 'the postmodern perception . . . that narrative inevitably breaks down. Looking for the reason for this leads us to see that the telling of tales is in effect a constant dialectic between remaining the same and becoming the other.'[19] This invites a kenotic theology that goes beyond meta-narrative, to present the story of Christ as a narrative which is constantly interrupted and broken up through the plurality of the languages and cultures it embraces, the ethical challenges that confront it, and the irruption of new situations that it cannot accommodate without change:

> the rupture of meta-narrative and of the hegemony of ritual opens the way to a new discovery of the abundance of language, as the truly open sign, in the interplay of metaphors, allowing speech to the marginal, and in ritual pointing to the location of divine power in the exchange of bread, wine, oil and water, for those who experience the rupture of their existence and of their expectations.[20]

But this opening up of language entails orality beyond the written word. To see 'sacramental celebration as excess', it is necessary to attend

> to the *saying*, the signifying, as process, rather than letting the tradition be constituted by the *said* or the signified . . . Such excess is impossible without emptying. To be open to the unsaid, the word has to be emptied of the said . . . Whenever the written is taken up into a process of oral expression and inter-subjective exchange, it is in a sense emptied through a process of hermeneutic and recovery that is allied to the lives of those who *are speaking, saying*.[21]

It is this bodily speaking and acting out of the language of sacramentality, an emptying of meaning into the speaking body of the other, that Irigaray refuses, for sacramental meaning is dependent upon materiality, upon the presence of bodies, of fluids, of speaking beyond writing, and of matter beyond speaking. Sacramentality breaks open the text to the radical presence of the material other, situated as it is in an unstable and volatile space of encounter and transformation between the world and the word. It cannot be reduced to symbolism alone, for it draws the symbol into a temporal, material act by way of which both symbol and matter (including the matter of the human body) are mutually transformed. Thus there can be no sacrament without the conscious marrying together of language and matter through the signifying functions of speech and gesture.

For Balthasar, angels 'make visible the social character of the Kingdom of Heaven, into which the cosmos is to be transformed'.[22] If Irigaray's angels are to perform this task of making visible, they must be permitted to manifest themselves through their participation in the liturgical gestures and sacramental presences that mediate between bodily humans and language in order to weave together relationships of love, worship, commitment and community.

Irigaray's angels circle ceaselessly within the text, opening up new, incorporeal meanings, but resisting that movement by which the body might enter into the space that opens up, to discover itself anew in relation to the mystery of the human and divine Other. Irigaray's readers, to play her game, must either open themselves to the otherness of a God who whispers through her texts, or they must defend their individuality and resist such otherness by ensuring that there is, as Derrida suggests, 'nothing outside of the text'.[23]

Yet, what might happen if Irigaray's symbolic language of a new parousia became viscous with unintended desires in the space between the body of the reader and the body of the text? What if her angels found wings to slip through the confines of the text, enabling her words to find sacramental expression through their incorporation into the performances of gender and identity that animate the postmodern, liturgical body? It is with these questions in mind that I now turn to the significance of the worshipping body, a body at play with the angels, a body kissed by God, a body becoming God.

The liturgical body

Raschke refers to Derrida's nihilism – 'the nihilism of an ongoing textual commentary no longer capable of signification'.[24] He argues that theology has yet to recognize the potential inherent in what David Levin refers to as the 'metaphoric postmodern', as opposed to the 'analytic postmodern'.[25] He associates the 'metaphoric postmodern' with 'Eco's understanding of semiotics as "carnival" in the sense of ribald and "polyform" aesthetic display',[26] and also with Kristeva's 'somatology'.[27] The metaphoric postmodern 'ultimately harks back to the desire of Nietzsche's Zarathustra to *dance* . . . It is the transcendence of nihilism.'[28] This transcendence of nihilism is to be found, not in the intellectualism of academic postmodernism, but in a popular culture that has rediscovered the value of performativity and the carnivalesque. The 'end of the book' and therefore of metaphysics is not brought about by yet more textual theories, but by the bodily performance of the signifier: 'Body becomes a metaphor for the dance of signification.'[29] This invites attentiveness to the phenomenon of religion in twentieth-century culture, so that

> a theological thinker privy to the aesthetics and the poetics of the postmodern can begin to envision 'sacrality' not simply as a complex of stock theological emblems or representations, but as a veritable marquee flashing with the evanescent tokens and hints of religious sentimentality in the twentieth century . . . Sexuality and popular religion, for instance . . . cannot be disentangled from each other because of their very 'carnivality' (in Eco's sense), or 'in-carnality' from a broader semiotic perspective.[30]

It is here that Raschke sees 'the unveiling of a new epoch in the historicity of Being' as Heidegger proposed, but in order to see this, one has to recognize with Ferdinand Saussure and Eco that 'signs "work" exclusively because they set in motion the play of differences . . . The moment of difference now discloses the transcendental backlighting of immanent everydayness; it is the *signature* of a pure presencing.'[31] This is 'the time of *parousia*',[32] brought about by the struggle of all that has been concealed, silenced and unsaid, as it 'writhes towards articulation in the wilderness of contemporary culture'.[33] It is, suggests Raschke, 'the Heideggerian "unsaid", or at a deeper, "speculative" level, the "unthought"', understood in terms of Lyotard's 'differend', in which 'something "asks" to be put into phrases, and suffers from the wrong of not being able to be put into phrases in the right way'.[34]

If the postmodern, sexual body has become the site of a signifying 'carnivality' that is also an 'in-carnality', this is potentially a sacramentality as well. If 'popular culture . . . is held together by the power of multiple, and often ambiguous, significatory functions',[35] might this also be true of the 'Mass culture' of Catholic Christianity, where it is the silenced, non-signifying female body that today 'writhes towards articulation', that 'suffers from the wrong of not being able to be put into phrases in the right way'? Beyond the nostalgia for the pre-modern that is marked by the totalizing trend of the modern in neo-orthodoxy, beyond the masked political power that hides behind the liberalism of much feminist theology, is there a postmodern sacramentality that might re-ignite the Mass so that it once again becomes a space of encounter within the 'fire and abyss',[36] of God's love, a shining darkness which glimmers through the bodily music of the liturgy so that it becomes our carnivalesque dancing with God? What new forms must language take to allow us to speak lightly of this darkness, to allow this darkness to shine among us?

I have referred to the widespread perception – which is not confined to conservatives – that the Second Vatican Council brought about the modernization of the Church, at the expense of the mystical potency of her sacramental life. David Torevell argues that the Council's liturgical reforms manifest a modernizing and rationalizing tendency that emphasizes conscious participation in the liturgy over the subliminal sensual potency inherent in sacred ritual. He refers to 'the devaluation of the importance of ritualized liturgy since the 1960s, in favour of a much more cognitivist, disembodied approach, centred around the engagement of the minds of the congregation'.[37] Godfried Cardinal Danneels also criticizes the over-intellectualization of the modern liturgy: 'A liturgy which is almost exclusively oriented to the intellect is . . . not likely to involve the human body in the celebration to any great extent.'[38] He goes on to describe liturgy as 'a global, symbolic activity which belongs to the order of the "playful". The uniqueness of "play" is the fact that one "plays in order to play", one plays for the sake of playing.'[39] Balthasar also invokes the image of 'play', in arguing that the postconciliar Church is a thoroughly masculinized institution:

> The idea of the Church developed in evolutionary theology was the first step towards the view that what was of ultimate importance was to make use of the erotic forces for the development of the world; if anything is a male need, then it is this desire to subject everything to a purpose. The flow of love between the sexes has *meaning*, but this meaning transcends any purpose; the play of children has meaning but it is not intended to fulfil any purpose. Great art has meaning, but no purpose. The power of Amor cannot be made to drive turbines, no more than can the power of the *caritas* between Christ and the Church.[40]

The Mass, then, might be likened to the gestures of lovers or of children at play. It is a bodily acting out of desires and roles which is an end in itself. Children do not play in order to achieve something else, nor is our lovemaking orientated to an end other than the mutual expression of love.[41] These meanings are sufficient in themselves. But if we are 'at play' in our worship, what is the nature of the game we are playing?

According to the Vatican II Constitution on Sacred Liturgy, 'In the earthly liturgy we take part in a foretaste of that heavenly liturgy which is celebrated in the Holy City of Jerusalem toward which we journey as pilgrims.'[42] Michael Kunzler, in his study of liturgy, refers to 'The many-faceted idea . . . of the unity of the earthly and heavenly liturgy'.[43] This means that

> If the liturgy celebrated on earth is a communication between God and the creature, then it is always a participation in the eternal feast of the heavenly liturgy in the fullness of the life of the triune God into which the heavenly Church of the angels and saints has already found an entry.[44]

The Eucharist, then, is first and foremost a taste of heaven on earth. It is a communal enactment of the heavenly wedding feast described in the Book of Revelation:

> Then I saw a new heaven and a new earth; for the first heaven and the first earth had passed away, and the sea was no more. And I saw the holy city, the new Jerusalem, coming down out of heaven from God, prepared as a bride adorned for her husband. And I heard a loud voice from the throne saying,
> 'See, the home of God is among mortals.
> He will dwell with them;
> they will be his peoples,
> and God himself will be with them;
> he will wipe every tear from their eyes.
> Death will be no more;
> mourning and crying and pain will be no more,
> for the first things have passed away.'
>
> (Rev. 21: 1–4)

This is a vision that promises transformation and healing, a recapitulation of the human story that begins with the creation of the sexes in the Garden of Eden, and culminates in the marriage of heaven and earth, God and humankind, in the New Jerusalem. It is a story which encompasses creation and destruction, birth and sacrifice, incarnation and redemption, tragedy and hope, written into the pages of human history and inscribed in the psyche of every human being. So in the meeting of heaven and earth in the Mass, there is a richly textured, volatile sacramentality that allows for the unfolding of meanings and possibilities, creating spaces in which every body might play according to his or her way of encountering Christ at this particular moment, which is both a moment in time and time out of time, for it constitutes what Kunzler calls 'the hallowing of time'.[45]

The Mass is a dramatic performance that is at one and the same time an incarnation, a crucifixion, a resurrection, a birth, a wedding and a feast. We come to

Christ with different needs at different times, and each time we experience a different facet of the marriage between the human and the divine in him and therefore in ourselves. Sometimes we come as those crucified by suffering or by shame, sometimes we come pregnant with vision and promise, sometimes we come yearning for nourishment, sometimes we come as mystical lovers, filled with erotic desire for the nameless, boundless Other, sometimes we come in nuptial celebration, sometimes we come in funeral mourning, and every time we incarnate him and he divinizes us. To quote Kunzler,

> [T]hat which God basically places in man, and causes to grow until the eschatological completion, is something uncreated, it is he himself as communicating with his creature. Without obliterating man in his created identity, he permits him to share in his uncreated, unalterable fullness of life. Therefore man becomes 'God by grace' by means of deification.[46]

Here, then, is the divinization of the human that Irigaray and Jantzen seek. In the Mass, we play at being the God we are becoming, and yet there is also being and letting be: in becoming God, we are no less ourselves; in intimate communion with us, God does not cease to be other than us. But this playing at being God, this playing with God, is a bodily participation in God. According to Torrevel,

> We 'learn' to share in the divine life of Christ primarily by the engagement of our bodily senses, not by increasing attention being given to the stimulation of our minds. The power of ritual is achieved through the symbolic use of the body.[47]

In Girardian terms, this constitutes the circulation of mimetic desire, modelled not on the violent rivalry of the social order but on the peace-making forgiveness and joy of Christ, in which we discover what it means to have faith – to love God – through our love for one another.

With other critics of modern liturgy, Torrevel attributes the loss of liturgical significance to a process of abstraction and intellectualization. The remedy, therefore, lies in a revitalized sense of sacramentality, capable of evoking meanings and responses beyond our rational, conscious thought processes.

However, we have seen that the neo-orthodox solution to this problem is to emphasize the sacrificial nature of the Mass, the essential masculinity of the priesthood, and the nuptial significance of the Church, in a way that creates a false mystique rather than a true mysticism – enveloping the liturgy in a miasma of sexual and sacrificial meanings that may indeed have considerable spiritual potency, because they play on the deeply repressed fears and fantasies of the unconscious. Might the ordination of women be the key that is needed to unlock a healthier but no less mystical sense of sacramentality and spirituality, through a deepened appreciation of our capacity for silence, mystery and unknowability, made possible by the insights of psychoanalysis? And until the female body can participate fully in the process of deification that unfolds in liturgical time, how can we tell the story of the wedding feast, which is surely a celebration of sexuality, desire and fecundity, when one body is permanently assigned to the role of bystander, a guest who watches the consummation of divine love without herself being necessary to the act?

The maternal priest

At present, the debate about women's ordination tends to divide along liberal/conservative lines. I have explored in some depth the arguments against women's ordination, in order to demonstrate the extent to which these appeal to highly problematic sexual stereotypes, which nevertheless have profound psychological resonance. As we have seen with Balthasar and Speyr, this can result in an intensely felt psychosomatic spirituality, which feeds on dark bodily fantasies of sexuality, suffering and death, fantasies that are experienced by way of a somatic mysticism by her and interpreted by way of a theological narration by him. Those in favour of women's ordination are concerned with questions of equality and justice, so that the symbolic significance of the priest is understood primarily in social rather than psychological terms. But sacramentality surely needs to encompass both of these dimensions: by way of the body, it invites each individual into a space of spiritual otherness – a state of mystical holiness – which finds social expression in love of one's neighbour, in an ongoing process of personal transformation, a process of 'becoming divine'. This inseparability of the mystical from the ethical is a hallmark of Christian mysticism. Consider, for example, Catherine of Siena, expressing this ethos in richly maternal imagery:

> Virtue, once conceived, must come to birth. Therefore, as soon as the soul has conceived through loving affection, she gives birth for her neighbors' sake. And just as she loves me in truth, so also she serves her neighbors in truth. Nor could she do otherwise, for love of me and love of neighbor are one and the same thing: Since love of neighbor has its source in me, the more the soul loves me, the more she loves her neighbors.[48]

There should, then, be no rupture between a rich sacramental life and a commitment to social justice. In our own time as well as Catherine's, this entails bodily worship and bodily participation in the quest for justice, because 'Every action, whether good or evil, is done by means of the body.'[49]

The female priest might be the key to a recovered, bodily spirituality of the sacraments as well as to a renewed social ethos, because she embodies so many profound meanings associated with sacrality and embodiment. The arguments against women priests that I have explored in this book feed on the fears that this provokes and seek to legitimize them, and we have seen that this leads to multiple contradictions and acts of rhetorical violence against the female body. But Girard and feminist psycholinguists offer insights which, taken together, might allow for a sacramentality that is charged with the potency of life and death, through the capacity of the female priest to give corporeal expression to that which is currently repressed, hidden and denied in the expression of Catholic spirituality, thus liberating a new form of sacramental energy that derives its communicative power from the liturgical expression of what is negated and denied in our social interactions.

Psychoanalysis tells us that the maternal body is associated with desires and drives that overflow the boundaries of our orderly, rationalized identities and institutions. Balthasar's theo-drama is premised upon a violent struggle between the two – the masculine self in encounter with its feminized other, the institutional Petrine Church in encounter with the feminine perfection of the Marian Church. This struggle finds expression in a sacrifice that plays out repeatedly on the bodies of men and women trapped in its deadly dynamics, not least in the imagery of the *casta meretrix* by which a male Christ conquers his carnal, sexual bride. But when we search for the maternal body that might transform the violence of desire into the love and loss that constitute our bodily yearning for God, first awakened (according to Balthasar) by the mother's presence, we find that there is nothing there – in Lacan, a Real that is only a void, in Balthasar, a burning abyss of the imagination in which the female sex burns to extinction, so that the male body can take his and her place as priest and Bride of Christ.

When the female body steps into this void as maternal priest, the Christian revelation of the mystery of God becomes complete. God, who is beyond all, is and is not father and mother, male and female, dazzlingly revealed and also concealed in the play of differences between Christ and the Church, father and mother, male and female, Word and flesh, made present in the sacraments. If we seek consistency with the arguments that have been offered so far in defence of the male priesthood, while also asking what kind of theological vision is needed to accommodate woman's priesthood as equal but different to man's, we might ask if the motherhood of the female priest is to the Church what the fatherhood of the male priest is to God. She is not the Mother, just as he is not the Father. She does not need to be a mother, any more than he needs to be a father. She is a sexual body, a graced body, enacting a presence beyond herself – a presence that can be experienced only in absence, and an absence that can be acknowledged only in naming and signification.

The Church is the phallic mother, the cosmic Mother, representing a dream of wholeness, a longing for bliss, experienced as an intangible body of the shared Catholic psyche which is before and beyond sexual difference, capable of accommodating all bodies within herself. She is the 'body' that comes into being at the crossroads where death yields to birth and sacrifice becomes fecundity on Calvary, where the male body of Christ reveals once and for all the power-in-vulnerability of God's love, by giving birth to and becoming the maternal body of the Church. Thus male and female body together experience their redemption in the presence of the birthing body of the man on the cross and the grieving love of the mother at the foot of the cross. The wound in the side of Christ becomes the vagina through which God gives birth to the new creation:

> The heart is capable of sacrifice.
> So is the vagina.
> The heart is able to forgive and repair.
> It can change its shape to let us in.
> It can expand to let us out.
> So can the vagina.
> It can ache for us and stretch for us, die for us
> and bleed and bleed us into this difficult,
> wondrous world.
> So can the vagina.[50]

The birth of the Church from the body of Christ is beyond logic, beyond explanation, but it is one of the most ancient and enduring truths of the Catholic faith, repeated from Tertullian to Balthasar, but never yet accepted in all its fullness. In the play of difference between the paternal priest who is not God and the maternal priest who is not the Church, might the sacramental imagination be inspired anew with the mystery of God, whose absence it celebrates in its carnivalesque naming and knowing of God?

Fecundity and sacrifice

In a critique of what she sees as Girard's exclusively masculine representation of religion as sacrifice, Irigaray asks if what has been sacrificed is a religious world represented by women, in which nature, the seasons and the earth's fertility would form the focus of worship and celebration, rather than sacrifice. She asks,

> At what point in time are nature, men, and gods consecrated by certain ritual acts and words? At what point does cosmic time get divided up into the periodicity of ritual? How does it come about that men cease to regulate their meetings, their communities, their prayers exclusively in accordance with natural cycles: morning, noon, and night; the different seasons; the solar and lunar periods; the various positions of the earth, or other plants, etc.?[51]

This refiguration of religious symbolism around fertility and nature rather than sacrifice has implications for the understanding of the crucifixion and the celebration of the Eucharist. Irigaray argues that the history of patriarchy, including its religious manifestations, can be traced back to the destruction of the mother–daughter relationship, symbolized by mythical figures such as Demeter and Kōrē / Persephone but also to some extent potentially by figures such as Mary and Anne: 'In a patriarchal regime, religion is expressed through rites of *sacrifice* or *atonement*. In women's history, religion is entangled with cultivation of the earth, of the body, of life, of peace.'[52] With regard to the Eucharist, Irigaray suggests that a female priesthood might rehabilitate the maternal body that has been sacrificed by patriarchal religion, giving rise to a new understanding of Eucharistic symbolism:

> when the minister of that one and only God, that God-Father, pronounces the words of the Eucharist: 'This is my body, this is my blood,' according to the rite that celebrates the sharing of food and that has been ours for centuries, perhaps we might remind him that he would not be there if our body and our blood had not given him life, love spirit. And that he is also serving us up, we women-mothers, on his communion plate. But this is something that must not be known. That is why women cannot celebrate the Eucharist . . . If they were to do so, something of the truth that is hidden in the communion rite would be brutally unmasked.

At the same moment the human race would be absolved of a great offence. If a woman were to celebrate the Eucharist with her mother, giving her a share of the fruits of the earth blessed by them both, she might be freed from all hatred or ingratitude toward her maternal genealogy, and be hallowed in her identity as a woman.[53]

Irigaray's critique of Girard is problematic in some of its claims, not least in its simplistic appeal to eastern practices ('yoga, tai chi, karate, song, dance, the tea ceremony, flower arranging'[54]) as examples of non-sacrificial religion. However, her attempt to refigure the cross beyond sacrifice has considerable resonance with Girard's reading of the significance of the cross. She suggests that 'Christ's own responsibility for the crucifixion is limited to his being faithful to his incarnation'.[55] Elsewhere, she describes Christ's death as

> Active vigilance to guard against the irruptions of hatred, passive consent to its violence when no avoidance is possible, except by denying oneself.

> Seen in this light, his life would herald an age of love, with the crucifixion marking the testing and failure of that age. At that moment in history? Hatred triumphs. Has the upper hand. The man who did not wish to enter violently

into the body of the other dies pierced with thorns, nails, lance. The environment created by the incarnation yields to the play of hostile forces. Does it succumb to the reaction secreted by any powerful establishment? Any word built up simply by a will for power?[56]

In interpreting the cross as a sign of Christ's faithfulness to his incarnation, which requires a refusal of all forms of violence and therefore makes him a victim of society's hatred, Irigaray shares considerable common ground with Girard. Girard suggests that 'A non-violent deity can only signal his existence to mankind by having himself driven out by violence – by demonstrating that he is not able to establish himself in the Kingdom of Violence.'[57] The cross, then, is not a religious or cultic sacrifice: it is a profanity that exposes the violence of the sacred as a mask for human hatred, and in that act of exposure through the innocent suffering of Christ it reveals the non-violent love of God. Both Irigaray and Girard recognize that, in opposing Christ to Dionysus and in affirming the violent excess of Dionysian religion over the suffering and vulnerability advocated by Christianity, Nietzsche paradoxically comes closer than any other thinker to recognizing the inherently non-violent nature of the Christian faith.[58]

They also both suggest that the 'death of God' and the decline of Christianity in the West signals a moment of opportunity, when Christianity might at last discover the true meaning of the Gospels. However, this is where they also differ as to what that meaning entails. Girard writes:

> What is in fact finally dying is the sacrificial concept of divinity preserved by medieval and modern theology – not the Father of Jesus, not the divinity of the Gospels, which we have been hindered – and still are hindered – from approaching, precisely by the stumbling block of sacrifice. In effect, this sacrificial concept of divinity must 'die', and with it the whole apparatus of historical Christianity, for the Gospels to be able to rise again in our midst, not looking like a corpse that we have exhumed, but revealed as the newest, finest, liveliest and truest thing that we have ever set eyes upon.[59]

Yet for Girard, this unmasking of sacrifice also entails a recognition of the cost of Christian discipleship. To refuse to collude in the violence that sustains the social order is to risk making oneself a social outcast. The consequence of greater Christian fidelity to its own truth, then, might be persecution and martyrdom – in effect, an increase rather than a decrease of violence and vengeance. The relationship between culture and violence is such that the refusal of violence always brings with it the threat of greater violence, because 'people fail to understand that they are indebted to violence for the degree of peace that they enjoy'.[60] To model oneself on Christ is to risk his fate:

How can non-violence become fatal? Clearly it is not so in itself; it is wholly directed towards life and not towards death! How can the rule of the Kingdom come to have mortal consequences? This becomes possible and even necessary because others refuse to accept it. For all violence to be destroyed, it would be sufficient for all of mankind to decide to abide by this rule . . . If all men loved their enemies, there would be no more enemies. But if they drop away at the decisive moment, what is going to happen to the one person who does not drop away? For him the word of life will be changed into the word of death . . . It is absolute fidelity to the principle defined in his own preaching that condemns Jesus. There is no other cause for his death than the love of one's neighbour lived to the very end, with an infinitely intelligent grasp of the constraints it imposes. 'Greater love has no man than this, that a man lay down his life for his friends' (John 15:13).[61]

From a Girardian perspective, Irigaray is utopian because she refuses to recognize what Girard sees as the inherently violent nature of the social order. From her perspective, sacrifice is not intrinsic to all society and religion but only to societies and religions dominated by masculine values. With Kristeva, she points to the sacrifice of the mother that underlies all other sacrifice, but unlike Kristeva, she seeks not to overcome but to affirm the significance of sexual difference through the rehabilitation of the maternal body to language and culture. Thus, while Irigaray agrees with Girard that it is necessary to attribute responsibility for Christ's death not to God but to society, she understands this specifically in terms of masculine society, and therefore the central revelation of the incarnation lies not in the cross but in the affirmation and divinization of the sexually differentiated body. The historical failure of Christianity is associated with its celebration of sacrifice at the expense of fecundity, but that in itself is symptomatic of a more fundamental failure: the failure to recognize the female as well as the male body as an incarnation of the divine in every human person.

Irigaray interprets the Nietzschean contrast between Christ, Dionysos and Apollo as more of a Girardian double, in which both Dionysos and Apollo become the monstrous doubles of Christ. Christ thus becomes 'the fragile little brother of the god of Greek desire',[62] with Dionysos representing 'the vigorous double of a degenerate Christ-child', and Apollo representing the triumph of an aesthetic Christian vision which transforms the brutality of crucifixion into religious ecstasy:

> Dying becomes desirable. The pain of sacrifice stirs the senses, blurs the mind. Gives comfort for the pain of living. Happy oblivion – of suffering and laughter. The horror of immolation is changed into ecstatic contemplation. The passion of the crucifixion spreads like a celestial horizon. Murder becomes rapture in which blood ransoms past and future. A tableau

surpassing any other show. Nailing the gesture. Paralyzing the sculptor himself . . . A *pathein* that has submitted to the order and the will of the Father.[63]

Over and against this necrophiliac aestheticism of the Christian tradition, Irigaray proposes an alternative reading of the death of Christ, in which the resurrection represents, not the deferral of the body's fulfilment to the life hereafter, but the body's overcoming of the 'tombs' of law and language within which it has been trapped: 'It was necessary for Christ to be made into a corpse in order for the resurrection to reveal that, in him, the flesh overcomes the walls of the tombs.'[64] To recognize this affirmation of the body's potential would also be finally to recognize that the incarnation involves a couple (Mary and Christ) and therefore includes the female body, in such a way that every body now has the potential to become divine. The 'death of God' thus paves the way for the coming into being of sexual difference, through a renewed understanding of the Christian message:

> Does the 'death of God' not mean, therefore, the end of the security lodged with, of the credit accorded to, those who thus suspend meaning in the letter? Those who immobilize life in something that is merely the traces of life? The preachers of death who paralyze the becoming of peoples? Those who indefinitely repeat the identical, because they are unable to discover difference?
>
> *Et incarnatus est.* Must this coming be univocally understood as a redemptory submission of the flesh to the Word? Or else: as the Word's faithfulness to the flesh? With the penetration of the word into a body still recalling and summoning the entry of that body into a word. Exit from the tombs. Access to a beyond here now. Passage from body-corpses to a saying that transfigures them – pulls them out of the walls of their death. Crossing their own frontiers in a meeting with the flesh of the other. Living, if she speaks. She too incarnating the divine.
>
> *Et incarnatus est* manifesting a different relationship between flesh and word. Approach into a touch that no longer drains bodies of their animation by the saying of them – either in acts or in words. Bonds in which human and divine are wedded.[65]

This, I have suggested, is the missing gesture in Balthasar's theology of hell. His Christ does indeed 'overcome the walls of the tombs', but in crossing the frontiers the 'meeting with the flesh of the other' becomes an act of ongoing annihilation. Only if Balthasar's theology – and the theology of the Church as a whole – can at last allow woman to incarnate the divine, only if the heavenly wedding feast truly becomes a consummation of the reconciliation of all things in Christ, will it be possible to go beyond sacrifice, to the peace of Christ. But if, as I have suggested, this reconciling move lies in a recognition of a maternal priesthood alongside the masculine theology of priesthood, then the resources for such a transformation lie within the Catholic tradition itself.

I have written elsewhere about René Laurentin's two-volume study of the history and theology of the Marian priesthood, but it is worth reiterating that summary here, for it is important in the insights it refuses.[66] Laurentin concludes that there are 'two antinomical tendencies' running through the Marian tradition, with no clear resolution between the two:

> the propensity to affirm the Marian priesthood is a *logical* process. The censure is an *intuitive* process. A thousand reasons lead towards affirming the priesthood of Mary; a sort of diktat which does not give its reasons blocks the affirmation.[67]

Laurentin describes this as 'a spontaneous movement of recoil, like the instinctive flight of an animal at the first encounter with an enemy of its breed'.[68] There is, suggests Laurentin, a mysterious silence surrounding the reasons for this resistance, but his study leads him to conclude that the affirmation of Mary's priesthood is blocked by the fact that she is a woman.

Laurentin then goes on to offer theological justification for this resistance, appealing to concepts of masculinized divinity and feminized humanity that we have encountered again and again through this book:

> In Christian doctrine, the symbol of man and woman expresses the rapport between God and the redeemed creature. The man represents God: initiative, authority, stability, creative power. The woman represents humanity: power of welcome and receptivity where the all-powerful initiative of God ripens and bears fruit.[69]

The argument against the Marian priesthood can therefore be shown to rest upon a philosophical claim that is insupportable in terms of the Christian understanding of God and the human made in the image of God: the identification of woman with humanity and man with God. If we clear away this obstacle, then Laurentin's study becomes an almost fully developed doctrine, unfolding gradually through the life of the Church, in support of a maternal, Marian, sacramental priesthood. He argues that the one feature which all the authors in his study have in common is the identification of Mary's priesthood with motherhood: 'that which is priestly in her is an aspect of her maternity'.[70]

Laurentin's suggestion that intuition and logic come into conflict over this issue points to something of the same dynamic that we have seen in Balthasar's theology, where the logic of his narrative leads towards an acknowledgement of God's maternal creative power and of the mutual capacity of man and woman to represent the difference and desire that constitute the dynamics of theo-drama, but an intuitive resistance to this idea leads to a violent struggle to block such possibilities. By allowing the female body to play her part in the sacramental life of the Church, we might go beyond the violence generated by this resistance, to a new birthing of God for us and among us.

God's grandeur and the body's grace

On the world's stage, our sexuality positions us in relationships of love and vulnerability, commitment and responsibility, desire and frustration, satisfaction and loss. We discover ourselves to be less than we dreamed of becoming, and more than we have words to express. But in the drama of the liturgy, our sexuality becomes part of the performance, and we play at being what we are not. We should not take ourselves too seriously in these roles, lest we fail to see the God who is becoming in us.

The male and female priest stand before us, signifiers of an absence that is marked not by nihilism but by anticipation: it is the absence of that which is yet to come, not the absence of that which has never been. In them, the Motherhood of the Church and the Fatherhood of God are expressed in a fertile union which draws us into a space of mystical encounter between the Bride and the Groom, the Mother and the Father, which we glimpse in the space of difference opening into mystery. As men and women, we affirm our personhood as bodily, sexual beings before God in relation to these priestly signifiers, in a tradition which, in its eastern and western manifestations, both affirms and denies that our sexuality has eternal significance. For western Catholicism, sexual difference is ontological and eternal. For eastern Orthodoxy, sexual difference is contingent and historical. Rather than seeing this as a contradiction, we need to see it as part of the mystery, part of the excess, so that we encounter something of the otherness of God in the strange uncanniness of our bodily encounters with otherness and difference, which constitute the volatile, unstable, constantly shifting space of our becoming before God. By opening up to the play of difference – not a parody of men in drag, but a genuine coming together of male and female, adult and child, priest and people, old and young – the Mass might yet become again the liturgical enactment of a promise that is both now and not yet, an eschatological celebration of a way of being that is deeply embodied in daily life by way of a spiritual ethos capable of expressing the desires and conflicts of our being in the world, including the ineluctably elusive but persistent claims of our sexuality.

The doctrine of the incarnation tells us that truth is revealed in that turbulent, incomprehensible encounter between Word and flesh. It is to be discovered in the space where marrow, blood and milk encounter adjective, noun and verb, where nature seeps through culture's gaps, where earth, womb and tomb form the hidden underbelly of language, thought and subjectivity, where angels mediate the divine mystery to the human spirit in sacramental encounters which whisper peace through the porous boundaries of heaven and earth, self and other. That is where we must go to, if we seek redemption, incarnation and resurrection of the body into a new space of gendered becoming. This involves nothing less than a transfiguration of theology, allowing a graced vision to emerge which enables us to see the divine luminosity shimmering beyond and within all that is, so that the material world becomes an icon of God:

> The World is charged with the grandeur of God.
> It will flame out, like shining from shook foil;
> It gathers to a greatness, like the ooze of oil
> Crushed. Why do men then now not reck his rod?
> Generations have trod, have trod, have trod;
> And all is seared with trade; bleared, smeared with toil;
> And wears man's smudge and shares man's smell: the soil
> Is bare now, nor can foot feel, being shod.
>
> And for all this, nature is never spent;
> There lives the dearest freshness deep down things;
> And though the last lights off the black West went
> Oh, morning, at the brown brink eastward, springs —
> Because the Holy Ghost over the bent
> World droops with warm breast and with ah! bright wings.
> ('God's Grandeur', Gerard Manley Hopkins)

Notes

Preface

1 Arthur Schopenhauer, 'On Women', in T.D. Saunders (ed.), *Schopenhauer Selections*, New York: Charles Scribner, 1928, quoted in Beverley Clack (ed.), *Misogyny in the Western Philosophical Tradition: A Reader*, Basingstoke and London: Macmillan, 1999, p. 187.

Introduction

1 Although I concentrate on western Catholicism in this book, it is important to recognize the increasing importance of non-western cultures and traditions for the formation of Catholic practice and doctrine. In seeking to explore the spiritual malaise which afflicts western Catholicism, and in asking if it is possible to develop a more life-affirming sacramental theology, I hope that I am addressing an issue which has implications for the Church as a whole, even although I remain focused on western theologians and theorists.
2 For a survey of the voting records of candidates in the 2004 American election, including John Kerry, across a range of domestic and international issues, see the website 'On the Issues' at http://www.issues2000.org / default.htm (last accessed 20 May 2005).
3 Peter J. Boyer, 'A Hard Faith', *The New Yorker*, 16 May 2005.
4 Pope Benedict XVI, 'Homily of His Holiness Benedict XVI', Mass for the Inauguration of the Pontificate of Pope Benedict XVI, Sunday 24 April 2005, *Libraria Editrice Vaticana*, at http://www.vatican.va/holy_father/benedict_xvi/homilies/documents/hf_ben-xvi_hom_20050424_inizio-pontificato_en.html (last accessed 21 May 2005).
5 Ibid.
6 I sometimes use the term 'neo-orthodox' instead of 'conservative' to describe the kind of Catholic theology that emerged under the influence of Pope John Paul II. Neo-orthodoxy does not refer simply to a reactionary form of conservatism, but to a new way of thinking theologically that, although profoundly problematized in this book, seeks a serious engagement with the issues of contemporary feminist and postmodernist culture.
7 In this respect, see Mary McClintock Fulkerson, *Changing the Subject: Women's Discourses and Feminist Theology*, Minneapolis: Fortress Press, 1994.

8 Rebecca S. Chopp, 'From Patriarchy into Freedom: A Conversation Between American Feminist Theology and French Feminism', in Maggie C.W. Kim, Susan St Ville, and Susan M. Simonaitis (eds), *Transfigurations: Theology and the French Feminists*, Minneapolis: Fortress Press, 1993, p. 32.
9 Ibid., p. 48.
10 Ibid., p. 45.
11 See Jacques Derrida, 'Plato's Pharmacy', *Dissemination*, Chicago: University of Chicago Press, 1981 [1968].
12 Ibid., p. 71.
13 Nancy A. Dallavalle, 'Toward a Theology that is Catholic and Feminist: Some Basic Issues', *Modern Theology*, Vol. 14, 4, October 1998: 535–53, p. 540.
14 Ibid., p. 548.
15 Susan Parsons, 'Accounting for Hope: Feminist Theology as Fundamental Theology', in Susan Parsons (ed.), *Challenging Women's Orthodoxies in the Context of Faith*, Aldershot, Burlington USA, Singapore, Sydney: Ashgate, 2000, p. 17.
16 Ibid., p. 18.
17 Ibid.
18 Ibid., p. 11.
19 Ibid.
20 Ibid., p. 5.
21 For a discussion of the implicit atheism of feminist theology, as well as Parsons, see Daphne Hampson, *Theology and Feminism*, Oxford UK and Cambridge MA: Blackwell, 1990, and Francis Martin, *The Feminist Question: Feminist Theology in the Light of Christian Tradition*, Edinburgh: T. & T. Clark, 1994. For a more positive and interesting analysis of Ruether's nihilism, see Marta Frascati-Lochhead, *Kenosis and Feminist Theology: The Challenge of Gianni Vattimo*, Albany NY: State University of New York Press, 1998. I do not engage with Frascati-Lochhead's argument since ultimately I think her post-Heideggerian/Nietzschean reading of Ruether as the most radical of postmodern, deconstructive feminist theologians is unconvincing, but nevertheless she raises challenging questions about power, representation and faith which make her book a worthwhile and undeservedly neglected contribution to feminist theology.
22 Rosemary Radford Ruether, *Women and Redemption: A Theological History*, London: SCM Press, 1998, p. 223.
23 Martin Heidegger, 'The Onto-theo-logical Constitution of Metaphysics', *Identity and Difference*, San Francisco, 1974, p. 72.
24 Jacques Derrida, *Of Grammatology*, translated by Gayatri Chakravorty Spivak, Baltimore: Johns Hopkins University Press, 1976, p. 162.
25 See Gillian Rose, 'Diremption of Spirit', in Philippa Berry and Andrew Wernick (eds), *Shadow of Spirit: Postmodernism and Religion*, London and New York: Routledge, 1992; and Gillian Rose, *The Broken Middle: Out of Our Ancient Society*, Oxford UK and Cambridge MA: Blackwell, 1992.
26 Michele M. Schumacher (ed.), *Women in Christ: Toward a New Feminism*, Grand Rapids MI and Cambridge UK: William B. Eerdmans, 2004.
27 Rebecca S. Chopp and Sheila Greeve Davaney (eds), *Horizons in Feminist Theology: Identity, Tradition, and Norms*, Minneapolis: Fortress Press, 1997.

28 See Sarah Coakley, 'Kenosis and Subversion: On the Repression of "Vulnerability" in Christian Feminist Writing', in *Powers and Submissions: Spirituality, Philosophy and Gender*, Oxford: Blackwell, 2002.
29 See Pamela Sue Anderson, *A Feminist Philosophy of Religion*, Oxford: Blackwell, 1998.
30 Michelle Gonzalez, 'Hans Urs von Balthasar and Contemporary Feminist Theology', *Theological Studies*, Vol. 65, 3, September 2004: 566–95, p. 578.
31 See Hans Urs von Balthasar, *First Glance at Adrienne von Speyr*, translated by Antje Lawry and Sr Sergia Englund Lawry OCD, San Francisco: Ignatius Press, 1981 [1968], pp. 11–12.

1   Catholicism, feminism and faith

1 Nancy A. Dallavalle, 'Toward a Theology that is Catholic and Feminist: Some Basic Issues', *Modern Theology*, Vol. 14, 4, October 1998: 535–53, 541. Dallavalle offers a brief but helpful summary of the perspectives of Catholic feminist theology.
2 Pope John Paul II, *Evangelium Vitae, Encyclical Letter on the Value and Inviolability of Human Life*, London: Catholic Truth Society, 1995, n. 99. The term 'new feminism' has also been used in a secular context. See Natasha Walter, *The New Feminism*, London: Virago Press, 1999.
3 Congregation for the Doctrine of the Faith, 'Letter to the Bishops of the Catholic Church on the Collaboration of Men and Women in the Church and in the World', 31 May 2004 at http://www.vatican.va / roman _ curia / congregations / cfaith / documents / rc _ con _ cfaith _ doc _ 20040731 _ collaboration _ en.html (last accessed 11 June 2005). See also Tina Beattie, 'Feminism Vatican Style', *The Tablet*, Vol. 7, August 2004; Fergus Kerr, 'Comment: Women', *New Blackfriars*, Vol. 85, 1000, November 2004: 579–82.
4 Pioneering feminist works affirming the relationality of women in contrast to the autonomous individualism of masculine models of subjectivity include Carol Gilligan, *In a Different Voice: Psychological Theory and Women's Development*, Cambridge MA: Harvard University Press, 1982, and Nel Noddings, *Caring: A Feminist Approach to Ethics and Moral Education*, Berkeley: University of California Press, 1984. For more recent debates and perspectives, see the essays in Catriona Mackenzie and Natalie Stoljar (eds), *Relational Autonomy: Feminist Perspectives on Autonomy, Agency, and the Social Self*, New York and Oxford: Oxford University Press, 2000.
5 For a profile of the CDF, see http://www.vatican.va/roman_curia/congregations/cfaith/documents/rc_con_cfaith_pro_14071997_en.html (last accessed 11 June 2005).
6 Michele M. Schumacher, 'An Introduction to a New Feminism', in M. Schumacher (ed.), *Women in Christ: Toward a New Feminism*, Grand Rapids MI and Cambridge UK: William B. Eerdmans, 2004, p. xi.
7 Ibid., p. ix.
8 Elizabeth Fox-Genovese, 'Equality, Difference, and the Practical Problems of a New Feminism', in Schumacher (ed.), *Women in Christ*, p. 297.
9 Beatriz Vollmer Coles, 'New Feminism: A Sex–Gender Reunion', in Schumacher (ed.), *Women in Christ*, p. 55.

10 Ibid., p. 55.
11 Ibid., p. 59.
12 Fox-Genovese, 'Equality, Difference', p. 300.
13 See Prudence Allen RSM, *The Concept of Woman: The Aristotelian Revolution 750 BC – AD 1250,* Grand Rapids MI and Cambridge UK: William B. Eerdmans, 1997 [1985]; and Prudence Allen RSM, *The Concept of Woman: Early Humanist Reformation, 1250–1500,* Grand Rapids MI and Cambridge UK: William B. Eerdmans, 2002.
14 Prudence Allen RSM, 'Can Feminism be a Humanism?' in Schumacher (ed.), *Women in Christ*, pp. 283–4.
15 Ibid., p. 102.
16 I discuss these questions further in Tina Beattie, 'Global Sisterhood or Wicked Stepsisters: Why Don't Girls with God-Mothers Get Invited to the Ball?' in Deborah F. Sawyer and Diane M. Collier (eds), *Is There a Future for Feminist Theology?* Sheffield: Sheffield Academic Press, 1999; and Tina Beattie, 'Religious Identity and the Ethics of Representation: The Study of Religion and Gender in the Secular Academy', in Ursula King and Tina Beattie (eds), *Religion, Gender and Diversity: New Perspectives*, London and New York: Continuum, 2004.
17 Rebecca S. Chopp, 'Theorizing Feminist Theory', in R. Chopp and Sheila Greeve Davaney (eds), *Horizons in Feminist Theology: Identity, Tradition, and Norms*, Minneapolis: Fortress Press, 1997, p. 230.
18 Ibid.
19 See Mary McClintock Fulkerson, 'Contesting the Gendered Subject: A Feminist Account of the Imago Dei', in Chopp and Davaney (eds), *Horizons in Feminist Theology*.
20 Mary McClintock Fulkerson, *Changing the Subject: Women's Discourses and Feminist Theology*, Minneapolis: Fortress Press, 1994, p. 114.
21 Ibid., p. 102.
22 Ibid., p. 102–3, referring to Michel Foucault, ed. Colin Gordon, 'Truth and Power', *Power/Knowledge: Selected Interviews and Other Writings, 1972–1977*, New York: Pantheon Books, 1980, pp. 109–33.
23 Fulkerson, *Changing the Subject*, p. vii.
24 Ibid., p. 16.
25 Emily R. Neill, 'Roundtable Discussion: From Generation to Generation. Horizons in Feminist Theology or Reinventing the Wheel?' *The Journal of Feminist Studies in Religion*, Vol. 15, 1, 1999: 102–38, pp. 104–5.
26 Ibid., p. 107.
27 In this context, see the debate about Butler's performative theory of gender in Seyla Benhabib, 'Feminism and Postmodernism: An Uneasy Alliance', in Seyla Benhabib, Judith Butler, Drucilla Cornell and Nancy Fraser (contributors), *Feminist Contentions: A Philosophical Exchange*, New York and London: Routledge, 1995.
28 Janet Martin Soskice, 'General Introduction', in Soskice and Diana Lipton (eds), *Feminism and Theology*, Oxford: Oxford University Press, 2003, pp. 7–8.
29 Lorraine Code, *What Can She Know? Feminist Theory and the Construction of Knowledge*, Ithaca and London: Cornell University Press, 1991, p. 26.
30 Ibid., quoting Michel Foucault, 'The Discourse on Language', *The Archaeology of Knowledge*, New York: Pantheon, 1972, p. 223.

316 Notes

31 For a survey of the philosophical background, see Genevieve Lloyd, *The Man of Reason: 'Male' and 'Female' in Western Philosophy*, London: Methuen, 1984.
32 J.B. Schneewind, *The Invention of Autonomy: A History of Modern Moral Philosophy*, Cambridge: Cambridge University Press, 1998, p. 3.
33 Ibid., p. 4.
34 Ibid., p. 7.
35 See Penelope Margaret Magee, 'Disputing the Sacred: Some Theoretical Approaches to Gender and Religion', in Ursula King (ed.), *Religion and Gender*, Oxford UK and Cambridge USA: Blackwell, 1995.
36 Ibid., p. 114.
37 Ibid., p. 115.
38 Ibid., p. 117.
39 Ibid.
40 See Caroline Walker Bynum, *Jesus as Mother: Studies in the Spirituality of the High Middle Ages*, Berkeley, Los Angeles, London: University of California Press, 1984 [1982]. Bynum argues that the 'sharp line between sacred and secular, spiritual and material' emerged during the twelfth century as a consequence of the Gregorian Reform movement of the mid-eleventh century. She writes,

> From the world of the early Middle Ages, in which the supernatural may break into everyday life at any moment and anything may be a sign or 'sacrament' of the holy, we move in the twelfth century into a world in which what we today call the material or secular is increasingly seen as having its own laws and operations, as *other than* the spiritual and perhaps even corrupting to it.
>
> (p. 14)

See also the discussion in Chapter III, 'Did the Twelfth Century Discover the Individual?' Bynum argues that the twelfth century 'did in some sense discover – or rediscover – the self, the inner mystery, the inner man, the inner landscape' (p. 106), but this was accompanied by a concern to establish appropriate social models and groups in which the self could operate, and therefore it cannot be equated with the meaning attached to the idea of the individual in a modern sense.

41 Nominalism, the belief that there are no universals but that each act of naming is arbitrary insofar as it refers to an individual entity that shares no common essence or grouping with other similar entities, can be traced back to the influence of Duns Scotus but is usually associated particularly with William of Ockham. Francis Martin argues that Ockham, in positing an opposition between the unknowability of the content of faith and the propositional function of theology, brought about 'the final step in the dismantling of the vision of faith as a light that provided a prophetic interpretation of all reality because it gave us a share in the very knowledge God has of himself' (Francis Martin, *The Feminist Question: Feminist Theology in the Light of Christian Tradition*, Edinburgh: T. & T. Clark, 1994, p. 54). John Milbank writes,

> In the thought of the nominalists, following Duns Scotus, the Trinity loses its significance as a prime location for discussing will and understanding in God and the relationship of God to the world. No longer is the world participatorily enfolded

within the divine expressive *logos*, but instead a bare divine unity starkly confronts the other distinct unities which he has ordained.

(John Milbank, *Theology and Social Theory: Beyond Secular Reason*, Oxford UK and Malden MA: Blackwell, 1998, p. 14)

42 George Steiner, *Heidegger*, edited by Frank Kermode, 2nd edn, Fontana Modern Masters, London: Fontana Press, 1992 [1978], p. 62.
43 See Jacques Derrida, *Acts of Religion*, edited and with an introduction by Gil Anidjar, New York and London: Routledge, 2002. See also John D. Caputo, *The Prayers and Tears of Jacques Derrida: Religion without Religion*, Bloomington and Indianapolis: Indiana University Press, 1997; Harold Coward and Toby Foshay (eds), *Derrida and Negative Theology*, New York: State University of New York Press, 1993.
44 Denys Turner, 'Apophaticism, Idolatry and the Claims of Reason', in Oliver Davies and Turner (eds), *Silence and the Word: Negative Theology and Incarnation*, Cambridge: Cambridge University Press, 2002, p. 11.
45 Luce Irigaray, *An Ethics of Sexual Difference*, translated by Carolyn Burke and Gillian C. Gill, London: The Athlone Press, 1993, p. 61.
46 Ibid., p. 62. Secular feminists have not welcomed this turn to religion in Irigaray, although her work has from the beginning been informed by a Catholic sensibility that has tended to be screened out by feminists engaging with her ideas. See the discussion in Beattie, 'Global Sisterhood or Wicked Stepsisters'.

2   Feminist bodies and feminist selves

1 Judith Butler, *Gender Trouble: Feminism and the Subversion of Identity*, 2nd edn, New York and London: Routledge, 1999 [1990], p. 173.
2 Judith Butler, *Bodies That Matter: On the Discursive Limits of 'Sex'*, New York and London: Routledge, 1993 [1990], p. 9.
3 Seyla Benhabib, 'Feminism and Postmodernism: An Uneasy Alliance', in Seyla Benhabib, Judith Butler, Drucilla Cornell and Nancy Fraser (contributors), *Feminist Contentions: A Philosophical Exchange*, New York and London: Routledge, 1995, p. 21.
4 Ibid.
5 Ibid., p. 22.
6 Butler, *Gender Trouble*, p. xxiii.
7 Sarah Coakley, 'The Eschatological Body: Gender, Transformation and God', in *Powers and Submissions: Spirituality, Philosophy and Gender*, Oxford: Blackwell, 2002, p. 159.
8 Ibid., p. 160.
9 Butler, *Gender Trouble*, p. xx.
10 Beatriz Vollmer Coles, 'New Feminism: A Sex–Gender Reunion', in Michele M. Schumacher (ed.), *Women in Christ: Toward a New Feminism*, Grand Rapids MI and Cambridge UK: William B. Eerdmans, 2004, p. 57.
11 Coakley, 'The Eschatological Body', p. 161.
12 Butler, *Gender Trouble*, p. xxvi. It is interesting in this context that Butler's 'bodies' are always defined in terms of their transgressive, conformist or imposed sexuality. Her world appears not to be peopled by children's bodies, sick bodies, elderly bodies, celibate bodies, pregnant bodies, foetal bodies.

13 Ibid.
14 Ibid.
15 Coakley, 'The Eschatological Body', p. 161.
16 Ibid., p. 161.
17 I discuss Lacan's work in more detail in Chapter 10.
18 Butler, *Bodies That Matter*, p. 188.
19 Ibid., p. 198.
20 Ibid.
21 Ibid., pp. 199–200.
22 Ibid., p. 201, quoting Slavoj Žižek, *The Sublime Object of Ideology*, London: Verso, 1989, p. 50.
23 Coakley, 'The Eschatological Body', p. 166.
24 Ibid., p. 164.
25 Ibid., p. 165.
26 Ibid., p. 165, quoting Rowan Williams, 'Macrina's Deathbed Revisited: Gregory of Nyssa on Mind and Passion', in Lionel Wickham and Caroline P. Bammel (eds), *Christian Faith and Greek Philosophy in Late Antiquity*, Leiden: E.J. Brill, 1993, p. 244.
27 Ibid., p. 166.
28 Michele M. Schumacher, 'The Nature of Nature in Feminism, Old and New: From Dualism to Complementary Unity', in Schumacher (ed.), *Women in Christ,* p. 17.
29 Ibid., p.19.
30 Ibid., p. 20.
31 Ibid., pp. 32–3.
32 Ibid., p. 23.
33 Ibid.
34 Ibid., p. 28. See Simone de Beauvoir, *The Second Sex*, translated by H.M. Parshley, Harmondsworth: Penguin Books, 1986 [1949], p. 295.
35 Schumacher, 'The Nature of Nature', p. 28.
36 Ibid., p. 28.
37 From Schumacher's own perspective, one would have to agree that a nature opposed to reason and freedom is not in fact nature but a cultural construct of 'nature' and therefore 'nature as man has conceived it', for in the Catholic understanding nature works with and not against reason and freedom. Certainly there is in Beauvoir's work no celebration of the female body and its reproductive functions such as one finds in the writings of some romantic feminists and of the Catholic new feminists. But nowhere does Beauvoir deny that 'woman – like man – is a being rooted in nature' (*The Second Sex,* p. 285) and she is clear that

> this means that her relations to her own body, to that of the male, to the child, will never be identical with those the male bears to his own body, to that of the female, and to the child; those who make much of 'equality in difference' could not with good grace refuse to grant me the possible existence of differences in equality.
>
> (*The Second Sex,* p. 740)

38. Beauvoir, *The Second Sex*, p. 15.
39. Butler, *Bodies That Matter*, p. 14.
40. Schumacher, 'The Nature of Nature', p. 29.

41 Ibid.
42 Ibid., p. 31, quoting Jean Borella, *The Sense of the Supernatural*, translated by G. John Champoux, Edinburgh: T. & T. Clark, 1998, p. 155.
43 Ibid., p. 29.
44 Nancy A. Dallavalle, 'Neither Idolatry nor Iconoclasm: A Critical Essentialism for Catholic Feminist Theology', *Horizons*, Vol. 25, 1, 1998: 23–42, p. 24.
45 Ibid., p. 31.
46 Ibid., p. 33.
47 Ibid., p. 37.
48 Ibid., p. 39.
49 Ibid.
50 Ibid., p. 40.
51 Ibid.
52 Christine Battersby, *The Phenomenal Woman: Feminist Metaphysics and the Patterns of Identity*, Cambridge: Polity Press, 1998, p. 23.
53 Ibid., p. 50.
54 Ibid., p. 26.
55 Ibid., p. 3.
56 Ibid., p. 19.
57 Ibid., p. 38.
58 Ibid., p. 39.
59 Ibid., p. 38.
60 Ibid., p. 34.
61 Ibid., p. 123.
62 Ibid., p. 122.
63 Ibid., p. 124.
64 See Sarah Jane Boss, *Empress and Handmaid: On Nature and Gender in the Cult of the Virgin Mary*, London and New York: Cassell, 2000; Carolyn Merchant, *The Death of Nature: Women, Ecology and the Scientific Revolution*, San Francisco: Harper & Row, 1990 [1980].
65 Pope John Paul II, *Original Unity of Man and Woman: Catechesis on the Book of Genesis*, Boston MA: St Paul Books & Media, 1981, p. 102.
66 See ibid., pp. 106–12.
67 Ibid., p. 99.
68 Ibid., p. 74.
69 Ibid., p. 110.
70 Ibid., p. 89.
71 Ibid., p. 164.
72 Ibid., p. 40.
73 Ibid., p. 62. I have explored these reflections at some length in engagement with Irigaray. See Tina Beattie, 'Carnal Love and Spiritual Imagination', in Jon Davies and Gerard Loughlin (eds), *Sex These Days: Essays on Theology, Sexuality and Society*, Studies in Theology and Sexuality, Sheffield: Sheffield Academic Press, 1997.
74 Schumacher, 'The Nature of Nature', pp. 33–4.
75 Schumacher, 'An Introduction to A New Feminism', in Schumacher (ed.), *Women in Christ*, p. xii.

76 Ibid.
77 Hanna-Barbara Gerl-Falkovitz, 'Gender Difference: Critical Questions concerning Gender Studies', in Schumacher (ed.), *Women in Christ*, p. 4.
78 Schumacher, 'The Nature of Nature', p. 30.
79 Ibid., p. 20.

3 Gender, knowledge and being

1 For a helpful survey of Heidegger's continuing impact on Christian theology, see John D. Caputo, 'Heidegger and Theology', in Charles Guignon (ed.), *The Cambridge Companion to Heidegger*, Cambridge: Cambridge University Press, 1993.
2 Susan Parsons, 'To Be or Not To Be: Gender and Ontology', *Heythrop Journal*, Vol. 45, 3, July 2004: 340.
3 Ibid.
4 Ibid.
5 Marta Frascati-Lochhead, *Kenosis and Feminist Theology: The Challenge of Gianni Vattimo*, Albany NY: State University of New York Press, 1998, p. 3.
6 Friedrich Nietzsche, 'The Gay Science' in Walter Kaufmann (ed.), *The Portable Nietzsche*, translated by Walter Kaufmann, New York, London, Ringwood, Toronto and Auckland: Penguin Books, 1982 {1954}, p.95.
7 Ibid.
8 Luce Irigaray, *Marine Lover of Friedrich Nietzsche*, translated by Gillian C. Gill, New York: Columbia University Press, 1991, p. 188.
9 Mary Daly, *Beyond God the Father: Towards a Philosophy of Women's Liberation*, London: The Women's Press, 1986 [1973], p. 19.
10 George Steiner, *Heidegger*, edited by Frank Kermode, 2nd edn, Fontana Modern Masters, London: Fontana Press, 1992 [1978], p. 36.
11 Ibid., p. 65.
12 Ibid., p. 18. For a discussion of the differentiation between being and Being in English translation through the capitalization of the second 'B', see Steiner, *Heidegger*, p. 26 and pp. 45–9.
13 See Martin Heidegger, *Being and Time*, translated by John Macquarrie and Edward Robinson, Oxford: Blackwell, 1980 [1927], pp. 26–7.
14 Ibid., p. 321.
15 See ibid., p. 174.
16 See ibid., p. 84.
17 Ibid.
18 Martin Heidegger, 'Recollection in Metaphysics', *The End of Philosophy*, New York, Evanston, San Francisco, London: Harper & Row, 1973, p. 75.
19 Ibid., p. 76.
20 Ibid., p. 79.
21 Ibid., p. 80.
22 Martin Heidegger, 'Letter on Humanism', in David Farrell Krell (ed.), *Basic Writings*, London: Routledge, 1993 [1947], p. 442, quoting Goethe, *Maxims and Reflections*, No. 993.

23 Ibid., p. 442.
24 Ibid., p. 445.
25 Luce Irigaray, *An Ethics of Sexual Difference*, translated by Carolyn Burke and Gillian C. Gill, London: The Athlone Press, 1993, p. 5. For an analysis of Heidegger's influence on Irigaray, see Tina Chanter, *Ethics of Eros: Irigaray's Rewriting of the Philosophers*, New York and London: Routledge, 1995, pp. 127–69.
26 Lorraine Code, *What Can She Know? Feminist Theory and the Construction of Knowledge*, Ithaca and London: Cornell University Press, 1991, pp. 8–9.
27 Parsons, 'To Be or Not To Be', p. 337.
28 Ibid., p. 338.
29 Jacques Derrida, 'Geschlecht: Sexual Difference, Ontological Difference', in Peggy Kamuf (ed.), *A Derrida Reader: Between the Blinds*, Hemel Hempstead: Harvester Wheatsheaf, 1991, p. 399, quoted in Parsons, 'To Be or Not To Be', p. 338.
30 Parsons, 'To Be or Not To Be', p. 339.
31 Ibid.
32 Ibid.
33 Ibid.
34 Ibid., p. 337.
35 Heidegger, 'Letter on Humanism', p. 217.
36 Seyla Benhabib, 'Feminism and Postmodernism: An Uneasy Alliance', in Seyla Benhabib, Judith Butler, Drucilla Cornell and Nancy Fraser (contributors), *Feminist Contentions: A Philosophical Exchange*, New York and London: Routledge, 1995, p. 24.
37 Ibid.
38 Ibid.
39 See Francis Martin, *The Feminist Question: Feminist Theology in the Light of Christian Tradition*, Edinburgh: T. & T. Clark, 1994, pp. 38–74. See also Jean-Luc Marion, 'Thomas Aquinas and Onto-theo-logy', in Michael Kessler and Christian Sheppard (eds), *Mystics: Presence and Aporia*, Chicago and London: University of Chicago Press, 2003.
40 Luce Irigaray, *This Sex Which Is Not One*, translated by Catherine Porter with Carolyn Burke, Ithaca NY: Cornell University Press, 1985, p. 74.
41 Margaret Whitford, *Luce Irigaray: Philosophy in the Feminine*, London and New York: Routledge, 1991, p. 70.
42 Fergus Kerr, *After Aquinas: Versions of Thomism*, Malden MA and Oxford: Blackwell, 2002, p. 27.
43 Ibid., p. 30.
44 Ibid.
45 Ibid., p. 31.
46 Martin, *The Feminist Question*, p. 173, quoting Thomas Aquinas, *In Boethius de Trinitate* 2, 4 and 5 in Thomas Aquinas, *Faith, Reason and Theology*, translated by Armand Maurer, Toronto: Pontifical Institute of Medieval Studies, 1987, p. 50.
47 See Thomas Aquinas, *Summa Theologiae*, I, q.1.1. Unless otherwise indicated, all quotations from Thomas Aquinas, *Summa Theologiae* (*ST*), are taken from the following editions: Latin text: produced in electronic hypertext form (*Corpus Thomisticum*) by Roberto Busa SJ from Leonine edition and adapted by Enrique Alarcón; English text: *Sancti Thomae Aquinatis – Summa Theologiae, Literally translated by Fathers of the English*

Dominican Province, 2nd and revised edn, 1920, available at http://krystal.op.cz/sth/sth.php (last accessed 23 May 2005). This website offers the full text of the *Summa Theologiae* with parallel versions available in English and Latin.
48 *ST* I, q.12.11.
49 *ST* I, q.12.12.
50 *ST* I, q.12.5.
51 *ST* I, q.12.13.
52 *ST* I, q.12.5.
53 *ST* I, q.12.13.
54 *ST* I, q.1.8.
55 Denys Turner, 'Apophaticism, Idolatry and the Claims of Reason', in Oliver Davies and Turner (eds), *Silence and the Word: Negative Theology and Incarnation*, Cambridge: Cambridge University Press, 2002, p. 29.
56 Ibid., p. 30.
57 *ST* I, q.3, preface, quoted in Elizabeth Johnson, *She Who Is: The Mystery of God in Feminist Theological Discourse*, New York: Crossroad, 1995 [1992], p. 109.
58 Ibid., p. 110.
59 Ibid., p. 120.
60 Ibid., p. 39.
61 Ibid., p. 108.
62 Ibid.
63 Ibid., p. 4, quoting Martin Luther, *Large Catechism*, in *The Book of Concord*, translated by Theodore Tappert, Philadelphia: Fortress, 1959, p. 365.
64 Ibid., p. 113.
65 Martin, *The Feminist Question*, p. 262.
66 Ibid.
67 Ibid., p. 181.
68 Johnson, *She Who Is*, pp. 61–7.
69 Ibid., p. 62.
70 Ibid.
71 Ibid., p. 63.
72 Ibid.
73 Ibid.
74 Ibid., p. 64.
75 Ibid.
76 Ibid.
77 Ibid.
78 Ibid., p. 67.
79 Ibid., p. 68.
80 Ibid.
81 Cf Harvey Cox, *Fire from Heaven: The Rise of Pentecostalism Spirituality and the Reshaping of Religion in the Twenty-first Century*, London: Cassell, 1996.
82 See Julia Kristeva, *Strangers to Ourselves*, translated by Leon S. Roudiez, Hemel Hempstead: Harvester, 1991 [1989].
83 Turner, 'Apophaticism', p. 17.
84 Ibid., p. 18.

85 Ibid., pp. 19–20, quoting *Pseudo-Dionysius, The Complete Works*, translated by Colm Luibheid, New Jersey: Paulist Press, 1987: first quotation – *Divine Names*, 817D, p. 98; second quotation – *Mystical Theology* 997B, p. 135.
86 Ibid., p. 23.
87 Ibid.
88 Jacques Lacan, 'God and the *Jouissance* of The Woman', in Juliet Mitchell and Jacqueline Rose (eds), *Feminine Sexuality: Jacques Lacan and the école freudienne*, Basingstoke and London: Macmillan, 1982 [1975], p. 144. I discuss this claim in more detail in Chapter 10.
89 See Sarah Coakley, 'Kenosis and Subversion: On the Repression of "Vulnerability" in Christian Feminist Writing', in *Powers and Submissions: Spirituality, Philosophy and Gender*, Oxford: Blackwell, 2002, p. 36. Coakley's reference to the 'semiotic' is a reference to contemporary French feminist theory, which informs the theology of much of the second and third parts of this book.
90 Nicola Slee, *Praying Like a Woman*, London: SPCK, 2004, p. 141.

4 Knowledge, desire and prayer

1 Timothy McDermott, 'Introduction', in Aquinas (edited), *Summa Theologiae: A Concise Translation*, London: Methuen, 1992 [1989], p. xlii.
2 As a relevant aside, it is worth pointing out that Aquinas has a more positive anthropology than Augustine, whose idea of original sin, closely associated with the concupiscence of sexual passion, leads to a highly pessimistic outlook with regard to our human capacity to do good because of the fundamental distortion of our desire, Aquinas has a more positive understanding of the role of desire in motivating us towards moral goodness. For Aquinas, all desire is fundamentally oriented towards the good, even if we can be deeply misguided as to the nature of what is good. Sin for Aquinas is what McDermott calls 'a grand fiction' (ibid.) since it constitutes the setting up of the self against God, which amounts to a misdirection of being away from its natural orientation, which is God. This is why it is necessary to cultivate virtue, in order to strengthen our will and our capacity to love, and thus to liberate our natural desire from its deceptions and distortions.
3 McDermott, 'Introduction', p. xli.
4 George Steiner, *Heidegger*, edited by Frank Kermode, 2nd edn, Fontana Modern Masters, London: Fontana Press, 1992 [1978], p. xviii.
5 Martin Heidegger, 'Letter on Humanism', in David Farrell Krell (ed.), *Basic Writings*, London: Routledge, 1993 [1947], p. 445.
6 Ibid.
7 Ibid., pp. 217–18.
8 Ellen L. Fox, 'Seeing through Women's Eyes: The Role of Vision in Women's Moral Theory', in Eve Browning Cole and Susan Coultrap-McQuin (eds), *Explorations in Feminist Ethics: Theory and Practice*, Bloomington and Indianapolis: Indiana University Press, 1992, p. 111.
9 Ibid., p. 111.
10 Ibid., p. 112.

324 Notes

11 Simone Weil, 'Reflections on the Right Use of School Studies with a View to the Love of God', *Waiting for God*, New York: G.P. Putnam's Sons, 1951, p. 115, quoted in Fox, 'Seeing through Women's Eyes', p. 112.
12 Fox, 'Seeing through Women's Eyes', p. 113.
13 Weil, 'Reflections', p. 115, quoted in Fox, 'Seeing through Women's Eyes', p. 112.
14 Fox, 'Seeing through Women's Eyes', pp. 112–13.
15 Valerie Saiving, 'The Human Situation: A Feminine View', in Carol P. Christ and Judith Plaskow (eds), *Womanspirit Rising: A Feminist Reader in Religion*, San Francisco: HarperSanFrancisco, 1992, p. 26.
16 Ibid., p. 37.
17 In this context, see Marilyn Friedman's thoughtful feminist critique of communitarianism and the ambiguities that women face in terms of communal and familial relationships. Marilyn Friedman, 'Feminism and Modern Friendship: Dislocating the Community', in Eve Browning Cole and Susan Coultrap-McQuin (eds), *Explorations in Feminist Ethics: Theory and Practice*, Bloomington and Indianapolis: Indiana University Press, 1992.
18 Elizabeth Johnson, *She Who Is: The Mystery of God in Feminist Theological Discourse*, New York: Crossroad, 1995 [1992], p. 4.
19 Daphne Hampson, *Theology and Feminism*, Oxford UK and Cambridge MA: Blackwell, 1990, p. 155, quoted in Sarah Coakley, 'Kenosis and Subversion: On the Repression of "Vulnerability" in Christian Feminist Writing', in *Powers and Submissions: Spirituality, Philosophy and Gender*, Oxford: Blackwell, 2002, p. 3. Coakley's emphasis.
20 Coakley, 'Kenosis and Subversion', p. 10.
21 Ibid., p. 11.
22 Ibid., p. 10. See Ruether's lyrical midrash on the *kenosis* of God the Father in Rosemary Radford Ruether, *Sexism and God-Talk: Towards a Feminist Theology*, London: SCM Press, 1992 [1983], pp. 2–3.
23 Coakley, 'Kenosis and Subversion', p. 25.
24 Ibid., p. 30.
25 Ibid.
26 Ibid., pp. 30–1.
27 Ibid., p. 32.
28 Ibid.
29 Ibid., p. 33.
30 Ibid., p. 34.
31 Ibid., p. 37.
32 Ibid., p. 39.
33 Ibid., p. 35.
34 Weil, 'Reflections', p. 55.
35 Ibid.
36 Pamela Sue Anderson, *A Feminist Philosophy of Religion*, Oxford: Blackwell, 1998, p. 22.
37 Ibid., p. 36.
38 Ibid., p. 19.
39 Ibid., p. 22.
40 See Tina Beattie, 'Religious Identity and the Ethics of Representation: The Study of Religion and Gender in the Secular Academy', in Ursula King and Tina Beattie (eds),

Religion, Gender and Diversity: New Perspectives, London and New York: Continuum, 2004; Tina Beattie, 'Redeeming Mary: The Potential of Marian Symbolism for Feminist Philosophy of Religion', in Pamela Sue Anderson and Beverley Clack (eds), *Feminist Philosophy of Religion: Critical Readings*, London and New York: Routledge, 2004.
41 Anderson, *A Feminist Philosophy of Religion*, p. 20.
42 Ibid., p. xi.
43 Catherine of Siena, *The Dialogue*, translation and introduction by Suzanne Noffke OP, preface by Giuliana Cavallini, New York, Mahwah: Paulist Press, 1980, pp. 365–6.
44 Hans Urs von Balthasar, *The Glory of the Lord, Vol.V: The Realm of Metaphysics in the Modern Age*, translated by Oliver Davies, Edinburgh: T. & T. Clark, 1991, p. 92.
45 Cf Grace M. Jantzen, *Power, Gender and Christian Mysticism*, Cambridge: Cambridge University Press, 1995.
46 Catherine of Siena, *The Dialogue*, p. 325.
47 Ibid., p. 325.
48 Ibid., p. 50.
49 Luce Irigaray, *Marine Lover of Friedrich Nietzsche*, translated by Gillian C. Gill, New York: Columbia University Press, 1991, p. 176.
50 Nicola Slee, *Praying Like a Woman*, London: SPCK, 2004, p. 1.
51 For further discussion of this idea, see Tina Beattie, 'The Baptism of Eros', *Theology and Sexuality*, Vol. 9, 2, 2003: 167–79.
52 Gregory of Nyssa, *Commentary on the Song of Songs*, translated with introduction by Casimir McCambley OCSO, Brookline MA: Hellenic College Press, 1987, pp. 206–8.
53 See Grace M. Jantzen, *Becoming Divine: Towards a Feminist Philosophy of Religion*, Manchester: Manchester University Press, 1998.
54 Catherine of Siena, *The Dialogue*, p. 365.
55 Fergus Kerr, *After Aquinas: Versions of Thomism*, Malden MA and Oxford: Blackwell, 2002, p. 30.
56 Luce Irigaray, *This Sex Which Is Not One*, translated by Catherine Porter with Carolyn Burke, Ithaca NY: Cornell University Press, 1985, p. 74.

5   Incarnation, difference and God

1 Cf the essays in Lucy Gardner, David Moss, Ben Quash and Graham Ward (eds), *Balthasar at the End of Modernity*, Edinburgh: T. & T. Clark, 1999.
2 Graham Ward, 'Kenosis: Death, Discourse and Resurrection', in Gardner *et al.* (eds), *Balthasar at the End of Modernity*, p. 67.
3 Hans Urs von Balthasar, *The Glory of the Lord, Vol.V: The Realm of Metaphysics in the Modern Age*, translated by Oliver Davies *et al.*, Edinburgh: T. & T. Clark, 1991, p. 449.
4 Ibid., p. 450.
5 Ibid., p. 46.
6 Ibid., p. 47.
7 Ibid.
8 Lucy Gardner and David Moss, 'Something like Time; Something like the Sexes – an Essay in Reception', in Gardner *et al.* (eds), *Balthasar at the End of Modernity*, p. 73.

9 Hans Urs von Balthasar, 'Women Priests? A Marian Church in a Fatherless and Motherless Culture', *Communio*, Vol. 22, Spring 1995: 164–70, pp. 165–6.
10 Luce Irigaray, *Thinking the Difference – For a Peaceful Revolution*, translated by Karin Montin, London: The Athlone Press, 1994 [1989], p. 7.
11 Hans Urs von Balthasar, *Elucidations*, translated by John Riches, London: SPCK, 1975, p. 69.
12 Luce Irigaray, *This Sex Which Is Not One*, translated by Catherine Porter with Carolyn Burke, Ithaca NY: Cornell University Press, 1985 [1977], p. 171.
13 Luce Irigaray, *Je, tu, nous: Toward a Culture of Difference*, translated by Alison Martin, New York and London: Routledge, 1993 [1990], p. 12.
14 Balthasar, 'Women Priests?' p. 165.
15 Hans Urs von Balthasar, *Theo-Drama: Theological Dramatic Theory, Vol. II: The Dramatis Personae: Man in God*, translated by Graham Harrison, San Francisco: Ignatius Press, 1990 [1976], p. 365.
16 Luce Irigaray, *An Ethics of Sexual Difference*, translated by Carolyn Burke and Gillian C. Gill, London: The Athlone Press, 1993 [1984], p. 13.
17 See ibid.
18 Irigaray, *This Sex Which Is Not One*, p. 78.
19 Irigaray, *Ethics of Sexual Difference*, p. 100.
20 Ibid., p. 127.
21 John O'Donnell SJ, *Hans Urs von Balthasar*, London: Geoffrey Chapman, 1992, p. 57.
22 Hans Urs von Balthasar, 'A Riddle unto Itself', *Das Weizenkorn*, 25, in *The Von Balthasar Reader*, edited by Kehl Medart SJ and Werner Loser SJ, Edinburgh: T. & T. Clark, 1985, p. 63.
23 Balthasar, 'Speech', *Verbum Caro* 86–89, in *The Von Balthasar Reader*, p. 70.
24 For a summary of this aspect of Irigaray's work, see Tina Chanter, *Ethics of Eros: Irigaray's Rewriting of the Philosophers*, New York and London: Routledge, 1995, pp. 251–2.
25 Irigaray, *Ethics of Sexual Difference*, p. 33.
26 Ibid., p. 115.
27 For a critical appraisal of feminist responses to Irigaray's religiosity, see Tina Beattie, 'Global Sisterhood or Wicked Stepsisters: Why Don't Girls with God-Mothers Get Invited to the Ball?' in Deborah F. Sawyer and Diane M. Collier (eds), *Is There a Future for Feminist Theology?* Sheffield: Sheffield Academic Press, 1999.
28 Luce Irigaray, *Sexes and Genealogies*, New York: Columbia University Press, 1993 [1987], p. 71.
29 Ibid., p. 67.
30 Ibid.
31 Ibid.
32 Ibid., p. 64.
33 Ibid., p. 62.
34 Margaret Whitford, *Luce Irigaray: Philosophy in the Feminine*, London and New York: Routledge, 1991, p. 140.
35 Serene Jones, 'This God Which Is Not One: Irigaray and Barth on the Divine', in Maggie C.W. Kim, Susan St Ville, and Susan M. Simonaitis (eds), *Transfigurations: Theology and the French Feminists*, Minneapolis: Fortress Press, 1993, p. 137.

36 Ibid., p. 138.
37 Ibid., p. 139.
38 Ibid.
39 Ibid., p. 141.
40 Balthasar, *The Glory of the Lord V*, p. 447.
41 Fergus Kerr points out that this claim is insufficiently explained by Balthasar. See Fergus Kerr, *After Aquinas: Versions of Thomism*, Malden MA and Oxford: Blackwell, 2002, p. 91.
42 Balthasar, *The Glory of the Lord V,* pp. 447–8.
43 Kerr, *After Aquinas*, p. 93.
44 Balthasar, *Theo-Drama II*, p. 428.
45 O'Donnell, *Hans Urs von Balthasar*, p. 56.
46 Ibid.
47 Balthasar, *Theo-Drama II*, p. 271.
48 Hans Urs von Balthasar, *Theo-drama III: The Dramatis Personae: the Person in Christ*, trans. Graham Harrison, San Francisco: Ignatius Press, 1992 [1978], p. 132.
49 Balthasar, *Theo-Drama II*, p. 187.
50 Hans Urs von Balthasar, *Theo-Drama: Theological Dramatic Theory, Vol. I: Prolegomena*, trans. Graham Harrison, San Francisco: Ignatius Press, 1988 [1983], p. 20.
51 Balthasar, *Theo-Drama II*, p. 187.
52 Ibid., p. 228.
53 Ibid., p. 355.
54 Ibid., p. 335.
55 Ibid., p. 17.
56 See Hans Urs von Balthasar, *Theo-Dramatik II. Die Personen des Spiels. Teil I: Der Mensch in Gott*, Einsiedeln: Johannes Verlag, 1976; Hans Urs von Balthasar, *Theo-Dramatik II. Die Personen des Spiels. Teil 2: Die Personen in Christus*, Einsiedeln: Johannes Verlag, 1978.
57 See Balthasar, *Der Mensch in Gott*, pp. 334–50; Balthasar, *Die Personen in Christus*, pp. 260ff.
58 It should be noted that the volume numbering in the English translation is different from the original German publications.
59 Balthasar, *Theo-drama III,* p. 292.
60 Ibid., p. 290.
6 Gardner and Moss, 'Something Like Time', p. 86.
62 Ibid., p. 87.
63 Balthasar, *Theo-Drama II*, p. 365.
64 Ibid., p. 365, p. 366.
65 Ibid., p. 372.
66 Ibid.
67 Ibid., p. 372.
68 Ibid., p. 373.
69 Ibid.
70 Ibid., pp. 373–4.
71 See Phyllis Trible, *God and the Rhetoric of Sexuality*, Philadelphia: Fortress Press, 1978, Chapter 4, 'A Love Story Gone Awry'.
72 See Pope John Paul II, *Original Unity of Man and Woman: Catechesis on the Book of Genesis*, Boston MA: St Paul Books & Media, 1981.

73 Balthasar, *Theo-drama III*, p. 333.
74 Ibid., p. 327.
75 Ibid., p. 325. I discuss this idea of suprasexuality in more detail in Chapter 11.
76 Ibid., p. 351.
77 Ibid., p. 352.
78 Hans Urs von Balthasar, *The Glory of the Lord: A Theological Aesthetics I: Seeing the Form*, trans. Erasmo Leiva-Merikakis, edited by Joseph Fessio, Edinburgh: T. & T. Clark, 1982 [1961], p. 20, his italics.
79 Balthasar, *Theo-drama III*, p. 288.
80 Ibid., pp. 288–9.
81 Ibid., p. 338.
82 Balthasar, *Theo-Drama I*. p. 340.
83 Ibid., p. 341.
84 Ibid., p. 557.
85 Ibid.
86 Ibid.
87 Ibid., p. 558.
88 Balthasar, *Theo-drama III*, p. 286.
89 Ibid., p. 287.
90 Ibid., p. 290.
91 Irigaray, *This Sex Which Is Not One*, p. 26.
92 Ibid. Ellipses and italics in original.
93 Balthasar, *Theo-drama III*, p. 287.
94 Ibid.
95 Ibid., pp. 287–8.
96 Ibid., p. 288.
97 Balthasar, *Theo-Drama II*, p. 373, quoting E. Przywara, *Mensch, typologische Anthropologie I*, Nuremberg: Glock und Lutz, 1958, pp. 140–1.

6 Masculinity, femininity and God

1 For a study of the ways in which pre-modern gender roles, understood primarily in terms of their social functions, came to be interpreted through an appeal to scientific theories of a fundamental biological difference between the sexes, see Thomas Laqueur, *Making Sex: Body and Gender from the Greeks to Freud*, Cambridge MA and London: Harvard University Press, 1992.
2 Hans Urs von Balthasar, *Theo-Drama III: The Dramatis Personae: The Person in Christ*, translated by Graham Harrison, San Francisco: Ignatius Press, 1992 [1978], pp. 283–4.
3 Ibid., p. 287.
4 Ibid., p. 284.
5 With apologies to Madonna.
6 Luce Irigaray, *Speculum of the Other Woman*, translated by Gillian C. Gill, Ithaca NY: Cornell University Press, 1985 [1974], p. 165.
7 Virginia Burrus, *'Begotten, Not Made': Conceiving Manhood in Late Antiquity*, Stanford CA: Stanford University Press, 2000, p. 185.

8 Interestingly, in Balthasar's study of Gregory he makes little of the pervasive sexual imagery and eroticism to be found in Gregory's mystical theology. Perhaps this is because the book on Gregory was published in 1942, at the beginning of his relationship with Adrienne von Speyr and before her influence became apparent. But that is to anticipate. See Hans Urs von Balthasar, *Presence and Thought: An Essay on the Religious Philosophy of Gregory of Nyssa*, translated by Mark Sebanc, San Francisco: Ignatius Press, 1995 [1988].
9 Burrus, *'Begotten, Not Made'*, p. 80, quoting Hélène Cixous, 'Tancredi Continues', in Deborah Jenson (ed.), *'Coming to Writing' and Other Essays*, Cambridge MA: Harvard University Press, 1991.
10 Burrus, *'Begotten, Not Made'*, p. 83, quoting Hélène Cixous, 'The Author in Truth', in Jenson (ed.), *'Coming to Writing'*, pp. 147–8.
11 Burrus, *'Begotten, Not Made'*, p. 84, quoting Nicole Loraux, *The Experiences of Tiersias: The Feminine and the Greek Man*, translated by Paula Wissing, Princeton NJ: Princeton University Press, 1995, pp. 14–15.
12 See Gregory of Nyssa, 'The Life of Saint Macrina' and 'On the Soul and Resurrection', in *Saint Gregory of Nyssa: Ascetical Works*, The Fathers of the Church: A New Translation, Washington DC: The Catholic University of America Press, 1967.
13 Hans Urs von Balthasar, *First Glance at Adrienne von Speyr*, translated by Antje Lawry and Sr Sergia Englund, OCD, San Francisco: Ignatius Press, 1981 [1968], p. 13.
14 Gregory of Nyssa, *Commentary on the Song of Songs*, translated by with introduction by Casimir McCambley OCSO, Brookline MA: Hellenic College Press, 1987, pp. 145–6.
15 Cf Kari Elisabeth Børresen, 'God's Image, Man's Image? Patristic Interpretation of Gen. 1,27 and I Cor. 11,7', in Børresen (ed.), *Image of God and Gender Models in Judaeo-Christian Tradition*, Oslo: Solum Forlag, 1991, p. 198.
16 Cf the brief but illuminating discussion re Gregory's Trinitarian language in Sarah Coakley, '"Persons" in the "Social" Doctrine of the Trinity: Current Analytic Discussion and "Cappadocian" Theology', in *Powers and Submissions: Spirituality, Philosophy and Gender*, Oxford: Blackwell, 2002.
17 Ibid., p. 124.
18 In this brief survey I sketch only the main contours of Gregory's theology. For further reading, see the essays in Sarah Coakley (ed.), *Re-thinking Gregory of Nyssa*, Oxford: Blackwell, 2003. See also Giulia Sfameni Gasparro, 'Image of God and Sexual Differentiation in the Tradition of *Enkrateia*', in Børresen (ed.), *Image of God and Gender Models in Judaeo-Christian Theology*; Rosemary Radford Ruether, 'Misogynism and Virginal Feminism in the Fathers of the Church', in Ruether (ed.), *Religion and Sexism – Images of Women in the Jewish and Christian Traditions*, New York: Simon and Schuster, 1974.
19 For an analysis of this encratite tradition in early Christian writings, see Gasparro, 'Image of God and Sexual Differentiation'. See also Andrew Louth, 'The Body in Western Catholic Christianity', in Sarah Coakley (ed.), *Religion and the Body*, Cambridge, New York and Melbourne: Cambridge University Press, 1997.
20 See Sarah Coakley, 'Creaturehood Before God: Male and Female', in *Powers and Submissions: Spirituality, Philosophy and Gender*, Oxford: Blackwell, 2002.
21 See Børresen, 'God's Image, Man's Image?' pp. 199–205, Louth, 'The Body in Western Catholic Christianity'. See also Tina Beattie, *God's Mother, Eve's Advocate: A*

Marian Narrative of Women's Salvation, London and New York: Continuum, 2002 [1999], pp. 55–6.
22 Børresen, 'God's Image, Man's Image?' p. 204, quoting Augustine, *De civitate Dei*, Book 22, Chapter 17, CCSL 48,835–6. See Augustine, *Concerning the City of God against the Pagans*, translated by and edited by David Knowles and Henry Bettenson, London: Penguin Books, 1981 [1467], p. 1058.
23 Augustine, *City of God*, Book 22, Ch. 17, p. 1057.
24 Børresen, 'God's Image, Man's Image?' p. 203.
25 Augustine, *The Trinity*, translated by Stephen McKenna CSsR, vol. 45, The Fathers of the Church: A New Translation, Washington DC: The Catholic University of America Press, 1963, Book 12, Ch. 7, n. 10.
26 Ruether, 'Misogynism and Virginal Feminism', pp. 153–4.
27 Gasparro, 'Image of God and Sexual Differentiation', p. 156, quoting Gregory of Nyssa, PG 46, 148 C–149 A.
28 Augustine, *De Sermone Dom. in Monte*, 41, quoted in Ruether, 'Misogynism and Virginal Feminism', p. 161.
29 Coakley, 'Creaturehood Before God', p. 65.
30 Penelope Deutscher, *'Operative Contradiction in Augustine's Confessions'*, *Yielding Gender: Feminism, Deconstruction and the History of Philosophy*, London and New York: Routledge, 1997, p. 144.
31 Ibid., p. 145.
32 Ibid., p. 161.
33 Ibid.
34 Børresen, 'God's Image, Man's Image?' p. 199.
35 Ibid., p. 205.
36 Ibid.
37 Rosemary Radford Ruether, *Sexism and God-Talk: Towards a Feminist Theology*, London: SCM Press, 1992 [1983], p. 94.
38 Ibid., p. 111.
39 Ibid.
40 Mary McClintock Fulkerson, 'Contesting the Gendered Subject: A Feminist Account of the Imago Dei', in Rebecca Chopp and Sheila Greeve Davaney (eds), *Horizons in Feminist Theology: Identity, Tradition, and Norms*, Minneapolis: Fortress Press, 1997, p. 108.
41 Ibid., p. 109.
42 Ibid., p. 107.
43 Ibid., p. 103.
44 Ibid., p. 106.
45 Ibid., p. 109.
46 Ibid.
47 Ibid., p. 114.
48 Ibid.
49 Nancy A. Dallavalle, 'Neither Idolatry nor Iconoclasm: A Critical Essentialism for Catholic Feminist Theology', *Horizons*, Vol. 25, 1, 1998: 23–42, p. 41.
50 Burrus, *'Begotten, Not Made'*, p. 193.
51 Of course, one would need to ask to what extent this sublimation of desire found expression through outlets such as art, poetry and music. I am not suggesting that

creativity and sensuality were entirely banished from Protestant culture, but they were to a very great extent banished from Protestant worship in the Reformed churches, eventually finding expression in the development of Pentecostal and charismatic forms of Protestantism.

7   *Cherchez la femme*: gender, Church and priesthood

1 Luce Irigaray, *Marine Lover of Friedrich Nietzsche*, translated by Gillian C. Gill, New York: Columbia University Press, 1991 [1990], p. 182.
2 Ibid., p. 188.
3 Nancy Frankenberry, 'Feminist Approaches: Philosophy of Religion in Different Voices', in Pamela Sue Anderson and Beverley Clack (eds), *Feminist Philosophy of Religion: Critical Readings*, London and New York: Routledge, 2004, p. 15.
4 Cf Manfred Hauke, *Women in the Priesthood? A Systematic Analysis in the Light of the Order of Creation and Redemption*, translated by David Kipp, San Francisco: Ignatius Press, 1988 [1986], and John Wijngaard, *The Ordination of Women in the Catholic Church: Unmasking a Cuckoo's Egg Tradition*, London: Darton, Longman & Todd, 2001, for two very different perspectives. Hauke argues from history and tradition in defence of the Church's rejection of women's ordination. Wijngaard argues from history and tradition in favour of women's ordination.
5 Congregation for the Doctrine of the Faith, '*Inter Insigniores*: Declaration on the Question of the Admission of Women to the Ministerial Priesthood', 15 October 1976 at http://www.womenpriests.org / church / interlet.asp (last accessed 7 April 2005). This website includes links to a range of excellent essays by biblical scholars and theologians, questioning the arguments and claims of the Declaration. In 1994, Pope John Paul II issued an apostolic letter, *Ordinatio Sacerdotalis*, in which he reaffirms the position of *Inter Insigniores*. His final paragraph seeks to silence further discussion of the question of women's ordination by declaring 'that the Church has no authority whatsoever to confer priestly ordination on women and that this judgment is to be definitively held by all the Church's faithful'. This stops just short of a pronouncement of infallibility, but it gives considerable power to those who would silence any debate or discussion about women's ordination. (See Pope John Paul II, '*Ordinatio Sacerdotalis*: Apostolic Letter on Reserving Priestly Ordination to Men Alone', n. 4, 22 May 1994, at http://www.womenpriests.org / church / ordinati.asp [last accessed 7 April 2005].)
6 Sara Butler, 'The Priest as Sacrament of Christ the Bridegroom', *Worship*, Vol. 66, 6, November 1992: 498–517.
7 *Inter Insigniores*, 31.
8 *Inter Insigniores*, 33.
9 John Paul II, *Mulieris Dignitatem*: Apostolic Letter on the Dignity and Vocation of Women, London: Catholic Truth Society, 1988, n. 25.
10 Ibid.
11 Hans Urs von Balthasar, *Theo-Drama III: The Dramatis Personae: The Person in Christ*, translated by Graham Harrison, San Francisco: Ignatius Press, 1992 [1978], p. 358.
12 Ibid., p. 359.

13 Ibid., p. 354.
14 Ibid.
15 Ibid., p. 355.
16 Ibid.
17 Ibid., p. 356.
18 Ibid., p. 357.
19 Ibid., p. 358. Balthasar is referring to Newman, *The Prophetical Office in the Church* (1837, reprinted in *Via Media I*, 1877).
20 See Stephan Ackermann, 'The Church as Person in the Theology of Hans Urs von Balthasar', *Communio*, Vol. 29, 2, 2002: 238–49, for an analysis of Balthasar's idea of the personhood of the Church.
21 Hans Urs von Balthasar, *The Office of Peter and the Structure of the Church*, translated by Andrée Emery, San Francisco: Ignatius Press, 1986 [1974], p. 185.
22 See Balthasar, *Theo-Drama III*, p. 327.
23 Ibid., p. 371.
24 Edward T. Oakes, *Pattern of Redemption: The Theology of Hans Urs von Balthasar*, New York: Continuum, 1997, p. 261.
25 Balthasar, *Theo-Drama III*, p. 359.
26 Ibid., p. 29.
27 Ibid.
28 Ibid. Writing this at a time when Cardinal Ratzinger has just been elected Pope Benedict XVI, it is not difficult to see how this kind of ecclesiology encourages an unwielding authoritarianism in the Church hierarchy.
29 Hans Urs von Balthasar, *Heart of the World*, translated by Erasmo S. Leiva, San Francisco: Ignatius Press, 1979 [1954], pp. 193–4.
30 Ibid., p. 197.
31 Oakes, *Pattern of Redemption*, p. 262.
32 See Sara Butler, 'Second Thoughts on Ordaining Women', *Worship*, Vol. 63, 2, March 1989: 157–64.
33 See David N. Power OMI, 'Representing Christ in Community and Sacrament', in Donald J. Goergen OP (ed.), *Being a Priest Today*, Collegeville MN: The Liturgical Press, 1992.
34 Butler, 'The Priest as Sacrament', p. 505.
35 Ibid.
36 Ibid., p. 506.
37 Ibid., p. 507.
38 Ibid.
39 Ibid.
40 Ibid.
41 Ibid., p. 511.
42 Ibid., pp. 511–12.
43 Ibid., p. 512.
44 Michele M. Schumacher, 'The Unity of the Two: Toward a New Feminist Sacramentality of the Body', in Schumacher (ed.), *Women in Christ: Toward a New Feminism*, Grand Rapids MI and Cambridge UK: William B. Eerdmans, 2004, p. 226.

45 Susan A. Ross, 'God's Embodiment and Women', in Catherine Mowry LaCugna (ed.), *Freeing Theology: The Essentials of Theology in Feminist Perspective*, San Francisco: HarperCollins, 1993, p. 206, quoted in Schumacher, 'The Unity of the Two', p. 201.
46 Rosemary Radford Ruether, 'Women's Difference and Equal Rights in the Church', *Concilium*, Vol. 6, December 1991: 11–18, p. 14, quoted in Schumacher, 'The Unity of the Two', pp. 203–4.
47 Schumacher, 'The Unity of the Two', p. 211.
48 John Paul II, general audience of 20 February 1980. English translation from *The Theology of the Body: Human Love in the Divine Plan*, Boston: Daughters of St Paul, 1997, p. 76, quoted in Schumacher, 'The Unity of the Two', p. 206. This is the same catechesis on the Book of Genesis that I referred to earlier, published under the title *Original Unity of Man and Woman*.
49 Ibid.
50 Hans Urs von Balthasar, *A Theological Anthropology*, New York: Sheed and Ward, 1967, pp. 312–13, quoted in Schumacher, 'The Unity of the Two', p. 208.
51 Schumacher, 'The Unity of the Two', p. 209, quoting Balthasar, *A Theological Anthropology*, p. 313.
52 Schumacher, 'The Unity of the Two', p. 205.
53 Balthasar, *A Theological Anthropology*, p. 313, quoted in Schumacher, 'The Unity of the Two', pp. 215–16.
54 Michele M. Schumacher, 'The Nature of Nature in Feminism, Old and New: From Dualism to Complementary Unity', in Schumacher (ed.), *Women in Christ*, p. 38.
55 Butler, 'The Priest as Sacrament', p. 514, referring to Power, 'Representing Christ', p. 114.
56 Butler, 'The Priest as Sacrament', p. 515.
57 Ibid., p. 513.
58 Ibid.
59 Adrienne von Speyr, *The Handmaid of the Lord*, London: The Harvill Press, 1956, p. 84. One wonders if Speyr ever read the Magnificat, in which Mary gives eloquent prophetic expression to the meaning of God's revelation in Christ.
60 Monica Migliorino Miller, *Sexuality and Authority in the Catholic Church*, Scranton: University of Scranton Press; London and Toronto: Associated University Presses, 1995, p. 106.
61 Balthasar, 'The Uninterrupted Tradition of the Church', *L'Osservatore Romano*, 24 February 1977: 6–7, quoted in ibid., pp. 108–9. Miller's emphasis.
62 Ibid., p. 107.
63 Walter Ong, *Fighting for Life*, London: Cornell University Press, 1981, p. 77 quoted in Miller, *Sexuality and Authority*, p. 107.
64 I consider more nuanced aspects of Ong's position, which Miller does not refer to, in Chapter 12.
65 Ong, *Fighting for Life*, p. 62, quoted in Miller, *Sexuality and Authority*, p. 109.
66 Miller, *Sexuality and Authority*, p. 110.
67 Ibid., p. 112.
68 Balthasar, *Elucidations*, p. 349. See also the discussion in Tina Beattie, *God's Mother, Eve's Advocate: A Marian Narrative of Women's Salvation*, London and New York: Continuum, 2002 [1999], pp. 80–1.

334 *Notes*

69 Miller, *Sexuality and Authority*, p. 113.
70 Brendan Leahy, *The Marian Profile in the Ecclesiology of Hans Urs von Balthasar*, London: New City, 2000, pp. 180–1.
71 Hans Urs von Balthasar, 'Women Priests? A Marian Church in a Fatherless and Motherless Culture', *Communio*, Vol. 22, Spring 1995: 164–70, p. 169.
72 Ibid., p. 170.
73 Luce Irigaray, *This Sex Which Is Not One*, translated by Catherine Porter with Carolyn Burke, Ithaca NY: Cornell University Press, 1985 [1977], p. 74.
74 Ibid.

8   Desire, death and the female body

1 Hans Urs von Balthasar, *Theo-Drama III: The Dramatis Personae: The Person in Christ*, translated by Graham Harrison, San Francisco: Ignatius Press, 1992 [1978], p. 325.
2 Hans Urs von Balthasar, *Theo-Drama: Theological Dramatic Theory, Vol. II: The Dramatis Personae: Man in God*, translated by Graham Harrison, San Francisco: Ignatius Press, 1990 [1976], p. 382.
3 Aidan Nichols OP, *No Bloodless Myth: A Guide Through Balthasar's Dramatics*, Edinburgh: T. & T. Clark, 2000, p. 86.
4 Balthasar, *Theo-Drama II*, pp. 413–14.
5 See, for example, Gerard Loughlin's discussion of Balthasar's writing on Dante. Loughlin points out that, although Balthasar claims that Dante's *Divina Commedia* represents 'the compatibility of earthly and heavenly desire . . . Dante and Beatrice didn't do it. Flesh is glorified, made to participate in the divine effulgence, but only so long as it is not touched, fondled or caressed' (Gerard Loughlin, *Alien Sex: The Body and Desire in Cinema and Theology*, Malden MA and Oxford: Blackwell, 2004, p. 173). For Balthasar on Dante, see various references in Hans Urs von Balthasar, *The Glory of the Lord, Vol. V: The Realm of Metaphysics in the Modern Age*, translated by Oliver Davies, Edinburgh: T. & T. Clark, 1991.
6 Balthasar, *Theo-Drama II*, p. 412.
7 See Chapter 7. See also Lucy Gardner and David Moss, 'Something like Time; Something like the Sexes – an Essay in Reception', in Gardner *et al.* (eds), *Balthasar at the End of Modernity*, Edinburgh: T. & T. Clark, 1999.
8 Balthasar, *Theo-Drama III*, p. 290.
9 Ibid., p. 294.
10 Ibid., p. 295.
11 See Luce Irigaray, *An Ethics of Sexual Difference*, translated by Carolyn Burke and Gillian C. Gill, London: The Athlone Press, 1993. See also Tina Chanter, *Ethics of Eros: Irigaray's Rewriting of the Philosophers*, New York and London: Routledge, 1995, pp. 146–51.
12 Luce Irigaray, *Speculum of the Other Woman*, translated by Gillian C. Gill, Ithaca NY: Cornell University Press, 1985 [1974], p. 245.
13 Balthasar, *Theo-Drama III*, p. 292.
14 Ibid., p. 293.
15 Ibid., p. 305.

16   Ibid., p. 306.
17   Ibid., p. 310.
18   Ibid.
19   See ibid., pp. 317–18.
20   Ibid., p. 342.
21   Ibid., p. 348.
22   Ibid., p. 351.
23   Balthasar, *Theo-Drama II*, p. 374, quoting Fichte, *Angewendete Philosophie*, Vorlesungen, 1813, 521–2.
24   Ibid., p. 377, quoting Thomas Aquinas, *Summa Theologiae*, q.98, a I c, translated by the Dominican Fathers, London: Burns, Oates and Washbourne, 1912–36.
25   Loughlin, *Alien Sex*, p. 154.
26   For Loughlin's nuanced deconstruction of Balthasar's sexual polarities, see ibid., pp. 143–61.
27   Hans Urs von Balthasar, *Explorations in Theology III: Creator Spirit*, translated by Brian McNeil CRV, San Francisco: Ignatius Press, 1993 [1967], p. 19.
28   Ibid., p. 20.
29   Nichols, *No Bloodless Myth*, p. 219. See the discussion of Heidegger and death in Hans Urs von Balthasar, *Theo-Drama: Theological Dramatic Theory, Vol. V: The Last Act*, translated by Graham Harrison, San Francisco: Ignatius Press, 1998 [1983], pp. 323–6.
30   For an exploration of these ideas, see Balthasar, *Theo-Drama V*, pp. 191–369.
31   John O'Donnell SJ, *Hans Urs von Balthasar*, London: Geoffrey Chapman, 1992, p. 31.
32   Balthasar, *Theo-Drama V*, p. 521. This final section of *Theo-Drama V* offers a helpful summary of many of Balthasar's ideas – see pp. 489–521.
33   Graham Ward, 'Kenosis: Death, Discourse and Resurrection', in Lucy Gardner *et al.* (eds), *Balthasar at the End of Modernity*, Edinburgh: T. & T. Clark, p. 35.
34   Ibid., p. 39.
35   Ibid., pp. 35–6.
36   Ibid., p. 36.
37   Ibid.
38   Ibid., p. 44.
39   Ibid.
40   Ibid., p. 45.
41   Balthasar, *Theo-Drama II*, p. 418.
42   Balthasar, *Theo-Drama V*, p. 504.
43   Ibid. See Anders Nygren, *Agape and Eros*, translated by Philip S. Watson, London: SPCK, 1982.
44   Balthasar, *Theo-Drama V*, p. 505.
45   Ibid.
46   Ibid.
47   Ibid., p. 506.
48   See Sarah Coakley, 'Kenosis and Subversion: On the Repression of "Vulnerability" in Christian Feminist Writing', in Coakley (ed.), *Powers and Submissions: Spirituality, Philosophy and Gender*, Oxford: Blackwell, 2002, p. 29, referring to Richard Swinburne, *The Christian God*, Oxford: Clarendon Press, 1994, and 'Could God Become Man?' in G. Vesey (ed.), *The Philosophy in Christianity*, Cambridge: Cambridge University Press, 1989.

336 Notes

49 Ibid., p. 30.
50 Ibid., p. 37.
51 Ibid., pp. 12–13.

9 Sex, death and melodrama

1 Johann Roten SM, 'The Two Halves of the Moon: Marian Anthropological Dimensions in the Common Mission of Adrienne von Speyr and Hans Urs von Balthasar', in David L. Schindler (ed.), *Hans Urs von Balthasar: His Life and Work*, San Francisco: Communio Books, Ignatius Press, 1991, p. 83.
2 Ibid., p. 85.
3 Ibid., pp. 85–6.
4 Angelo Scola, *Hans Urs von Balthasar: A Theological Style*, Edinburgh: T. & T. Clark, 1995 [1991], p. 11.
5 Michelle Gonzalez, 'Hans Urs von Balthasar and Contemporary Feminist Theology', *Theological Studies*, 65, 3, 2004: 566–95, p. 579.
6 Hans Urs von Balthasar, *First Glance at Adrienne von Speyr*, translated by Antje Lawry and Sr Sergia Englund OCD, 1981 [1968], p. 68.
7 Ibid.
8 Ibid., pp. 34–5.
9 Ibid., p. 35.
10 Ibid., p. 44.
11 Ibid., p. 69.
12 Ibid.
13 Ibid., p. 73, referring to Adrienne von Speyr, *Erde und Himmel. Teil II: Die Zeit der grossen Diktate* (1944–9), paragraphs 1645 and 1729.
14 Ibid., referring to Speyr, *Erde und Himmel II*, 1645.
15 See ibid., pp. 72–3.
16 Ibid., p. 74, quoting Speyr, *Erde und Himmel II*, 1215, 1265, 1325.
17 Ibid., p. 75.
18 Ibid., referring to Speyr, *Erde und Himmel*, Teil I: *Einübungen* (1940–4), paragraph 123.
19 See Teresa Brennan, *The Interpretation of the Flesh: Freud and Femininity*, London and New York: Routledge, 1992. In Brennan's study of Freud, she argues that his female analysands psychosomatically internalized his own rejected femininity that he projected onto them, so that they in turn projected it back at him, thus confirming his stereotypes of femininity by their behaviour and symptoms.
20 Balthasar's writings on death and hell are widely regarded as the most original and provocative aspect of his theology, particularly with regard to what some see as his universalism. Although he is careful to distance himself from the concept of *apokatastasis* – the certainty that everything will be saved – he also argues that the New Testament does not necessarily support the idea of a populated hell, and his understanding of the ultimate pattern or form of Christian redemption leads him to argue strongly in favour of the hope of universal salvation. See Hans Urs von Balthasar, *The Glory of the Lord, Vol. V: The Realm of Metaphysics in the Modern Age*, translated by Oliver Davies, Edinburgh: T. & T. Clark, 1991, pp. 269–90. For a summary of Balthasar's

eschatology and his response to critics, see Hans Urs von Balthasar, *Dare We Hope 'that all men be saved?' with, A Short Discourse on Hell*, translated by David Kipp and Lothar Krauth, San Francisco: Ignatius Press, 1992. See also the discussion in James T. O'Connor, 'Von Balthasar and Salvation', *Homiletic & Pastoral Review*, July 1989: 10–21. For a helpful survey, see Geoffrey Wainwright, 'Eschatology', in Edward T. Oakes and David Moss (eds), *The Cambridge Companion to Hans Urs von Balthasar*, Cambridge: Cambridge University Press, 2004. For a more critical analysis, see Ben Quash, 'Drama and the Ends of Modernity', in Lucy Gardner *et al.* (eds), *Balthasar at the End of Modernity*, Edinburgh: T. & T. Clark, 1999.

21 Graham Ward, 'Kenosis: Death, Discourse and Resurrection', in Lucy Gardner *et al.* (eds), *Balthasar at the End of Modernity*, p. 48.
22 Hans Urs von Balthasar, *Mysterium Paschale: The Mystery of Easter*, translated by Aidan Nichols OP, Edinburgh: T. & T. Clark, 1990, p. 150.
23 Ben Quash, 'Drama and the Ends of Modernity', in Lucy Gardner *et al.* (eds), *Balthasar at the End of Modernity*, p. 167.
24 Luce Irigaray, *Speculum of the Other Woman*, translated by Gillian C. Gill, Ithaca NY: Cornell University Press, 1985 [1974], pp. 191–2.
25 Balthasar, *Mysterium Paschale*, p. 151.
26 Ibid., p. 151.
27 Ibid., p. 153.
28 Ibid.
29 Ibid., p. 154.
30 Ibid., p. 165.
31 Ibid., p. 173.
32 Ibid.
33 Ibid., p. 173.
34 Ibid., pp. 173–4, referring to the following sources: L. Eizenhöfer, 'Taetrum chaos illabitur', ALW 2 (1952), pp. 94 ff; Peter Chrysologus, Sermo 74, 'Movetur chaos' (PL 52, 409C); Eriugena, *De Divisionibus Naturae* V. 6 (PL 122, 873c); A. Gügler, 'Die Hölle' in *Nachgelassene Schriften* V, Lucerne, 1836, pp. 545–69.
35 Andrew Louth, 'The Place of *Heart of the World* in the Theology of Hans Urs von Balthasar', in John Riches (ed.), *The Analogy of Beauty: The Theology of Hans Urs von Balthasar*, Edinburgh: T. & T. Clark, 1986, p. 148.
36 Peter Henrici SJ, 'A Sketch of von Balthasar's Life', in David L. Schindler (ed.), *Hans Urs von Balthasar: His Life and Work*, San Francisco: Communio Books, Ignatius Press, 1991, p. 31.
37 Erasmo Leiva, 'Translator's Note' in Hans Urs von Balthasar, *Heart of the World*, translated by Erasmo Leiva, San Francisco: Ignatius Press, 1979 [1954], p. 7.
38 Ibid.
39 Cf ibid., p. 142, when the narrative voice becomes Isaac pleading to Abraham – 'Do not, my Father, draw out your knife over me!' with an implicit suggestion that this is Christ's voice.
40 Ibid., p. 135.
41 Ibid., p. 138.
42 Ibid., p. 142.
43 Ibid., p. 142.

44 Ibid., p. 148.
45 Ibid., p. 151.
46 Ibid., p. 152.
47 Ibid.
48 Ibid., pp. 152–3.
49 Louth, 'The Place of *Heart of the World*', p. 158.
50 Irigaray, *Speculum*, p. 196.
51 Balthasar, *Heart of the World*, p. 176.
52 Ibid., p. 177.
53 Ibid., p. 185.
54 Ibid., p. 192.
55 Ibid., pp. 194–7.
56 Catherine of Siena, *I, Catherine: Selected Writings of Catherine of Siena*, translated by and edited by Kenelm Foster OP and Mary John Ronayne OP, London: Collins, 1980, p. 71.
57 Ibid., p. 72.
58 Hans Urs von Balthasar, *Explorations in Theology II: Spouse of the Word*, San Francisco: Ignatius Press, 1991 [1961], p. 196.
59 Ibid., pp. 196–8, referring to H. Riedlinger's transcription in *Hoheliedkommentare des MA* (1958), pp. 255 f.
60 J. Cheryl Exum, *Plotted, Shot, and Painted: Cultural Representations of Biblical Women*, Sheffield: Sheffield Academic Press, 1996, p. 102.
61 Ibid., p. 115.
62 Ibid., pp. 118–19.
63 Ibid., p. 120, quoting Robert C. Carroll, 'Desire under the Terebinths: On Pornographic Representation in the Prophets – a Response', in Athalya Brenner (ed.), *A Feminist Companion to the Latter Prophets*, Sheffield: Sheffield Academic Press, 1995, pp. 275–307, p. 285.
64 Ibid., quoting Carroll, 'Desire under the Terebinths', p. 292.
65 Ibid.
66 Balthasar, *First Glance*, p. 172.
67 Ibid.
68 Ibid., pp. 174–5.
69 The idea that a confessor could compel someone to reveal the secrets of the confessional as an act of obedience should in itself raise questions about Balthasar's priestly integrity in relation to Speyr.
70 Balthasar, *First Glance*, p. 178.
71 Hans Urs von Balthasar, *Theo-Drama: Theological Dramatic Theory, Vol. II: The Dramatis Personae: Man in God*, translated by Graham Harrison, San Francisco: Ignatius Press, 1990 [1976], p. 198.
72 Balthasar, *First Glance*, p. 44–5.
73 Roten, 'The Two Halves of the Moon', p. 74, quoting Speyr, *Erde und Himmel II*, 1680.
74 See ibid., pp. 78 ff.
75 Ibid., p. 80.
76 Ibid., p. 79.

77 According to Roten she died of bowel cancer, but she was also blind, obese and housebound for most of the years Balthasar spent with her.
78 Roten, 'The Two Halves of the Moon', p. 68.
79 Balthasar, *Spouse of the Word*, pp. 238 f.
80 Ibid., p. 239.
81 Ibid.
82 Ibid.
83 Ibid., p. 243.
84 Ibid., p. 241.
85 'Jewish Christian Relations', 'Negative images of Judaism in Christian Art ó Ecclesia and Synagoga', at http://www.sprezzatura.it/Arte/Ecclesia_Synagoga/res/art1.htm (last accessed 11 January 2005). See also Sara Lipton, 'The Temple is my Body: Gender, Carnality, and Synagoga in the Bible Moralisée', in Eva Frojmovic (ed.), *Imaging the Self, Imaging the Other: Visual Representation and Jewish–Christian Dynamics in the Middle Ages and Early Modern Period*, Cultures, Beliefs, and Traditions, Leiden: Brill, 2002.
86 See Richard L. Rubenstein and John K. Roth (eds), *Approaches to Auschwitz: The Holocaust and its Legacy*, Atlanta GA: John Knox Press, 1987.
87 In this respect, see also Philippa Berry's critique of Irigaray's metaphors of fire in Philippa Berry, 'The Burning Glass', in Carolyn Burke, Naomi Schor and Margaret Whitford (eds), *Engaging with Irigaray*, New York: Columba University Press, 1994.
88 Donald MacKinnon, 'Some Reflections on Hans Urs von Balthasar's Christology with Special Reference to *Theodramatik II/2* and *III*, including Appendix', in John Riches (ed.), *The Analogy of Beauty: The Theology of Hans Urs von Balthasar*, Edinburgh: T. & T. Clark, p. 165.
89 MacKinnon, 'Reflections', p. 179. Mackinnon is referring in particular to the last volume of *Theo-Drama*.
90 Alan Ecclestone, *Yes to God*, London: Darton, Longman & Todd, 1990 [1975], p. 93. See Hans Urs von Balthasar, *Prayer*, translated by A.V. Littledale, London: SPCK, 1973.
91 Quash, 'Drama and the Ends of Modernity', p. 167. See also Thomas G. Dalzell SM, 'Lack of Social Drama in Balthasar's Theological Dramatics', *Theological Studies*, Vol. 60, 1999: 457–75.
92 Balthasar, *Theo-Drama II*, p. 27.
93 Ibid.
94 Aristotle Papanikolaou, 'Person, Kenosis and Abuse: Hans Urs von Balthasar and Feminist Theologies in Conversation', *Modern Theology*, Vol. 19, 1, January 2003: 41–65, p. 42.
95 It is interesting to note that Michelle Gonzalez, although offering a restrained feminist critique of Balthasar, gives a positive interpretation to Papanikolaou's interpretation. Even approaching him as a critical feminist reader, Gonzalez fails to problematize the violence in Balthasar's language. See Gonzalez, 'Hans Urs von Balthasar'.
96 See Tina Beattie, *God's Mother, Eve's Advocate: A Marian Narrative of Women's Salvation*, London and New York: Continuum, 2002 [1999], pp. 45–70.
97 See Gillian Rose, *The Broken Middle: Out of Our Ancient Society*, Oxford UK and Cambridge MA: Blackwell, 1992.
98. Irigaray, *Marine Lover*, pp. 67–72.

10   Being beyond death

1. See Tina Beattie, 'Redeeming Mary: The Potential of Marian Symbolism for Feminist Philosophy of Religion', in Pamela Sue Anderson and Beverley Clack (eds), *Feminist Philosophy of Religion: Critical Readings*, London and New York: Routledge, 2004 for a development of this suggestion.
2. Cf Melanie Klein, 'Some Theoretical Conclusions Regarding the Emotional Life of the Infant', in Joan Riviere (ed.), *Developments in Psycho-Analysis*, London: The Hogarth Press and the Institute of Psycho-Analysis, 1952. See also Juliet Mitchell (ed.), *The Selected Melanie Klein*, Harmondsworth: Penguin Books, 1986.
3. Diane Jonte-Pace, 'Situating Kristeva Differently: Psychoanalytic Readings of Woman and Religion', in David R. Crownfield (ed.), *Body/Text in Julia Kristeva: Religion, Women, and Psychoanalysis*, Albany NY: State University of New York, 1992, p. 21.
4. Beverley Clack, *Sex and Death: A Reappraisal of Human Mortality*, Cambridge: Polity Press, 2002, p. 3.
5. Ibid.
6. Ibid.
7. Ruether remains 'agnostic' with regard to what form, if any, life might take beyond death. However, in her feminist critique of Christian eschatology, she too argues that the quest for transcendence associated with Christian beliefs about life after death results in hostility towards female carnality and the physical world. See Rosemary Radford Ruether, *Sexism and God-Talk: Towards a Feminist Theology*, London: SCM Press, 1982 [1983], pp. 235–58. In *Women and Redemption*, she develops this idea by focusing on the shift to a 'this-worldly progressive hope' (p. 274) in some nineteenth- and twentieth-century theologies. See Ruether, *Women and Redemption: A Theological History*, London: SCM Press, 1998, pp. 273–5.
8. Clack, *Sex and Death*, pp. 134–5.
9. Annie Dillard, 'The Book of Luke', in *The Annie Dillard Reader*, New York: HarperCollins, 1995 [1994], p. 265.
10. See Grace M. Jantzen, *Becoming Divine: Towards a Feminist Philosophy of Religion*, Manchester: Manchester University Press, 1998, pp. 129–31.
11. Ibid., p. 129.
12. Freud first introduced the idea of the death drive in 1920 in *Beyond the Pleasure Principle* after which time it becomes an integral part of his psychoanalytic theory (see Sigmund Freud, 'Beyond the Pleasure Principle', *On Metapsychology: The Theory of Psychoanalysis*, The Penguin Freud Library, Harmondsworth: Penguin Books, 1991 [1920]). *Eros*, or the sex drive, is associated with the desire for life and integration, but it must always struggle against *thanatos*, which is the desire for death and dissolution. Cf Sigmund Freud, 'Anxiety and Instinctual Life', in James Strachey (ed.), *New Introductory Lectures on Psychoanalysis*, The Penguin Freud Library, Harmondsworth: Penguin Books, 1991 [1933].
13. Cf Sigmund Freud, 'Femininity', in James Strachey (ed.), *New Introductory Lectures on Psychoanalysis*. This essay gives excellent insights into Freud's continuing bewilderment with regard to the workings of the female psyche. The essay concludes with the admission that it is 'incomplete and fragmentary and does not always sound friendly' (p. 169). In the final sentence, Freud recommends, 'If you want to know more about

femininity, inquire from your own experiences of life, or turn to the poets, or wait until science can give you deeper and more coherent information' (p. 169). It is this combination of denigration and bafflement in Freud's evaluation of femininity that provides the basis of Irigaray's extensive critique.
14 Jantzen, *Becoming Divine*, p. 44.
15 Sigmund Freud, 'The Future of an Illusion', in James Strachey (ed.), *New Introductory Lectures on Psychoanalysis*.
16 Ibid., p. 195.
17 Hans Urs von Balthasar, *Mysterium Paschale: The Mystery of Easter*, translated by Aidan Nichols OP, Edinburgh: T. & T. Clark, 1990, p. 39.
18 Ibid., p. 150.
19 Jantzen, *Becoming Divine*, p. 45.
20 Ibid.
21 Like other French theorists such as Irigaray, Kristeva and Derrida, and unlike Anglo-American secular thinkers, Lacan weaves themes of religion and God into his thinking in a way that makes it impossible to isolate particular texts. However, an excellent selection of his work relevant to the themes of woman, God, sexuality and death can be found in Juliet Mitchell and Jacqueline Rose (eds), *Feminine Sexuality: Jacques Lacan and the école freudienne*, Basingstoke and London: Macmillan, 1982. See also Jacques Lacan, *Écrits: A Selection*, translated by Alan Sheridan, London: Tavistock/Routledge, 1977 [1966].
22 Jantzen, *Becoming Divine*, p. 46.
23 See Jacqueline Rose, 'Introduction – II', in Mitchell and Rose (eds), *Feminine Sexuality*, p. 37.
24 For a helpful summary of the mirror stage, see Jonathan Scott Lee, *Jacques Lacan*, Boston MA: Twayne Publishers, 1990, pp. 17–25.
25 See ibid., pp. 135–70.
26 See Rose, 'Introduction – II', p. 38.
27 Ibid.
28 See ibid., p. 48; Lee, *Jacques Lacan*, pp. 143–5.
29 Lee, *Jacques Lacan*, pp. 66–7.
30 Luce Irigaray, *Sexes and Genealogies*, translated by Gillian C. Gill, New York: Columbia University Press, 1993 [1987], p. 21.
31 Rose, 'Introduction – II', p. 49.
32 Jacques Lacan, 'God and the *Jouissance* of The Woman', in Mitchell and Rose (eds), *Feminine Sexuality*, p. 143.
33 Ibid., p. 142. For an interesting critique of Lacan's mystification of the word *jouissance*, see Toril Moi, 'From Femininity to Finitude: Freud, Lacan, and Feminism, Again', *Signs*, Vol. 29, 3, Spring 2004: 841–78.
34 Lacan, 'God and the *Jouissance* of The Woman', p. 138.
35 Ibid., p. 140.
36 Ibid.
37 Ibid., p. 141.
38 Ibid., p. 142.
39 Ibid.
40 Ibid., p. 143.

41 Ibid.
42 Ibid.
43 Jantzen, *Becoming Divine*, p. 50.
44 Ibid.
45 Lacan, 'God and the *Jouissance* of The Woman', p. 147. Lacan's emphasis.
46 Ibid.
47 Rose, 'Introduction – II', p. 34.
48 Lacan, *Écrits*, p. 104 quoted in Jantzen, *Becoming Divine*, p. 46.
49 Malcolm Bowie, *Lacan*, Fontana Modern Masters, London: HarperCollins, 1991, p. 162, quoted in Jantzen, *Becoming Divine*, p. 46.
50 Lacan, 'The Direction of the Treatment', *Écrits*, 642/276–7, quoted in Lee, *Jacques Lacan*, p. 92.
51 See ibid., pp. 91–9.
52 Ibid., p. 92.
53 Ibid., p. 96.
54 Ibid., p. 80.
55 Ibid., p. 81.
56 Ibid., p. 80, quoting Lacan, *Écrits*, 408/121.
57 Lacan, 'God and the *Jouissance* of The Woman', p. 144.
58 Heidegger, *Being and Time*, p. 294.
59 Cf ibid., pp. 295–6.
60 Ibid., p. 307.
61 Jantzen, *Becoming Divine*, p. 245.
62 Ibid., p. 246, quoting Seyla Benhabib, *The Reluctant Modernism of Hannah Arendt* London: Sage, 1996, p. 56.
63 Heidegger, *Being and Time*, p. 294.
64 Ibid.
65 Jantzen, *Becoming Divine*, p. 133.
66 For a helpful overview of Girard's thought, see René Girard, 'Generative Scapegoating', in Robert Hamerton-Kelly (ed.), *Violent Origins: Walter Burkert, René Girard and Jonathan Z. Smith on Ritual Killing and Cultural Formation*, Stanford: Stanford University Press, 1987. For his most developed treatment of the relevance of his theory to Christianity, see René Girard, *Things Hidden Since the Foundation of the World*, translated by Stephen Bann and Michael Metteer, London: The Athlone Press, 1987 [1978].
67 René Girard, 'Freud and the Oedipus Complex', in James G. Williams (ed.), *The Girard Reader*, New York: Crossroad, 1996, p. 228, referring to Freud's 1923 essay, *The Ego and the Id* (Freud, *Standard Edition*, vol. 19).
68 Ibid., p. 242. For a more extended critique of Lacan, see Girard, *Things Hidden*, pp. 402–5.
69 See Girard, 'Freud and the Oedipus Complex', p. 242, referring to Lacan's article, 'Aggression in Psychoanalysis', in *Écrits* (Paris: Seuil, 1966). Girard quotes Lacan's observation that 'The structural effect of the identification with the rival does not follow naturally, except perhaps in mythic thinking' (p. 117).
70 Girard's theory repeats the androcentrism of Freud's theory here. Readers may or may not be persuaded by the editor's defensive preface which rejects feminist criticisms of

Girard as ill-informed and politically motivated. See James G. Williams in *The Girard Reader*, p. 227. I say more in Chapter 11 about feminist interpretations of Girard.
71 Ibid., p. 232.
72 Girard, *Things Hidden*, p. 291.
73 Girard, 'Freud and the Oedipus Complex', p. 233.
74 Ibid., p. 234.
75 Ibid.
76 Hans Urs von Balthasar, *Heart of the World*, translated by Erasmo S. Leiva, San Francisco: Ignatius Press, 1979 [1954], p. 148.
77 Girard, *Things Hidden*, p. 299.
78 See ibid., p. 327. Girard is cautious about describing this as 'masochism', because he seeks to maintain a distance between his own theoretical position and that of psychoanalysis. Indeed, reading the extent of Girard's vitriol against psychoanalysis, one might wonder what kind of rivalrous relationship between model and disciple might be operating between Girard and Freud!
79 See ibid., pp. 326–51.
80 See René Girard, 'Sacrifice as Sacral Violence and Substitution' and 'Stereotypes of Perspection', in James G. Williams (ed.), *The Girard Reader*.
81 See René Girard, *Violence and the Sacred*, translated by Patrick Gregory, Baltimore: The Johns Hopkins University Press, 1977 [1972].
82 See René Girard, 'Mimesis and Violence', in James G. Williams (ed.), *The Girard Reader*.
83 Ibid., p. 18.
84 Girard, *Things Hidden*, p. 182.
85 Ibid., p. 219.
86 Ibid., p. 430.
87 Ibid., p. 431.
88 See Tina Beattie, 'A Roman Catholic's View on the Apostolicity of Women', in Harriet Harris and Jane Shaw (eds), *The Call for Women Bishops*, London: SPCK, 2004.

11   Maternal beginnings

1 I use the term 'Catholic' broadly here – Kristeva comes from an Orthodox background.
2 See René Girard, *Things Hidden Since the Foundation of the World*, translated by Stephen Bann and Michael Metteer, London: The Athlone Press, 1987 [1978].
3 Ibid., p. 404.
4 Sigmund Freud, *Standard Edition* XVIII, 16, quoted in ibid.
5 For a helpful summary of feminist responses to Girard, see Michael Kirwan, *Discovering Girard*, London: Darton, Longman & Todd, 2004. See also Susan Nowak, 'The Girardian Theory and Feminism: Critique and Appropriation', *Contagion: Journal of Violence, Mimesis and Culture*, Vol. 1, Spring 1994: 19–29; Pamela Sue Anderson, 'Sacrificed Lives: Mimetic Desire, Sexual Difference and Murder', *Cultural Values*, Vol. 4, 2, 2000: pp. 216–27.
6 René Girard, 'The Anthropology of the Cross: A Conversation with René Girard', in James G. Williams (ed.), *The Girard Reader*, New York: Crossroad, 1996, p. 276.

7 Girard, 'Freud and the Oedipus Complex', in James G. Williams (ed.), *The Girard Reader*, New York: Crossroad, 1996, p. 275.
8 Ibid.
9 Ibid., p. 276.
10 Martha Reineke, 'The Mother in Mimesis: Kristeva and Girard on Violence and the Sacred', in David R. Crownfield (ed.), *Body/Text in Julia Kristeva: Religion, Women, and Psychoanalysis*, Albany NY: State University of New York, 1992, p. 69.
11 Diane Jonte-Pace, 'Situating Kristeva Differently: Psychoanalytic Readings of Woman and Religion', in Crownfield (ed.), *Body/Text in Julia Kristeva*, p. 10.
12 See Julia Kristeva, 'Revolution in Poetic Language', in Toril Moi (ed.), *The Kristeva Reader*, Oxford and Cambridge MA: Blackwell, 1986 [1974]. See also Elizabeth Grosz, *Sexual Subversions: Three French Feminists*, St. Leonards NSW: Allen & Unwin, 1989, pp. 42–4.
13 Julia Kristeva, *In the Beginning was Love: Psychoanalysis and Faith*, translated by Arthur Goldhammer, New York: Columbia University Press, 1987 [1985], p. 5.
14 Julia Kristeva, *New Maladies of the Soul*, translated by Ross Guberman, New York and Chichester: Columbia University Press, 1995 [1993], p. 118.
15 Ibid., p. 119.
16 Ibid.
17 See Julia Kristeva, *Powers of Horror: An Essay on Abjection*, translated by Leon S. Roudiez, New York: Columbia University Press, 1982 [1980], p. 92. See also Mary Douglas, *Purity and Danger: An Analysis of the Concepts of Pollution and Taboo*, London and New York: Routledge, 1996 [1966].
18 See also Derrida's discussion of circumcision as a mark of identity and separation from the mother in Jacques Derrida, *Circumfession*, in Geoffrey Bennington and Derrida, *Jacques Derrida*, Chicago: University of Chicago Press, 1993.
19 Kristeva, *Powers of Horror*, p. 100. Italics in original.
20 Ibid., p. 106.
21 Ibid., p. 107.
22 Ibid., p. 112.
23 Ibid., p. 114.
24 Ibid.
25 Ibid., p. 115.
26 Ibid., p. 117.
27 Ibid., p. 120.
28 Ibid.
29 Ibid.
30 Reineke, 'The Mother in Mimesis', p. 79.
31 Kristeva, *Powers of Horror*, p. 122.
32 Ibid.
33 Ibid., p. 123.
34 Julia Kristeva, *Strangers to Ourselves*, translated by Leon S. Roudiez, Hemel Hempstead: Harvester, 1991 [1989].
35 Ibid., p. 183.
36 Ibid., p. 192.
37 Julia Kristeva, 'Women's Time', in *The Kristeva Reader*, p. 199.

38 Ibid., p. 189.
39 Ibid., p. 202.
40 Ibid., p. 204.
41 Ibid. Writing in the 1970s, Kristeva points to the involvement of women in terrorist groups such as the Baader-Meinhoff Gang, Palestinian commandos and the Red Brigades as evidence of this potential unleashing of anarchic and ultimately self-destructive violence. This raises questions about the extent to which women risk becoming drawn into both so-called acts of terror and the war on terror through their participation in resistance movements on the one hand, and in military institutions on the other.
42 Ibid., p. 205.
43 Ibid.
44 The late 1970s mark a significant transition between Kristeva's early, highly theoretical work on linguistics and her later, more lyrical work on themes of love, motherhood, religion and language. Some suggest that this change in emphasis is related to the birth of her child.
45 Kristeva, 'Women's Time', p. 206.
46 See Christine Battersby's development of these ideas in Christine Battersby, *The Phenomenal Woman: Feminist Metaphysics and the Patterns of Identity*, Cambridge: Polity Press, 1998.
47 Kristeva, 'Women's Time', p. 205.
48 Ibid., p. 209.
49 Ibid., p. 210. Her italics.
50 Reineke, 'The Mother in Mimesis', p. 81.
51 See Marina Warner, *Alone of All Her Sex: The Myth and Cult of the Virgin Mary*, London: Vintage, 2000 [1976].
52 Julia Kristeva, 'Stabat Mater', in *Tales of Love*, translated by Leon S. Roudiez, New York: Columbia University Press, 1987 [1983], p. 263.
53 Ibid.
54 Julia Kristeva, 'Freud and Love: Treatment and Its Discontents', in *Tales of Love*, p. 34.
55 Ibid., p. 33.
56 Reineke, 'The Mother in Mimesis', p. 74.
57 See Kristeva, 'Freud and Love', pp. 21–4.
58 David R. Crownfield, 'The Sublimation of Narcissism in Christian Love and Faith', in Crownfield (ed.), *Body/Text in Julia Kristeva*, p. 61. See the various essays on narcissism, Christianity and psychoanalysis in Kristeva, *Tales of Love*.
59 Kristeva, *New Maladies*, p. 4.
60 Ibid., pp. 7–8.
61 Ibid., pp. 124–5.
62 Kristeva, *In the Beginning was Love*, p. 18.
63 Ibid., p. 19.
64 Crownfield, 'The Sublimation of Narcissism', p. 63.
65 Ibid.
66 Ibid.

12 Redeeming fatherhood

1 Cf Janet Martin Soskice, 'Can a Feminist Call God "Father"?' in Teresa Elwes (ed.), *Women's Voices: Essays in Contemporary Feminist Theology*, London: HarperCollins, 1992.
2 Hans Urs von Balthasar, *Theo-Drama: Theological Dramatic Theory, Volume IV: The Action*, translated by Graham Harrison, San Francisco: Ignatius Press, 1994 [1980], p. 299. See also John O'Donnell SJ, *Hans Urs von Balthasar*, London: Geoffrey Chapman, 1992, pp. 105–8; Michael Kirwan, *Discovering Girard*, London: Darton, Longman & Todd, pp. 108–10.
3 Balthasar, *Theo-Drama IV*, p. 308.
4 Ibid., p. 309.
5 See ibid.
6 Ibid., pp. 309–10.
7 Ibid., p. 309, referring to Raymund Schwager, *Brauchen wir einen Sündenbock? Gewalt und Erlosung in den biblischen Schriften*, München: Kosel, 1978; English translation: *Must There be Scapegoats? Violence and Redemption in the Bible*, San Francisco: Harper & Row, 1987.
8 Ibid., p. 501.
9 Donald MacKinnon, 'Some Reflections on Hans Urs von Balthasar's Christology with Special Reference to Theodramatik II/2 and III, including Appendix', in John Riches (ed.), *The Analogy of Beauty: The Theology of Hans Urs von Balthasar*, Edinburgh: T. & T. Clark, 1986, p. 165; Andrew Louth, 'The Place of *Heart of the World* in the Theology of Hans Urs von Balthasar' in Riches (ed.), *The Analogy of Beauty*, p. 165.
10 See Hans Urs von Balthasar, *Theo-Drama: Theological Dramatic Theory, Vol. II: The Dramatis Personae: Man in God*, translated by Graham Harrison, San Francisco: Ignatius Press, 1990 [1976], pp. 33–6.
11 Ibid., p. 32.
12 Ibid., p. 33.
13 Ibid.
14 Ibid.
15 Ibid., p. 34.
16 Ibid., p. 35.
17 Ibid.
18 Synod of Bishops, XI Ordinary General Assembly, 'The Eucharist: Source and Summit of the Life and Mission of the Church', Lineamenta, *Libreria Editrice Vaticana*, quoting John Chrysostom, *De Sacerdotio*, III, 4: SCh 272, 142–44, at http://www.vatican.va/roman_curia/synod/documents/rc_synod_doc_20040528_lineamenta-xi-assembly_en.html#_ftnref41 (last accessed 30 December 2004).
19 Another Catholic woman wrote to me after reading something I had written on the Mass and sacrifice, admitting that for many years she had been troubled by the Church's language of sacrifice, but had been afraid to say anything in case she caused offence. She expressed great relief to discover that she was not alone in her reservations.
20 Walter Ong, *Fighting for Life*, London: Cornell University Press, p. 169.
21 Ibid.

22 Ibid.
23 Ibid., p. 170.
24 Ibid., p. 171.
25 Ibid., p. 168.
26 Ibid., p. 169.
27 Ibid., p. 171.
28 Ibid. It should be noted that Miller reads Ong in an entirely anti-feminist way, so she makes no mention of this positive evaluation of the influence of feminism.
29 Ibid., p. 178.
30 Ibid.
31 Ibid.
32 Ibid., p. 179.
33 Ibid., pp. 179–80.
34 Ibid., p. 180.
35 Ibid.
36 Ibid.
37 Ibid., pp. 180–2.
38 Hans Urs von Balthasar, *A Short Primer for Unsettled Laymen*, translated by Sister Mary Theresilde Skerry, San Francisco: Ignatius Press, 1985 [1980], p. 90.
39 Ibid., p. 91.
40 Paul Ricoeur, 'Fatherhood: From Phantasm to Symbol', in Don Ihde (ed.), *The Conflict of Interpretations*, Evanston: Northwestern University Press, 1974, p. 486.
41 Justin Martyr, *First Apology n. 33 in The First and Second Apologies*, ed., Walter J. Burghardt, John J. Dillon and Dennis D. McManus, with notes by Leslie William Barnard, vol. 56, Ancient Christian Writers: The Works of the Fathers in Translation, New York and Mahwah NJ: Paulist Press, 1997, p. 46.
42 Luce Irigaray, *Speculum of the Other Woman*, translated by Gillian C. Gill, Ithaca NY: Cornell University Press, 1985 [1974], p. 300.
43 Ibid., p. 169. Quotations from Plotinus are taken from the Sixth Tractate of the Third Ennead, 'The Impassivity of the Unembodied', and the edition used in the English translation is *Plotinus' Enneads*, translated by Stephen MacKenna, 2nd edn, revised B.S. Page, London: Faber & Faber, 1956, pp. 201–22. MacKenna's complete translation is available online at the University of Adelaide ebooks website: http://etext.library.adelaide.edu.au/p/p72e/ (last accessed 12 June 2005).
44 Ibid.
45 Ibid., p. 179. Ellipses indicate my editing of the quoted material.
46 Luce Irigaray, *Sexes and Genealogies*, translated by Gillian C. Gill, New York: Columbia University Press, 1993 [1987], pp. 14–16.
47 Ibid., p. 19.
48 Ricoeur, 'Fatherhood', p. 468.
49 Ibid., p. 490.
50 Ibid., p. 491.
51 Ibid.
52 Ibid.
53 Ibid., pp. 492–3.
54 Ibid., p. 493.

55 The idea of the imaginary father is explored in the collection of essays in Julia Kristeva, *Tales of Love*, translated by Leon S. Roudiez, New York: Columbia University Press, 1987 [1983].
56 Ibid., p. 26.
57 Ibid., p. 141.
58 Ibid.
59 See ibid., pp. 146–7.
60 Ibid., p. 149.
61 Ricoeur, 'Fatherhood', p. 496.
62 Julia Kristeva, *Powers of Horror: An Essay on Abjection*, translated by Leon S. Roudiez, New York: Columbia University Press, 1982 [1980], p. 15.
63 See Ricoeur, 'Fatherhood', pp. 493–5.
64 Ibid., p. 495.
65 Kristeva, *Tales of Love*, pp. 261–2.
66 Peter Chrysologus, 'Sermon 147', *The Divine Office: The Liturgy of the Hours According to the Roman Rite*, London, Glasgow, Sydney, Dublin: Collins, E.J. Dwyer, Talbot, 1974, p. 88.

13   Redeeming motherhood

1 Balthasar, *Theodramatik IV*, Einsiedeln: Johannes Verlag, 1983, p. 75, quoted in David L. Schindler, 'Catholic Theology, Gender, and the Future of Western Civilization', *Communio*, Vol. 20, Summer 1993: 200–39, p.204.
2 Ibid., p.205.
3 Ibid., p. 210, quoting Balthasar, *You Crown the Year with Your Goodness*, San Francisco: Ignatius Press, 1989, p. 223. Note here once again the emphasis on pain in Balthasar's thought, rather than a possible emphasis on the fecundity and joy of motherhood.
4 Ibid., p. 211.
5 Ibid., p. 212.
6 Ibid., p. 231.
7 The title of this essay reveals more than it intends, perhaps, of the link between a certain kind of Catholic conservatism and a certain kind of global politics, again, bearing in mind the alliance between conservative Catholicism and Republican politics in the 2004 American elections, an allegiance primarily formed around issues of sexual politics.
8 Schindler, 'The Future of Western Civilization', pp. 238–9.
9 Hans Urs von Balthasar, *Theo-Drama: Theological Dramatic Theory, Vol. II: The Dramatis Personae: Man in God*, translated by Graham Harrison, San Francisco: Ignatius Press, 1990 [1976], p. 315.
10 Hans Urs von Balthasar, *Theo-Drama III: The Dramatis Personae: The Person in Christ*, translated by Graham Harrison, San Francisco: Ignatius Press, 1992 [1978], p. 518.
11 Ibid.
12 Ibid., p. 527.
13 Hans Urs von Balthasar, 'Women Priests? A Marian Church in a Fatherless and Motherless Culture', *Communio*, Vol. 22, Spring 1995: 164–70, p. 168.

14 Balthasar, *Creator Spirit*, p. 15.
15 Ibid., p. 32.
16 Ibid., p. 23.
17 Ibid., p. 27.
18 Balthasar, *Theo-Drama II*, p. 402.
19 Ibid., p. 403.
20 Balthasar, *Creator Spirit*, p. 30.
21 Ibid., p. 31.
22 Ibid.
23 Ibid.
24 Ibid., p. 36.
25 Ibid., pp. 33–4.
26 Christine Battersby, *The Phenomenal Woman: Feminist Metaphysics and the Patterns of Identity*, Cambridge: Polity Press, 1998, p. 39.
27 Ibid., p. 3.
28 Ibid., p. 19.
29 Ibid., p. 23.
30 Ibid., p. 38.
31 Grace Jantzen, *Becoming Divine: Towards a Feminist Philosophy of Religion*, Manchester: Manchester University Press, 1998, p. 275.
32 See especially the essay 'Divine Women' in Luce Irigaray, *Sexes and Genealogies*, translated by Gillian C. Gill, New York: Columbia University Press, 1993 [1987], pp. 55–72.
33 Jantzen, *Becoming Divine*, p. 243.
34 Ibid., p. 157.
35 Ibid.
36 Ibid., p. 217.
37 Ibid., p. 269.
38 Ibid., p. 10.
39 Ibid., p. 270.
40 Ibid., p. 271.
41 Ibid., p. 78.
42 Luce Irigaray, *Speculum of the Other Woman*, translated by Gillian C. Gill, Ithaca NY: Cornell University Press, p. 245.
43 Ibid., p. 311.
44 See Tina Beattie, 'Mary, Eve and the Church: Towards a New Ecclesiology', *Maria: A Journal of Marian Studies*, February 2001: 5–20.
45 Henri de Lubac, *The Motherhood of the Church*, translated by Sr Sergia Englund OCD, San Francisco: Ignatius Press, 1982 [1971], p. 69, quoting Louis Bouyer, *Le sens de la vie monastique*, Paris: Desclée, 1950, pp. 89–90, and John 11:53.
46 Ibid., p. 72.
47 Ambrose, 'On Virgins', 5.22 in Boniface Ramsey, *Ambrose*, London and New York: Routledge, 1997, p. 79.
48 Tertullian, *De oratione*, c. 2 (CSEL, 20:182) quoted in Lubac, *Motherhood*, p. 115.
49 Has not the witness of the mother always been necessary to guarantee the father's paternity, at least until male scientists discovered a way round the problem with DNA testing, thus eliminating one more vital maternal function from our modern culture?

50 Monica Migliorino Miller, *Sexuality and Authority in the Catholic Church*, Scranton: University of Scranton Press; London and Toronto: Associated University Presses, p. 142.
51 Ibid., p. 138, quoting St Augustine, *Sermon 216*, 8, translated by Sr Mary Sarah Muldowny RSN, *Fathers of the Church*, vol. 38, New York: Fathers of the Church, 1959, 157–8 (PL 38.1081). Miller's emphasis.
52 Ibid., p. 139.
53 For a development of this idea about the disruption of the incest taboo and family relationships, see Tina Beattie, 'Virgin and Mother, Daughter and Bride – The Queer Queen of Heaven', in Gerard Loughlin (ed.), *Queer Theology: New Perspectives on Sex and Gender*, Oxford: Blackwell, 2006 (forthcoming).
54 Lubac, *Motherhood*, p. 79.
55 Pope John XXIII, *Mater et Magistra* in Michael Walsh and Brian Davies (eds), *Proclaiming Justice and Peace: Documents from John XXIII to John Paul II*, London: CAFOD and Collins, 1984: 1–44, n. 1, p. 4.
56 Pastoral Constitution on the Church in the Modern World, *Gaudium et Spes*, in Austin Flannery OP (ed.), *Vatican Council II: The Conciliar and Post Conciliar Documents*, Dublin: Dominican Publications; New Town, NSW: E. J. Dwyer, 1992: 903–1001, n. 1, p. 903.
57 Hans Urs von Balthasar, *Elucidations*, translated by John Riches, London: SPCK, p. 70.
58 Charlene Spretnak, *Missing Mary: The Queen of Heaven and Her Re-Emergence in the Modern Church*, New York and Basingstoke: Palgrave Macmillan, 2004, p. 9.
59 Ibid., p. 5.
60 Ibid., p. 3.
61 Ibid.
62 Ibid.
63 Ibid., p. 4.
64 One might contrast this with the argument in David L. Schindler, 'Creation and Nuptiality: A Reflection on Feminism in Light of Schmemann's Liturgical Theology', *Communio*, Vol. 28, 2001: 265–95. Focusing on the work of Elizabeth Johnson, Schindler argues with some justification that her 'democratic-feminist' (p. 292) representation of Mary lacks a symbolic or cosmic perspective. However, in arguing this, he resorts to the kind of sexual and nuptial cosmology that we have already seen in Balthasar – appealing to an essentially feminine, womanly creation redolent with stereotypes of Mary's feminine dependence and 'littleness' on which her power depends. Spretnak's cosmic Mary is an altogether more potent and mystical symbol, with a capacity to dissolve these time- and culture-bound stereotypes.
65 Spretnak, *Missing Mary*, p. 97.
66 Ibid., p. 101.
67 Ibid.
68 Sarah Jane Boss, *Empress and Handmaid: On Nature and Gender in the Cult of the Virgin Mary*, London and New York: Cassell, 2000, p. 18.
69 Ibid., p. 40.
70 Sarah Jane Boss, *Mary*, New Century Theology, London and New York: Continuum, 2003.
71 Spretnak, *Missing Mary*, p. 203.
72 Lubac, *Motherhood*, p. 55.

73 See Gillian Rose, 'Diremption of Spirit', in Philippa Berry and Andrew Wernick (eds), *Shadow of Spirit: Postmodernism and Religion*, London and New York: Routledge, 1992, p. 53. See also Rose, *The Broken Middle: Out of Our Ancient Society*, Oxford UK and Cambridge MA: Blackwell, 1992.
74 Rose, 'Diremption of Spirit', p. 53.
75 See Balthasar, *Theo-Drama III*, p. 308. See also Tina Beattie, *God's Mother, Eve's Advocate: A Marian Narrative of Women's Salvation*, London and New York: Continuum, 2002 [1999], pp. 150–5.
76 Sarah Coakley, 'The Eschatological Body: Gender, Transformation and God' in *Powers and Submissions: Spirituality, Philosophy and Gender*, Oxford: Blackwell, 2002, p. 163.
77 Peter Chrysologus, *Sermon 64*, *T. 52*, p. 380. *Patr. Lat. Migne*, quoted in Thomas Livius, *The Blessed Virgin in the Fathers of the First Six Centuries*, London, New York, Cincinnati, Chicago: Burns and Oates/Benziger Brothers, 1893, p. 57. For the patristic association of the biblical women with the Church as New Eve, see Beattie, *God's Mother, Eve's Advocate*, pp. 103–9.
78 See Trible, *God and the Rhetoric of Sexuality*, Chapter 4, 'A Love Story Gone Awry'.
79 Severian, *De Mundi Creatore*, Orat. vi. 10. Int. Opp. S. Chrysost. Tom. vi. p. 497, Migne, in Livius, *The Blessed Virgin*, p. 56. For further discussion on the relationship between Eve and Mary, see Beattie, *God's Mother, Eve's Advocate*, pp. 164–93.

14   Redeeming language

1 Luce Irigaray, *Sexes and Genealogies*, translated by Gillian C. Gill, New York: Columbia University Press, 1993 [1987], p. 10.
2 Monica Migliorino Miller, *Sexuality and Authority in the Catholic Church*, Scranton: University of Scranton Press; London and Toronto: Associated University Presses, 1995, p. 48.
3 Irigaray, *Sexes and Genealogies*, pp. 15–16.
4 Ibid., p. 16.
5 The clitoris is pure in purpose. It is the only organ in the body designed purely for pleasure. The clitoris is simply a bundle of nerves: 8,000 nerve fibres, to be precise. That's a higher concentration of nerve fibres than is found anywhere else in the body, including the fingertips, lips, and tongue, and it is twice . . . twice . . . twice the number in the penis.
   (from *Woman An Intimate Geography* by Natalie Angier, ellipses as given, quoted in Eve Ensler, *The Vagina Monologues*, London: Virago, 2003 [2001], p. 51)

See also Beattie, 'Carnal Love and Spiritual Imagination', in Jon Davies and Gerard Loughlin (eds), *Sex These Days: Essays on Theology, Sexuality and Society*, Sheffield: Sheffield Academic Press, 1997.
6 Graham Ward, 'Kenosis: Death, Discourse and Resurrection', in Lucy Gardner *et al.* (eds), *Balthasar at the End of Modernity*, Edinburgh: T. & T. Clark, 1999, p. 47.
7 Ibid., p. 48.
8 Ibid., p. 63, quoting Julia Kristeva, *New Maladies of the Soul*, translated by Ross Guberman, New York and Chichester: Columbia University Press, 1995 [1993], p. 44.

352   Notes

9   Ward, 'Kenosis', p. 65.
10 Ward, 'Kenosis', pp. 66–7.
11 Luce Irigaray, *An Ethics of Sexual Difference*, translated by Carolyn Burke and Gillian C. Gill, London: The Athlone Press, 1993, p. 100.
12 Hans Urs von Balthasar, *Theo-Drama V: Theological Dramatic Theory, Vol. V: The Last Act*, translated by Graham Harrison, San Francisco: Ignatius Press, 1998 [1983], p. 260. Quotations are taken from the following works by Adrienne von Speyr, all published by Johannes Verlag, Einsiedeln: *Kath. Briefe* Vols 1 and 2; *Johannes* Vols 2–4; *Kolosser; Passion nach Matthäus; Gleichnisse des Herrn; Die Beichte; Bergpredigt; Des Angesicht des Vaters*.
13 Ibid., p. 261, quoting Speyr, *Johannes* Vol. 2; *Epher (Kinder des Lichtes)*.
14 Julia Kristeva, *Powers of Horror: An Essay on Abjection*, translated by Leon S. Roudiez, New York: Columbia University Press, 1982 [1980].
15 Julia Kristeva, *In the Beginning was Love: Psychoanalysis and Faith*, translated by Arthur Goldhammer, New York: Columbia University Press, 1987 [1985], p. 40.
16 Ibid.
17 Ibid., pp. 40–1.
18 Pope John Paul II, 'At the Root of the Eucharist is the Virginal Heart of Mary', *L'Osservatore Romano* (13 June 1983), 2, quoted in Miller, *Sexuality and Authority*, p. 155.
19 Pope John Paul II, 'At the Root of the Eucharist', quoted in ibid., p. 159.
20 Adrienne von Speyr, *The Handmaid of the Lord*, London: The Harvill Press, 1956, p. 84.
21 Hans Urs von Balthasar, *Mysterium Paschale: The Mystery of Easter*, translated by Aidan Nichols OP, Edinburgh: T. & T. Clark, p. 163.
22 Ibid.
23 Ibid.
24 Ibid.
25 Kristeva, *Powers of Horror*, p. 11.
26 See ibid., pp. 88–9.
27 Balthasar, *Mysterium Paschale*, p. 173.
28 Hans Urs von Balthasar, *Heart of the World*, translated by Erasmo S. Leiva, San Francisco: Ignatius Press, 1979 [1954], p. 148.
29 Kristeva, *Powers of Horror*, pp. 3–4.
30 Balthasar, *Heart of the World*, p. 141.
31 Sarah Jane Boss, *Mary*, New Century Theology, London and New York: Continuum, 2003, p. 87.
32 Ibid., p. 86.
33 Ibid., p. 88.
34 Ibid., p. 89. Boss's emphasis.
35 Ibid.
36 Ibid., p. 4–5.
37 Ibid., p. 91.
38 Ibid.
39 Ibid., p. 116.
40 Ibid.
41 Ibid., p. 142.

42 Balthasar, *Mysterium Paschale*, p. 173.
43 Catherine of Siena, *The Dialogue*, translated by and introduction by Suzanne Noffke OP, preface by Giuliana Cavallini, New York and Mahwah NJ: Paulist Press, 1980, p. 297.
44 Ibid.
45 Ibid., p. 73.
46 Balthasar, *Mysterium Paschale*, p. 168.
47 Ibid., p. 167.
48 Ibid., p. 174.
49 Kristeva, *Powers of Horror*, p. 15.
50 Balthasar, *Heart of the World*, pp. 202–3.
51 Augustine, *Concerning the City of God against the Pagans*, trans. Henry Bettenson, London: Penguin Books, 1972 [1467], XIX.13, p. 870.

15   Redeeming sacramentality

1 'The Gospel of Bartholomew', II: 1–5 in E. Hennecke, *New Testament Apocrypha*, translated and edited by W. Schneemelcher, vol. 1, London: Lutterworth Press, 1963, pp. 484–503.
2 Luce Irigaray, *Speculum of the Other Woman*, translated by Gillian C. Gill, Ithaca NY: Cornell University Press, 1985 [1974], p. 197.
3 René Girard, *Things Hidden Since the Foundation of the World*, translated by Stephen Bann and Michael Metteer, London: The Athlone Press, 1987 [1978], p. 441.
4 Carl Raschke, 'Fire and Roses, or the Problem of Postmodern Religious Thinking', in Philippa Berry and Andrew Wernick (eds), *Shadow of Spirit: Postmodernism and Religion*, London and New York: Routledge, 1992, pp. 93–4.
5 Jacques Lacan, *Écrits: A Selection*, translated by Alan Sheridan, London: Tavistock/Routledge, 1977 [1966], p. 104.
6 Luce Irigaray, *Marine Lover of Friedrich Nietzsche*, translated by Gillian C. Gill, New York: Columbia University Press, p. 190.
7 Raschke, 'Fire and Roses', pp. 105–6.
8 T.S. Eliot, *Four Quartets*, New York: Harcourt Brace Jovanovich, 1971, p. 59, quoted in Raschke, 'Fire and Roses', p. 106.
9 See Barbara G. Walker, *The Woman's Encyclopedia of Myths and Secrets*, London: HarperCollins, 1983, p. 868.
10 Catherine of Siena, *The Dialogue*, translated by and introduction by Suzanne Noffke OP, preface by Giuliana Cavallini, New York and Mahwah NJ: Paulist Press, 1980, p. 365.
11 Luce Irigaray, *Sexes and Genealogies*, translated by Gillian C. Gill, New York: Columbia University Press, 1993 [1987], p. 47.
12 Luce Irigaray, *An Ethics of Sexual Difference*, translated by Carolyn Burke and Gillian C. Gill, London: The Athlone Press, 1993, pp. 15–16.
13 Irigaray, *Marine Lover*, pp. 171–2.
14 Thomas Aquinas, *ST* I, q.12.4.
15 *ST* I, q.50.1.
16 Irigaray, *Ethics of Sexual Difference*, p. 16.

17 David N. Power OMI, 'The Language of Sacramental Memorial: Rupture, Excess and Abundance', in L. Boeve and L. Leussen (eds), *Sacramental Presence in a Postmodern Context*, Leuven, Paris, Sterling VA: Leuven University Press, 2001, p. 144.
18 Ibid., p. 138.
19 Ibid., p. 140.
20 Ibid., p. 149.
21 Ibid., pp. 149–50.
22 Hans Urs von Balthasar, *The Glory of the Lord: A Theological Aesthetics I: Seeing the Form*, translated by Erasmo Leiva-Merikakis, edited by Joseph Fessio, Edinburgh: T. & T. Clark, 1982 [1961], p. 675. See also Graham Ward, 'Kenosis: Death, Discourse and Resurrection' in Lucy Gardner *et al.* (eds), *Balthasar at the End of Modernity*, Edinburgh: T. & T. Clark, pp. 67–8.
23 Jacques Derrida, *Of Grammatology*, translated by Gayatri Chakravorty Spivak, Baltimore: Johns Hopkins University Press, 1976, p. 158.
24 Raschke, 'Fire and Roses', p. 95.
25 Ibid., p. 101, referring to David Levin, 'Postmodernism in Dance: Dance, Discourse, Democracy', in Hugh J. Silverman (ed.), *Postmodernism – Philosophy and the Arts*, New York: Routledge, 1990.
26 Ibid., p. 102.
27 Ibid., p. 103.
28 Ibid., p. 102.
29 Ibid., p. 103.
30 Ibid., pp. 104–5.
31 Ibid., p. 105.
32 Ibid.
33 Ibid., p. 100.
34 Ibid., quoting Jean-François Lyotard, *The Differend: Phrases in Dispute*, translated by Georges Van Den Abbeele, Minneapolis: University of Minnesota Press, 1988, p. 13.
35 Raschke, 'Fire and Roses', p. 104.
36 Catherine of Siena, *The Dialogue*, p. 365.
37 David Torevell, *Losing the Sacred: Ritual, Modernity and Liturgical Reform*, Edinburgh: T. & T. Clark, 2000, p. 5. See also Laurence Paul Hemming, 'A Response Article to Andrew Cameron-Mowat on "Polarisation & Liturgy"', *The Pastoral Review*, Vol. 1, 1, January/February 2005: 70–4.
38 Godfried Cardinal Danneels, 'Liturgy Forty Years after the Second Vatican Council: High Point or Recession', in Keith Pecklers SJ (ed.), *Liturgy in a Postmodern World*, London and New York: Continuum, 2003, p. 17.
39 Ibid., p. 17.
40 Hans Urs von Balthasar, *Elucidations*, translated by John Riches, London: SPCK, 1975, p. 70.
41 It should be noted that Balthasar poses a challenge to the Church's insistence that sexual intercourse is purposeful insofar as it is intended for procreation as well as for the expression of love. Sex can be an end in itself. Does the liturgy suffer when the Church refuses to understand sexuality as 'play', when every sexual encounter must be invested with the procreative function? Does our worship too become caught up in the ecclesial politics of production?

42. 'The Constitution on the Sacred Liturgy, *Sacrosanctum concilium*', in Austin Flannery OP (ed.), *Vatican Council II: The Conciliar and Post Conciliar Documents*, Leominster: Fowler Wright Books, 1975 [4 December 1963], p. 5.
43. Michael Kunzler, *The Church's Liturgy*, translated by Henry O'Shea OSB, Placed Murray OSB and Cilian Ó Sé OSB, Amateca: Handbooks of Catholic Theology, London and New York: Continuum, 2001, p. 19.
44. Ibid.
45. Ibid., pp. 324–444.
46. Ibid., p. 71.
47. Torevell, *Losing the Sacred*, pp. 194–5.
48. Catherine of Siena, *The Dialogue*, p. 36.
49. Ibid., p. 86.
50. Ensler, *The Vagina Monologues*, pp. 124–5.
51. Irigaray, *Sexes and Genealogies*, p. 76.
52. Luce Irigaray, *Thinking the Difference – For a Peaceful Revolution*, translated by Karin Montin, London: The Athlone Press, 1994 [1989], p. 11. For further exploration of Irigaray's representation of the mother–daughter relationship in relation to Mary, see Tina Beattie, *God's Mother, Eve's Advocate: A Marian Narrative of Women's Salvation*, London and New York: Continuum, 2002 [1999], pp. 141–63.
53. Irigaray, *Sexes and Genealogies*, p. 21.
54. Ibid., p. 77.
55. Ibid., p. 78.
56. Irigaray, *Marine Lover*, pp. 183–4.
57. Irigaray, *Sexes and Genealogies*, p. 219.
58. See René Girard, 'Nietzsche versus the Crucified', in James G. Williams (ed.), *The Girard Reader*, New York: Crossroad, 1996; Irigaray, *Marine Lover*, pp. 164–90.
59. Girard, *Things Hidden*, pp. 235–6.
60. Ibid., p. 211.
61. Ibid.
62. Irigaray, *Marine Lover*, p. 184. See also Girard, 'Mimesis and Violence', in *The Girard Reader*.
63. Irigaray, *Marine Lover*, pp. 184–5.
64. Ibid., p. 185.
65. Ibid., p. 169.
66. See René Laurentin, *Marie, l'Église et le Sacerdoce: Maria, Ecclesia, Sacerdotium: Essai sur la Développement d'une Idée Religieuse*, vol. 1, Paris: Nouvelles Éditions Latines, 1952; René Laurentin, *Marie, l'Église et le Sacerdoce: Étude Théologique*, vol. 2, Paris: Nouvelles Éditions Latines, 1953. See Beattie, *God's Mother, Eve's Advocate*, pp. 198–202.
67. Laurentin, *Maria, Ecclesia, Sacerdotium*, p. 630.
68. Ibid., p. 632.
69. Ibid., p. 644.
70. Laurentin, *Maria, Ecclesia, Sacerdotium*, p. 200.

Bibliography

Ackermann, Stephan. 'The Church as Person in the Theology of Hans Urs von Balthasar', *Communio*, 29, 2, 2002: 238–49.
Allen, Prudence, RSM. *The Concept of Woman: The Aristotelian Revolution 750 BC–AD 1250*, Grand Rapids MI and Cambridge UK: William B. Eerdmans, 1997 [1985].
—— *The Concept of Woman: Early Humanist Reformation, 1250–1500*, Grand Rapids MI and Cambridge UK: William B. Eerdmans, 2002.
—— 'Can Feminism Be a Humanism?' in Michele M. Schumacher (ed.), *Women in Christ: Toward a New Feminism*, Grand Rapids MI and Cambridge UK: William B. Eerdmans Publishing Co., 2004, pp. 251–84.
Anderson, Pamela Sue. *A Feminist Philosophy of Religion*, Oxford: Blackwell, 1998.
Aquinas, Thomas. *Summa Theologiae, a concise translation*, ed. Timothy McDermott. London: Methuen, 1989.
Augustine. *The Trinity*, trans. Stephen McKenna CSsR, Vol. 45, *The Fathers of the Church, a new translation*, Washington DC: The Catholic University of America Press, 1963.
—— *Concerning the City of God against the Pagans*, trans. and edited by David Knowles and Henry Bettenson, London: Penguin Books, 1981 [1467].
Balthasar, Hans Urs von. *A Theological Anthropology*, New York: Sheed and Ward, 1967.
—— *Prayer*, trans. A.V. Littledale, London: SPCK, 1973.
—— *Elucidations*, trans. John Riches, London: SPCK, 1975.
—— *Theo-Dramatik II. Die Personen des Spiels. Teil I: Der Mensch in Gott*, Einsiedeln: Johannes Verlag, 1976.
—— *Theo-Dramatik II. Die Personen des Spiels. Teil 2: Die Personen in Christus*, Einsiedeln: Johannes Verlag, 1978.
—— *Heart of the World*, trans. Erasmo S. Leiva, San Francisco: Ignatius Press, 1979 [1945].
—— *First Glance at Adrienne von Speyr*, trans. Antje Lawry and Sr Sergia Englund OCD, San Francisco: Ignatius Press, 1981 [1968].
—— *The Glory of the Lord: A Theological Aesthetics I: Seeing the Form*, trans. Erasmo Leiva-Merikakis, edited by Joseph Fessio, Edinburgh: T. & T. Clark, 1982 [1961].
—— *A Short Primer for Unsettled Laymen*, trans. Sister Mary Theresilde Skerry, San Francisco: Ignatius Press, 1985 [1980].
—— *The Von Balthasar Reader*, edited by Kehl Medart SJ and Werner Loser SJ, Edinburgh: T. & T. Clark, 1985.
—— *The Office of Peter and the Structure of the Church*, trans. Andrée Emery, San Francisco: Ignatius Press, 1986 [1974].

—— *Theo-Drama: Theological Dramatic Theory, Vol. I: Prolegomena*, trans. Graham Harrison, San Francisco: Ignatius Press, 1988 [1983].
—— *Mysterium Paschale: The Mystery of Easter*, trans. Aidan Nichols OP, Edinburgh: T. & T. Clark, 1990.
—— *Theo-Drama: Theological Dramatic Theory, Vol. II: The Dramatis Personae: Man in God*, trans. Graham Harrison, San Francisco: Ignatius Press, 1990 [1976].
—— *The Glory of the Lord, Vol. V: The Realm of Metaphysics in the Modern Age*, trans. Oliver Davies, Andrew Louth, Brian McNeil CRV, John Saward, John Riches and Rowan Williams, Edinburgh: T. & T. Clark, 1991.
—— *Explorations in Theology II: Spouse of the Word*, San Francisco: Ignatius Press, 1991 [1961].
—— *Theo-drama III: The Dramatis Personae: The Person in Christ*, trans. Graham Harrison, San Francisco: Ignatius Press, 1992 [1978].
—— *Dare We Hope 'that all men be saved?' with, A Short Discourse on Hell*, trans. David Kipp and Lothar Krauth, San Francisco: Ignatius Press, 1992.
—— *Explorations in Theology III: Creator Spirit*, trans. Brian McNeil CRV, San Francisco: Ignatius Press, 1993 [1967].
—— *Theo-Drama: Theological Dramatic Theory, Volume IV: The Action*, trans. Graham Harrison, San Francisco: Ignatius Press, 1994 [1980].
—— *Presence and Thought: An Essay on the Religious Philosophy of Gregory of Nyssa*, trans. Mark Sebanc, San Francisco: Ignatius Press, 1995 [1988].
—— 'Women Priests? A Marian Church in a Fatherless and Motherless Culture', *Communio*, 22, 1995: 164–70.
—— *Theo-Drama: Theological Dramatic Theory, Vol. V: The Last Act*, trans. Graham Harrison, San Francisco: Ignatius Press, 1998 [1983].
Battersby, Christine. *The Phenomenal Woman: Feminist Metaphysics and the Patterns of Identity*, Cambridge: Polity Press, 1998.
Beattie, Tina. 'Carnal Love and Spiritual Imagination', in Jon Davies and Gerard Loughlin (eds), *Sex These Days: Essays on Theology, Sexuality and Society*, Sheffield: Sheffield Academic Press, 1997.
—— 'Global Sisterhood or Wicked Stepsisters: Why Don't Girls with God-Mothers Get Invited to the Ball?' in Deborah F. Sawyer and Diane M. Collier (eds), *Is There a Future for Feminist Theology?* Sheffield: Sheffield Academic Press, 1999.
—— 'Mary, Eve and the Church: Towards a New Ecclesiology' in *Maria: A Journal of Marian Studies*, 2001: 5–20.
—— *God's Mother, Eve's Advocate: A Marian Narrative of Women's Salvation*, London and New York: Continuum, 2002 [1999].
—— 'Feminism Vatican Style', *The Tablet*, 7, August 2004.
—— 'Redeeming Mary: the Potential of Marian Symbolism for Feminist Philosophy of Religion', in Pamela Sue Anderson and Beverley Clack (eds), *Feminist Philosophy of Religion: Critical Readings*, London and New York: Routledge, 2004.
—— 'Religious Identity and the Ethics of Representation: The Study of Religion and Gender in the Secular Academy', in Ursula King and Tina Beattie (eds), *Religion, Gender and Diversity: New Perspectives*, London and New York: Continuum, 2004.
—— 'A Roman Catholic's View on the Apostolicity of Women', in Harriet Harris and Jane Shaw (eds), *The Call for Women Bishops*, London: SPCK, 2004.

—— 'Virgin and Mother, Daughter and Bride – The Queer Queen of Heaven', in Gerard Loughlin (ed.), *Queer Theology: New Perspectives on Sex and Gender*, Oxford: Blackwell, 2006 (forthcoming).

Beauvoir, Simone de. *The Second Sex*, trans. H.M. Parshley, Harmondsworth: Penguin Books, 1986 [1949].

Benhabib, Seyla. 'Feminism and Postmodernism: An Uneasy Alliance', in Seyla Benhabib, Judith Butler, Drucilla Cornell and Nancy Fraser (contributors). *Feminist Contentions: A Philosophical Exchange*, New York and London: Routledge, 1995.

Bennington, Geoffrey, and Jacques Derrida. *Jacques Derrida*, Chicago: University of Chicago Press, 1993.

Berry, Philippa. 'The Burning Glass', in Carolyn Burke, Naomi Schor and Margaret Whitford (eds), *Engaging with Irigaray*, New York: Columbia University Press, 1994.

Børresen, Kari Elisabeth. 'God's Image, Man's Image? Patristic Interpretation of Gen. 1,27 and I Cor. 11,7' in Børresen (ed.), *Image of God and Gender Models in Judaeo-Christian Tradition*, Oslo: Solum Forlag, 1991.

Boss, Sarah Jane. *Empress and Handmaid: On Nature and Gender in the Cult of the Virgin Mary*, London and New York: Cassell, 2000.

—— *Mary*, New Century Theology, London and New York: Continuum, 2003.

Bowie, Malcolm. *Lacan*, Fontana Modern Masters, London: HarperCollins, 1991.

Boyer, Peter J. 'A Hard Faith', *The New Yorker*, 16 May 2005.

Brennan, Teresa. *The Interpretation of the Flesh: Freud and Femininity*, London and New York: Routledge, 1992.

Burrus, Virginia. *'Begotten, Not Made': Conceiving Manhood in Late Antiquity*, Stanford CA: Stanford University Press, 2000.

Butler, Judith. *Bodies That Matter: On the Discursive Limits of 'Sex'*, New York and London: Routledge, 1993 [1990].

—— *Gender Trouble: Feminism and the Subversion of Identity*, 2nd edn, New York and London: Routledge, 1999 [1990].

Butler, Sara. 'Second Thoughts on Ordaining Women', *Worship*, 63, 2, March 1989: 157–65.

—— 'The Priest as Sacrament of Christ the Bridegroom', *Worship*, 66, 6, 1992: 418–517.

Bynum, Caroline Walker. *Jesus as Mother: Studies in the Spirituality of the High Middle Ages*, Berkeley, Los Angeles, London: University of California Press, 1984 [1982].

Caputo, John D. 'Heidegger and Theology', in Charles Guignon (ed.), *The Cambridge Companion to Heidegger*, Cambridge: Cambridge University Press, 1993.

—— *The Prayers and Tears of Jacques Derrida: Religion without Religion*, Bloomington and Indianapolis: Indiana University Press, 1997.

Catherine of Siena. *I, Catherine: Selected Writings of Catherine of Siena*, trans. and edited by Kenelm Foster OP and Mary John Ronayne OP, London: Collins, 1980.

—— *The Dialogue*, trans. and introduction by Suzanne Noffke OP, preface by Giuliana Cavallini, New York and Mahwah NJ: Paulist Press, 1980.

Chanter, Tina. *Ethics of Eros: Irigaray's Rewriting of the Philosophers*, New York and London: Routledge, 1995.

Chopp, Rebecca S. 'From Patriarchy into Freedom: A Conversation Between American Feminist Theology and French Feminism', in Maggie C.W. Kim, Susan St Ville, and Susan M. Simonaitis (eds), *Transfigurations: Theology and the French Feminists*, Minneapolis: Fortress Press, 1993, pp. 31–48.

—— 'Theorizing Feminist Theory', in Rebecca S. Chopp and Sheila Greeve Davaney (eds), *Horizons in Feminist Theology: Identity, Tradition, and Norms*, Minneapolis: Fortress Press, 1997.

—— and Sheila Greeve Davaney (eds). *Horizons in Feminist Theology: Identity, Tradition, and Norms*, Minneapolis: Fortress Press, 1997.

Chrysologus, Peter. 'Sermon 147', in *The Divine Office: The Liturgy of the Hours According to the Roman Rite*, London and Glasgow: Collins; Sydney: E.J. Dwyer; Dublin: Talbot, 1974.

Cixous, Hélène. 'The Author in Truth', in Deborah Jenson (ed.), *'Coming to Writing' and Other Essays*, Cambridge MA: Harvard University Press, 1991.

—— 'Tancredi Continues', in Deborah Jenson (ed.), *'Coming to Writing' and Other Essays*, Cambridge MA: Harvard University Press, 1991.

Clack, Beverley (ed.). *Misogyny in the Western Philosophical Tradition: A Reader*, Basingstoke and London: Macmillan, 1999.

—— *Sex and Death: A Reappraisal of Human Mortality*, Cambridge: Polity Press, 2002.

Coakley, Sarah. 'Creaturehood Before God: Male and Female', in *Powers and Submissions: Spirituality, Philosophy and Gender*, Oxford: Blackwell, 2002.

—— 'The Eschatological Body: Gender, Transformation and God', in *Powers and Submissions: Spirituality, Philosophy and Gender*, Oxford: Blackwell, 2002.

—— 'Kenosis and Subversion: On the Repression of "Vulnerability" in Christian Feminist Writing', in *Powers and Submissions: Spirituality, Philosophy and Gender*, Oxford: Blackwell, 2002.

—— '"Persons" in the "Social" Doctrine of the Trinity: Current Analytic Discussion and "Cappadocian" Theology', in *Powers and Submissions: Spirituality, Philosophy and Gender*, Oxford: Blackwell, 2002.

—— (ed.). *Re-thinking Gregory of Nyssa*, Oxford: Blackwell, 2003.

Code, Lorraine. *What Can She Know? Feminist Theory and the Construction of Knowledge*, Ithaca and London: Cornell University Press, 1991.

Coles, Beatriz Vollmer. 'New Feminism: A Sex–Gender Reunion', in Michele M. Schumacher (ed.), *Women in Christ: Toward a New Feminism*, Grand Rapids MI and Cambridge UK: William B. Eerdmans, 2004.

Congregation for the Doctrine of the Faith at http://www.vatican.va/roman_curia/congregations/cfaith/documents/rc_con_cfaith_pro_14071997_en.html (last accessed 11 June 2005).

—— 'Letter to the Bishops of the Catholic Church on the Collaboration of Men and Women in the Church and in the World', 31 May 2004 at http://www.vatican.va/roman curia/congregations/cfaith/documents/rc_con_
cfaith_doc_20040731_collaboration_en.html (last accessed 11 June 2005).

—— '*Inter Insigniores*: Declaration on the question of the admission of women to the ministerial priesthood', 15 October 1976 at http://www.womenpriests.org/church/interlet.asp (last accessed 7 April 2005).

Coward, Harold, and Toby Foshay (eds). *Derrida and Negative Theology*. New York: State University of New York Press, 1993.

Cox, Harvey. *Fire from Heaven: The Rise of Pentecostalism Spirituality and the Reshaping of Religion in the Twenty-first Century*, London: Cassell, 1996.

Crownfield, David R. 'The Sublimation of Narcissism in Christian Love and Faith', in Crownfield (ed.), *Body/Text in Julia Kristeva: Religion, Women, and Psychoanalysis*, Albany NY: State University of New York, 1992.

Dallavalle, Nancy A. 'Neither Idolatry nor Iconoclasm: A Critical Essentialism for Catholic Feminist Theology', *Horizons*, 25, 1998: 23–42.

—— 'Toward a Theology that is Catholic and Feminist: Some Basic Issues', *Modern Theology*, 14, 4, 1998: 535–53.

Daly, Mary. *Beyond God the Father: Towards a Philosophy of Women's Liberation*, London: The Women's Press, 1986 [1973].

Dalzell, Thomas G., SM. 'Lack of Social Drama in Balthasar's Theological Dramatics', *Theological Studies*, 60, 1999: 457–75.

Danneels, Godfried Cardinal. 'Liturgy Forty Years after the Second Vatican Council: High Point or Recession', in Keith Pecklers SJ (ed.), *Liturgy in a Postmodern World*, London and New York: Continuum, 2003.

Derrida, Jacques. *Of Grammatology*, trans. Gayatri Chakravorty Spivak, Baltimore: Johns Hopkins University Press, 1976.

—— 'Plato's Pharmacy', in *Dissemination*, Chicago: University of Chicago Press, 1981 [1968].

—— 'Geschlecht: Sexual Difference, Ontological Difference', in Peggy Kamuf (ed.), *A Derrida Reader: Between the Blinds*, Hemel Hempstead: Harvester Wheatsheaf, 1991.

—— *Acts of Religion*, edited and with an introduction by Gil Anidjar, New York and London: Routledge, 2002.

Deutscher, Penelope. 'Operative Contradiction in Augustine's *Confessions*', in *Yielding Gender: Feminism, Deconstruction and the History of Philosophy*, London and New York: Routledge, 1997.

Dillard, Annie. *The Annie Dillard Reader*, New York: HarperCollins, 1995 [1994].

Douglas, Mary. *Purity and Danger: An Analysis of the Concepts of Pollution and Taboo*, London and New York: Routledge, 1996 [1966].

Ecclestone, Alan. *Yes to God*, London: Darton, Longman & Todd, 1990 [1975].

Eliot, T.S. *Four Quartets*, New York: Harcourt Brace Jovanovich, 1971.

Ensler, Eve. *The Vagina Monologues*, London: Virago, 2003 [2001].

Exum, J. Cheryl. *Plotted, Shot, and Painted: Cultural Representations of Biblical Women*, Sheffield: Sheffield Academic Press, 1996.

Flannery, Austin OP (ed.). 'The Constitution on the Sacred Liturgy, *Sacrosanctum concilium*', in *Vatican Council II: The Conciliar and Post Conciliar Documents*, Leominster: Fowler Wright Books, 1975.

—— (ed.). *Vatican Council II: The Conciliar and Post Conciliar Documents*, Dublin: Dominican Publications; New Town, NSW: E.J. Dwyer, 1992.

Foucault, Michel. 'The Discourse on Language', in *The Archaeology of Knowledge*, New York: Pantheon, 1972.

—— 'Truth and Power', in Colin Gordon (ed.), *Power/Knowledge: Selected Interviews and Other Writings, 1972–1977*, New York: Pantheon Books, 1980.

Fox, Ellen L. 'Seeing through Women's Eyes: The Role of Vision in Women's Moral Theory', in Eve Browning Cole and Susan Coultrap-McQuin (eds), *Explorations in Feminist Ethics: Theory and Practice*, Bloomington and Indianapolis: Indiana University Press, 1992.

Fox-Genovese, Elizabeth. 'Equality, Difference, and the Practical Problems of a New Feminism', in Michele M. Schumacher (ed.), *Women in Christ: Toward a New Feminism*, Grand Rapids MI and Cambridge UK: William B. Eerdmans, 2004.

Frankenberry, Nancy. 'Feminist Approaches: Philosophy of Religion in Different Voices', in Pamela Sue Anderson and Beverley Clack (eds), *Feminist Philosophy of Religion: Critical Readings*, London and New York: Routledge, 2004.

Frascati-Lochhead, Marta. *Kenosis and Feminist Theology: The Challenge of Gianni Vattimo*, Albany NY: State University of New York Press, 1998.

Freud, Sigmund. 'Anxiety and Instinctual Life', in James Strachey (ed.), *New Introductory Lectures on Psychoanalysis*, Harmondsworth: Penguin Books, 1991 [1933].

— 'Beyond the Pleasure Principle', in James Strachey (ed.), *On Metaphyschology: The Theory of Psychoanalysis*, Harmondsworth: Penguin Books, 1991 [1920].

— 'Femininity', in James Strachey (ed.), *New Introductory Lectures on Psychoanalysis*, 145–69, Harmondsworth: Penguin Books, 1991 [1933].

— 'The Future of an Illusion', in James Strachey (ed.), *New Introductory Lectures on Psychoanalysis*, 179–241, London: Penguin Books, 1991 [1927].

Friedman, Marilyn, 'Feminism and Modern Friendship: Dislocating the Community', in Eve Browning Cole and Susan Coultrap-McQuin (eds), *Explorations in Feminist Ethics: Theory and Practice*, Bloomington and Indianapolis: Indiana University Press, 1992.

Fulkerson, Mary McClintock. *Changing the Subject: Women's Discourses and Feminist Theology*, Minneapolis: Fortress Press, 1994.

— 'Contesting the Gendered Subject: A Feminist Account of the Imago Dei', in Rebecca S. Chopp and Sheila Greeve Davaney (eds), *Horizons in Feminist Theology: Identity, Tradition, and Norms*, Minneapolis: Fortress Press, 1997.

Gardner, Lucy, and David Moss. 'Something like Time; Something like the Sexes – an Essay in Reception', in Lucy Gardner, David Moss, Ben Quash and Graham Ward (eds), *Balthasar at the End of Modernity*, Edinburgh: T. & T. Clark, 1999.

Gardner, Lucy, David Moss, Ben Quash and Graham Ward (eds). *Balthasar at the End of Modernity*. Edinburgh: T. & T. Clark, 1999.

Gasparro, Giulia Sfameni. 'Image of God and Sexual Differentiation in the Tradition of Enkrateia', in Kari Elisabeth Børresen (ed.), *Image of God and Gender Models in Judaeo-Christian Tradition*, Oslo: Solum Forlag, 1991.

Gerl-Falkovitz, Hanna-Barbara. 'Gender Difference: Critical Questions concerning Gender Studies', in Michele M. Schumacher (ed.), *Women in Christ: Toward a New Feminism*, Grand Rapids MI and Cambridge UK: William B. Eerdmans, 2004.

Gilligan, Carol. *In a Different Voice: Psychological Theory and Women's Development*, Cambridge MA: Harvard University Press, 1982.

Girard, René. *Violence and the Sacred*, trans. Patrick Gregory, Baltimore: The Johns Hopkins University Press, 1977 [1972].

— 'Generative Scapegoating', in Robert Hamerton-Kelly (ed.), *Violent Origins: Walter Burkert, René Girard and Jonathan Z. Smith on Ritual Killing and Cultural Formation*, Stanford: Stanford University Press, 1987.

— *Things Hidden Since the Foundation of the World*, trans. Stephen Bann and Michael Metteer, London: The Athlone Press, 1987 [1978].

— *The Girard Reader*, edited by James G. Williams, New York: Crossroad, 1996.

Gonzalez, Michelle. 'Hans Urs von Balthasar and Contemporary Feminist Theology', *Theological Studies*, 65, 3, 2004: 566–95.

Gregory of Nyssa. 'The Life of Saint Macrina', in *Saint Gregory of Nyssa: Ascetical Works*, The Fathers of the Church, a New Translation, trans. Virginia Woods Callahan, Washington DC: The Catholic University of America Press, 1967.

—— 'On the Soul and the Resurrection', in *Saint Gregory of Nyssa: Ascetical Works*, The Fathers of the Church, a New Translation, trans. Virginia Woods Callahan, Washington DC: The Catholic University of America Press, 1967.

Grosz, Elizabeth. *Sexual Subversions: Three French Feminists*, St Leonards NSW: Allen & Unwin, 1989.

Hampson, Daphne. *Theology and Feminism*, Oxford UK and Cambridge MA: Blackwell, 1990.

Hauke, Manfred. *Women in the Priesthood? A Systematic Analysis in the Light of the Order of Creation and Redemption*, trans. David Kipp, San Francisco: Ignatius Press, 1988 [1986].

Heidegger, Martin. 'Recollection in Metaphysics', in *The End of Philosophy*, trans. Joan Stambaugh, New York, Evanston, San Francisco, London: Harper & Row, 1973.

—— 'The Onto-theo-logical Constitution of Metaphysics', in *Identity and Difference*, trans. Joan Stambaugh, San Francisco: Harper & Row, 1974.

—— *Being and Time*, trans. John Macquarrie and Edward Robinson, Oxford: Blackwell, 1980 [1927].

—— 'Letter on Humanism', in David Farrell Krell (ed.), *Basic Writings*, London: Routledge, 1993 [1947].

Hemming, Laurence Paul. 'A Response Article to Andrew Cameron-Mowat on "Polarisation & Liturgy"', *The Pastoral Review*, 1, 1, 2005: 70–4.

Hennecke, E. *New Testament Apocrypha*, trans. and ed. W. Schneemelcher, Vol. 1, London: Lutterworth Press, 1963.

Henrici, Peter SJ. 'A Sketch of von Balthasar's Life', in David L. Schindler (ed.), *Hans Urs von Balthasar: His Life and Work*, San Francisco: Communio Books, Ignatius Press, 1991.

Irigaray, Luce. *Speculum of the Other Woman*, trans. Gillian C. Gill, Ithaca NY: Cornell University Press, 1985 [1974].

—— *This Sex Which Is Not One*, trans. Catherine Porter with Carolyn Burke, Ithaca NY: Cornell University Press, 1985 [1977].

—— *Marine Lover of Friedrich Nietzsche*, trans. Gillian C. Gill, New York: Columbia University Press, 1991.

—— *An Ethics of Sexual Difference*, trans. Carolyn Burke and Gillian C. Gill, London: The Athlone Press, 1993 [1984].

—— *Je, tu, nous: Toward a Culture of Difference*, trans. Alison Martin, New York and London: Routledge, 1993 [1990].

—— *Sexes and Genealogies*, trans. Gillian C. Gill, New York: Columbia University Press, 1993 [1987].

—— *Thinking the Difference – for a Peaceful Revolution*, trans. Karin Montin, London: The Athlone Press, 1994 [1989].

Jantzen, Grace M. *Becoming Divine: Towards a Feminist Philosophy of Religion*, Manchester: Manchester University Press, 1998.

Jewish Christian Relations, 'Negative images of Judaism in Christian Art ó Ecclesia and Synagoga' at http://www.sprezzatura.it/Arte/Ecclesia_Synagoga/res/art1.htm (last accessed 11 January 2005).

Johnson, Elizabeth. *She Who Is: The Mystery of God in Feminist Theological Discourse*, New York: Crossroad, 1995 [1992].

Jones, Serene. 'This God Which Is Not One: Irigaray and Barth on the Divine', in Maggie C.W. Kim, Susan St Ville, and Susan M. Simonaitis (eds), *Transfigurations: Theology and the French Feminists*, Minneapolis: Fortress Press, 1993.

Jonte-Pace, Diane. 'Situating Kristeva Differently: Psychoanalytic Readings of Woman and Religion', in David R. Crownfield (ed.), *Body/Text in Julia Kristeva: Religion, Women, and Psychoanalysis*, Albany NY: State University of New York, 1992.

Kaufmann, Walter (ed.). *The Portable Nietzsche*, trans. Walter Kaufmann, New York, London, Ringwood, Toronto and Auckland: Penguin Books, 1982 [1954].

Kerr, Fergus. *After Aquinas: Versions of Thomism*, Malden MA and Oxford: Blackwell, 2002.

—— 'Comment: Women', *New Blackfriars*, 85, 1000, 2004: 579–82.

Kirwan, Michael. *Discovering Girard*, London: Darton, Longman & Todd, 2004.

Klein, Melanie. 'Some Theoretical Conclusions Regarding the Emotional Life of the Infant', in Joan Riviere (ed.), *Developments in Psycho-Analysis*, London: The Hogarth Press and the Institute of Psycho-Analysis, 1952.

Kristeva, Julia. *Powers of Horror: An Essay on Abjection*, trans. Leon S. Roudiez, New York: Columbia University Press, 1982 [1980].

—— *The Kristeva Reader*, edited by Toril Moi, Oxford and Cambridge MA: Blackwell, 1986.

—— *Tales of Love*, trans. Leon S. Roudiez, New York: Columbia University Press, 1987 [1983].

—— *In the Beginning was Love: Psychoanalysis and Faith*, trans. Arthur Goldhammer, New York: Columbia University Press, 1987 [1985].

—— *Strangers to Ourselves*, trans. Leon S. Roudiez, Hemel Hempstead: Harvester, 1991 [1989].

—— *New Maladies of the Soul*, trans. Ross Guberman, New York and Chichester: Columbia University Press, 1995 [1993].

Kunzler, Michael. *The Church's Liturgy*, trans. Henry O'Shea OSB, Placed Murray OSB, Cilian Ó Sé OSB, *Amateca: Handbooks of Catholic Theology*, London and New York: Continuum, 2001.

Lacan, Jacques. *Écrits: A Selection*, trans. Alan Sheridan, London: Tavistock/Routledge, 1977 [1966].

—— 'God and the *Jouissance* of The Woman', in Juliet Mitchell and Jacqueline Rose (eds), *Feminine Sexuality: Jacques Lacan and the école freudienne*, Basingstoke and London: Macmillan, 1982 [1975].

Laqueur, Thomas. *Making Sex: Body and Gender from the Greeks to Freud*, Cambridge MA and London: Harvard University Press, 1992.

Laurentin, René. *Marie, l'Église et le Sacerdoce: Maria, Ecclesia, Sacerdotium: Essai sur la Développement d'une Idée Religieuse*, Vol. 1, Paris: Nouvelles Éditions Latines, 1952.

—— *Marie, l'Église et le Sacerdoce: Étude Théologique*. Vol. 2, Paris: Nouvelles Éditions Latines, 1953.

Leahy, Brendan. *The Marian Profile in the Ecclesiology of Hans Urs von Balthasar*, London: New City, 2000.

Lee, Jonathan Scott. *Jacques Lacan*, Boston MA: Twayne Publishers, 1990.

Lipton, Sara. 'The Temple is my Body: Gender, Carnality, and Synagoga in the Bible Moralisée', in Eva Frojmovic (ed.), *Imaging the Self, Imaging the Other: Visual*

Representation and Jewish–Christian Dynamics in the Middle Ages and Early Modern Period, Leiden: Brill, 2002.

Livius, Thomas. *The Blessed Virgin in the Fathers of the First Six Centuries*, London: Burns and Oates; New York, Cincinnati, Chicago: Benziger Brothers, 1893.

Lloyd, Genevieve. *The Man of Reason: 'Male' and 'Female' in Western Philosophy*, London: Metheun, 1984.

Loughlin, Gerard. *Alien Sex: The Body and Desire in Cinema and Theology*, Malden MA and Oxford: Blackwell, 2004.

Louth, Andrew. 'The Place of *Heart of the World* in the Theology of Hans Urs von Balthasar', in John Riches (ed.), *The Analogy of Beauty: The Theology of Hans Urs von Balthasar*, Edinburgh: T. & T. Clark, 1986, pp. 147–63.

—— 'The Body in Western Catholic Christianity', in Sarah Coakley (ed.), *Religion and the Body*, Cambridge, New York and Melbourne: Cambridge University Press, 1997.

Lubac, Henri de. *The Motherhood of the Church*, trans. Sr Sergia Englund OCD, San Francisco: Ignatius Press, 1982 [1971].

Lyotard, Jean-François. *The Differend: Phrases in Dispute*, trans. Georges Van Den Abbeele, Minneapolis: University of Minnesota Press, 1988.

Mackenzie, Catriona, and Natalie Stoljar (eds), *Relational Autonomy: Feminist Perspectives on Autonomy, Agency, and the Social Self*, New York and Oxford: Oxford University Press, 2000.

MacKinnon, Donald. 'Some Reflections on Hans Urs von Balthasar's Christology with Special Reference to Theodramatik II/2 and III, including Appendix', in John Riches (ed.), *The Analogy of Beauty: The Theology of Hans Urs von Balthasar*, Edinburgh: T. & T. Clark, 1986.

Magee, Penelope Margaret. 'Disputing the Sacred: Some Theoretical Approaches to Gender and Religion', in Ursula King (ed.), *Religion and Gender*, Oxford UK and Cambridge MA: Blackwell, 1995.

Marion, Jean-Luc. 'Thomas Aquinas and Onto-theo-logy', in Michael Kessler and Christian Sheppard (eds), *Mystics: Presence and Aporia*, Chicago and London: University of Chicago Press, 2003.

Martin, Francis. *The Feminist Question: Feminist Theology in the Light of Christian Tradition*, Edinburgh: T. & T. Clark, 1994.

Martyr, Justin. *First Apology n. 33* in *The First and Second Apologies*, edited by Walter J. Burghardt, John J. Dillon and Dennis D. McManus, with notes by Leslie William Barnard, Vol. 56, *Ancient Christian Writers: The Works of the Fathers in Translation*, New York and Mahwah NJ: Paulist Press, 1997.

Merchant, Carolyn. *The Death of Nature: Women, Ecology and the Scientific Revolution*, San Francisco: Harper & Row, 1990 [1980].

Milbank, John. *Theology and Social Theory: Beyond Secular Reason*, Oxford UK and Malden MA: Blackwell, 1998.

Miller, Monica Migliorino. *Sexuality and Authority in the Catholic Church*, Scranton: University of Scranton Press; London and Toronto: Associated University Presses, 1995.

Mitchell, Juliet (ed.) *The Selected Melanie Klein*, Harmondsworth: Penguin Books, 1986.

Mitchell, Juliet, and Jacqueline Rose (eds), *Feminine Sexuality: Jacques Lacan and the école freudienne*, Basingstoke and London: Macmillan, 1982.

Moi, Toril. 'From Femininity to Finitude: Freud, Lacan, and Feminsim, Again', *Signs*, 29, 3, 2004: 841–78.
Neill, Emily R. 'Roundtable Discussion: From Generation to Generation. Horizons in Feminist Theology or Reinventing the Wheel?' *The Journal of Feminist Studies in Religion*, 15, 1, 1999: 102–38.
Nichols, Aidan OP. *No Bloodless Myth: A Guide Through Balthasar's Dramatics*, Edinburgh: T. & T. Clark, 2000.
Nietzsche, Friedrich. *A Nietzsche Reader*, trans. selection and translation R.J. Hollingdale Introduction, London: Penguin Books, 1977.
Noddings, Nel. *Caring: A Feminist Approach to Ethics and Moral Education*, Berkeley: University of California Press, 1984.
Nowak, Susan. 'The Girardian Theory and Feminism: Critique and Appropriation', *Contagion: Journal of Violence, Mimesis and Culture*, 1994: 19–29.
Nygren, Anders. *Agape and Eros*, trans. Philip S. Watson, London: SPCK, 1982.
Nyssa, Gregory of. *Commentary on the Song of Songs*, trans. with introduction by Casimir McCambley OCSO, Brookline MA: Hellenic College Press, 1987.
Oakes, Edward T. *Pattern of Redemption: The Theology of Hans Urs von Balthasar*, New York: Continuum, 1997.
O'Connor, James T. 'Von Balthasar and Salvation', *Homiletic & Pastoral Review*, 1989: 10–21.
O'Donnell, John SJ. *Hans Urs von Balthasar*, London: Geoffrey Chapman, 1992.
'On the Issues' at http://www.issues2000.org / default.htm (last accessed 20 May 2005).
Ong, Walter. *Fighting for Life*, London: Cornell University Press, 1981.
Papanikolaou, Aristotle. 'Person, Kenosis and Abuse: Hans Urs von Balthasar and Feminist Theologies in Conversation', *Modern Theology*, 19, 1, 2003: 41–65.
Parsons, Susan. 'Accounting for Hope: Feminist Theology as Fundamental Theology', in Susan Parsons (ed.), *Challenging Women's Orthodoxies in the Context of Faith*, Aldershot, Burlington USA, Singapore, Sydney: Ashgate, 2000.
—— 'To Be or Not To Be: Gender and Ontology', *Heythrop Journal*, 45, 3, 2004: 327–43.
Plotinus, *The Six Enneads*, trans. Stephen MacKenna and B.S. Page, The University of Adelaide Library Electronic Texts Collection, eBooks @ Adelaide 2004, at http://etext.library.adelaide.edu.au/p/p72e/ (last accessed 12 June 2005).
Pope Benedict XVI, 'Homily of his Holiness Benedict XVI', Mass for the Inauguration of the Pontificate of Pope Benedict XVI, Sunday, 24 April 2005, *Libraria Editrice Vaticana*, at http://www.vatican.va/holy_father/benedict_xvi/homilies/documents/hf_ben-xvi_hom_20050424_inizio-pontificato_en.html (last accessed 21 May 2005).
Pope John Paul II. *Original Unity of Man and Woman: Catechesis on the Book of Genesis*, Boston MA: St Paul Books & Media, 1981.
—— '*Ordinatio Sacerdotalis*: Apostolic Letter on Reserving Priestly Ordination to Men Alone', 22 May 1994 at http://www.womenpriests.org / church / ordinati.asp (last accessed 7 April 2005).
Power, David OMI. 'Representing Christ in Community and Sacrament', in Donald J. Goergen OP (ed.), *Being a Priest Today*, Collegeville MN: The Liturgical Press, 1992.

— 'The Language of Sacramental Memorial: Rupture, Excess and Abundance', in L. Boeve and L. Leussen (eds), *Sacramental Presence in a Postmodern Context*, Leuven, Paris, Sterling VA: Leuven University Press, 2001.

Quash, Ben. 'Drama and the Ends of Modernity', in Lucy Gardner, David Moss, Ben Quash and Graham Ward (eds), *Balthasar at the End of Modernity*, Edinburgh: T. & T. Clark, 1999.

Ramsey, Boniface. *Ambrose*, London and New York: Routledge, 1997.

Raschke, Carl. 'Fire and Roses, or the Problem of Postmodern Religious Thinking', in Philippa Berry and Andrew Wernick (eds), *Shadow of Spirit: Postmodernism and Religion*, London and New York: Routledge, 1992.

Reineke, Martha. 'The Mother in Mimesis: Kristeva and Girard on Violence and the Sacred', in David R. Crownfield (ed.), *Body/Text in Julia Kristeva: Religion, Women, and Psychoanalysis*, Albany NY: State University of New York, 1992.

Ricoeur, Paul. 'Fatherhood: From Phantasm to Symbol', in Don Ihde (ed.), *The Conflict of Interpretations*, Evanston IL: Northwestern University Press, 1974.

Rose, Gillian. *The Broken Middle: Out of Our Ancient Society*, Oxford UK and Cambridge MA: Blackwell, 1992.

— 'Diremption of Spirit', in Philippa Berry and Andrew Wernick (eds), *Shadow of Spirit: Postmodernism and Religion*, London and New York: Routledge, 1992.

Rose, Jacqueline. 'Introduction – II', in Juliet Mitchell and Jacqueline Rose (eds), *Feminine Sexuality: Jacques Lacan and the école freudienne*, Basingstoke and London: Macmillan, 1982.

Ross, Susan A. 'God's Embodiment and Women', in Catherine Mowry LaCugna (ed.), *Freeing Theology: The Essentials of Theology in Feminist Perspective*, San Francisco: Harper-Collins, 1993.

Roten, Johann SM. 'The Two Halves of the Moon: Marian Anthropological Dimensions in the Common Mission of Adrienne von Speyr and Hans Urs von Balthasar', in David L. Schindler (ed.), *Hans Urs von Balthasar: His Life and Work*, San Francisco: Communio Books, Ignatius Press, 1991, pp. 65–86.

Rubenstein, Richard L., and John K. Roth (eds), *Approaches to Auschwitz: The Holocaust and its Legacy*, Atlanta GA: John Knox Press, 1987.

Ruether, Rosemary Radford. 'Misogynism and Virginal Feminism in the Fathers of the Church', in Rosemary Radford Ruether (ed.), *Religion and Sexism – Images of Women in the Jewish and Christian Traditions*, New York: Simon and Schuster, 1974.

— 'Women's Difference and Equal Rights in the Church', *Concilium*, 6, 1991: 11–18.

— *Sexism and God-Talk: Towards a Feminist Theology*, London: SCM Press, 1992 [1983].

— *Women and Redemption: A Theological History*, London: SCM Press, 1998.

Schindler, David L. 'Catholic Theology, Gender, and the Future of Western Civilization', *Communio*, 20, 1993: 200–39.

— 'Creation and Nuptiality: A Reflection on Feminism in Light of Schmemann's Liturgical Theology', *Communio*, 2001: 265–95.

Schneewind, J.B. *The Invention of Autonomy: A History of Modern Moral Philosophy*, Cambridge: Cambridge University Press, 1998.

Schopenhauer, Arthur. 'On Women', in T.D. Saunders (ed.), *Schopenhauer Selections*, New York: Charles Scribner, 1928.

Schumacher, Michele M. 'An Introduction to a New Feminism', in Michele M. Schumacher (ed.), *Women in Christ: Toward a New Feminism*, Grand Rapids MI and Cambridge UK: William B. Eerdmans, 2004, pp. ix–xvi.
— 'The Nature of Nature in Feminism, Old and New: From Dualism to Complementary Unity', in Michele M. Schumacher (ed.), *Women in Christ: Toward a New Feminism*, Grand Rapids MI and Cambridge UK: William B. Eerdmans, 2004, pp. 17–51.
— 'The Unity of the Two: Toward a New Feminist Sacramentality of the Body', in Michele M. Schumacher (ed.), *Women in Christ: Toward a New Feminism*, Grand Rapids MI and Cambridge UK: William B. Eerdmans, 2004, pp. 210–31.
— (ed.) *Women in Christ: Toward a New Feminism*, Grand Rapids MI and Cambridge UK: William B. Eerdmans, 2004.
Scola, Angelo. *Hans Urs von Balthasar: A Theological Style*, Edinburgh: T. & T. Clark, 1995 [1991].
Slee, Nicola. *Praying Like a Woman*, London: SPCK, 2004.
Soskice, Janet Martin. 'Can a Feminist Call God "Father"?' in Teresa Elwes (ed.), *Women's Voices: Essays in Contemporary Feminist Theology*, London: HarperCollins, 1992.
— 'General Introduction', in Janet Martin Soskice and Diana Lipton (eds), *Feminism and Theology*, Oxford: Oxford University Press, 2003.
Speyr, Adrienne von. *The Handmaid of the Lord*, London: The Harvill Press, 1956.
Spretnak, Charlene. *Missing Mary: The Queen of Heaven and Her Re-Emergence in the Modern Church*, New York and Basingstoke: Palgrave Macmillan, 2004.
Steiner, George. *Heidegger*, edited by Frank Kermode, 2nd edn, Fontana Modern Masters, London: Fontana Press, 1992 [1978].
Synod of Bishops, XI Ordinary General Assembly, 'The Eucharist: Source and Summit of the Life and Mission of the Church', Lineamenta, Libreria Editrice Vaticana, at http://www.vatican.va/roman_curia/synod/documents/rc_synod_doc_20040528_lineamenta-xi-assembly_en.html#_ftnref41 (last accessed 30 December 2004).
Thomas Aquinas, *Sancti Thomae Aquinatis – Summa Theologiae,* literally translated by the Fathers of the English Dominican Province, 2nd and revised edn, 1920, Latin text produced in electronic hypertext form (*Corpus Thomisticum*) by Roberto Busa SJ from Leonina edition and adapted by Enrique Alarcón, at http://krystal.op.cz / sth / sth.php (last accessed 23 May 2005).
Torevell, David. *Losing the Sacred: Ritual, Modernity and Liturgical Reform*, Edinburgh: T. & T. Clark, 2000.
Trible, Phyllis. *God and the Rhetoric of Sexuality*, Philadelphia: Fortress Press, 1978.
Turner, Denys. 'Apophaticism, Idolatry and the Claims of Reason', in Oliver Davies and Turner (eds), *Silence and the Word: Negative Theology and Incarnation*, Cambridge: Cambridge University Press, 2002, pp. 11–34.
Wainwright, Geoffrey. 'Eschatology', in Edward T. Oakes and David Moss (eds), *The Cambridge Companion to Hans Urs von Balthasar*, Cambridge: Cambridge University Press, 2004.
Walker, Barbara G. *The Woman's Encyclopedia of Myths and Secrets*, London: HarperCollins, 1983.
Walsh, Michael, and Brian Davies (eds), *Proclaiming Justice and Peace: Documents from John XXIII to John Paul II*, London: CAFOD and Collins, 1984.
Walter, Natasha. *The New Feminism*, London: Virago Press, 1999.

Ward, Graham. 'Kenosis: Death, Discourse and Resurrection', in Lucy Gardner, David Moss, Ben Quash and Graham Ward (eds), *Balthasar at the End of Modernity*, Edinburgh: T. & T. Clark, 1999.

Warner, Marina. *Alone of All Her Sex: The Myth and Cult of the Virgin Mary*, London: Vintage, 2000 [1976].

Whitford, Margaret. *Luce Irigaray: Philosophy in the Feminine*, London and New York: Routledge, 1991.

Wijngaard, John. *The Ordination of Women in the Catholic Church: Unmasking a Cuckoo's Egg Tradition*, London: Darton, Longman & Todd, 2001.

Index

abjection 6, 10, 37, 171, 202, 211–22, 241–4, 274–9, 282; *see also* Kristeva, Julia
abortion 1, 4, 24, 25
Ackermann, Stephen 332 n20
Allen, Prudence 24, 25
analogy 38, 61, 62, 107, 109, 112, 117, 123, 127, 132, 134, 159, 243, 251, 272, 276 *see also* Balthasar, Hans Urs von
Anderson, Pamela Sue 12, 76–80, 209
androcentrism 40, 43, 51, 58, 61, 119, 123, 210
androgyny 102, 104, 120, 248
angels 6, 116, 118, 122, 289, 293–97, 300, 310
apophaticism 9, 32, 62, 66, 67, 117, 248
Aquinas, Thomas 4, 9, 12, 48, 57, 58–61, 66, 68, 75, 85, 86, 108, 155, 235, 252, 255, 263, 295
Aristotle 43, 52, 57, 86, 155, 182, 235
Augustine 62, 118–23, 125, 155, 189, 235, 258, 259, 277, 288
autonomy 29, 30, 32, 34, 41, 45, 47, 58, 63, 64, 70, 72, 76, 105, 107, 178, 196, 209, 212, 213, 215, 265, 275

Balthasar, Hans Urs von 3, 9, 11, 13, 14, 24, 73, 80, 85, 86, 87, 91–6, 98–111, 112–16, 117, 119, 120, 122, 128, 129, 130, 132, 133–7, 138, 139, 140, 141, 143, 144, 145–8, 149–62, 163–83, 187–94, 196–7, 200, 202–3, 206, 207, 208–9, 215, 221, 225–9, 230, 233, 234–5, 238, 242, 244, 246–53, 261–2, 264, 265, 267, 268, 269, 271–80, 282, 283, 284, 285, 286, 290, 293, 297, 299, 302, 303, 304, 308, 309; Adrienne von Speyr 116, 163–71, 176–9, 194, 202–3, 273, 276–7, 279, 302; analogy 107, 109, 112, 117, 159, 251, 272; bodiliness 95–6; *casta meretrix* 14, 136, 146, 173–81, 191, 265, 280, 303; ecclesiology 133–37, 145–47, 151, 152–5, 261–62, 265, 275, 299; eros 160–1, 272; Girard, René 226–9; Heidegger, Martin 91–2, 95, 98–9, 158–9; hell 167–73, 267, 268, 271–2, 276–80, 282, 283–7, 290, 293, 308; Holy Saturday 167, 171–2, 174, 271; *kenosis* 73, 104, 129, 158–62, 182, 196, 225, 249, 271–2; motherhood of God, 246–53, 286; sacrifice 226–9, 244, 276, 278, 285–6; sex and death 150–1, 155–58, 272, 302; sin 105, 111, 137, 149–50, 169–81, 187, 202–4, 215, 225, 226, 228, 267, 273–4, 276–80, 283, suprasexuality

105, 135, 141, 150–1, 154, 160, 163, 167, 271; theo-drama 99–101; three polarities of human existence 11, 100, 101, 103, 111, 114, 127, 133, 155–7, 200, 209, 231, 264; virginity 157, 160, 161, 165, 166, 177, 179, 187, 280
Barth, Karl 97–8
Battersby, Christine 43–45, 253–4, 345 n46
Beauvoir, Simone de 40–41, 254, 318 n37
Benedict XVI, Pope 1, 2, 25, 332 n28, *see also* Ratzinger, Cardinal
Benhabib, Seyla 34, 56–7, 199, 315 n27
Berry, Philippa 339 n87
Børresen, Kari Elisabeth 118–19, 122–3, 125, 329 n15, 329 n21
Boss, Sarah Jane 14, 45, 26–4, 280–3, 285
Bowie, Malcolm 197
Boyer, Peter J. 1
Brennan, Teresa 166, 336 n19
broken middle 11–12, 183, 264
Burrus, Virginia 115–16, 122, 126, 130, 156
Butler, Judith 12, 24, 28, 33–40, 41, 44, 45, 69, 73, 83, 124, 129, 287; *see also* Coakley, Sarah
Butler, Sara 131, 137–8, 142
Bynum, Caroline Walker 316 n40

Caputo, John D. 317 n43, 320 n1
casta meretrix, *see* Balthasar, Hans Urs von
castration 37, 38, 127, 145, 147, 192–5, 237, 238, 239, 240, 270
cataphaticism 67. 126
Catherine of Siena 4, 9, 79–81, 85, 101, 117, 166, 174, 283, 302
celibacy 4, 46, 151, 163, 168, 169, 223, 229, 271, 280
Chanter, Tina 321 n25, 326 n24
chaos 64, 78, 158, 172–4, 177, 192, 196, 204, 263, 267, 269, 273, 274, 276, 278, 279–85
Chopp, Rebecca S. 3, 4, 12, 26
Christine de Pizan 24
Cixous, Hélène 115
Clack, Beverley 14, 157, 188–89, 190, 206
Clement of Alexandria 123
clitoris 108, 145, 153, 270, 271; *see also* orgasm, female
Coakley, Sarah 12, 35–7, 39, 67, 73–75, 76, 120, 161–2, 182, 227, 245, 266, 329 n16, 329 n18, 329 n20; Butler, Judith: 35–7, 39; kenosis 161–2
Code, Lorraine 29, 54
Coles, Beatriz Vollmer 24
Congregation for the Doctrine of the Faith (CDF) 2, 12, 20–3, 36, 131, 314 n5
contraception 4, 25
conversion 4, 63–4, 215, 240, 244, 257
Coward, Harold and Toby Foshay 317 n43
Cox, Harvey 322 n81
Crownfield, David R. 222–3
Cyril of Alexandria 162

Dallavalle, Nancy 6, 19, 42–43, 126
Daly, Mary. 19, 21, 27, 51
Danneels, Godfried Cardinal 299
Dasein 49–50, 52–3, 55, 199; and death, 199–200; *see also* Heidegger, Martin
death of God 7, 50, 97, 243, 271, 285, 306, 308
deification 7, 60, 301, 302
Derrida, Jacques 5, 11, 32, 55–6, 95,

96, 146, 149, 183, 200, 210, 297, 298
Deutscher, Penelope 121–22, 126, 156
Dillard, Annie 189
Douglas, Mary 212
Dürr, Emil 164

Ecclestone, Alan 181
Eckhart, Meister 91
Eliot, T.S. 269, 293
Enlightenment 8, 11, 12, 26, 29–30, 40, 76, 127, 130, 149, 191, 215, 284
epistemology 6, 10, 12, 28, 31, 45, 58–62, 68, 70, 76–9, 85, 189
eros 39, 95, 127, 150, 160–1, 234, 241, 267, 271–2
eschatology 12, 15, 39, 100, 118–19, 125, 150, 153, 157, 173, 191, 200, 229, 264, 287, 289, 292, 301, 310
essentialism 12, 20, 33, 35, 42–4, 45, 48, 56, 66, 86, 112, 126, 147, 204, 218, 225, 232, 295,
Eucharist 130, 132, 136, 144, 147, 160, 161, 223, 226, 227, 229, 242, 257, 266, 275, 294, 300, 305
Exum, J. Cheryl 175–6

father, imaginary, *see* Kristeva, Julia
Fiorenza, Elisabeth Schüssler 3, 7, 19, 24
Foucault, Michel 27, 29, 37
Fox, Ellen L. 70–72, 85
Fox-Genovese, Elizabeth 24
Frascati-Lochhead, Marta 50, 313 n21,
Frankenberry, Nancy 130
Freud, Sigmund 31, 37, 80, 109, 159, 166, 189, 190–2, 196–202, 206, 208–10, 212, 215–6, 217–20, 221, 222, 232, 236, 237, 239, 240, 241, 243, 274, 257
Friedman, Marilyn 324 n17
Fulkerson, Mary McClintock 27, 64, 76, 123–6

Gardner, Lucy, 102 325n1, 334 n7
Gasparo, Giulia Sfameni 329 n18, 329 n19
Girard, René 14, 201–6; 209–11, 216, 218–20, 222, 225, 226–7, 229, 233, 290, 291, 301, 304–7; feminism 209–11; Irigaray, Luce 304–7; Kristeva, Julia 216–222; sacrifice 201–5, 210–11, 226–7, 290–1, 306;
Glendon, Mary Ann 23
Gonzalez, Michelle 13, 164, 339 n95
Gregorian Reform 31
Gregory of Nyssa 39, 83–5, 115–22, 125, 130, 266

Hampson, Daphne 73–4, 182, 313 n21
Hauke, Manfred 331 n4
Hegel, G. 44, 155, 159, 239, 243
Heidegger, Martin 9, 12, 31–2, 48, 49–58, 67, 68–70, 91, 92, 95, 96, 98, 129, 152, 153, 158, 159, 197–200, 210, 255, 293, 298
hell *see* Balthasar, Hans Urs von
Henrici, Peter 170
Herbert, George 71
heterosexuality 21, 33–6, 124–5, 130, 140, 141, 196, 208
Holocaust 180–1
Holy Saturday, *see* Balthasar, Hans Urs von
homosexuality 1, 21, 24, 92, 195, 248, 249

imago Dei, image of God 2, 7, 15, 23, 42, 47, 62, 85, 103, 104, 118, 119, 121, 123, 127, 159, 209, 227, 267, 309
Irigaray, Luce 4, 10, 13, 14, 24, 28, 30, 32, 44, 50, 54, 55–8, 66, 92–99, 100, 109, 111, 113, 127, 129, 147, 152, 168, 173, 183, 188,

193, 197, 198, 208, 211, 217, 235–8, 240, 253, 254, 255, 256–7, 269–70, 275, 284, 287, 289, 293–7, 301, 304–8; angels 293–97; female mysticism 57, 96, 167–68; Girard, René 304–8; God 96–98, 96–98, 235–38; maternal body 256–57, 269–70; sacrifice 236–8, 304–9; sensible transcendental 96, 127, 197, 255, 259

Jantzen, Grace M. 14, 157, 189, 190–2, 195–7, 199, 200, 206, 209, 254–6, 287, 301
John XXIII, Pope 350 n55
John Paul II, Pope 1, 3, 5–6, 19, 20, 24, 25, 46–7, 92, 105, 108, 132, 139, 157, 160, 275, 312 n6, 331 n5
Johnson, Elizabeth 61–64, 66, 73
Jones, Serene 9–8
Jonte-Pace, Diane 188, 211
jouissance 10, 81, 168, 195, 196, 215
Julian of Norwich 293
Justin Martyr 235

Kaegi, Werner 116, 164
Kant, Immanuel 29, 31, 79
Kantianism 29, 70, 78, 79
kenosis 12, 45, 64, 67, 72, 73–4, 104, 106, 129, 158–62, 182, 196, 225, 240, 244, 245, 249, 271, 274; *see also* Balthasar, Hans Urs von; Coakley, Sarah; orgasm, male
Kerr, Fergus 59, 85, 98, 314 n3, 327 n41
Kerry, John 1, 312 n2
Kirwan, Michael 343 n5
Klein, Melanie 188, 192
Kristeva, Julia 4, 10, 14, 44, 65, 80, 188, 208, 209, 211–22, 236, 240–4, 253, 271–2, 274–80, 283, 287–88, 289, 290, 291, 298, 307; abjection 211–22, 241–4, 274–9; Christianity, 220–2; cross of Christ, 274–5; imaginary father, 219–20, 240–2; maternal body, 211–15, 219; sacrifice 211–12, 216–20, 222, 241, 243, 278, 287–8, 307; sin 213–15, 244
Kunzler, Michael 300–1

Lacan, Jacques 4, 37, 41, 44, 57, 66, 159, 190, 192–96, 197–200, 201, 206, 208, 209, 212, ; mysti212, 217–8, 219, 237, 238, 240, 253, 259, 275, 303
Laclau, Ernesto 37
Laqueur, Thomas 328 n1
Laurentin, René 309–10
Leahy, Brendan 146
Lee, Jonathan Scott 193, 197, 198, 341 n24
Levinas, Emmanuel 32, 200
liturgy 2, 6, 14, 15, 46, 57, 58, 82, 130, 137, 144, 200, 206, 207, 209, 227–8, 234, 257, 262, 263, 266, 288–9, 291–2, 294, 296–297, 298–302, 303, 310
Lloyd, Genevieve 316 n31
Llull, Ramon 281
Loraux, Nicole 116
Loughlin, Gerard 156, 334 n5
Louth, Andrew 170, 172, 329 n19, 329 n21, 346 n9
Lubac, Henri de 257, 264
Luther, Martin 41, 62
Lyotard, Jean-François 298

MacKinnon, Donald 181, 22–8
McDermott, Timothy 68, 323 n2
Magee, Penelope Margaret 30
Marion, Jean-Luc 321 n39
Martin, Francis 23, 59, 62–3, 313 n21,

Mass 22, 142, 213, 227, 229, 275, 298–301, 310; as sacrifice 227–30
Maximus the Confessor 118
Merchant, Carolyn 45
Milbank, John 316–7 n41
Miller, Monica Migliorino 142–5, 258–9
mimesis 11, 33, 58, 82, 93, 129, 178, 201–3, 205, 210, 219, 227, 236, 272, 301
misogyny 4, 14, 163, 174, 182, 207, 210
mission 2, 100, 101, 106, 109, 112, 134, 142, 147, 152, 153, 154, 165, 166, 179, 227, 248, 249
Moi, Toril 341 n33
Moss, David 102, 334 n7
mysticism 9, 32, 51, 57, 61, 64, 67, 80, 83–5, 96, 117, 126, 131, 164–6, 168, 174, 194, 223, 230, 237, 261, 262, 265, 266, 272, 279, 284, 290, 293, 294, 299, 301, 302, 310; mystical theology 4, 32, 65, 147, ; *see also* apophaticism; Catherine of Siena; Gregory of Nyssa; Irigaray, Luce; Speyr, Adrienne von; Teresa of Avila

natality 25–5, 287; *see also* Jantzen, Grace
necrophilia 14, 157, 190, 230, 254, 269, 271, 287, 308
Neill, Emily R. 27, 28
Newman, Cardinal 332 n19
Nichols, Aidan 150, 158
Nietzsche, Friedrich 41, 44, 129, 159, 183, 216, 298, 306; Nietzschean 7, 31, 34, 50, 97, 307
nihilism 7, 25, 35, 48, 96, 129, 189, 196, 209, 223, 283, 298, 310
nominalism 31
Nowak, Susan 344 n5
Nygren, Anders 160

O'Connor, James T. 337 n20
Oedipus complex 2, 38, 191, 195, 200, 201–2, 204, 205, 210, 212, 217, 218–9, 220, 225, 237, 239, 240–4, 246, 259, 274–5
Ong, Walter 143–5, 158, 229–34, 245
ontology 33–5, 43, 50, 52, 54, 55, 69, 99, 102, 105, 113, 117, 118, 159, 253, 273, 310; ontotheology 9, 49, 52, 57, 117, 129
orgasm, as *jouissance* 196; female, 144–5; male, as *kenosis* 129, 144, 225; and death 151

paganism 14, 99, 144, 214–5, 221, 222, 235, 264, 274, 284
Papanikolaou, Aristotle 182
Parmenides, 53
Parsons, Susan 7, 8, 49, 5–5, 76
patriarchy 3, 24, 27, 38–9, 40, 42, 43, 44, 48, 50, 51, 58, 61, 65, 70, 74–6, 81, 83, 86, 123, 162, 200, 211, 225, 227, 231, 238, 239–45, 248–9, 272, 275, 305
patristic theology 13, 105, 120, 125–6, 130, 140, 151, 179, 187, 235, 263
Pentecostalism 64, 331 n51
Peter Chrysologus 245, 266
phallus 97, 109, 129, 192–6, 198, 199, 237, 238, 259–60, 270, 279, 303; phallocentrism 58, 98, 109; phallic 129, 152–3, 169, 172, 195, 197, 236, 244, 256, phallic mother 240, 269–70, 303; Lacanian 192–6, 238
pharmakon 5, 183
Plato 5, 52, 56, 95, 152, 160, 168, 169, 189, 212, 236, 238, 256, 284; Platonism 117, 204, 235, 236, 266; the cave, 152, 236–8, 256, 284
Plotinus 169, 235–7, 249

Index

Power, David N. 296
prayer 4, 5, 9, 12, 15, 26, 28, 31, 38, 45, 46, 47, 48, 51, 57, 64–67, 68–91, 108, 181, 189, 229, 263, 281, 285, 287, 289, 294, 304
procreation 15, 46, 104, 120, 131, 141, 144, 160, 206, *see also* reproduction
Protestantism 1, 6, 11, 127, 130, 188, 208, 209, 245, 254, 255–6, 257, 262,
theology, 11, 208; *see also* Reformation
Przywara, Erich 110
pseudo-Denys 65
purity and pollution 212–14, 270

Quash, Ben 167, 325 n1, 337 n20

rational passion 12, 77; *see also* Anderson, Pamela Sue
Ratzinger, Cardinal 2, 20, 25, 36; *see also* Benedict XVI, Pope
real, Lacanian 37–43, 192–3, 198, 209, 236, 282, 283, 303,
redemption 5, 7, 8, 105, 119, 123, 125, 147, 148, 149, 157, 169, 172, 182, 183, 187, 192, 206, 207, 222, 232, 233, 239, 247, 265, 267, 270–1, 273, 275, 280, 281, 282, 284, 285, 286, 287, 300, 304, 308, 311
Reformation 11, 31
reproduction 34, 36, 104, 108, 155, 160, 216, 250, 270; *see also* procreation
resurrection 7, 75, 116, 118–9, 145, 147, 148, 153, 154, 162, 167, 171–3, 190, 191, 205–6, 241, 243, 264, 267, 271, 276, 285, 300, 308, 311
revelation 4, 6, 9, 12, 26, 33, 34, 39, 42, 45, 46, 51, 57, 58–62, 65, 69, 70, 79, 86, 94, 101, 107, 108, 127, 137, 142, 149, 152, 158, 161, 183, 191, 197, 205, 206, 208, 209, 215, 220, 222, 227, 239, 243, 244, 245, 251, 255, 268, 273, 274, 276, 291, 293, 303, 307
Ricoeur, Paul 14, 235; fatherhood of God, 239–40, 243, 244
ritual 204, 211, 262, 276, 296, 299, 301, 304
Rose, Gillian 11–12, 264
Ross, Susan A. 139
Roten, Johann 163–6, 178–9
Roth, John K. 339 n86
Rubenstein, Richard L. 339 n86
Ruether, Rosemary Radford 3, 7, 9, 19, 24, 74, 119, 120, 122–5, 139, 145, 189, 239, 244, 324 n22, 329 n18, 340 n7

sacrifice 6, 9, 31, 50, 144, 147, 168, 181, 190, 201–5, 206, 209, 210–12, 216–20, 222, 225, 226–30, 234, 236–8, 240, 241, 243, 244, 246, 272, 275–8, 283, 284, 285–6, 287–8, 289, 290–1, 300, 301, 303, 304–9; Balthasar, Hans Urs von 226–9, 244, 276, 278, 285–6; Girard, René 201–5, 210–11, 226–7, 290–1, 306; Irigaray, Luce 236–8, 304–9; Kristeva, Julia 211–12, 216–20, 222, 241, 243, 278, 287–8, 307; the Mass 227–30
Saiving, Valerie 72
Sartre, Jean Paul 41, 159
Saussure, Ferdinand de 124, 298
scapegoat 203–4, 210–11, 218, 220, 222; *see also* Girard, René
Schindler, David L. 246–49, 350 n64
Schneewind, J.B. 29, 30
Schopenhauer, Arthur 155, 159, 326

Schumacher, Michele 12, 22, 23, 24, 26, 40–2, 47–8, 139–41, 295
Scola, Angelo 164
Second Vatican Council 3, 14, 19, 154, 229, 230, 260–2, 265, 284, 299, 300
secularism 6, 10, 12, 22–3, 25, 26, 29–31, 36–9, 41, 43, 45, 58–9, 70–2, 75, 81, 85, 96, 139, 160, 200, 217, 222–3, 287, 291
shame 46–7, 174, 202, 204, 301
sin 20, 47, 63–4, 68, 72, 105, 111, 137, 147, 149–50, 169–81, 187, 203, 213–15, 225, 226–8, 244, 259, 267, 270, 273–4, 276, 278–80, 283–4; Balthasar, Hans Urs von 105, 111, 137, 149–50, 169–81, 187, 202–4, 215, 225, 226, 228, 267, 273–4, 276–80, 283; Kristeva, Julia 213–15, 244; original sin 20, 259, 267; feminist critique 63–4, 72–3
Slee, Nicola 67, 82
Song of Songs 83, 96, 117, 131, 153
Soskice, Janet Martin 28, 346 n1
Speyr, Adrienne von 13, 14, 116, 142, 163–79, 194, 202–3, 209, 227, 272, 273, 275, 276–80, 284, 302; *see also* Balthasar, Hans Urs von
Spretnak, Charlene 262–63
Stein, Edith 24
Steiner, George 52, 69, 320 n12
suprasexuality, *see* Balthasar, Hans Urs von
Swinburne Richard 161

symbolic order 37, 192, 200, 212, 216, 241, 254
synagogue, ecclesia and synagogia 179–81

Teresa of Avila 117, 166
Tertullian 258, 264, 304
theo-drama *see* Balthasar, Hans Urs von
Thomism, *see* Aquinas, Thomas
Trible, Phyllis 327 n71
Trinity 61, 79–80, 81, 85, 99, 101, 110, 134, 158–62, 172, 226, 247–50, 271, 273–4, 281–2
Turner, Denys 32, 61, 65–6

vagina 108, 140–1, 191, 270, 271, 304; Vagina Monologues 304, 351 n5
Vatican 1, 6, 19, 20–2, 130; *see also* Second Vatican Council

Wainwright, Geoffrey 337 n20
Ward, Graham 161, 271–72, 325 n1
Warner, Marina 219
Weil, Simone 70–72, 75, 76, 80, 85
Whitford, Margaret, 58, 97
Wijngaard, John 331 n4
William of Auvergne 174, 180
Williams, Rowan 39
worship 6, 14, 15, 46, 57, 75, 79, 82, 12–7, 130, 200, 225, 227–8, 250, 265–6, 271, 289, 294, 297, 298–302, 304; *see also* liturgy, ritual

Žižek, Slavoj 37–8

eBooks – at www.eBookstore.tandf.co.uk

A library at your fingertips!

eBooks are electronic versions of printed books. You can store them on your PC/laptop or browse them online.

They have advantages for anyone needing rapid access to a wide variety of published, copyright information.

eBooks can help your research by enabling you to bookmark chapters, annotate text and use instant searches to find specific words or phrases. Several eBook files would fit on even a small laptop or PDA.

NEW: Save money by eSubscribing: cheap, online access to any eBook for as long as you need it.

Annual subscription packages

We now offer special low-cost bulk subscriptions to packages of eBooks in certain subject areas. These are available to libraries or to individuals.

For more information please contact webmaster.ebooks@tandf.co.uk

We're continually developing the eBook concept, so keep up to date by visiting the website.

www.eBookstore.tandf.co.uk